The Mystery of E Troop

Custer's Gray Horse Company at the Little Bighorn

Gregory Michno

D0036824

Mountain Press Publishing Company
Missoula, Montana
1994

Fourth Printing, March 2005

Front cover photo: Horse bones and "UNKNOWN" marker
on Custer Hill, taken by Stanley J. Morrow, 1879.
Little Bighorn Battlefield National Monument.

Back cover photo: Gravemarker on Deep Ravine Trail.
Copyright © 1988 by Bill and Jan Moeller.

Figures 1-5, 18 by Trudi Peek. Figures 15 and 17 by Carla Majernik.
Aerial photo of the battlefield used to prepare some figures
courtesy of Little Bighorn Battlefield National Monument.

Portions of this book appeared in the
January 1992 and January 1994 issues of
Research Review: The Journal of the Little Big Horn Associates.

Library of Congress Cataloging-in-Publication Data

Michno, Gregory, 1948–
    The mystery of E Troop : Custer's Gray Horse Company at the Little
Bighorn / Gregory Michno.
        p.   cm.
    Includes bibliographical references (p.   ) and index.
    ISBN 0-87842-304-4 : $15.00
    Little Bighorn, Battle of the, Mont., 1876—Personal narratives. 2. United
States. Army. Calvalry, 7th. Company E.—History—Sources. 3. Cheyenne
Indians—Wars, 1876—Personal narratives. 4. Dakota Indians—Wars,
1876—Personal narratives. 5. Little Bighorn Battlefield National Monument
(Mont.)—Antiquities.   I. Title.
E83.876.M53   1994
973.8'2—dc20   94-25545
                                                                              CIP

PRINTED IN THE U.S.A.

Mountain Press Publishing Company
P.O. Box 2399 • Missoula, MT 59806
406-728-1900

And I beheld a pale horse,
and the name of its rider was Death.
—Revelation

CONTENTS

4. White Accounts
The 7th Cavalry

The Montana and Dakota Columns

The Reburials and Post-Battle Accounts

Foreword

Most of America's national battlefields are preserved in such a beautiful state that it takes a determined effort to realize they were once the scenes of carnage and horror. The one exception is the broken hogback ridge where Lt. Col. George Armstrong Custer and five companies of the 7th U. S. Cavalry were wiped out on June 25, 1876. The white marble stones scattered across the dips, gullies, and rises beneath the summit of Last Stand Hill mark where 213 men fought, despaired, and died, giving those 600 acres the aura of a graveyard. Even casual tourists come away from Little Bighorn Battlefield National Monument haunted by the ghosts they seem to sense there amid the grass and sage.

Those marble markers are more than reminders of tragedy. They also stand as clues to what has long ranked as America's favorite mystery, the Battle of the Little Bighorn. Ever since the news first broke in the nation's newspapers, Americans have wondered how Custer and nearly half a regiment of regular cavalry could meet with such a total defeat. What tactics did Custer employ and what mistakes did he make? Was the fight really a quick panic rout, or did the trapped troopers sell their lives dearly?

For over a century, a veritable army of former Indian fighters, novelists, hack writers, Hollywood producers, and assorted buffs have attempted to reconstruct the final movements of Custer's doomed battalion, but almost all of these efforts rested on sheer speculation. Until relatively recently, most serious Custer students believed that no one would ever know the full truth about the Last Stand. After all, they reasoned with ethnocentric arrogance, all of the battle's white participants were killed in action, and the testimony of the Indian survivors was confused, contradictory, and unreliable.

Then, on August 10, 1983, a grass fire swept away enough foliage for archaeologists to try their hands at solving the Custer mystery. The thousands of artifacts recovered in various digs breathed new life into Custer studies, allowing researchers to finally start making sense out of Indian accounts, as well as the often confused and contradictory reports of the first white troops to view the scene of Custer's defeat. The past decade has seen the appearance of some of the most valuable contributions to the already vast literature on the Little Bighorn fight.

With *The Mystery of E Troop: Custer's Gray Horse Company at the Little Bighorn*, Greg Michno joins John S. Gray, Charles Kuhlman, Richard A. Fox Jr., Douglas D. Scott, and Jerome A. Greene as one of the leading interpreters of the movements of Custer's battalion. This book will take its place among the best in the lengthy Custer canon.

Exhibiting a remarkable grasp of the pertinent sources—white, Indian, and archaeological—Michno focuses his attention on Custer's most conspicuous company and clears up a number of long-standing misconceptions regarding the Last Stand. He explodes the myth of the 28 dead cavalrymen in Deep Ravine, offers additional support for the South Skirmish Line theory, and accurately assesses the impact of Lame White Man's charge on the beleaguered troopers. In his brief, novelized account of Company E's destruction, Michno restores the humanity and terror-filled agony of the men who fell with Custer.

The Mystery of E Troop is more than micro-history at its best. Having read widely on nineteenth-century American military tactics, politics, and society, Michno succeeds in placing the events he describes in their proper historical context. Michno's powers as a researcher and an analyst rival those of professional historians who have devoted a lifetime of study to Custer and the Indian Wars. Even those who do not completely agree with *The Mystery of E Troop* will be hard-pressed to marshall sufficient evidence to refute Michno's arguments.

GREGORY J. W. URWIN

Preface

For well over a century there has been vigorous speculation, interpretation, and argument concerning the fate of five troops of the 7th Cavalry led by Lt. Col. George Armstrong Custer on June 25, 1876. There were no white survivors to give a military accounting of the tactics used, the troop dispositions, or the soldiers' last desperate moments. Of course, there were Indian survivors, but their stories were not told with a military eye for strategy and tactics evidenced by red and blue pins on a battle map.

Indian accounts speak of individual action, of small-scale, eyewitness personal deeds, with little care or need for establishing a generalized picture. As such, it has been claimed that the Indian accounts are confusing and contradictory. However, many are no less confusing than some white accounts. The soldiers who were at the battle or visited the field later left their own contradictory stories. Confusion, distortion, perception variances, and perhaps outright lies were not the provenance of any race in recalling what happened that afternoon along the Little Bighorn River. Though there are both Indian and white accounts that must be used with caution, there is also much truth and insight to be gained from both sides.

One major problem with interpreting the fight on the Little Bighorn is not a lack of evidence, but an overabundance. Whereas historians often dealing with earlier times often face a scarcity of documents, those relying on sources printed during the last half century are plagued by a proliferation of documents of all sorts. It is no longer possible for historians to be acquainted with all of the printed material that is reasonably pertinent to their subject. Previously, a requirement of professional historiography has been to provide a more or less complete bibliography appended to the work to assist future scholars and to demonstrate the writer's acquaintance with virtually all of the material relating to the subject. Today we may have to resign ourselves to a novel condition: all modern historians will, of necessity, have a selective bibliography.[1]

This is particularly true in researching "Custeriana." Several attempts have been made to compile and update lists of all the Custer items in print. One entire book devoted 200 pages to list over 3,100 Custer-related books and articles.[2] William A. Graham, in his dedication in the opening pages of *The Custer Myth*, certainly illustrated the point. Almost jocularly, the good colonel collected the eyewitness accounts and left them for us to attempt to decipher "with malice aforethought."[3]

Unfortunately, the more one delves into the massive amount of Custer and Little Bighorn literature, the more the frustration tends to mount. Could it be possible that some of those accounts actually purported to be describing the same event? It is not unlike the story of the bank robbery that occurred in broad daylight and five eyewitnesses described the getaway car in five different colors. However, if four of the witnesses saw the car in blue-green tones, and one saw it as red, at least the investigating officer may be able to discard the latter testimony and concentrate on the blue-green.

So it is with the Little Bighorn researcher. One tries to discover where the evidence is more heavily weighted and then draw conclusions accordingly. However, the thousands of books and articles on the subject make the collection of evidence alone a Herculean labor. But Hercules, overworked chap that he was, at least knew what substance it was that clung to his boots when he attempted to clean out the Augean Stables; and Hercules had the assistance of a river to do the flushing. Sometimes the researcher has to use a little more finesse in sorting out the buffalo steaks from the buffalo chips.

What aspects of the Little Bighorn fight need sorting out? There have been enough general treatments and specific interpretations done (some of them very fine) that at first glance it would appear there is nothing left to rehash. It has all been done before. The major aspects of the fight are known as well as they're going to be. Therefore, perhaps the proper question might be, which aspect is intriguing enough, manageable in scope, and lends itself to solution?

For this writer, the search began some years ago during a visit to the battlefield. While browsing in the visitor center bookstore, an employee behind the counter was heard to remark something to the effect of ". . . and they still haven't found the twenty-eight bodies." Now that was intriguing! Which bodies were missing? Where were they? What happened to them? Why can't they be found? Here was a nice mystery that might be worth investigating.

It turns out that the missing troopers were thought to belong to Company E of the 7th Cavalry, known as the Gray Horse Troop. They rode with Custer's battalion that day. Their big gray horses were more easily seen by the Indians than the troops with the more nondescript mounts. They were seen by the river; they were seen on the bluffs; they were seen on Last Stand Hill. They, or their riders, were seen dead in a ravine after the battle. But which ravine? Why haven't archaeological excavations uncovered some of their remains? Why were soldiers who searched the area within a few years of the fight unable to find their bones? It is the purpose of this book to answer these questions and solve the mystery of the missing men of E Troop.

This is also perhaps an opportune time to address the choice of words in the title. It has been asserted that "troop" is not the correct word to use when referring to the organizational units being studied here. According to 7th Cavalryman Charles Windolph, "company" was the term used by soldiers of his day,[4] but Windolph was in the infantry before he deserted. He later rejoined and was assigned to the cavalry. Did Windolph simply confuse the two service branches' preferred terminology? Today, the Custer Battlefield Historical and Museum Association, in a pamphlet concerning the submission of research papers, gives the warning not to fall into the supposedly anachronistic "troop" trap. Cavalry "companies" did not officially become "troops" until 1883, per historian Robert M. Utley, or was it 1882, per publisher Richard Upton, or was it 1880, per Col. Wilbur S. Nye and editor Jay Smith?[5]

However, another 7th Cavalryman, Capt. Albert Barnitz, indicated in his diary in 1867, nine years before the Battle of the Little Bighorn and a dozen or more years before the official changeover, that the cavalry used the word "troop" purposely to distinguish it from an infantry "company." George Custer himself used the words "troop" and "trooper" freely in the story of his Indian-fighting experiences on the plains, a narrative written in the early 1870s. Lt. Winfield S. Edgerly used "troop" to designate those units in 1881.[6] Can there be nothing connected with the Little Bighorn that does not generate controversy?

In any event, one tires of hearing "company" repeated over and over. This book will use "company" and "troop" interchangeably. Also remember that a trooper is a soldier, but a soldier isn't necessarily a trooper. For those readers not familiar with the story of the 7th Cavalry and Custer's last fight, the investigation begins with a brief sketch of the history of Company E, from its initial organization in 1866 to its near annihilation at the Little Bighorn in 1876. June 25, the last day, will be treated in a novelistic format, eschewing the footnotes. There will be those who will be critical of the technique, since no one knows what the troopers really thought or said. Others may enjoy the adventure of the moment and be more critical of the relative dryness of the historical accounts. In any case, no attempt was made to write of the last day's events until all the evidence was examined. Though it is true that one cannot possibly know the exact words spoken, all the various vignettes presented actually have a basis in fact or can be inferred from surrounding episodes. The rendition should paint a credible picture of events as they occurred in Company E's perspective that day. The purpose of the chapter is to acquaint the general reader with some background information in preparation for the remainder of the study.

The second chapter details some of the 1984-85 archaeological work done on the battlefield, particularly concentrating on the search in the Deep Ravine for the troopers of Company E.

The two central chapters detailing the Indian and white accounts of the fight are the essence of the investigation. This is the primary evidence that must be used in any study of this type. The accounts are examined to see if they can provide clues that will enable us to determine the actual resting places of the missing troopers and if their past assessors have interpreted those accounts correctly.

After studying the historical accounts, the archaeological work of 1989 will be briefly examined to see if the latest findings have shed any light on the mystery. Secondary, interpretive opinion will be presented. The question of whether or not troopers actually formed a "south skirmish line" below Custer Hill will be discussed, and several authors' ideas on the subject will be briefly reviewed.

Lastly, in a more speculative exercise, we will touch on the psychological aspects of stress and fear and their possible roles in the formation and perpetuation of the mystery. By that stage, readers may have already formulated their own theories concerning the solution of the problem. I hope they will accept some of my conclusions, but if not, perhaps this work still serves a positive purpose in suggesting new avenues of possible investigation. That, in the long run, may be the best lesson to learn in the search for historical truth.

A word of caution: though the first chapter should provide sufficient background information for the general reader, this book is not an adventure narrative about the 7th Cavalry and the Battle of the Little Bighorn. It would be helpful to possess at least a cursory familiarity of the colorful players and events detailed in these pages. Then again, reading the accounts without any preconceived notions may be the best way to successfully interpret the evidence and solve the mystery.

Acknowledgments

My thanks to Jim Schneider for his encouragement, for reading the manuscript, and for thinking it was a good idea in the first place. To Bruce Trinque for his many letters, suggestions, readings, and contributions. To the Little Big Horn Associates, who put some of my preliminary ideas into print. To Carl Katafiasz at the Monroe County Library for his resource and photo assistance. To the folks at the Little Bighorn Battlefield, including Kitty Deernose for her help with the photos, Doug McChristian for allowing my fieldwork, and John Doerner for letting me serve as a Deep Ravine Trail guide. To the staff at Lee Library, Brigham Young University, and Lilly Library, Indiana University, for helping me obtain copies of Walter M. Camp's notes and maps. To the hardworking people at Mountain Press who spent so much time and effort putting this together, and especially to Dan Greer, who had faith in the project from the beginning. Also to Susan, part-time researcher, Amanda, part-time reader, and Nathaniel, part-time fieldworker, who put up with me for the past few years.

1. The Long Road to Disaster

A New Regiment

1865. The Civil War was over. The news of the Northern victory had barely reached the smallest villages in the land before there was a clamor for the immediate demobilization of the Union Army. Of the 1,034,000 volunteers in service in May 1865, more than 800,000 were sent home by November. In addition to its old mission of patrolling the frontier, the army was now charged with occupying the Southern states and maintaining a show of force along the Mexican border. Yet by the end of 1865 the strength of the regular army had fallen to 38,545. It became apparent even in Washington that the army was not large enough to perform all its duties.

In July 1866, Congress authorized the reorganization of the 19 existing regiments of infantry into 45 regiments of 10 companies each. The cavalry, with six regiments, was authorized to form four more regiments of twelve companies each. The new postwar strength of the army was set at 57,000 officers and men.[7]

The 7th Cavalry was organized at Fort Riley, Kansas, in August 1866. The recruits came from every strata of society. There were the few former farmers, tradesmen, and laborers, but most were young adventurers, frontiersmen, ex-soldiers from the Civil War, outcasts from society, fugitives from the law, and immigrants recently arrived in the country. About half of this collection was foreign born, many from Ireland and Germany. A great number could barely speak English. This conglomeration was to be welded into a fighting unit able to meet the expert Indian horsemen of the plains.

The organization of the 7th was not complete until December. At that time the commanding officer of the regiment was Col. Andrew J. Smith; the second in command was Lt. Col. George A. Custer. Company E was organized September 10. By November it was already on duty at Fort Hays, Kansas. Its captain was Albert P. Morrow, and second in command was Lt. David W. Wallingford. By the end of the year the regiment totaled 15 officers and 963 enlisted men. There had already been one death from wounds and eleven from disease. Eighty men had deserted.[8]

The Civil War years had seen an intensification of Indian-white conflict on the frontier. Although some have assumed this was a result of the

Indians taking advantage of the removal of the regular army to fight in the east, such was not necessarily the case. The military role was taken up by the volunteers. Many of them were from western states and territories, and their outlook reflected accepted frontier viewpoints. They lacked the tact, inclination, or restraint to deal with the Indians as had the regulars. In fact, there were probably more soldiers on the frontier during the Civil War than before it. The problem resulted from their belligerent attitudes and the new level of brutality they brought to Indian campaigning. To many volunteers, the answer to the Indian problem was extermination.[9]

By 1867, the regular army was badly needed to restabilize the situation. That would not be easy when the commander of the upcoming campaign, Gen. Winfield S. Hancock, was rather belligerent himself. The Indian depredations would stop, he told their agents, or he would lead an army to the plains to whip them. If they wanted war, he would oblige them. If not, they had better get out of his way. "We go prepared for war. . . . No insolence will be tolerated."[10]

Since A. J. Smith also commanded the District of the Upper Arkansas, command of the 7th fell to the young Lieutenant Colonel Custer. He led the regiment from Fort Riley to Fort Harker and then to Fort Larned. Company E joined the column there on April 7. The first confrontation with the Cheyenne and Sioux came at their encampments on the North Fork of the Pawnee River about 30 miles west of Larned. After unsuccessful negotiations the Indians fled, fearing a repetition of the Sand Creek affair, the 1864 surprise attack on an unsuspecting Cheyenne camp by Colorado cavalry under Col. John M. Chivington. Custer was allowed to cut loose with the cavalry in pursuit.

The command marched north to the Smoky Hill River, then east to Fort Hays, and arrived in camp at Big Creek on April 19, out of forage for the horses and unable to continue for want of supplies. They hadn't caught a single Indian. It was a learning experience for the regiment. It was the first time that most of the men, including Custer, had seen a hostile Indian. It was the first independent command Custer led against the Indians. He also saw his first wild buffalo and, while hunting, accidentally shot his wife's favorite horse and a horse lent to him by one of his officers. The pursuit accomplished little in military terms, but it foreshadowed later events. Custer was criticized for overmarching his tired men and horses (as he would be again), and he undoubtedly came to believe that it was more difficult to catch the Indians than it would be to fight them.[11]

April and May were spent near Fort Hays recuperating, gathering supplies, and patrolling along the Smoky Hill route. Custer, impatient at the delays, used the time to drill and discipline the troops. During April alone, 85 men had deserted, 65 from the troops encamped at Big Creek.

Lt. Col. George Armstrong Custer, 7th Cavalry.
—Little Bighorn Battlefield National Monument

Capt. Albert Barnitz of Company G filled his diary with complaints: the camp was unpleasant; Custer was high-handed, injudicious, and obnoxious; the other officers were shirking their duties; men were deserting and the disciplinary punishments were cruel. On May 17, Custer ordered six men of Companies E and H to have half of their heads shaved, on one side of a line drawn from the nose to back of the neck. They had left the post

3

without a pass. On May 18, fourteen more men of E, H, and M Companies, armed and mounted, broke through the guards and departed.[12]

Custer himself was aware of the problems. He attributed the desertions to insufficient and inferior quality of the rations because of gross fraud by dishonest contractors. Bad provisions caused bad health. Scurvy and cholera appeared. Camp inactivity led to restlessness and dissatisfaction. Thus, stricter disciplines had to be applied.[13]

By June 1, the regiment was again ready to move. While some companies were detailed to other Kansas posts, Companies A, D, E, H, K, and M were ordered to leave the Smoky Hill route and march to the Platte. Captain Morrow had been promoted to major of the 9th Cavalry. Commanding Company E on this campaign would be Capt. Edward Myers.

Myers was born in Germany in 1830. He emigrated to the United States in 1857 and enlisted in the 1st Dragoons, where he attained the rank of sergeant. Myers was commissioned a second lieutenant in 1861, the same year the dragoons became the 1st Cavalry. He was brevetted a lieutenant colonel for his Civil War services at Todd's Tavern and Five Forks.[14]

The itinerary of the march had been to scout up to the Platte River in the vicinity of Fort McPherson, loop southward to the headwaters of the Republican River, head back to the Platte at Fort Sedgwick for supplies, then move south again to Fort Wallace. At Wallace they would follow the Smoky Hill route back to their starting point at Fort Hays. The distance of the scout would measure about 1,000 miles.[15]

Leaving Fort Hays, the command traveled north and west. On the morning of June 7, they had crossed the Republican River, three feet deep and 75 yards wide at that point. Seven miles after the crossing the regiment came upon a mounted band of about 100 warriors. The Indians wheeled around and headed westward. Custer ordered Captain Myers and Company E in pursuit. After several miles of pounding along in the tracks of the faster Indian horses, Myers pulled up. They were not going to catch them in a stern chase. Myers circled back to overtake the rest of the column some miles farther on.[16] Company E had experienced its first real Indian pursuit. It was exhilarating at first, but exhausting over the long term. Those were the only Indians seen between Fort Hays and the Platte.

The next day's march was hard, with much time spent seeking a crossing of Medicine Lake Creek, with its steep banks and soft, boggy bottom. The 20 wagons had to be corduroyed separately, and four hours were needed to cross. The men were exhausted when the regiment went into camp. More than a few would relish the moment to consume a little alcohol that may have been secreted away for just such a time. That may have been the circumstance on the evening of June 8, shortly after stable call, when a pistol shot was heard from the tent of Maj. Wickliffe Cooper.

The major, second in field command of the regiment, had been a problem drinker. He had formed a friendship with Captain Myers, and just the night before had bared his soul to the captain, coming to him "suffering from some bilious delirious complaint" and being haunted by ghosts who would come to his tent at night and whisper his wife's name to him.[17]

Myers had only left Cooper's tent for a few minutes when he heard the shot. He rushed back in to find Cooper dead, fallen from his knees, evidently after praying. The bullet crashed through his head, entering behind the right ear. The incident cast a pall of gloom over the command. Custer used it as a warning to his men that a similar fate might lie in store for those intemperate enough to fall into the clutches of the demon rum.[18]

The regiment moved north to Fort McPherson, bearing Cooper's pine box for burial. They remained near the fort, conferred with the Sioux Pawnee Killer, and received orders from General Sherman to have the Indian arrested—but too late. On June 18, the command moved south toward the Republican.

On June 22, after a march of 129 miles, the regiment reached the north fork of the Republican, in the vicinity of present-day Benkelman, Nebraska. At this point, they were about 75 miles southeast of Fort Sedgwick and the same distance north of Fort Wallace. Since the terrain to the south was better suited for wagons, Custer sent 12 of them, escorted by D Company, to Fort Wallace for supplies. Carrying dispatches, Maj. Joel A. Elliot took a detachment of 10 men north to Fort Sedgwick. At dawn on June 24, a picket near Custer's tent discovered Indians attempting to stampede the horses. He fired his carbine, alerting the troops and foiling the Indians, but received a bullet through the body for his efforts. The warriors stopped a mile away and Custer and a small party attempted to confer with them. It was Pawnee Killer's band, the same Indians that had professed peace back on the Platte. The talk accomplished little, and the Indians rode away with the troopers in pursuit. Once more the heavy cavalry horses proved unequal to the speed of the Indian ponies. Company E had been in its first, albeit minor, Indian fight.

Custer worried about the wagon train he had sent south to Fort Wallace. He sent Captain Myers with a squadron of men to meet Capt. Robert West's command scouting near Beaver Creek. Myers was to join West, find the train, and escort it back to the command. The train, meanwhile, had reached the post and had been resupplied. On its way back north the Indians attacked. Lt. William W. Cooke, in charge of the train, had the wagons form up in two parallel columns with the troopers marching in between. When the charge was made, the troopers deliberately worked their repeating Spencers and dropped several circling warriors. The fight had kept up for about three hours when the Indians suddenly broke off. From the north came the detachment of troops under West and

Myers.[19] It was one of the few times, contrary to the Hollywood movies, that Indians actually charged and circled around a wagon train and the defenders were saved in the nick of time by the cavalry. The wagons, with Companies E, D, and K, returned to the command on June 28.

On the same day, Major Elliot returned with a message from General Sherman for the regiment to continue north to the Platte and the vicinity of Fort Sedgwick. It was a long haul, including one day's march of 65 miles without a drop of water. The command struck the South Platte about 50 miles west of Fort Sedgwick, near Riverside Station. Telegraphing back to Sedgwick, Custer learned that Sherman had sent Lt. Lyman S. Kidder with a detachment of 10 men of Company M of the 2nd Cavalry with messages for Custer. Kidder had gone south to Custer's last known position at the forks of the Republican. Custer was telegraphed the same orders that Kidder was carrying to him: proceed to Fort Wallace.

The two days spent on the South Platte proved too much of a temptation for some of the troopers. The rough life of a cavalryman and the nearness of the Colorado goldfields prompted another 35 men to desert on the morning of July 7. There was no time for pursuit. The command started south, making 15 miles before the noon rest. At that point, 13 more soldiers, seven on horseback, openly deserted the command, heading rapidly north. This time Custer ordered a pursuit. Major Elliot, Lt. Tom Custer, Lieutenant Cooke, and seven men galloped after them. Those on horseback escaped. The six on foot were caught; three were shot down and the other three surrendered.[20] The incident would haunt Custer later, but the desertions were definitely curtailed for the time.

Back near the crossing of Beaver Creek on July 12, the tired command came upon the carcass of a dead white horse. About two miles farther on, another slain horse was discovered. Both were branded "M.2.C." Major Elliot remembered seeing a company of the 2nd Cavalry mounted on white horses at Fort Sedgwick. There, on the divide above Beaver Creek, there appeared to have been a chase. The trail left the plateau and dropped into the valley. About 700 yards down from the trail crossing and 40 yards north of the creek were the bodies of Lieutenant Kidder and his men, bristling with arrows, lying in an irregular circle. They had been brutally hacked, disfigured, and burned, their skulls broken and body parts cut off.[21] It was a horrible introduction to Indian warfare in its most graphic form. The men of Company E gazed upon the bodies. They had no reason to comment on the fact that Kidder and his men rode white horses. It would be 15 more months before they received theirs.

Later, in September of 1867, Custer was court-martialed for his conduct during the campaign. The charges included: absence without leave for vacating his post after the command reached Fort Wallace, for proceeding from Fort Wallace to Fort Hays with 75 men on private business without authority, for procuring eight mules and two ambulances to convey himself from Fort Hays to Fort Harker, for failure to pursue Indians that had killed two of his detachment, and for shooting deserters. A guilty verdict in November resulted in his suspension from rank and command for one year.[22]

The factions that would always be a hindrance to the smooth operations of the regiment were already well developed by this time. Even before the court convened, Custer began receiving letters regarding who would or would not support him. Only Weir, Brewster, Wallingford, Hamilton, and Moylan could be counted on. The Custerphobes included Elliot, Myers, Robbins, Barnitz, Commagere, Hale, Jackson, and Keogh.[23]

Major Elliot was now the field commander. Company E was engaged in routine scouting duties along the Saline River, back to Beaver Creek, and down to Fort Wallace again. In September, they went to their station at the new Fort Hays, rebuilt 15 miles west of the old location, which had been abandoned after Big Creek flooded the post in June. November found E Troop stationed back at Fort Leavenworth for winter quarters. They logged 2,105 miles of marching in 1867, the most of any company in the 7th Cavalry.[24]

To perhaps forestall the Indian raids that would come with the spring, Companies A, D, E, G, and K were ordered into the field in April 1868. Under Major Elliot they proceeded 20 miles west of Fort Hays to Ellis Station on the Kansas Pacific Railroad. There they laid out a site they named Camp Alfred Gibbs, in honor of the major that commanded the 7th in Custer's absence. They remained there until July.

Captain Myers had not been with Company E over the past several months. During the latter half of 1867, Myers was in and out of trouble. Apparently somewhat dull-witted and with a temper not fit for the requirements of military discipline, he almost lost his commission. At Fort Wallace in August 1867, he disobeyed orders from Major Elliot relating to quartermaster requisitions, refused to submit to arrest, and then broke his arrest. He twice drew a pistol on Lieutenant Robbins and once challenged him to a duel. He took exception with a doctor's decision to release a sick man from duty, called the doctor a "God damn fool," and returned the man to duty. Myers was tried by court-martial in December and sentenced to be cashiered. However, the judge advocate general disapproved the sentence in June of 1868, and Myers returned to duty.[25]

During Myers's absence in the spring of 1868, Company E was commanded by Lt. Algernon E. Smith. Algernon was sometimes called "Fresh" Smith, as a counter to another 7th Cavalry lieutenant, Walworth H. "Salty" Smith. Born in New York in 1842, Smith served in the 117th New York Infantry during the Civil War and emerged as a captain at war's end. He served on the staffs of Generals Ames, Ord, and Terry and participated in

Lt. Algernon E. Smith, Company E, 7th Cavalry. On temporary duty from Company A, he died on Custer Hill. —Little Bighorn Battlefield National Monument

the fights at Fort Wagner, Cold Harbor, Petersburg, Richmond, and Fort Fisher. At the latter battle, while on Terry's staff, Smith was severely wounded in the shoulder. In 1870 he applied for disability retirement because of the wound, which caused him persistent pain and limited the use of his arm, which he could not lift above his shoulder. However, after undergoing treatment, he withdrew the application. The "Benzine Boards," convened to weed out substandard officers, found him fit for service and restored him to duty.[26]

In the summer of 1868, the Cheyennes, Kiowas, Arapahoes, and Comanches began to gather at Fort Larned in expectation of the annual distribution of goods. The new commander of the District of the Upper Arkansas, Gen. Alfred Sully, ordered units to concentrate there in anticipation of trouble. Returning to duty, Captain Myers led Company E from Camp Alfred Gibbs to Larned.

No matter where the troops moved, it seemed the Indians would be free to raid elsewhere. From August through October, after receiving 160 pistols, 80 Lancaster rifles, and powder and lead at Larned, warrior bands struck at will. Ranches, farms, and way stations were attacked from the Saline and Solomon Rivers to Denver and Fort Lyon, and down to the Texas frontier. It appeared that a winter campaign would have to be attempted to catch the warriors while they were more or less immobile. Accordingly, troops would activate in Kansas and start probing south as a diversion, hoping to lure the hostiles away from the settlements. The 7th Cavalry and elements of the 3rd Infantry began to concentrate at Fort Dodge.

On September 7, General Sully led nine troops of the 7th under Major Elliot across the Arkansas toward the Cimmaron. Early on the morning of September 11, a party of Indians galloped into the camp and carried off two men of F Troop who were in the rear guard. Capt. Louis Hamilton of Company A, in command of the rear guard, prepared to rescue the men. The acting adjutant, Lt. Algernon Smith, as a representative of the commanding officer, took the responsibility of directing a squadron of troopers to wheel out of the column to support Hamilton. The Indians were pressed so closely that they were forced to release one prisoner, but not before severely wounding him. The troops were gaining on the retreating warriors when they received a preemptory order to end the pursuit and rejoin the column immediately. The second soldier was lost. For their efforts, Hamilton and Smith were summoned by General Sully, reprimanded, and placed under arrest for leaving the command without orders. Fortunately, wiser counsel prevailed and they were later released, to numerous compliments from their brother officers.[27]

The march continued on September 12. Near the North Fork of the Canadian at the Beaver River, the Indians made a stand. The troops dismounted to attempt to drive them from a stronghold in the surrounding sand hills. Action continued for about two hours, then the Indians withdrew. Private C. H. Tares of E Company was seriously wounded.[28] The next day Sully rode into a trap and nearly lost his supply train. While the company of 3rd Infantrymen protected the wagons, the cavalry again moved into the sand hills to fight, and the Indians were eventually dislodged. Sully then became convinced that the Indians had moved south to the Wichita Mountains, and he decided to return to Fort Dodge. It was not a very effective expedition. They had scouted about 255 miles and believed they had killed 20 to 30 warriors. The troop losses were three killed and six wounded.[29]

Fight on the Washita

A winter campaign would be necessary. The 7th went into camp on Bluff Creek, 45 miles southeast of Fort Dodge. On September 23, they marched 18 miles nearer to Dodge and constructed a new camp on a stream known as Cavalry Creek. Over the next month, the 7th operated from various locations along that stream while the commander of the Department of the Missouri, Gen. Philip H. Sheridan, prepared for the upcoming expedition. Since the Sully Campaign had failed, Sheridan cast about for a new commander, even offering Capt. Frederick Benteen the position. He declined. Lieutenant Colonel Custer was recalled from suspension and reinstated as field commander of the 7th Cavalry.[30]

Custer lost no time. Receiving a telegram from Sheridan on September 24, he packed and was at Fort Hays by September 30. Custer found the 7th demoralized and depleted by desertions, with many vacancies filled by raw recruits. He initiated an intensive training course to bring it back to fighting condition.[31]

Custer also made some radical changes in the cavalry's horseflesh. Back in Monroe, Michigan, during the past summer he had plenty of time to fish, hunt, read, and write. Custer's home library included 15 books on history, 6 on politics, 22 on the Civil War, and 28 more on other military subjects. Among the military books were those on Napoleonics, the theory and practice of warfare, and Delafield's and Jomini's studies on the art of war.[32] Whether Custer had been influenced by reading about European cavalry organization, or whether he simply wanted to revive an old practice begun in 1837 by Col. Stephen Watts Kearny of the 1st Dragoons,[33] Custer's next step after training was to "color the horses." He considered the change somewhat ornamental, but useful nevertheless. Prior to this move, the horses had been distributed among the troops indiscriminately. For uniformity of appearance, one day was devoted to a general exchange of horses. The troop commanders were assembled and allowed, in order of their rank, to select the color they preferred.[34]

The horses were led out and placed in groups. The grays and whites went to one place, the blacks to another, the browns and sorrels likewise, and also the bays, of which there was the greatest preponderance. There was difficulty categorizing some, especially those labeled chestnuts, roans, claybanks, duns, sorrels, buckskins, or bays. A sorrel ran from a light yellow-brown to a light red-brown. A buckskin was yellow-tan in color with black points, including mane and tail. A claybank was of a light copper color with mane and tail of a darker copper. A chestnut was red-brown.

A roan could be chestnut, sorrel, or bay sprinkled with gray to yellow-white markings. A dun was a dull gray-brown. A bay was of various shades of red-brown ranging from tan to dark mahogany, distinguished by black legs below the knee and a black mane and tail. Many of the mixed-color breeds could actually be more simply classified as bays.[35]

Obviously, there were not going to be definite color lines among some of the roans and duns. Custer called these the "brindles" and noted that the junior troop commander would be the reluctant recipient of these. Not everyone was happy with the changes. Captain Barnitz of Company G received what he called "chestnut colored horses." He bitterly opposed the scheme and called it foolish, unwarranted, and unjustifiable. Capt. Frederick Benteen of Company H received bays. He was disgusted. Captain Hamilton of Company A got blacks and liked the new arrangement. Sgt. John Ryan of Company M treated the entire affair with the resigned attitude of a "lifer." He simply said General Custer gave dark bays to Company A, light bays to B, sorrels to C, blacks to D, grays to E, light bays to F, H, I, L, and M, mixed colors to Company G, and sorrels to Company K. The band, the noncommissioned officers, and the trumpeters got grays.[36]

Custer thought the change was a great improvement, making the command very handsome in appearance. Among the most prominent and noticeable were the grays of E Troop. The company had received its identifying badge.

On November 12, 1868, eleven companies of the 7th Cavalry, three companies of the 3rd Infantry, one company of the 5th Infantry, one company of the 38th Infantry, and 450 wagons began the march south for Indian Territory. In the bright sunlight of the clear, cool morning, the colorful arrangement of the companies looked magnificent.[37]

On November 27, about 50 Cheyenne lodges were found at a timbered campsite along the banks of the Washita River. With the infantry remaining back at Camp Supply, Custer divided the cavalry into four units to surround the camp and strike simultaneously. Elliot would take Companies G, H, and M and swing around the hills north of the camp and attack from the northeast. Capt. William Thompson would take Troops B and F in from the south. Captain Myers would be in charge of Companies E and I. They would go to the right and come down the river from the southwest. Actually leading Company E that day would be Lt. John M. Johnson; Myers, with a severe case of snow blindness, had relinquished command. Custer would lead Companies A, C, D, and K, plus a sharpshooter unit under Lieutenant Cooke, across the river and in from the west. Lieutenant Smith, as acting regimental commissary, would ride with Custer's group. About 700 troopers participated.[38]

The men moved into their positions in the frigid darkness. The sunlight on the eastern horizon had just brightened when a shot was fired by an Indian who saw one of Elliot's men to the northeast. Custer had the bugle sounded. The band broke in with the rollicking tune of "Garryowen," but the music died after a few strains because the breath moisture froze in the instruments. Gunfire crackled on nearly all sides of the camp. The troops rushed in and the chaos began, with war cries, curses, screams, and gunfire. There was no quarter given. Captain Hamilton was killed by a bullet in the chest, and Captain Barnitz was severely wounded by a bullet in the abdomen. Major Elliot had cut loose to the east with 18 men of various troops in an attempt to stop the escape of Indians through the only open gap left in the encirclement. They remained missing after the battle. The regiment remained to gather up prisoners, burn the village, and shoot down the pony herd. The arrival of more Indians from numerous camps downriver forced the 7th to fall back to the north. They returned to Camp Supply on December 1.

Custer and elements of the 7th Cavalry, accompanied by General Sheridan, returned to the battlefield on December 11. The bodies of Major Elliot, Sgt. Maj. Walter Kennedy, and 15 other enlisted men were found. During the battle, Pvt. Frederick Klink of Company E received a slight wound in the left arm from a spent bullet. The return to the field proved that three other missing E Troopers were not so lucky. Cpl. Harry Mercer was found with several bullet holes, including one near the heart and three in the back, eight arrow wounds in the back, his right ear cut off, head scalped, skull fractured, gashes in both legs, and throat cut. Pvt. Thomas Christie had a bullet hole in his head, his right foot cut off, a bullet in the stomach, and his throat cut. Pvt. John McClernan may have been one of the three bodies that could not be identified. They were mutilated beyond recognition. All had accompanied Major Elliot, who allegedly shouted to Lt. Owen Hale, "Here goes for a brevet or a coffin" when he sallied after the fleeing Indians.

Elliot's body was eventually taken to Fort Arbuckle for interment. The remaining troopers were laid beneath the icy ground on a small knoll west of the battlefield. Later, interpreter Philip McCusker interviewed an Indian participant who spoke of seeing a group of fleeing Indians pursued by about 18 soldiers. The Indian thought the troopers "were all riding gray horses."[39]

Back on December 8, a wagon train left Camp Supply for Fort Dodge with 53 Indian captives and 115 sick and wounded 7th Cavalrymen. The remainder of the regiment, after finding Elliot, traveled to Fort Cobb, Indian Territory, where they ended the year of 1868. Company E had recorded 1,558 miles of marching that year, the second highest in the regiment.[40]

The winter of 1868-69 saw the 7th on duty between Fort Cobb and their camp on Medicine Bluff Creek near the spot that was to become Fort Sill. They rounded up Arapahoes, Kiowas, and Cheyennes who had had enough winter fighting and appeared willing to go to the reservations. On March 2, 1869, the last leg of the long campaign began when elements of the 7th Cavalry and 19th Kansas Volunteer Cavalry headed west to bring in the last Cheyenne holdouts. The 19th Kansas, however, because they had not been paid, were low on supplies, and had many poor mounts, much preferred to go home rather than begin another campaign. On March 6, because of the dissatisfaction and inability to supply such a large group while heading toward the Texas Staked Plains, Custer split up the command. He selected 800 men from both regiments and continued west. The remainder, including Captain Myers, Company E, and many of the wagons, headed for a supply depot near the old Washita battlefield.[41] Custer continued on and was successful in locating a Cheyenne village near Sweetwater Creek and freeing two white women captives while taking three Cheyenne captives himself. The Cheyennes eventually trickled in to Camp Supply. Custer crossed back into Kansas on April 1. The winter war of 1868-69 proved to be his most successful campaign.[42]

A Long Respite

The spring of 1869 began a period of relative quiet for the regiment. At least there were no major Indian outbreaks or long campaigns to contend with, but the troopers could not escape the never-ending routine duties of cavalrymen on the Great Plains. Company E went to Fort Wallace in May and was divided into detachments as escorts to surveying parties. In June, Company E formed up and went to Denver via Cheyenne Wells and Fort Lyon. In July they were back at Fort Wallace. In August, the troop escorted surveyors for the Union Pacific. In September and October they went to the Big Sandy and back to the Smoky Hill River. They went into winter quarters at Fort Wallace. Company E had marched 1,852 miles in 1869, again the highest total in the regiment.[43]

The year 1870 was to be spent in much of the same pursuits as 1869. The troops of the regiment were scattered in independent bands, marching many weary miles with no apparent objective. In May, the troop was protecting citizens and railroad employees in the vicinity of Cheyenne Wells, Colorado Territory. In June, they scouted the length of the Kansas Pacific Railroad for 630 miles and ended up in Denver in July. In the fall they were back in the Fort Lyon area chasing stolen stock and scouting in numerous directions. In October, they headed for winter quarters at Fort Leavenworth, passing through Fort Hays, Abilene, Fort Riley, and Topeka. Totaling up 2,965 miles in 1870, Company E had done the most marching in the regiment for three out of the past four years.[44]

In 1871 the 7th Cavalry's tour in the Department of Dakota was terminated, and early in the year its companies were distributed to different posts in the Department of the South. Leaving the garrison at Leavenworth in March, Company E shipped out to Louisville, Kentucky, thence by rail to Columbia, South Carolina. From there they proceeded to their station at Spartanburg.

While in South Carolina, Company E lost its commander of five years, Captain Myers, the only German-born officer that the 7th had during its Indian-fighting days. He had been in declining health for the past several years and died while still on duty with his troop.[45] In June, detachments under Lt. Thomas M. McDougall were sent in pursuit of local Ku Klux Klan members. McDougall had been with the regiment for six months. Born in 1845 in Prairie-du-Chien, Wisconsin, he served in the 48th U.S. Colored Infantry and the 14th U.S. Infantry and was in Grant's Vicksburg Campaign in 1863. McDougall was promoted to 1st lieutenant in 1867 and assigned to the 7th Cavalry on January 1, 1871.

In early July, men of Company E went on a scout to destroy illicit distilleries, and later in the month McDougall had them rounding up Ku Kluxers again. In August, McDougall and 20 men assisted the U.S. marshall in making arrests in Greencastle, and in September, McDougall and 24 troopers went to the old Revolutionary War battlefield site of Cowpens as a posse for the marshall, capturing six outlaws. In November, Lt. William T. Craycroft and McDougall helped round up 16 more fugitives. William Thomas Craycroft was a Kentuckian, born in 1847. He became a 2nd lieutenant and was assigned to the 7th Cavalry in 1869. The two lieutenants did an excellent job as constabularies. In December 1871 the troop moved to a new station at Unionville, South Carolina.[46]

The next year, 1872, was nearly a copy of the previous year's activities—assisting U.S. marshalls in arresting violators of the internal revenue laws and preventing violence done by night-riding Klansmen. These years saw the 7th Cavalry retire the tried and true Spencer carbines they had used since 1866. The seven-shot Spencer used a hefty .52 caliber rimfire cartridge. With the Blakeslee Quickloader system, the Spencer was the most desirable weapon in service after 1863. Its effective range was 400 yards and its battle range was 200 to 300 yards. One drawback was the dangerous way the cartridges nested in the magazine, nose to tail. A dropped carbine, butt first, could result in a disastrous discharge. Nevertheless, many officers who had experience with the Spencer were reluctant to give it up. Custer had led his Spencer-equipped 5th and 6th Michigan Cavalry at Gettysburg with devastating effect against J. E. B. Stuart's gray troopers.[47]

In 1870, trials were begun with a .50 and .52 caliber Sharps. It was a single shot, breech-loading weapon with an effective range of 500 yards and a battle range of 300 yards. Its rate of fire by an experienced marksman was said to be four shots per minute, much slower than the Spencer. The danger with the Sharps was the flashback. The sharp front breech block cut through the paper on the inserted cartridge for ignition by the percussion cap. After a time, loose powder would get ground between the breech and the block, and could cause an additional burn when fired. The powder could foul the works to such an extent that the lever couldn't even be forced back into position. Thus, the soldiers had to deal with the cost-conscious government. By mid-1871, all of Company E was equipped with the .50 caliber Sharps and .44 caliber Colt pistols.[48]

Back to the Plains

In 1873, the regiment was ordered out of the Department of the South and back to Dakota. Company E assembled at Memphis, Tennessee, in March. Reaching Cairo, Illinois, in April, they took the rails to Yankton, Dakota Territory. While in Yankton, waiting for wagons and for the ice to clear the river, the regiment experienced a whopper of a blizzard, the worst they had ever seen on the plains. It became known as "Custer's blizzard." In May the entire command marched for Fort Rice on the Missouri River. The 7th would accompany Col. David S. Stanley on an expedition to guide and protect engineering surveyors for the Northern Pacific Railroad. In August, along the Yellowstone above the mouth of the Tongue, the regiment had its first Indian fight in the past few years. Custer had one man wounded and one missing, but two others, the regiment's veterinarian, Dr. John Honsinger, and the sutler, Augustus Baliran, were caught alone on the prairie and killed.[49]

On August 11, near the mouth of the Bighorn, the Sioux appeared in greater force, perhaps a thousand of them attacking the 7th's 450 cavalrymen. Custer placed 30 of his best marksmen behind trees along the riverbank to fire on the Indians some 400 yards across the Yellowstone. The crack shot of the regiment was Company E's Pvt. Frank Tuttle. With uncanny accuracy, Tuttle dropped three warriors in a row. Then the Indians got him in a cross fire while he sighted from behind a tree and put a bullet through his head. He was the only trooper killed in the engagement.[50] A spirited charge by the 7th dispersed the Indians.

The regiment was detached from the expedition on August 29 and returned to Fort Abraham Lincoln on September 21. There, on the west bank of the Missouri five miles down and across from the little town of Bismarck, they would make their winter quarters. On November 1, Company E finally got to move out of their tents and into their new wooden barracks.

Eighteen seventy-four began with the usual round of garrison duties and occasional escorts. It was not until June that the major expedition of the year was organized. Custer would lead ten troops of the 7th, two companies of infantry, scouts, and scientists to explore the Black Hills and surrounding area. While in the Hills, a significant discovery of gold was

15

reported. Though the Fort Laramie Treaty of 1868 gave the Sioux the undisputed right to the Hills, the discovery almost guaranteed that they would eventually be forced out of the area by a "civilization" that always appropriated lands the Indians "did not need."[51] The expedition returned to Fort Lincoln in August after marching about 950 miles.

On September 29, 1874, six troops, including Company E, were reassigned to the Department of the Gulf. Company E was sent to Greensboro and then Opelika, Alabama, where they performed constabulary duty for the remainder of the year. The ordinance report for the third quarter of 1874 shows Company E had begun receiving the new issue .45 caliber Springfields and .45 caliber Colt pistols. By December the Sharps rifles were gone and the changeover was complete. Company E had on hand 83 Springfields, 81 Colts, and 75 light cavalry sabres.[52]

The selection of the Springfield was the end result of a long series of field trials that began in 1871. There were four main factors that went into the selection of a single-shot weapon over a repeater: manufacturing economy, ruggedness and reliability, efficient use of ammunition, and the selection of a similar weapon by European countries. A board of officers, which included Maj. Marcus A. Reno, was selected to study the tests and make recommendations. Weapons evaluated were submitted by Sharps, Peabody, Remington, Ward-Burton, Spencer, Springfield, Elliot, Freeman, and Mauser. The Springfield had the highest scores. It was a "trapdoor" breech-loading, single-shot weapon that weighed 7.1 pounds and fired a .45 caliber copper-cased cartridge over 1,000 yards with an effective range of 250 yards. It proved to be an effective service weapon throughout the Indian Wars. However, though the Springfield would have an advantage over the Spencer in long-range, selective fire, the repeating Spencer would certainly have been more useful at the Little Bighorn.[53]

Company E continued to assist the civil authorities in making arrests in the northeast counties of Alabama. In January, Craycroft and 15 troopers captured 15 distillers and seized their stills. Their duties in the Department of the Gulf ended in April, and they made the return trip from Alabama to the Department of Dakota in May 1875. Companies E, A, and H were stationed near Fort Randall on the Missouri River. They were engaged in ejecting miners and other unauthorized persons from the Black Hills until September. Company E then marched to their station at Fort Abraham Lincoln.[54] In December 1875, Lieutenant Craycroft was transferred to Company B. Lieutenant McDougall was promoted to captain.

Early in 1876, Companies E and L were stationed at Fort Totten, Dakota Territory. On April 17, they returned to Fort Lincoln to prepare for the Sioux expedition. Captain McDougall was transferred to Company B, and Lt. Algernon Smith had taken command of Company E. The expedition left Fort Lincoln on May 17, 1876, and marched west to Montana. The column was commanded by Gen. Alfred Terry. It consisted of Companies C and G of the 17th Infantry and Company B of the 6th Infantry, a platoon of three gatling guns from the 20th Infantry, and a detachment of 40 Indian scouts. There were 160 wagons and 1,694 horses and mules in the expedition. The main striking force of the Dakota Column was the 7th Cavalry, 32 officers and 792 enlisted men—all 12 companies assembled together for the first time since the regiment's organization in 1866.[55]

The 7th was a young regiment. Custer was one of the "old men" at 36 years. The average age of a recruit was 23 for first enlistments and 32 for reenlistments. Their average height was five feet seven and their average weight 140 pounds.[56] The average term of enlistment for a trooper was three years and eight months. Only 22 percent of the men had less than one year of service. This last statistic, the new recruits, remains a point of controversy. Col. William Graham believed the number was 30 to 40 percent, and Dr. John S. Gray figured them to be 11 percent trained recruits and 35 percent raw. Dr. Lawrence Frost thought the amount was 11 percent raw with less than six months' experience. Although the 7th was not a regiment of highly trained marksmen as it rode to the Little Bighorn in 1876, the number of new recruits was not large enough to significantly affect any battle they might have. Company E, with only two new recruits, had the highest percentage of veterans in the regiment.[57]

On June 7, Terry's column reached the junction of the Powder and Yellowstone. On the 10th, Major Reno led Companies B, C, E, F, I, and L on a scout up the Powder, then west to the Mizpah and Tongue Rivers, where he exceeded his orders and continued west to scout on the Rosebud before turning back to the Yellowstone, arriving on June 18. Reno's unauthorized trip showed that the hostiles had moved west toward the Bighorn. Men with broken-down mounts, band members, those detailed to care for the equipment, and some civilians, packers, and recruits were left behind on the Yellowstone. On June 22, the 7th Cavalry, with 31 officers, 586 soldiers, 33 Indian scouts, and 20 citizen employees, marched out alone, heading up the Rosebud. When Custer bid farewell, Col. John Gibbon remarked, "Now Custer, don't be greedy, but wait for us." Custer's enigmatic answer: "No, I will not."[58]

Each man was armed with a Springfield carbine with 100 rounds and a Colt pistol with 24 rounds. No sabres were taken. The pack mules carried 26,000 extra rounds of ammunition and 15 days' rations. On the 23rd the column passed three deserted Indian camps and marched 33 miles. At 5 A.M. on the 24th the regiment broke camp and continued up the Rosebud. They halted for lunch and rested until 5 P.M. At 7:45 P.M. they halted for coffee and hardtack after marching 28 miles since reveille.

After supper, the fires were extinguished and the men tried to bed down. In the deepening evening, scouts began to come in with news. The

trail diverged out of the valley of the Rosebud and over to the Little Bighorn. There was a large village beyond. Custer called for his officers at
9:25 P.M. and explained the situation. They would have to cross over the
divide from the Rosebud at night to avoid being discovered. They could
hide out in the hills and wait for Terry and Gibbon to move into position.
The attack would commence on the morning of June 26.

The march was wearily resumed about one in the morning; however,
about two hours later it was realized they would not make the divide
before daylight. The column again halted and unsaddled after a march of
eight more miles.[59] It was about 2:30 A.M. The first hint of dawn would
soon be painting streaks of orange over the mountains to the east. The
troops settled into a restless sleep. It was Sunday morning, June 25, 1876.
Company E had nearly come to the end of its long road.

The Last Day

The men still asleep were jostled awake by their companions going
up the line. It couldn't be time already, but, yes, there was the sun, already
partway up over the hills. Wasn't it just like the army—sleep in the day
and march at night. Up the Rosebud for three days. Stop before eight last
night. Eat. Sleep. Get up after midnight. March in the blackness until the
false dawn starts lighting the horizon. Halt. Dismount for a few hours of
shut-eye until it's too damn light to sleep anyway.

While some men sat up, rubbing the sleep out of their eyes, others
began munching glumly on a scrap of bacon or dry, ground coffee, washing the concoction down with a swig of bitter, alkaline water. You took
your nourishment when you could get it in this outfit . . . never knew
when you'd get a chance to eat again.

Daylight showed they were on the headwaters of some pitiful little
creek bed some ways up and out of the Rosebud Valley. Another day. One
more that promised to be a repetition of the interminable number that had
gone before and promised yet to be. The men of Company E grumbled,
scratched, relieved themselves, prepared their mounts. There was already
activity up ahead.

"Git up. Git moving." Sure. Get moving. Haul ass. Hurry up and wait.

First Sgt. Frederick Hohmeyer had been one of the first up. He always
was. It was his job and he was good at it. No Gott verdamnt soldats would
be slackers in his unit. He could put on a rough face when the occasion
warranted it, like when rousing up tired soldiers. The 27-year-old sergeant
from Darmstadt, Germany, was used to the routine. He had been sworn
in for his third enlistment just last year by Lieutenant McDougall, who
had commanded his company until earlier this year.

Hohmeyer stood up, combed back his sandy-colored hair with his
fingers, and stretched out to his full height. The perfect cavalryman, five

First Sgt. Frederick Hohmeyer, Company E. His body was identified after the battle by the name tag on his socks. —Little Bighorn Battlefield National Monument

feet seven from his head to his stockinged feet. That reminded him of something. Hohmeyer sat back down. Before tugging on those boots he would allow himself a little luxury. Ach! He peeled off those old, dirty, sweat-stained socks he had worn for weeks and pulled out a spare pair he had tucked away in his pack. They felt good and he admired them as he wiggled his toes. He'd been around a long time, and he knew how articles of clothing in the army had a way of disappearing. He smiled a bit when he looked at the "Hohmeyer" tags he had stitched onto them. At least his feet would be a bit more comfortable for the next few days.

19

Actually, it wasn't all that odd to stitch names into one's clothing. Young 2nd Lt. James Garland Sturgis always had his name on his shirts, trousers, and underclothes. It was something one got used to at the Point, and from years of schooling before that. It was something his mother used to do for him as a child. Sturgis's thoughts flashed back to his mother as he shared a coffee breakfast with some of the men. Military routines seemed to be a part of his life since he was born. Seemed forever, though it was only 22 short years. He'd do something someday to make his mother and father proud of him. Especially his father. After all, Pa, Col. Sam Sturgis, was the real commander of the 7th Cavalry, though Custer always seemed to take the regiment out in the field.

Young Jack Sturgis was lost in thought. Pa had always done things for him—at least when he wasn't off on duty somewhere. Pa got him into the Point. He had graduated a year and a week ago. Pa also got him on court-martial duty in St. Louis, far from any real action. But Jack had gotten out of it by October 1875 and marched north to Fort Rice with the other new recruits fresh out of Jefferson Barracks.

Sturgis was assigned to Company M, but he was riding with Company E during this campaign to assist Lieutenant Smith. Maybe now he'd have a chance to exercise command, maybe get rid of that "wet behind the ears" label, maybe show that he was just as good a soldier as Pa was. Sturgis downed the coffee and turned to look to the bluffs above them to the west. There were horses moving downhill.

Sgt. William James had roused himself up about the same time as Hohmeyer did. He dumped his coffee in the dirt. The water made it taste like hell. James was also 27 years old, but had enlisted his first time in Chicago four years ago. He had worked there for a time as a coachman, which was not much of a job, but the army was no great improvement. Then again, either was probably better than his prospects would have been had he remained in the small Welsh coal town where he was born.

James eyed Hohmeyer as he pulled on his boots. Where the hell'd the Dutchie get a fresh pair of socks? James scratched at his scraggly growth of whiskers and walked down the line of blankets to give each lump a not-so-gentle kick in passing.

The horse pulled back on its rope with a start, spooked by the clang of a dropped pot. Cpl. Thomas P. Eagan's eyes snapped open, his arm jerking awkwardly with the movement of the horse. He invariably slept that way while in the field, rope loosely wrapped around one arm. His mount would warn him of any untoward movement quicker than any human sentry could. Eagan rolled over and looked. The bright sun caught him full in the eyes and he slammed them shut again. When he next chanced admitting the daylight he saw Hohmeyer walking up.

Lt. James G. Sturgis, Company E, 7th Cavalry. On temporary duty from Company M, his body was never identified. —Little Bighorn Battlefield National Monument

"Already?" he thought, and grunted an acknowledgment. He stood up to soothe his mount. Eagan, 28 years old and five feet five inches tall, barely stood face to face with the big gray whose neck he patted. He chuckled. Hell, he was a giant compared to Pvt. John Heim, who barely stood five feet tall. That poor ol' boy had a rough time even getting on his horse.

Adjusting the saddle, Eagan thought a bit about home. Back in Ireland, his half sister, Ella, had only recently received the letter he had

21

written her back at Fort Totten in March. "We ar to start the 10th of this month for the Big horn country," he wrote. "The Indians are getting bad again. i think that we will have some hard times this summer. The old Chief Sitting Bull says that he will not make peace. . . . The weather very cold hear at preasent. . . . Ella, you need not rite to me. . . . As soon as i get back . . . i will rite you. That is if i do not get my hair lifted by some Indian. . . . From your loving brother, T.P. Eagan."

Pvt. William Davis jerked his head up. What the hell was that, a trumpet call? Couldn't be. He rolled back over. Probably a nightmare. Someone came by and kicked him. "Goddamn," he mumbled. If he'd been a little bit quicker last year, or a little smarter, he'd have been back home in Vandalia, Illinois, right now—or California. He always wanted to see California. The 25-year-old former laborer cursed his luck. For three days he was free. Three lousy days, last February of '75. He'd taken French leave, but they caught him before he could get transportation out of the area. He'd do it again, too, if he had a good chance. Someday he'd be relieved of the damn drudgery and discipline of this goddamn army. Someday he'd get to sleep as long as he wanted.

The troopers prepared their horses first. It was a routine that became second nature to them. A horse could be a man's salvation in a tight spot. It was a constant companion and was cared for as a family member. Many soldiers would share their own meager rations with their mount.

Lt. Algernon Smith watched one trooper hand-feed his gray a handful of oats and looked on approvingly. He was spared that duty, but he had so many other things to worry about. The scouts had been high up on the divide and had apparently seen an Indian camp, a huge camp in the valley of the Little Bighorn. It seemed he hadn't slept a wink in 24 hours, and that news probably meant he wouldn't sleep for a long time to come. There was an officers' call last night. Smith had to grope his way in the darkness by watching the feeble candlelight in the headquarters tent. Word was that they would probably come upon a village soon. They'd move out after midnight and cross the divide before daybreak, then hide out and wait, giving Terry a chance to come up. A combined attack would be made on the morning of the 26th. More hurry up and wait.

Smith wondered about Terry, his old commander back in the war. He had served on Terry's staff. Just the thought made him involuntarily lift his left arm and gingerly rotate the shoulder. His arm still wouldn't lift above the horizontal. He rubbed his shoulder with his right hand. There was his captain's brevet, his reward for the 1865 assault on Fort Fisher. Who's to judge whether or not the action was worth it? A man just does what he has to do.

There were enough other things to think about. Now, up near the divide, Custer had come down from what they called the "Crow's Nest,"

Capt. Thomas W. Custer, Company C, 7th Cavalry. Shown wearing his two Medals of Honor, he was so disfigured after the battle that he could only be recognized by the "T. W. C." tattoo on his arm. —Monroe County, Michigan, Library

and there was some activity. Horsemen were galloping back downhill. Another officers' call was held. There was a village, about 15 miles distant. They had seen Indians. Problem was, the Indians had seen them too. Even in the rear there was trouble. The general's brother, Capt. Thomas W. Custer of Company C, had just ridden up, passing the word. Seems that some men of F Troop had gone back to retrieve some equipment left behind at the last halt. There they found Indians rummaging through the discarded contents of the pack train. They fired and the Indians scattered.

23

There was no way to conceal their presence until the following morning now. The village would flee—or the warriors would come out looking for them. There was no other choice. It would be rather unprecedented, a midday attack on a large, alerted Indian village. But the 7th had always persevered before.

Smith rode back to Company E. They were mounted and waiting. Custer had called for one noncommissioned officer and about a half-dozen enlisted men to be detached and added to the escort for the pack train. Smith called out to Sgt. James F. Riley.

Sergeant Riley, 31 years of age, from Baltimore, Maryland, was in his second five-year enlistment. He only had about one and a half months to go before his discharge date, and he was looking forward to it. Ten years in the cavalry was enough for any man. He rode back down the line and selected the men who would eat dust with him for the day.

"Kimm . . . Berwald . . . Liddiard . . . Lange . . . James!" he yelled out as he trotted past. The men pulled out and went to the rear. Poland's contribution to the troop, 25-year-old Frank Berwald, was rather non-committal about the selection. He was a blacksmith by trade and would probably be of better use with the sometimes-ornery mules anyway. The German, Henry Lange, would do his job well, whatever it might be. John Kimm was a friend of Berwald's. He was a five foot ten New Yorker with gray eyes and black hair, 28 years of age and already in his third enlistment. Kimm would probably make the army his lifetime home. Pvt. John James, born in Rome, was 28 this year. He listed "soldier" as his previous occupation. James looked back over at Kimm, who just shrugged his shoulders. James spit in the dirt as Sergeant Riley rode back through the column.

Herod T. Liddiard was born in London. He was 25 years old and long removed from his boyhood aspirations of being a sailor on the rolling blue ocean. He had come a long way, in distance at least, but not so much in expectations realized. At five feet five and hardly able to see over his mount's big gray head, he was rolling across an ocean of prairie instead of climbing the rigging on a fast clipper ship rounding the Horn. Oh, for a breath of salt air and a sea breeze. Funny, Liddiard thought. There was his "Crow's Nest" and his masts, a grassy hilltop with scattered lodge-pole pines; his Cape Horn only the valley of the Little Bighorn. No ro-mance at all with this detail. He'd rather be in the action instead of daw-dling along in the dust with the godforsaken mule train.

Sergeant Riley nodded a greeting to Captain McDougall. They knew each other well. McDougall had led Company E for about five years, only moving to Company B with his promotion last March. The move was one in a set of shifts that sent Lt. Charles C. DeRudio to Company A and moved Lieutenant Smith to the command of Company E upon McDougall's departure. Now McDougall was slowest in preparing this morning and was rewarded by being stuck with escorting the mules. The assignments to the train, commanded by Lt. Edward G. Mathey of Company M, drained 126 soldiers from the fighting ranks.

The sun was directly overhead, glaring down from a crystal-blue Sunday sky. Cresting the divide, the sweating men and horses were the beneficiaries of a slight breeze lifting out of the valley to the west. A short distance beyond and there was another halt while the regiment was divided up into battalions. Company E moved to the right. They would go with Custer and Companies C, F, I, and L. Some thought Custer played favorites. Company C was in charge of his brother Tom. Company

Lt. James Calhoun, Company L, 7th Cavalry. Custer's brother-in-law, he gave his name to the hill he died defending.
—Monroe County, Michigan, Library

F was led by Capt. George Yates, whom Custer had helped get into the regiment. Company L was commanded by Lt. James Calhoun, Custer's brother-in-law, and Company I was headed by Myles Keogh, a hard-fighting, hard-drinking captain who would be good to have around in a tight spot.

Word was that E Troop was Custer's favorite. Certainly some of that reasoning went into Custer's determination not to let DeRudio command it. The 44-year-old Italian soldier of fortune with Baron Munchausen propensities was not to Custer's liking. DeRudio got his 1st lieutenant straps in December 1875, and the promotion made him commanding officer of Company E. Custer, however, believing DeRudio a gambler, a conspirator, and of inferior quality, requested that he not remain with Company E. DeRudio was sent to Company A, where he would be second in command to Capt. Myles Moylan. DeRudio was furious, but the end result was that he followed Moylan and Reno into the valley fight and would live to tell about it. Lieutenant Smith, previously the acting regimental quartermaster, rode to the heights with Custer in command of Company E.

Custer liked another lieutenant, Francis M. Gibson, and gave him the opportunity to come to Company E when Lieutenant Craycroft was sent on detached service. The transfer papers arrived at Fort Rice in March 1876. Gibson was ready to sign, but his wife, Katherine, pleaded with him not to. It was silly, she knew, but she had had a dream, or a premonition. Call it what you will, she explained, but please don't sign the papers. Something was going to happen, she felt it deep inside. Gibson angrily acquiesced. Today he would ride with Benteen's battalion.

William Van Wyck Reily, a 2nd lieutenant only one month older than Jack Sturgis, had transferred to the 7th Cavalry just five months ago. Though assigned to Company E to replace Lieutenant Craycroft, he was on detached duty with Company F to accommodate the other personnel changes. Reily was not with "E," but he was not far enough away from it either.

Capt. Frederick Benteen, the third senior officer with the regiment, cut out of the column on a slight left oblique. Following his lead were Companies D, H, and K. He was to search over the next ridge for any other campsites or any fleeing Indians. Within minutes, Benteen was approached by Chief Trumpeter Henry Voss. Actually a Company E man, Voss, another native German, rode with Custer's headquarters staff. He brought Benteen a message. If nothing was seen from the first ridge, Benteen was to proceed to the next ridge. Voss immediately turned and galloped away, trying to catch up with his receding battalion.

As Benteen left the first ridge and crossed the little valley on his ascent up the second ridge, he caught a glimpse of the Gray Horse Troop, riding, he thought, at a dead gallop as it followed along the creek two or more miles to the north. It was the last time Benteen would see any of those men alive.

Company E trotted only part of the time, so as not to outdistance Benteen. About four miles down the creek they passed a morass and picked up the pace. Three more miles and they sighted a single tepee. Some Ree Indian scouts had entered the Sioux lodge and appeared to be setting it ablaze. Civilian scout George Herendeen rode near Custer. Lieutenant Smith heard him shout something about "Indians running like devils." He saw Custer glance behind, as if looking for Benteen. Then he ordered Major Reno and Companies A, G, and M to continue down the stream and pursue any fleeing Indians. Custer would follow in support.

John Ogden, born in Massachusetts 31 years earlier, was having trouble keeping his mount in line. The horse was spooked by something—maybe the nearby Rees or the smell of the dead Sioux in the tepee. All he knew was that the bucking and rearing was getting damned aggravating. As a sergeant in his second enlistment, he should be making a better showing among the troopers, especially for the boys who had done less soldiering than he had. He talked to his horse, patted its neck. It did finally calm down. One of these days Ogden would have to get himself a horse not so flighty and easily spooked.

Cpl. Henry Mason watched Sergeant Ogden and his mount in disgust. "He don't like keepin' comp'ny with poor Mr. Lo," Mason wisecracked. A 29-year-old Hoosier and almost six feet tall, Mason thought he'd made a damn sight better appearance when he had his stripes. Of course that was about two years ago in the Black Hills. But he'd been busted. Goddamnit. Busted to private. "Gross neglect of duty," they said. Horseshit. Every man was entitled to a little mistake or two. Since then he'd already made it back to corporal. And he'd still be the best damn sergeant in the troop. All he needed was another chance to prove his mettle. One good fight. Maybe this one.

They were moving out now, leaving the creek valley and heading up into the hills to the north. They could see Reno's men disappear into the timber at the river. Then they lost sight of them as they climbed out of the valley.

After following the ascending eastern slope of the bluffs for one and one half miles, Custer bore to the left to the ridge top while the command continued. Trumpeter Thomas McElroy couldn't see anything below the rim of the bluff. He desperately wanted to know what was out there. Custer appeared agitated, prancing about on his sorrel, gesticulating, and calling out orders. There was a sergeant heading back to the rear, probably with a message. McElroy saw him depart as they trotted closer to the bluff's edge. They were on top for a short time, then immediately angled right,

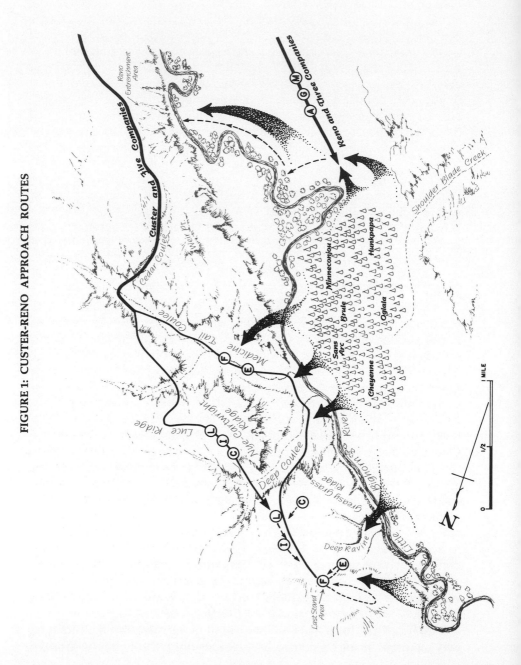

FIGURE 1: CUSTER-RENO APPROACH ROUTES

alongside another long knoll and down into a coulee. For those few brief minutes McElroy could see down in the valley.

"Holy mother o' Christ," he said, half out loud. His mind flashed to the valley in Ireland where he lived as a young boy. Not as green, this valley, but much bigger and almost filled as far as he could see with Indian lodges. It also looked like Reno's battalion was moving across the bottoms. A lump rose in his throat and he couldn't swallow it down. He'd come to America in 1863 and fought in its Civil War. He'd been in battle and he'd been wounded. But there was always that knot in the stomach, that lump in the throat that would appear before each fight, no matter how many times. Now, at 31 years of age and with a wife and a two-year-old son that he'd given his name to, there really was no need for him to be soldiering anymore. The army didn't need another trumpeter. Maybe he could go back home and teach music. He'd sure like to see Nora and little Tommy again. McElroy nervously fingered his wedding band. The grays left the bluff top and descended into a cedar-lined draw.

Custer had gone up to an even higher point on the bluffs, and the command stopped to await further word. They could see him coming down now, waving his hat. Some of the men cheered. Down at the bottom, the draw opened out into a larger coulee that headed left toward the river. Nothing much could be seen from there. They'd have to move closer or get up some hill. The adjutant, 1st Lt. William W. Cooke, wrote something and handed it to a man, another trumpeter probably, because he rode a gray. The messenger hightailed it rearward back up the draw. The battalion headed west, down the coulee. Still nothing much of the Indian camp could be seen from down there.

The Smiths found themselves all riding together. Pvt. James Smith from Massachusetts and Pvt. James Smith from Ireland and Pvt. Albert Smith from New York all rode close behind the other New York Smith, the lieutenant himself. Now Algernon could see Indians on horseback near the trees at the river, still maybe a mile or more ahead. They disappeared. The column halted. To the left, Lieutenant Smith could see the scout Mitch Bouyer and one of the Crows riding down from the high hill. Custer advanced to meet them and they talked. Ogden's horse was rearing up again. An orderly galloped up and gave the lieutenant the word. He was to advance his troop to the river with Captain Yates's command and determine the enemy's disposition. Were they running? Were they in force at the river to oppose a crossing? Make a demonstration and send back word. Custer and three companies cut out of the coulee and began climbing a ridge that paralleled the coulee to the north.

"Here we go, boys!" yelled Lieutenant Sturgis over his shoulder. He was answered by another cheer, but one not very enthusiastic, he thought.

Nearing the river, they pulled up short and fanned out to the right, downstream, staying on the cutbanks maybe 100 yards back from the water. Where were all the Indians? The village was massive, but not much could be seen with all the dust being kicked up.

Sturgis, Ogden, and several troopers continued down to the water's edge when several puffs of smoke appeared from the brush across the river. Warriors jumped up and screamed. The troops back up on the cutbank let go with some long-range carbine fire. Somewhere in the exchange, Ogden's horse caught a bullet. It was off in an instant, splashing into the stream, Ogden holding on for his life. Should he be unhorsed here, he would surely be brought down by the savages on the other bank. Just hold! Hold! Maybe he could get the brute under control. He'd be as good as dead on foot. The others watched, glued to the spectacle. The beast plunged, bucked, and charged forward. In a few seconds it was gone. The sergeant's hat was the only thing left, floating downstream in the current. They caught a glimpse of Ogden and the gray as both disappeared into the dust of the village.

Bullets whistled past Lieutenant Sturgis, snapping him out of his reverie. More Indians showed themselves, firing and ducking down. Some were on horseback, splashing across the river in the direction Ogden's hat had floated. Sturgis called out for the men to fall back to the rest of the company. They needed no urging. Sturgis was the last up from the water. It was like Pa would have wanted.

Things didn't look good to Lieutenant Smith. There was a ford all right, but there was no way they'd be crossing it into that camp. The firing along the banks increased. He could see Indians on the high hills to the south now too. The men kept up a ragged fire while remaining mounted. Yates was still partly back down the coulee. When he came up, they could increase their firepower, but Smith didn't think they'd be able to stay for too long.

The Indians dictated their next move. They crossed both up and downstream. The companies would have to pull out. They couldn't go back up the low coulee they had just emerged from with the Indians taking position on the hills to the south, and besides, Custer was heading north when they had separated. Just then a volley of gunfire echoed down from the hills to the east. Was it Custer signaling? By mutual agreement, Smith and Yates pulled back and angled north and east, up the banks of another coulee.

The shooting slackened somewhat as they moved away from the river, though the occasional warrior would fire from the left on a parallel ridge as they headed north. The column angled up the slopes of the coulee now, heading for higher ground. Pvt. John Darris, a 30-year-old former farmer from Goshen, New York, was just congratulating himself on his escape back at the river. Glory was fine and all that, but who needed to charge an Indian village with hundreds of screaming braves shooting at him? Amid the gunshots and the hoofbeats, no one even heard the nearly silent arrow that plunged down directly into Darris's spine, severing nerves and causing him to collapse and slide off his horse like an old used-up rag doll. He landed in a small ditch in the side of the coulee. E Troop kept on moving.

Up on the ridge, Smith could size up the situation better. As he moved north, he could see Custer coming down from some higher ground to the east. They'd intersect on the long knoll ahead. He could see the Indians coming up behind him, crossing the river where he'd been just a short time ago. He heard the crash of volley fire—Custer, up ahead, firing at some other target.

They converged on the hill, Smith and Yates with E and F Troops, and Custer with C, I, and L. It was Jim Calhoun that dismounted and formed an arcing line on the hill to hold back the Indians approaching up the coulee in C and F's wake. Company E took the lead, the handsome grays trotting north and west now, just below the crest of a long, narrow ridge.

At the northern terminus Company E dismounted and formed a line just beyond the end of the ridge. Company F, with Custer and the scouts, continued toward the river where it was thought there might be another ford. There was less activity on the northern end of the ridge than where Calhoun had deployed, but that probably wouldn't last long. Warriors could be seen coming up the ravines from the west and the southeast too. It didn't look good. What was Custer's plan?

As the warriors closed in, Company E sent ragged volleys in their direction. There was enough open ground to prevent their approaching too closely, or so it seemed. Troopers occasionally looked back down the ridge to where Calhoun and Keogh had deployed whenever the sound of battle crested from that direction. The firing tempo picked up. There was plenty of smoke and dust now.

Pvt. John S. Hiley placed a well-aimed shot at a warrior who exposed his head above a small draw. Hiley squeezed and the warrior dropped down. Did he hit him? Looked like it. But the warriors always popped up and down to draw the soldiers' fire. Hiley, rather John Stuart Forbes, was not too sure he had made the right decision at this point. Born in Rugby, England, of noble ancestry and listed in Foster's *Peerage and Baronetage,* he regretted the deed that brought him to America. Four years prior, at age 23, the noble Scotsman had come to New York and enlisted as a private, using his brother-in-law's last name. It was not that odd. Other men, seeking to hide some dark part of their past, often used aliases and joined the army. But Hiley-Forbes wasn't like other men. He was no common criminal. He'd just had a little gambling problem. He only had one year to go in his enlistment. Maybe he'd even skip out before that. There was nothing to keep him here anymore. Back at Fort Lincoln in his footlocker was the letter he had recently received from his mother. "You can return home now, as the trouble causing your departure has been settled." He'd do it. Just as soon as he got back to the post, he'd arrange a way out of this parched prairie land and return to the green meadows of home.

The troop mounted up. Indian pressure was making the position untenable, and something would have to be done. Custer had returned from his abortive search for a ford. More warriors were massing beyond a flat-topped hill toward the river and down in the lower reaches of a broad valley. Company E was called on to check their approach.

Lieutenant Sturgis relished his chance. Smith had directed him to take the company down the valley and form a skirmish line to check the warriors threatening from that direction. Smith would remain on the hilltop with Custer, his brother Tom, and Yates, waiting for further developments. Part of F Troop remained on the flat hill below to link with Sturgis's right.

About 150 paces down in the basin the young lieutenant called out orders. "Company as skirmishers, at ten paces. March!" Sturgis and Trumpeter George A. Moonie followed about 25 paces behind. At the appropriate time, Moonie was instructed to sound out "to the left." The line guided up the gentle ravine slope. The company covered the interval between F Troop and a low divide on the south end of the basin. Sturgis called out "Halt!" Then, "Prepare to fight—on foot!" He smiled. Without a hitch, trooper numbers one, two, and three passed their reins over their horses heads, numbers three handing them to four, tight slip knots fixed with about one foot of play, then they all faced to the front. "Into—line!" The command moved about 12 paces forward and halted. Nicely done, Sturgis thought.

Holding mounts were Cpl. Albert H. Meyer and Pvts. Robert Barth, James Brogan, and Edward Connor, among others—some of the company's most experienced soldiers. There was no volleying. The braver or more reckless warriors out in front of the main host fell back at the troop's approach. But this was no charge. The Indians ceased their flight when they saw the troopers dismount. Now they returned even bolder. Sturgis called out to fire at will. Targets of opportunity. The lieutenant rode the line. If Pa could only see him now.

At the line's far left, Pvt. Andy Knecht made his way to the top of the divide and peered over. From here he could get a view none of the others had farther back down the slope. The 24-year-old former butcher from Cincinnati, Ohio, almost had his heart jump up in his throat. Injuns! Maybe hundreds more, down another ravine, a deeper one, just a couple of hundred yards away and moving uphill to their left and rear. He drew back the hammer of his carbine and fired in the direction of the gulch. It's like throwing a stone into an anthill, he thought.

Knecht turned around, saw Sergeant James, and yelled out. At least his mouth was open, but the voice seemed to stick in his throat. "Sergeant!" he bellowed, but he couldn't even hear himself in all the godawful screeching and shooting. "Sergeant!" His legs were like rubber. Suddenly James was running to him. When he reached the crest, there was no need for Knecht to attempt to say anything else.

James's jaw slackened. Then he turned to Knecht and shouted, "Don't just stand there, man. Work that carbine!" He ran back, waving at Lieutenant Sturgis. The lieutenant was dismounted now. He listened, took in the situation quickly, and shifted a handful of men to the left. The move made gaps in the center. Things were just not working the way they were supposed to in the tactics manuals. Indians were rising up all along his front now. And what? At the far right of his line, coming down the flat-topped hill, were mounted Indians! They weren't stopping. They were charging right into the troopers' fire, right into the lines. My God, were they crazy? What was he supposed to do now?

Near the center of the line, Trumpeter McElroy was working his Springfield as fast as his nimble musician's fingers would allow when a bullet smashed into his carbine right where his left hand cradled the weapon. The impact tore the barrel out of his hand. He held up his wounded hand in front of his face, dazed, staring. He saw his wedding band twinkle in the hot sun. The next bullet found more flesh to rip into. The missus back home became a widow.

It was all too quick, too crazy. The Indians were on them. Sergeant Hohmeyer released the horses' reins. It was a desperation move. There was no turning back now. Every carbine was needed on the line. Can't shoot and hold the Gottdamnt horses. Meyer released, and Connor and the others. The grays were gone in an instant, charging wildly downhill toward the river.

Some of the troopers drifted left, away from the attack of the crazy mounted warriors who came into the broad depression on the right. Knecht was still on the low divide. "The Injuns is behind us!" he screamed, but didn't know if his words made any sound or not.

After the Indians approached up that deep gully, they had swung left and hit the troopers from the rear. Knecht looked back down the little valley to see Lieutenant Sturgis fall. A naked warrior was standing tall above him, lifting his war club up and bringing it down, up and down, up and down, driving the stone over and over into the lieutenant's face. Knecht was mesmerized. Smoke blew into his eyes. There was a roaring in his ears. Several gray horses went running by him. The next thing he knew, he had dropped his carbine and was running along with them. Running. Running as fast as his overweight, five foot six frame could carry him.

Both James Smiths went down, hit almost at the same instant. So too went Privates Rood, Van Sant, and Stella. Corporal Eagan wasn't dead. He knew it. When you're dead there wasn't any pain, or so he'd been told. But he couldn't move. He lay on his face, choking in the dirt. If he could only lift up and get some air. Something hard forced his head deeper into the dirt—a terrible pressure on the back of his neck. Then his skull felt like it burst aflame. My God! Was his head being torn off? Eagan's scream was muffled as his open mouth was jammed farther down into the buffalo grass. Then everything went black and the pain stopped.

Sykes Henderson and William Torrey were gone. John Heim, too. He watched the mounted warriors charge down the hill right at him. He fired. They kept coming. Heim tried to eject the casing and place another cartridge in the chamber, but his fingers wouldn't work. He dropped the carbine and reached for his pistol. Too late. The Indian pony's hoofs were as high as his face. Heim's knees buckled and he went down in the dust.

Corporal Mason was the last one fighting up near the divide. He'd show 'em. Bust me, will they? He'd get his stripes back after this. Maybe they'd make him a lieutenant. Or a captain. They ought to make him a Goddamn captain for this stand. But he couldn't load fast enough. If he had his Goddamn Spencer yet, maybe, but no, not in this Goddamn army. Mason dropped his Springfield and went to the Colt. At least he'd get maybe six more shots.

The line was gone. Lieutenant Smith looked down the valley at the swarming Indians, then in anguish up at Custer. The lieutenant colonel didn't notice him. Smith glanced downhill again. There were survivors. A handful, maybe a half dozen. His company was gone, shattered. Yates's troop crumbled and fell back too, and some of Tom Custer's men. There were soldiers of every unit here. Smith heard a trumpet call. It was Voss of E, sounding recall. For what, Smith thought? The fugitives were already flying toward the guidon here on the hill.

They shot more of the horses for barricades and crouched behind them, the bays of Company F, the remaining grays, and a few sorrels of Company C that made it there from Calhoun's position. Smith lay behind his dead mount. Shots crashed out around his head. Every warrior that chanced to stick his head up received prompt attention. The soldiers were good now. Even the recruits had become professionals. They'd sell it as dearly as possible. Suddenly, a band of braves burst over the hill from the back side. Lieutenant Smith was using his pistol. Crouched low, he barely caught a glimpse of the swift blur over his left shoulder. He tried to spin and ward off the blow with his arm. The damaged shoulder refused to allow for a successful parry. The warclub caught part of his arm and then glanced up into his left cheekbone.

Back on Reno's hilltop position things had been quiet for a time, but now they were getting lively again. The pack train had come up. Benteen directed some of the escort into firing positions. There were a few Indians on a low knoll to the north, firing into the exposed troopers.

"We'll get 'em, sir," Liddiard said. Several troopers responded by sending some long-range bullets in the Indians' direction. Liddiard lay down. He wondered where the rest of his company had gone. Over the hills somewhere to the north they said. He was out of the action again. Maybe he could make up for it. He wasn't a bad shot. Pretty damn good in fact, for an ex-boatman. He took careful aim at a puff of smoke he could see on the knoll.

Where the hell was Custer, anyway? Probably watering his horses in the Little Bighorn, one trooper suggested. No, said another. He abandoned us, just like he did Elliot at the Washita. He's probably in a spot just like we're in here, said a third. "What do you say, Liddiard?"

There was no answer. The boatman lay unmoving, still sighting along the barrel of his carbine. "Hey, Liddiard!" a trooper called. Then he noticed the dark, wet stain welling up around the prone trooper's hatbrim. A soldier knelt beside him and shook his shoulder. Liddiard's head tilted to the side at an awkward angle as his chin slipped off the gunstock. Blood coursed down in a line across his eye and cheek. The bullet had gone clean through his forehead and out the back.

There was a lull in the fight back on the hill. Hohmeyer watched the warriors burst over the men and disappear back down another gulch. He shot once, twice, and the targets were gone. Except on the farther hills. Mein Gott! There were hundreds of them. Poor Mary. And little William, and Lizzie and Lena and Nellie. He'd never see any of them again. He looked to the south in the direction they had come up, and then down in the valley to the west. Where the hell was Benteen! And that hosen-scheisser Reno! Mein Gott im Himmel!

Who was left? Hohmeyer shifted his gaze quickly left and right. Several pairs of eyes met his. Somewhere on the hill a trooper was mounting a Company C sorrel brought in by the men that had made it from Calhoun's position. He tore off to the south, clinging to the horse's mane and with his head bowed like he was riding through a hailstorm.

Where was Custer? There were no standing figures to be seen. Another trooper popped up and began to run. Hohmeyer looked around at the several men watching him. "Ach! Up! Raus! Raus!"

They jumped up and began to run. There was Corporal Meyer and Privates Farrell and Rees and Moonie and Huber. There was Custer's color sergeant, Robert Hughes. There was Mitch Bouyer too, the half-breed scout.

He was wounded, but still game. There were several others of various troops. Hohmeyer paid no attention now. He ran as fast as he could, neck and neck with his countryman Corporal Meyer.

They tore off downhill, awkwardly stumbling, leaping, terror-stricken, legs pumping wildly over the uneven, sage-covered slope. One fired his pistol at the sky as he ran. Another threw his gun away as if the extra weight would slow him down too much. Hohmeyer saw one man downslope still alive, sitting with his legs crossed and crying like a baby. The man put a pistol to his head. Hohmeyer left him in the dirt. Maybe they could get to the river, to the cutbanks, to the brush. But it was so far. They seemed to be running in slow-motion.

The warriors chased them down. One by one they fell. Along what had been E Company's skirmish line, among the other bodies, past the sprawled forms of Privates Boyle and Baker, Walker and Smallwood. Past the now-unrecognizable smashed head of young Jack Sturgis. Bouyer made it up near the divide before he fell. A few feet away lay the outstretched form of Corporal Mason, empty-handed, his pistol now in the possession of a jubilant warrior.

Some troopers burst over the divide and headed downhill toward a deep ravine. Maybe if they could get there they'd be safe. Pvt. William H. Rees had outdistanced them all. Although he was 38 years old, his lanky six foot one frame allowed him to lead the pack. Rees was about the tallest man in the regiment, but right now he wished he was only one inch high. He felt like the center dot in a bull's-eye. There were more Indians down in this direction. He slowed his run, turned one way, then another. Something ripped into his back. Rees looked down to his chest and saw an arrowhead protruding from his rib cage. He crumpled down onto the grass.

The last handful of stampeding men literally flew into the deep gully, almost landing on a wounded Indian. One trooper put a bullet into him and another finished him off with the warrior's own knife. Hohmeyer was there, and Meyer, Farrell, Huber, Hughes, and a few others. Hohmeyer almost shouted in exultation. They caught their breath for a few seconds and then headed down the ravine—only to come upon more warriors moving toward them not 50 yards away. The troopers turned to dash back up the gully, but now there were Indians on the banks above them too.

Pvt. Andy Knecht had lain near the edge of the gully for, God, it seemed like hours now . . . maybe days. At least his breathing had calmed and his chest wasn't heaving like it had been. He had been wounded, his scalp grazed. It knocked him dizzy and he went to his knees. Then the thought flashed to him. He collapsed. The blood trickled slightly down his forehead. He rubbed it around to make his cheek good and red, then closed his eyes. Maybe he could lie this way until dark.

Two squaws saw a soldier with a full set of clothes still on. They could use them. They approached the *wasichu*. One grasped his pant legs while another unfastened his trouser buttons. They yanked them off in no time. Knecht almost screamed inside. Dead. Dead. I'm dead. He remained limp and lifeless as could be. They'd take his clothes and go away. His shirt and underdrawers were peeled off. They dropped his legs back down. The squaws had been talking nonstop, but they had suddenly become silent. The silence rang in his ears. It was too much. Knecht cracked open one dirt-encrusted eyelid just in time to see the big-bladed knife in the squaw's hand. She was kneeling over his midsection and was just about to grab his . . .

"No!" The *wasichu* bounded back to life, nearly startling the women into flight themselves. One recovered her wits in time to grab Knecht by the wrist. He ran and she swung behind him in a macabre dance. Some warriors watched the spinning couple and thought it one of the funniest sights they had ever seen, the squaw dancing with the naked *wasichu*. Another woman, not so enthralled with the scene, ran up and drove her blade deep into Knecht's back.

Then the mutilations began.

FIGURE 2: MAIN BATTLEFIELD LOCATIONS

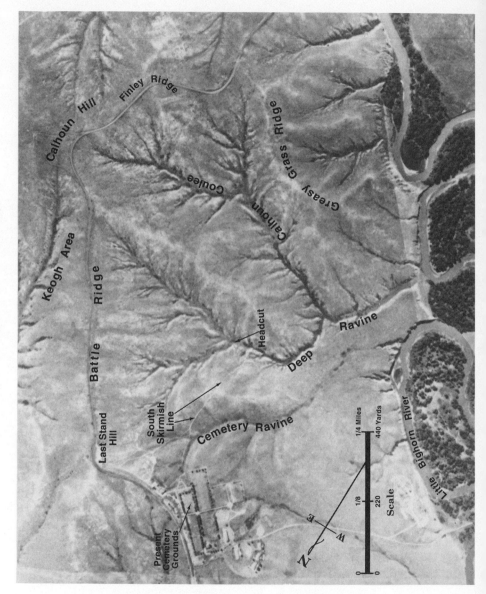

2. The 1984-85 Dig

Origin of the Mystery

Thus the men of Company E, who had gone through ten years and thousands of miles of marching and fighting, came to the end of the trail within the confines of one square mile of Montana prairie. The great majority of the company fell on Custer Hill (Last Stand Hill) and down toward the Little Bighorn, along 700 or 800 yards of rolling hill and vale covered with buffalo grass and speckled with sagebrush.

Standing atop Custer Hill and looking out over the valley of the Little Bighorn, one notices the stark white tombstones dotting the grassy slopes. It is the only battlefield in the nation where the gravestones dot the fields marking where individual men fell fighting. Clusters here and there indicate where groups of cavalrymen fell. Paired and individual stones mark more isolated deaths. Walking along the heights and hollows is both serene and eerie, for ghosts still seem to haunt the hills and valleys along the Little Bighorn. The line of stones stretching obliquely across the gentle vale downslope from the hilltop represents many of the men of Company E. They are instructive. There are no secrets in the somber white markers facing the setting sun. Or are there?

Somewhere, sometime between the first cursory burials on June 28, 1876, the reburials of 1877 and 1879, the removal of the bones in 1881, and the placing of the tombstones in 1890, we seem to have lost track of a good portion of Company E. Today, the consensus is that approximately 28 bodies are missing. How were these bodies lost? Where were they when they disappeared?

The mystery begins with the reports of the survivors of the commands of Maj. Marcus A. Reno and Capt. Frederick W. Benteen, detailed to bury Custer's troopers. Traveling three miles north from the area where they had been besieged, they came upon Custer's field. Riding together, Lt. Edward S. Godfrey of K Company and Capt. Thomas B. Weir of Company D first noticed what appeared to be a large number of boulders scattered across the field. Field glasses soon defined the objects with crystal clarity. They were bodies. "Oh, how white they look!" exclaimed Captain Weir. Occasionally there was a body with a bloody undershirt, a pair of trousers or a boot with the leather uppers cut away, but most of the men were stripped, mutilated, and almost unrecognizable. Godfrey thought the field was a scene of "sickening, ghastly horror!" The survivors of the 7th Cavalry, with few available tools, began the interment.[60]

The battlefield was divided into five sectors. The company commanders went over the field to find the bodies of the commissioned officers, and the first sergeants of each company advanced the men over their sector to identify the bodies, bury them, and keep a count of the number. Company B was on the extreme left closest to the river, then Company A to their right.[61] Companies G, M, and K had the central area and Companies D and H covered the right farthest back from the river. They swept north, burying and counting. The company sectors were very much intermingled by the time they reached Last Stand Hill.

In one location south and west of the main battle ridge there was mention of a deep ravine where many bodies were clustered. Of course, there are many ravines in the area—ravines, coulees, gullies, dozens of them. The ravine in question, however, has been designated "Deep Ravine." It is truly the deepest ravine in the area and appears to be the spot where our mystery begins.

Many of the Indians who witnessed the troopers' deaths and the soldiers who later buried the bodies spoke of finding a significant number of men in this ravine, down from Custer Hill toward the river. First Sgt. John Ryan of Company M saw where about 18 or 20 men of Smith's Gray Horse Company got into a ravine where they couldn't get out, were shot by the Indians, and fell back into the ravine.[62] Capt. Frederick Benteen of Company H testified at the Reno Court of Inquiry that he thought there were about 22 bodies in a ravine down near the river. Capt. Myles Moylan of Company A testified at the same court that he saw about 20-odd bodies of E Company in a ravine with scramble marks in the dirt halfway up the bank.[63] Lt. Edward Godfrey wrote that about 28 men of Smith's troop were found in a ravine near the river.[64] Lt. Luther R. Hare of Company K gave testimony that 28 bodies of Lieutenant Smith's company were in a coulee in skirmish order.[65] Sgt. Daniel Knipe of Company C told interviewer Walter M. Camp that he rode along the edge of a deep gully and counted 28 bodies in there. Lt. Richard Thompson of the 6th Infantry told Camp he saw maybe 34 bodies in a gully.[66] First Lt. Edward Maguire of the Engineers drew a map and reported that in one ravine 28 bodies were found.[67] Lt. Edward McClernand of the 2nd Cavalry recorded that 28 bodies from Smith's troop were found at the lower end of the line in a deep coulee.[68] Col. John Gibbon of the 7th Infantry noted that some 40 or 50 bodies were found in a valley running perpendicular to the river.[69]

There were fewer Indians that could substantiate the number. Apparently they were not so concerned with the totals as were the white men, or perhaps, they saw the events differently. Walter Camp interviewed Good

Voiced Elk, a Hunkpapa Sioux, who said 25 to 30 died in a gully. In a conversation with He Dog, an Oglala, Camp asked if 28 bodies were in the gully and the Indian corroborated the number.[70]

The totals vary from 18 to 50, but 28 seems to be most often repeated. So what is the mystery of 28-odd bodies in a deep ravine? The first burial on the 28th was a slipshod affair. Lack of spades and other tools prevented deep, thorough interments. Bodies were covered as well as could be, scraping up the hard, dry Montana soil with whatever was available. If a hand, a knee, or a foot stuck out, so be it. A little more dirt and a ripped-up piece of sagebrush on the mound and it would be out of sight. The bodies in less accessible places were simply left as they lay. Hauling them to another place was well-nigh impossible. "Many times in taking hold of a body to lift it into the grave the skin would slip from the wrist, or the shoulders became dislocated," wrote Cpl. John E. Hammon of G Company.[71] According to Pvt. Theodore Goldin, also of G Company, the ground was so hard a pick was needed to make an impression in it. The bodies were in such a state of mortification they couldn't be moved. There were times "where men taking hold of an arm often found it to come loose from the body."[72] All they could do was to "remove a little dirt in a low place, roll in a body and cover it with dirt," said Pvt. William C. Slaper of M Company.[73]

Out of sight, out of mind. There were still men with wounds to attend to and an evacuation to be carried out. There were still hostiles about, obviously undefeated and perhaps still ready to fight. The dead would be of second priority. The soldiers pulled out.

Over the succeeding months the elements and the animals would have their play with the hastily buried troopers. In the summer of 1877, an expedition under Lt. Col. Michael V. Sheridan and Capt. Henry J. Nowlan of the 7th Cavalry's Company I was sent to the field to gather up the remains of the officers for reinterment in cemeteries back in the States. They identified and removed the bodies as best as they could. They also staked the graves of the enlisted men. They set no stakes in Deep Ravine.

During that same summer an inspection tour was made by Gen. Philip H. Sheridan, Gen. George Crook, the generals' staffs, and members of the 5th Cavalry. Although arriving less than one month after his brother Michael, General Sheridan was embarrassed by the condition of the field, had the area skirmished again for any exposed remains, and had the graves remounded and re-marked.

In 1879, Capt. George K. Sanderson of the 11th Infantry was sent to the field. He built a cordwood mound and filled it with more exposed remains, human and equine. Sanderson replaced headboards and repainted the inscriptions on them all. He did no replacing or painting in Deep Ravine.

In 1881, there was another re-reburial by Lt. Charles F. Roe of the 2nd Cavalry. Roe erected the granite monument that stands atop Custer Hill today. He collected all the enlisted mens' remains and reinterred them at the base of the monument. He again planted stakes so future visitors could see where the men fell. He planted no stakes in Deep Ravine.

In 1890, Capt. Owen Sweet led men of the 25th Infantry to the Custer battlefield to set 246 marble gravestones for all the men that fell there. Sweet planted no stones in Deep Ravine.

All the above expeditions will be examined in detail in a subsequent chapter. At this time it is sufficient simply to reiterate that the soldiers of 1876 saw and reported about 28 bodies in a deep ravine, yet all ensuing burial and inspection details found no indications of bodies in Deep Ravine.

In this book the "Deep Ravine" referred to will be the narrow, steep-walled channel coursing up from the Little Bighorn about 700 yards to the headcut area below the forks of the upper ravine (fig. 3). It does not include the upper Deep Ravine watershed. The Deep Ravine proper is where contemporary authors have assumed the 28 bodies fell, and it is where subsequent archaeological expeditions have concentrated their attention in searching for those bodies.

What happened to the bodies? All those reports were made of dead men in a deep ravine and there are no gravemarkers set in Deep Ravine to show their death spots. Was there a mistake made? Are many of those stones on Custer Hill and stretching down the valley along what is sometimes called the South Skirmish Line erroneous? Do many of those stones actually belong in Deep Ravine? Two respected contemporary researchers, Richard G. Hardorff and the late John S. Gray, support exactly that contention.[74] Another argued that 88 percent of the stones on Custer Hill and the South Skirmish Line are misplaced, and contain markers that belong in Deep Ravine.[75] Charles Kuhlman, the man probably most responsible for the South Skirmish Line concept, also thought there ought to be markers in Deep Ravine where there were none.[76] As early as 1920, researcher Walter Mason Camp was writing that there were too many stones between the monument and the river and none in the deep gully where 28 ought to have been.[77]

How could those Micawbers of the late nineteenth century apparently be so optimistic that their job was well done, yet so negligent as to leave Deep Ravine unmarked? There were obviously some discrepancies between the record and the actual state of affairs, but were the discrepancies the fault of the participants or the interpreters?

The Park Service was aware of the problem, but there was no sense in ignoring the attraction of a good mystery. Deep Ravine's potential as a drawing card was viable enough by the summer of 1979 to be included as a regular addition to the interpretive battle descriptions given the park

FIGURE 3: CEMETERY RAVINE AND DEEP RAVINE DIVISIONS

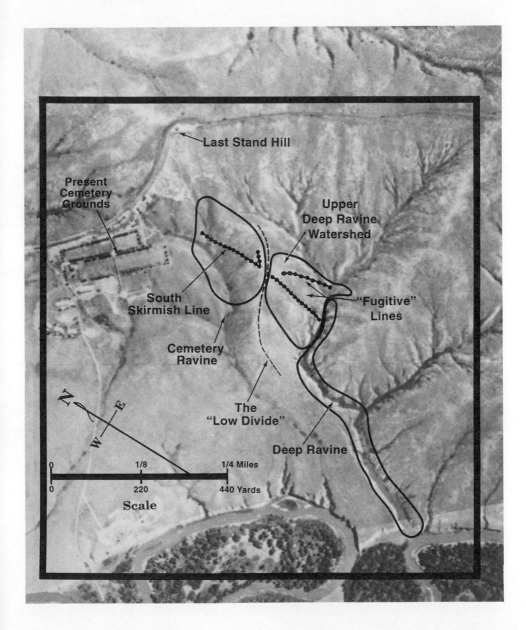

visitors. In 1980, the ravine was featured in a new battlefield tour, and the trails around it were improved in 1981.[78] In 1983, however, an event occurred that had the potential of finally solving the Deep Ravine mystery.

The Fire

The Custer battlefield lies within the shortgrass prairie of eastern Montana. One of the most significant features of the shortgrass prairie is the slight amount of precipitation it receives, the annual averaging as low as 10 to 12 inches. Although most of the precipitation occurs during the growing season of May through July, the desiccating property of the winds and the high temperatures soon use the moisture up. With the climate less congenial to growth, the plants go into a state of dormancy during the summer.

One of the dominant grasses of the prairie here is buffalo grass, which spreads by stolons, or above-ground stems, taking root as they spread and sending up tufts of green grass. They can grow an inch or two a day and can colonize a bare site quite easily. Blue grama grass is taller than the buffalo grass, its delicate, arched stalks growing between six and twenty inches high. Also present in the shortgrass prairie are western wheatgrass and needle-and-thread, its fibrous end tufts curling around and through each other in resemblance of its namesake.

Other shortgrass prairie plants found in the area are the locoweed, plains wallflower, gumweed, prairie clover, and sunflower. Silvery gray-leaved sagebrush speckles the hillsides through much of the battle area. Even prickly pear cacti and yucca can be found occasionally.[79]

Shunning the hilltops because of sun, wind, and dryness, the trees of the area are concentrated almost exclusively in the sheltered coulees and along the riverbanks. By far the most common to the Custer battlefield area is the cottonwood, heavy and massive at times, its pale, heavily furrowed bark seen lining much of the banks of the Little Bighorn River. In lesser profusion will be found the aspen, chokecherry, mesquite, or an occasional juniper snaking up the numerous gullies from the river. Soldiers of the nineteenth century also spoke of using cedar stakes to mark gravesites, while others cut ash along the Little Bighorn to build a derrick to help erect the granite monument.

The trees, shrubs, and grasses indigenous to the prairie are there because they have adapted to the climatic conditions. One of the agents that aids in tipping the balance between grass or tree cover is fire. Most trees are killed or weakened by fire, but grasses have adapted to thrive on it, and may even grow better after a conflagration.[80] The shortgrass prairie on the Custer battlefield got a chance to renew itself in the summer of 1983.

It was a dry year. Rain seldom disturbed the visitors, and the opinion was expressed that the ridges and coulees hadn't been so tinder dry in five years. Naturally the prairie vegetation thrived, having nearly reached the top of the three-foot marble markers. On August 9, a grass fire scorched the ground north of the battlefield along Highway 212. It consumed 100 acres before Crow Indians and employees of the Bureau of Indian Affairs checked it.

Sometime overnight, however, the wind picked up and fanned to life some undead embers. Before noon on the 10th, battlefield employees noticed a cloud of smoke towering up east of Calhoun Hill. The flames raced across the hill, along the battlefield road, and toward the river. The area was cleared as quickly as possible, a job that included finding some people who had disappeared in the smoke down the Deep Ravine Trail. They were quickly ushered out. From the museum the flames could be seen, 15 feet high and a half-mile long. The ground sprinklers were turned on, the fire hoses broken out, and the buildings and grounds around the cemetery were doused. The quick action of the employees and a little luck with the wind saved the visitor center and environs, the only damage to the cemetery being some scorched trees on the east edge. The rest of the field didn't fare so well. It was described as being "black as a freeway," or looking like "a Safeway parking lot."[81]

The fire could have been a calamity, but it was actually the catalyst that set off a chain of events that led to a thorough archeological examination of the battlefield. There had been artifacts collected in and around the battlefield for years, but no one had ever done a controlled study to determine what historical materials might still lie hidden beneath the surface of the prairie. Also, the accuracy of the placement of the marble markers, perhaps the most distinctive feature of the field, had been questioned many times. Now the field lay bare, begging examination before hardy buffalo grasses began to recolonize the area. A dig was organized to begin in the spring of 1984.

The First Excavations

Archaeology is said to be the handmaiden of history, but the one branch of study is not always subordinate to the other. History depends on the availability and accuracy of the written record.[82] Sometimes the record is incomplete, and possibly biased or speculative. Archaeology can reveal much of what might be left out of the written record. In this instance it might be able to correlate the written record of the eyewitnesses with the physical record in the ground.

The research objectives of the Custer battlefield dig were shaped with this realization in mind. There does exist a behavioral relationship between historical events and the physical remains of those events. Battlefield behavior can be understood by exposing the physical remains and evaluating them in their historical context. The first objective would be to analyze the nature of the armaments used in the fight. Second, perhaps the troop deployments could be traced and accounted for in behavioral terms. Third, the skeletal remains would be analyzed to determine demographic data such as disease, diet, age, physical condition, the extent of mutilations, and possible identities of the cavalrymen. The fourth objective would be to evaluate the equipment used on a field campaign of that time. The last objective would be to determine the whereabouts of the 28 missing soldiers supposedly buried in Deep Ravine, in order to correctly analyze the progress of the fight itself. Only after their whereabouts were discovered could the circumstances of their presence be addressed.[83]

The battlefield historian, Neil Mangum, put the Deep Ravine aspects of the dig in a more succinct perspective: "We want to satisfy the question of were there any bodies down there, and if not, where did the missing soldiers fall and where are they buried."[84]

There was reason for optimism. In the past there had been success with relic hunting in the area, but because the digging wasn't controlled, many opportunities to answer questions had the artifacts been recorded in situ were lost forever. Yet, some positive information did emerge.

In 1928, J. A. Blummer, a local resident who ran the store at Garryowen, was told by Frank Bethune, a member of the Crow Nation, of the discovery of some bones south of Custer's field. Blummer searched up the draw (Deep Coulee) from the marker thought to be the death site of Company L Sgt. James Butler.[85] Working his way toward Custer's field, Blummer went to the place where Bethune had found a skeleton with an arrow sticking in the backbone and a gun scabbard with initials that appeared to be R. D. In that same area, Blummer had discovered a boot with the initials J. D. that contained human bones. He searched farther up Deep Coulee toward Custer's field and was rewarded by finding 17 shells on the east side of a small ridge about three-fourths of a mile southeast of the southeast corner of the field. The shells were strung out in a line about 150 yards long.[86]

The discovery was one of the first to provide solid proof that there was firing done some distance east of Medicine Tail ford. The announcement was the catalyst that sent many others to the area looking for relics. In 1929, Blummer and his friend, R. G. Cartwright of Lead, South Dakota, went up to the ridge and found 28 more cartridges. When Blummer moved out of the area, Cartwright was left alone with the information. His attempts to bring it to the attention of historians were futile, and he was labeled a "screwball." It was a decade later that Cartwright guided Col. Elwood L. Nye of the 4th Cavalry to the area. They picked up seven more casings.[87]

In 1943, Cartwright found two more shells and showed the position to retired 7th Cavalry Capt. Edward S. Luce, then the superintendent of the Custer battlefield. Luce continued southeast along the ridge, following the trail of shells. After a half-mile gap he began finding more shells, this time 48. They were spread at three- to four-yard intervals, which Luce thought designated a dismounted skirmish line. A few weeks later, Luce brought another official in, whom he called "my boss from Yellowstone Park." They found a brass buckle, a canteen, a spur, and a hat ornament.[88]

In July 1946, Cartwright, Luce, Nye, and author Charles Kuhlman explored the area. Letters from these individuals indicate an abundance of artifacts were discovered, Cartwright estimating "nearly two hundred" and Luce writing "over 400" expended cartridges had been found during the past several years. Cartwright also indicated that Kuhlman picked up one shell and nearly broke down and cried. Finding battle evidence there had nearly destroyed his entire thesis.[89]

The discoveries along what have come to be known as Nye-Cartwright and Luce Ridges (fig. 1) have detracted from some of the early Indian accounts, particularly those of the Cheyennes, who claimed there was a substantial conflict at the river's edge.[90] Yet, the Medicine Tail ford area has produced its own relics. In 1958 and 1959, researcher Jesse W. Vaughn and park historian Don Rickey Jr. found 17 items 50 yards west of the present battlefield road near the ford, including shells, arrowheads, buttons, screws, tent pins, and a knife. A short way up Deep Coulee (north fork of Medicine Tail Coulee) they found 11 more shells, of various calibers.[91]

The known artifact finds total over 70 within a half-mile arc east of the mouth of the Medicine Tail. More than 400 artifacts were found along the mile or so length of Luce and Nye-Cartwright Ridges.[92] The amounts are sufficient to show action occurred in both areas. Those who would seek to explain the battle in terms of a unified, five-company Custer battalion would bump up against the hard artifact evidence with whatever route they propounded. It did not make sense, and there was not the time, for all five companies to come to the river, fight, retrace their route to the eastern ridges, fight again, then make their way to the Calhoun Hill position. The Indian accounts tell of no such thing, and the artifacts show convincingly that Custer's companies were split, part going to the river and part staying on the eastern ridges. The relic finds showed that some seemingly contradictory historical records were not so contradictory or irreconcilable after all. Perhaps a thorough, controlled examination of Custer's field would also provide insights concerning the troop movements and the course of the battle, even more so than the discoveries near Medicine Tail ford and on Luce and Nye-Cartwright Ridges.

The 1984 dig began by dividing the field up into a grid system for reference; it was then marked by professional land surveyors. The inventory phase consisted of three operations: survey, recovery, and recording. Metal detector operators swept each designated grid area, walking at 15-

Excavation site on Last Stand Hill, with marked-off graves and sifter box. —Little Bighorn Battlefield National Monument

foot intervals across the field. Following behind the detectors, other volunteers would place a pin flag on the spot of each find. Recovery crews then followed up by excavating at each flagged location. Whenever bone, leather, or wood was encountered, the excavators would call an archaeologist, who would decide whether to continue excavating or cover the site for more extensive probing at a later date. Recorders followed the recovery crew to mark and catalog all the finds. The marble markers were also surveyed because their locations had not been accurately mapped since the U.S. Geological Survey in 1891.

There were three testing techniques used during the fieldwork. Standard small-scale block excavations consisted of one-by-two-meter or two-by-two-meter square units, which were dug in areas of suspected battle activity or around a sampling of marble gravemarkers to check the validity of marker and burial correlations. These were essentially layered, horizontal excavations generally no more than six to eight inches deep. Other techniques used in Deep Ravine were shovel and auger tests. The shovel tests were concentrated on suspicious-looking mounds that might have represented graves. They weren't confined to the standard meter pattern, could be of different dimensions, and went down as far as three feet. The auger tests were utilized to locate any human remains in Deep Ravine. They were placed at regular intervals along both walls of the ravine. The auger bit was 10 inches in diameter and four feet long. After the first sweep of the field, certain units were selected to be reinventoried and subjected to extensive searches for anything that might have been missed in the first sweep. Each 100-meter square selected yielded about twice the number of artifacts that were uncovered in the first sweep.[93]

In 1985, Deep Ravine was subjected to even more testing. To understand the ravine's stratigraphic history, a backhoe with a mechanical arm that could extend down to six feet was brought in. Eleven trenches were dug along the length of the ravine, nine of them wall to wall. Seven major

Testing in progress in Deep Ravine. Looking south in the "bend" area. Gravemarker 5 is on upper left bank. —Little Bighorn Battlefield National Monument

Excavations in progress in the upper Deep Ravine watershed. Looking north along the lower South Skirmish Line.
—Little Bighorn Battlefield National Monument

geologic strata were revealed and the physical configuration of the ravine was established.[94]

After two seasons of detecting, locating, excavating, collecting, and analyzing, the results were quite impressive. A number of magazines ran stories about the dig's accomplishments. *Natural History* claimed 2,200 artifacts were found, including 300 human bones and 200 animal bones. *National Parks* announced that over 3,000 relics were found during the two-year project. *National Geographic* said that over 4,000 items were found, including a great number of bullets and cartridges, arrowheads, weapon pieces, buttons, and bones. The "official" book of the dig, written by those who organized and participated in the project, claimed that their efforts unearthed over 5,000 items.[95]

Considering the years and number of times the field had been skirmished, cleaned, picked over, and scavenged by soldiers, park personnel, and civilians, the great number of artifacts found was amazing. They were located on Greasy Grass Ridge, on Calhoun Hill, and at a position southeast of Calhoun Hill where so many .44 caliber Henry cartridges were found it was dubbed "Henryville." They were found along Battle Ridge and in the gully where Keogh fell, at Last Stand Hill, down along the South Skirmish Line, and at numerous places in between. In fact, artifacts were found almost everywhere—except in Deep Ravine!

The concentrations of battle-related relics shown in figure 4 were compiled from reports of the archaeologists, park employees, and independent collectors.[96] Other artifacts were found between the circled areas, but not in great enough concentrations to warrant a separate label. All areas had a mix of both Indian and army relics, while some had a predominance of one type over another to mark it as either a soldier or Indian position. Indian positions were held along Greasy Grass Ridge, particularly in the southern portion, at Henryville, at what is now the cemetery, and to a lesser extent at the "bend" of Deep Ravine and at north Custer Hill. Soldier positions were strongest at Custer Hill and to a lesser extent at Calhoun Hill. Mixed areas were in Calhoun Coulee, Finley, Keogh, and the South Line. The latter two, with heavy artifact concentrations, show there was much Indian and army activity in the area.

Why were there no artifacts in the steep-walled gulch of Deep Ravine? No one seemed to know. All those accounts existed about men dying in Deep Ravine, yet absolutely no evidence of bodies was discovered. It was puzzling to all those concerned. The archaeological crew was at a loss to explain why there were no remains of any of the missing men. There was little evidence, they concluded, of any fighting in or around Deep Ravine.[97] The author of the *National Parks* article espoused a similar opinion. The Deep Ravine evidenced "few artifacts to suggest a lengthy battle" in its environs.[98] Lengthy? There were few artifacts to suggest *any* battle in Deep Ravine (fig. 17).

The archaeological crew suggested several possible reasons for their inability to find evidence of remains: (1) the areas searched were the wrong locations, (2) the remains had been scoured away by erosion, (3) the remains were buried too deeply by alluvial deposition, (4) the alternate wet and dry deposits in the ravine and the high-alkaline soils destroyed the bones, and (5) the historical record had been misinterpreted and the remains had already been recovered.[99]

What manner of terrain, what type of geological Charybdis, was this Deep Ravine that would swallow up 28 bodies without a trace? Beneath the grasses lie several layers of sediments formed from the decomposition and erosion of the underlying bedrock. That bedrock consists of sandstones and shales of what has been labeled the Fort Union formation. There is disagreement about which geologic era this terrain should be classified under. The archaeological team responsible for the dig said the parent rock is shale of the Fort Union formation dating from the Cretaceous period, which ended about 60 million years ago.[100] A Montana geology handbook claims the Fort Union belongs to the Tertiary era, formed after the extinction of the dinosaurs and younger than 60 million years old. Most of eastern and central Montana is underlaid by the Fort Union rock, if it can be called "rock" in some cases. Much of it can be so soft, it might more accurately

FIGURE 4: ARTIFACT CONCENTRATIONS ON CUSTER'S FIELD

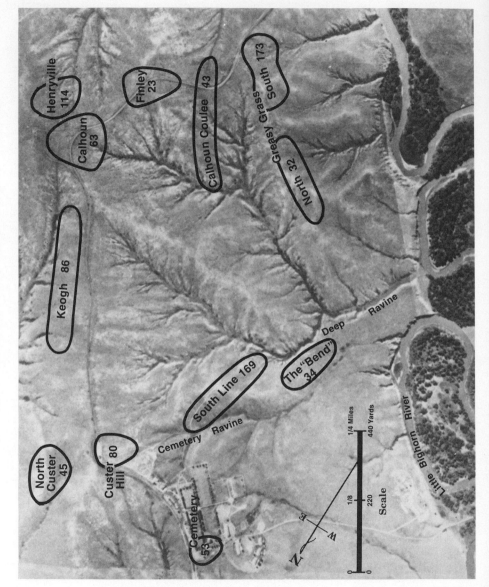

be called mud and sand, and working in it may be easier with a shovel than a hammer. The Fort Union consists of three zones. The lowest and oldest is the Tullock member, mostly thinly bedded sandstone and mudstone. Next is the Lebo shale, which also can erode into vast plains. At the top is the Tongue River member, formed mostly of thick sandstone layers that can be seen in cliffs along the riverbeds and as outcrops in the rugged hills of the area. The entire formation can be between two and three thousand feet thick.[101]

Regardless of the exact age of the Fort Union bedrock under Deep Ravine, once any trenching hits it, the digging can be considered done for that location. Any historical artifacts of 100 years ago could not have worked their way into the 55 to 60 million-year-old bedrock. Two trenches, numbers 5 and 6, hit bedrock. Nothing was found.

The backhoe trenching cut across several layers of sands, gravels, and silty sands of different consistencies that ranged in color from light yellow and orange to olive to brown. Dr. C. Vance Haynes Jr. conducted the geomorphological investigation in Deep Ravine. Examining and radiocarbon dating the various layers, he eliminated most of them as being prehistoric, which also precluded the deep burial of the missing troopers. Only one layer looked promising enough, being the right age and thickness, to possibly conceal the bones. He labeled it unit "F." All of the trenches cut well below that unit. Still no remains were found.[102]

After completing eight trenches and coming up empty, three more were dug in the upper Deep Ravine area near what is called the "headcut." Trench 9 contained the usual silt and sand, but had the extra deposit of one-half foot of trash, glass, crockery, pipe, wood, and cobbles dating from the 1930s. The trash was thought to have been placed there as "riprap," a crude dam to prevent further erosion of the headcut. Trench 10, about 16 feet upstream, showed only the natural strata again. Trench 11, about 26 feet downstream from trench 9, exposed only sand and cobbles. Again no remains (fig. 5). What next? Below trench 11, the north wall of the ravine had slumped, doubling the width of the ravine at that point. Perhaps the extra dirt that collapsed there had covered the bodies. The archaeologists didn't know for certain, but the slump area appeared to be a likely site for the remains. Unfortunately, Haynes concluded, the water table was too high there and they were unable to dig.[103]

While volunteers combed the area with their metal detectors, Dan Larson, a "dowser" from Antioch, California, walked and crawled through Deep Ravine with two nylon tubes. Dowsing is more commonly known as "water witching," but Larson claimed to have used the technique with success in locating lost graves in California. Because of this he was invited to participate in the search. Some mounds in the ravine had already been marked as possible gravesites by archaeologist Richard Fox Jr. and a psychic

FIGURE 5: DEEP RAVINE EXCAVATIONS

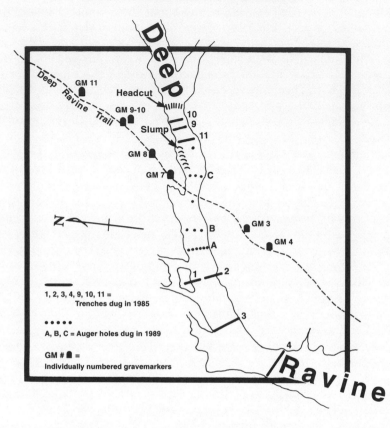

from Denver. Larson also found three additional sites that he thought might be graves. All the sites were unearthed. Again, no body remains were found.[104]

It was rather anticlimactic. There had been 11 major backhoe trenches, 200 auger holes, shovel tests on suspicious areas, metal detector sweeps, and dowsings. The result: a suggestion by Haynes that the bodies still might be in a spot where no one had looked. The mystery was no nearer a solution than when the dig began two years earlier. The searchers already knew the bodies had to be somewhere they hadn't looked.

What about the archaeological team's five suggested possible reasons for not finding any of the 28 bodies? Number two, the suggestion that perhaps the remains were scoured away by erosion, does not appear valid. Deep Ravine extends about 700 yards from the headcut area downstream to its mouth at the Little Bighorn. The floor is from five to fifteen yards wide and has grassy sloping banks about three to six yards high and angling up between 40 and 60 degrees. The floor of the ravine below the headcut slopes only about one degree, a 2 percent grade, and is thus nearly flat. The area is regularly visited by heavy rain and hailstorms, and great "gullywashers" are not uncommon. Could one of these have flushed the remains down to the Little Bighorn? Dr. Haynes said no. Though the sides had a sufficient grade to be washed clean, the flat bottom would still be too big an obstacle for erosion of the floor. Far from eroding out, sediments have been deposited in Deep Ravine.[105]

Perhaps then, possibility number three is the answer: the remains have been buried too deeply by alluvial deposition. This explanation might be valid for someone searching the ravine 100 years after the battle, but it does not provide a logical reason for the inability of searchers to find any remains within five years of the battle. We have already mentioned that the Sheridan, Sanderson, and Roe expeditions did no reburying, removing, or marking of graves in Deep Ravine from 1877 to 1881. One researcher has gone so far as to suggest that those work details couldn't have found any bodies because they were already buried too deep under a layer of silt and grass within a year or two of the battle.[106] A body laid out flat would need about a foot of dirt over it to hide it completely from sight. To suggest one foot of deposition per year is fantastic. It would mean the ravine itself would have nearly disappeared from view about the time Captain Sweet went there in 1890 looking for places to plant his gravestones. Or, to carry on the suggestion to an even more fantastic conclusion, after over 100 years of such deposition the "ravine" would be 80 feet higher than the terrain surrounding it.

Archaeologist Robert T. Bray, who excavated the Reno-Benteen battlefield in 1958, made some pertinent observations. The dead on Reno Hill were given much deeper burials than those on Custer's field, yet in no place did Bray find any relic associated with the battle deeper than twenty inches into the soil. In fact, almost every human bone found was consistently between six and twelve inches deep.[107] Sgt. John Ryan, who helped bury George Custer, said his grave was only eighteen inches deep, and that was the best-dug grave of them all.[108]

The depths of the artifacts on Custer's field were consistent with excavations at other Indian battle sites on the High Plains. During the 1970s the Adobe Walls site in northern Texas was examined. Artifacts numbering in the thousands were unearthed, from bullets, beads, buttons, and bones to shoes, shells, scrapers, and screws. Though a high water table in the bottomland had deteriorated much of the ferrous metals, objects such as tin cans were still found nearly at the surface with the grass roots growing through them. Other objects that were once inside the buildings were buried by a foot or two of additional overburden, a result of the sod roofs collapsing. Nonetheless, the searchers had little trouble uncovering the relics. Bones, about 450 of them, were especially well preserved.[109]

At the Summit Springs battle site in northeast Colorado, one even more similar to the Little Bighorn than Adobe Walls, the relic hunters found hundreds of spoons, shards, shot, and shell spread one mile along the creek where the Cheyenne Tall Bull's village once stood. The artifacts were found from near the surface to twenty inches deep, the average recovery depth being from four and one-half to five inches.[110]

Right lower leg with 1872 cavalry boot found at gravemarker 128 at the south end of Finley Ridge. The remains at this location were dubbed "Trooper Mike."
—Little Bighorn Battlefield National Monument

Finger bone still encircled by a wedding ring. Found near gravemarker 42. —Little Bighorn Battlefield National Monument

The relics were there for the picking at Adobe Walls and Summit Springs. They were also there for the picking on Custer's field. In May of 1985, on Greasy Grass Ridge at gravemarker 128, searchers uncovered 150 bones from a trooper, including an articulated leg with foot bones still encased in a boot, the tip just an inch or two below the ground surface. Since this find was at excavation "M," the remains were later dubbed "Trooper Mike."[111] One of the biggest finds of the 1984 dig was made only about 200 yards down the South Skirmish Line from the visitor center. Near gravemarker 42, only two inches below the grass roots, a human finger bone was found, still encircled by a wedding band.[112]

Of the six non-gravemarker sites excavated on Calhoun Hill, all the artifacts they yielded were found within one to four inches of the ground surface, essentially within the root zones of the native grasses.[113]

The above examples all illustrate just how near the surface these relics still remain. They are obviously not buried irretrievably beneath tons of prairie soil. The bones have not been buried too deeply to be discovered today, and certainly they weren't buried too deeply to be discovered within five years of the battle.

Perhaps possibility number four is the answer: the alternate wet and dry deposits in the ravine and the high alkaline content of the soil have destroyed the bones. If the bones had become exposed from their protective covering they could have bleached white and disintegrated completely within several years. If they remained covered, the process of chemical and biological decay would depend on the presence of moisture, warmth, oxygen, and the acid or alkaline content of the environment. In acid soils or humid, tropical conditions, bone will be poorly preserved. In alkaline soils or desert climes, bone is preserved and may even become semifossilized. Bones covered in soil of the right chemical balance will stay intact almost indefinitely. Even objects as potentially fragile as dinosaur eggs have been found by the hundreds in the fossil-preserving, dry, alkaline, upland Montana soils in the Hell Creek Formation only 150 miles from the Little Bighorn.[114] The detritus, the eroded layers of the Fort Union sandstone and shale on the Custer battlefield, are alkaline. The bones have not disintegrated.

The two-year dig produced over 5,000 artifacts, including 411 bones and teeth. Of the remainder, the majority consisted of different types of cartridges, cartridge cases, and bullets, but there were also numbers of weapons parts, arrowheads, buckles, buttons, coins, spurs, nails, rivets, saddle and tack parts, and various other army accoutrements. The artifacts were found everywhere in greater or lesser concentrations—in gullies, on ridges, and along slopes. The bones and other relics are obviously not disintegrated, eroded away, or buried too deep.

Is Deep Ravine just too large an area to search? Are 28 skeletons too small a number to reasonably be expected to be found? The Custer battlefield measures approximately one mile square. A mile is 1,760 yards in length and thus contains 3,097,600 square yards. There were about 2,000 artifacts found on Custer's field. This averages about one artifact every 1,548 square yards. There were 411 bones and teeth found, 20 percent of the artifact total. This averages only one human relic per 7,536 square yards. The team did a tremendous job finding the proverbial needle in a haystack.

Deep Ravine is about 700 yards long from its mouth to the headcut. Its width averages about eight yards. Thus, its area is about 5,600 square yards, or less than one-fifth (.18 percent) of 1 percent of the entire fenced-in area. In this ravine there are supposed to be 28 skeletons. One skeleton consists of about 206 bones. Thus, there should be 5,768 bones in an area of 5,600 square yards, more than one bone per square yard. If the searchers could find one bone per 7,536 square yards on the rest of the field, Deep Ravine should theoretically have a 7,000 percent greater relic concentration and represent a veritable goldmine of bones.

But the archaeological team was fairly convinced, per the historical record and the limits of the physical configuration of the ravine itself, that the bodies must lie between the headcut and the lower Deep Ravine Trail crossing, a distance of about 35 yards. The ravine is much narrower here, maybe five yards across at the most. Now the area to be considered shrinks to 175 square yards. If the 28 bodies lie in this area, there should be about 33 bones per square yard. Also remember that the bones on the rest of the field represented only 20 percent of the total artifacts. If this proportion were anything similar in Deep Ravine, the total number of artifacts there would be truly phenomenal. It would be the mother lode of all Indian War boneyards.

Just for argument's sake, let us assume that all 28 bodies are there and were laid out evenly in line, between the headcut and the lower trail crossing. The 28 bodies, side by side, would take up about one yard each. We've just covered 28 of the 35 yards in our suspected area. Three backhoe trenches were dug within this 35 yards. Trench 9 was in the middle. Sixteen feet above it was trench 10. Twenty-six feet below it was trench 11 (fig. 5). There is no way around the fact that there was a possibility that all three trenches *could* have hit the bodies, that two trenches *should* have hit bodies, and that one absolutely *had* to hit bodies.

But the corpses were probably not laid side by side, for some accounts mentioned bodies piled up on each other. How high? Certainly the men, before dying, did not crawl up on each other in a tidy little pyramid, nor were they later stacked like cordwood. If they died in this part of Deep Ravine, they died scattered about haphazardly, perhaps several close enough to have an arm or leg resting across the torso of another. A tall stack of bodies is preposterous; it would still be protruding above the floor of the ravine. A random scattering is more likely, but then they would have been discovered in at least one of the three backhoe trenches.

So where are the bones? We have disposed of three of the five possibilities suggested by the archaeological team. Two remain: (1) the areas searched were the wrong locations and (5) the historical record has been misinterpreted and the remains were recovered. We shall see in a later chapter that the suggestion that the remains were recovered will not bear up to examination. The accounts of Michael Sheridan, Henry Nowlan, Hugh Scott, and others will show that no such body removal was attempted. The first part of possibility number five, that the historical record has been misinterpreted, may be exactly the case. It is this writer's contention that this is the very essence of the mystery: the bodies have not been located because the historical record has been misinterpreted and the search has been conducted in the wrong place. This wrong place does not simply mean the wrong place in Deep Ravine. The entire search has been focused in the wrong ravine!

What of all those accounts, all those descriptions of bodies in a deep ravine? Could we have been misinterpreting them for over 100 years?

Yes. The following two chapters will focus on those very historical accounts, Indian and white, that spoke of the Gray Horse Troop or men being killed in a ravine. What did the eyewitness participants and later visitors to Custer's field really have to tell us? By placing our preconceptions and assumptions on the shelf and by avoiding quick quotes taken out of context, we may very well find that a radically altered picture will emerge. Perhaps a more thorough examination of the historical accounts will provide the answer to why no soldiers' remains can be found in Deep Ravine. Perhaps no remains can be found there because no bodies were there to begin with.

Stand again near the monument on Custer Hill and look toward the river. Directly in front is a ravine. It arrows up toward the observer and broadens downslope to an abrupt tablelike bank, rimmed with a cottonwood canopy beyond. To the right rises the national cemetery ground. To the left swells the divide that separates this ravine's watershed from that of Deep Ravine. In fact, Deep Ravine is barely visible in the picture from this vantage point—certainly its floor and steepest sides are completely obscured. The tiny white tombstones that stretch from the lower left on the divide to the near right below the cemetery delineate the South Skirmish Line. The viability of this line has been accepted by some and rejected by others. The main branch of the line consists of 44 gravemarkers. It rightly belongs in context with the unnamed ravine it diagonally crosses. This unnamed ravine will be salient in our examination. Since it drains Custer Hill and receives the runoff from the eastern and southern portions of the cemetery, we will name it Cemetery Ravine. In Cemetery Ravine, not Deep Ravine, the 28 bodies were once consigned.

Heretofore, consensus interpretations have argued that only a handful of soldiers, perhaps up to a dozen, fell along the slopes in the upper Deep Ravine watershed and in what we have termed Cemetery Ravine, while 28 or more fell in Deep Ravine (fig. 3). Corollary to those interpretations, the gravestones found along the South Skirmish Line are said to be improperly placed, the majority needing to be relocated in Deep Ravine. It is a contention of this study that the great majority of soldiers fell in Cemetery Ravine and in the upper Deep Ravine watershed, with very few dying in Deep Ravine. Thus, the markers placed along the South Skirmish Line and the "fugitive" lines are very representative of where the soldiers actually fell. Further searches for the remains of 28 men in Deep Ravine should prove futile.

A view down Cemetery Ravine toward the Little Bighorn River.

3. Indian Accounts

In this chapter we will analyze those accounts of Indian participants in the Battle of the Little Bighorn that mentioned soldiers dying in a ravine on the river side of Custer Hill. We will also include narratives that mention gray horses with the hope that they will enable us to trace the battlefield movements of Lt. Algernon Smith's Company E. These handsome horses were easier for the Indians to follow through the action than the more nondescript bays and sorrels. The Gray Horse Troop gallops ghostlike through many Indian accounts of the fight.[115] The gray horse movements as seen by the Indians, taken in conjunction with the soldier accounts, can provide a very intelligible outline of the fight and provide us with a perspective on the story of E Troop.

There are many other Indian accounts that spoke of various aspects of the battle but did not specifically mention the ravines in question or the gray horses and those will not concern us here. There have been some researchers who have washed their hands of the Indian accounts. Col. William A. Graham would not use them in his story of the battle, saying that they ". . . differ so widely that little satisfactory information can be culled from them. Their stories cannot be reconciled." Graham showed them to Gen. Hugh L. Scott to help him out of his dilemma. The general studied them "and threw up his hands."[116] Earl Brininstool said Indians only gave their stories under pressure, and thus were not dependable. Researcher Fred Dustin also preferred the white stories, particularly the officers', crediting them with "the traditional truthfulness of their class."[117] Yet the court recorder at Reno's Inquiry, Lt. Jesse M. Lee, writing about these very same officers in a letter to Custer's widow, was convinced they lied. He was shocked by the jealousies and self-interests that unloosed such calumnies from their tongues.[118]

There have also been authors such as Stanley Vestal, George Bird Grinnell, Thomas B. Marquis, and David H. Miller that relied almost entirely on Indian tales and excluded most white accounts. Gen. George Crook, after twenty years of experience, thought you could not be sure when an Indian was telling the truth. He and the white man may lie to you. "But if you make it to the Indian's interest to tell the truth, you get correct information; a white man will lie intentionally, and mislead you unintentionally."[119]

It appears that the sane solution would be to honor both sides of the ledger. Instead of making a contest out of finding whether the whites or the Indians were the more prolific liars, we can accept the accounts for what they are. The great, great majority of eyewitnesses did nothing but report what they observed on their small portion of the battlefield. A noted expert on Cheyenne history and customs, Dr. Thomas B. Marquis, said that every Indian narrative of the battle centers mainly on that Indian's personal movements, on where he went or what he did or didn't do.[120] And so they should. The Indian who said he fired at a soldier attempting to cross the river at Medicine Tail ford should have his veracity questioned no more than the white man who said he fired at an Indian from the timber in the valley. Both saw what was pertinent to them in their relatively small field of vision. Neither could give testimony as to what occurred at the same moment on the other side of the hill. If, however, we can piece together bits of evidence that may seem contradictory at times, we can still perhaps present a comprehensible story. If we steer away from stories where personal honor is at stake, we are more assured of getting the truth, for men's stories tend to change when their honor is in question.[121] Those Indian accounts unconcerned with individual bravery and relating only to general field actions, of where the white soldiers rode their horses and where they died, should be of much use to the researcher.

1. Gall (Pizi) *Hunkpapa Lakota*

Gall, born in 1838, was a warrior chief of above-average skills and leadership abilities who gained much notoriety after his deeds in the Custer battle became publicized. He had no admiration of Sitting Bull and often commented that Bull was usually nowhere to be seen once the gunfire had begun, calling him a coward and a fraud. Gall was made an Indian judge and was officially favored by the U.S. Government. His cooperation with the whites during his reservation life made him an accessible source of information on the Custer fight.[122]

Gall attended the 10th reunion at the battlefield, and his stories were recorded by several interviewers. A Chicago newspaper printed June 26, 1886, said that Gall went over the entire field with the newsmen and soldiers and described the battle scenes in an intelligent and straightforward manner. He said that Custer did not reach the river, but was met about a half a mile up a ravine (Medicine Tail). The Indians were in the coulees behind and in front of Custer as he moved up the ridge to take his final position. Keogh and Calhoun dismounted to fight on foot. The warriors fired specifically at the horse holders, then stampeded the horses by waving their blankets. Many horses ran to the river and were captured by the squaws. Some soldiers ran away down a ravine, crossed the river, came back again, and were killed.[123]

Gall, Hunkpapa Lakota. Photo by D. F. Barry, c. 1881. —Little Bighorn Battlefield National Monument

The St. Paul *Pioneer Press* of June 25, 1886, reported that Gall said Custer was attacked half a mile from the river and forced back step by step. Shells stuck in the soldiers' rifles and they had to fight with "little guns." Keogh's and Calhoun's men were the first to dismount and fight on foot. The troops "were shot down in line where they stood." They fought desperately hard and never surrendered. "They fought standing," Gall repeated. "They fought in line along the ridge."[124]

In the *Pioneer Press* of July 18, 1886, a reporter wrote that Gall said Custer was attacked fully three-fourths of a mile from the river and was forced back by an attack that came from the left, in the direction of the high ground now called Weir Point. That was the nearest Custer got to the river. He stopped in the ravine (Medicine Tail) for a time to await the coming of the rest of the command, but was forced to the summit where the monument now stands. Only Keogh's and Calhoun's companies fought in formation and held their positions. They were the last to die. The others were shot down in confusion. The soldiers fought on foot while one held the horses and others fired. The Indians scared the horses down a coulee, and Cheyenne women caught many of them at the river.[125]

Attending the 1886 gathering was Edward S. Godfrey, a lieutenant in K Company at the time of the battle. After sitting for some time near the monument, apparently several people became restive at the interpreter's inability to give satisfactory translations of the Indian testimony. Gall motioned to Godfrey to follow him. They rode over to Calhoun Hill, where Gall began to indicate—by sign language, pantomime, and by placing Godfrey in several positions to represent the troops—just how the battle developed. Gall indicated that Custer never got nearer to the river than his final position on the ridge. His route was far back east. The tracks at the ford were from Indian ponies and captured cavalry horses. Keogh's and Calhoun's men fought dismounted, and their horses were held at a spring in the upper reaches of Deep Coulee. Smith's men deployed as skirmishers and took position on the ridge, his right on Custer Hill and left toward Keogh. Smith's men held their gray horses and remained in groups of fours. Bodies scattered between the ridge and the river were not early victims, but those that had survived the fighting and attempted to escape to the river. Twenty-eight were found in a big gully near the river. Gall personally was in the attack against Keogh and Calhoun from the ravines to the south and east. The Indians didn't make many large-scale attacks from the river, but had defensive forces in the ravines to destroy those who left Custer's line.[126]

Also attending the 1886 reunion was David F. Barry, who photographed and recorded much of the proceedings. Barry recorded that Gall said the soldiers approached east of the high bluffs. They were first noticed two miles from the village about two hours past noon, kicking up a dust cloud as they headed for the Cheyenne camp. "They were mounted on white horses and it was a nice sight to see this parade across the river to our East." They marched along on the high land going northwest and not directly toward the camp, and so the Indians were not sure whether they meant to fight.

While Gall was helping chase Reno's men away, Crazy Horse and Crow King raced after Custer. Crow King turned right before he got to the north end of the camp and went up a deep gully where Custer's men could not see him. "Ride down there and you will see that this gully is so deep that no one can see you from here," Gall said. The upper part of the gully brought Crow King close to the soldiers. "Crazy Horse went to the extreme north end of the camp and then turned to his right and went up another very deep ravine and by following it, which he did, he came very close to the soldiers on their north side. Crow King was on their South side."

It was about two-thirty when this part of the battle began. The soldiers headed for the camp but only got halfway from the ridge to the river. They never crossed the river. Crow King shot at them from the south. They tried to get back up the hill, but Crazy Horse was behind them and shot at them from the north. The Indians were on foot because their horses were in the ravine where Crazy Horse was. The soldiers fought well, but they could not hit the warriors in the gully and ravine. The dust and smoke was black as evening. Soon all the soldiers' horses were killed or captured and the last of the soldiers were killed.[127]

Gall's accounts are definite in stating Custer did not get to the river, but either chose a route or was forced to follow a route far back from the Little Bighorn. It was not too far back, however, for Gall commented on how nice the white horses looked as they paraded past him. It is evident that Gall had much influence on Godfrey's conception of the battle. Although Godfrey wrote several accounts of the affair, we can be sure that it was Gall who provided most of the insight on the troop movements. We can see that the troops fought in lines along the ridges and we can determine that Smith's dismounted troopers came down from their position on the ridge and went toward the river, only to be killed for their efforts. About 28 of them died in a gully. We cannot be sure if Godfrey or Gall supplied the number, but from Gall's last account as recorded by David Barry, we can gain insight as to which gully those 28 died in. It was Crow King and his warriors who were hiding to the south, out of sight of the soldiers on the ridge. The troops came down from the hill, were surprised by the warriors in the ravine, and were killed or driven back. It appears the majority of Smith's men did not get into Deep Ravine, but Gall's accounts are not quite definite enough to categorize.

2. Crow King (Kangi-yatipika) *Hunkpapa Lakota*

Crow King's story was given to the Leavenworth *Weekly Times* when reporters visited the reservation Indians at Fort Yates, Dakota Territory, on the Missouri River. It was printed August 18, 1881. Crow King said the first soldier attack came against the Hunkpapa camp at the upper end of the village. The Indians drove them to the hill when the second band of white warriors came (Custer). The Indians commenced firing at long range. Crow King had about 80 warriors that followed him. The greater portion of all the warriors rushed at them while others rode around them until they were surrounded. "When they saw they were surrounded they dis-

Crow King, Hunkpapa Lakota. Photo by D. F. Barry, 1881.
—Montana Historical Society

mounted. They tried to hold on to their horses, but as we pressed closer they let go their horses. We crowded them toward our main camp and killed them all. They kept in order and fought like brave warriors as long as they had a man left."[128]

Crow King told of the action in brief. Gall provided more detail of Crow King's deeds than the latter did himself. Another Hunkpapa, Moving Robe Woman, also corroborated Crow King's attack from the south.[129] Unfortunately, we cannot determine anything of the Gray Horse Trooper's movements or of where they might have died from Crow King's story. It is significant, however, that he said the soldiers were attacked in a manner that "crowded them toward our main camp," which precludes an attack from the south and seems to contradict Gall and Moving Robe Woman. Crow King thus indicated that one of the main directions of the Indian thrust was from out of the north and/or east.

Here we are confronted with one of the difficulties inherent in assessing the historical accounts. Many of the battle descriptions revolve directionally around the long ridge that Custer marched along during the latter stages of the action, generally called Custer Ridge or Battle Ridge. The ridge actually trends from the Calhoun Hill end in the southeast to the Custer Hill end in the northwest. Depending on one's orientation or sense of direction, action on the far, or land, side of the ridge may be correctly labeled either north or east. Likewise, action on the river side may be labeled either south or west. Each individual saw the ridge as lying either north-south or east-west. Gall and Moving Robe Woman most likely viewed the ridge as lying east-west, hence the statements of Crazy Horse attacking from the north and Crow King from the south. Of course, Crow King himself said nothing of the kind. Driving the enemy toward the camp would mean an attack out of the north or east. This illustrates the caution necessary in any interpreting of the battle accounts.

3. Runs The Enemy (Tok kahin hpe ya) *Two Kettle Lakota*

Runs The Enemy told his story to Dr. Joseph K. Dixon at the great Indian council at the Custer Battlefield in 1909. Runs The Enemy had seen Custer's approach and tried to circle around him. The Cheyennes had already circled around on the north, west, and east. All his group of warriors could do was to fill in a gap on the south. While Custer was being surrounded there was not much firing until the Sioux made a charge from the rear, but they had to retreat because the soldiers' fire was too strong. Runs The Enemy then went around to the north where the monument now stands. There were hundreds of dismounted Indians in the coulees all around. They charged through the soldier line just below the monument area, captured many horses, and drove them down to the river. The horses were so thirsty they stopped to drink as soon as they reached the water, and the ammunition could be easily removed from their saddle packs.

When Runs The Enemy returned to the fight the soldiers made a rush down a ravine toward the river and a great roll of smoke seemed to go down the ravine. The soldiers were met by an advance of Indians from the river and were driven back to the hill. The soldiers back at the hill made a stand all in a bunch. The Indians charged again and the soldiers retreated along the line of the ridge. Runs The Enemy and his band of warriors met the soldiers along the ridge. They broke and divided, some troops going down the eastern slope of the hill and some going down to the river. A few others went back to where the final stand was made on the hill. The last gathered in a group where the monument now stands. One final charge was made, a mountain of smoke rolled up overhead, and the soldiers were dead, piled on top of each other.[130]

Taken alone, Runs The Enemy's story does not specifically identify which ravine the soldiers ran down on their way to the river. It does indicate that a significant portion of the troops did head downhill, where they were met and repulsed by warriors in the ravines. However, the ravine could have been Deep Ravine or Calhoun Coulee (the south fork of Deep Ravine), or both.

4. Good Voiced Elk *Hunkpapa Lakota*

One of Walter Camp's informants was Good Voiced Elk. He was interviewed in 1909. Good Voiced Elk indicated that Custer was going down the right side of the river and the Indians who had fought Reno were going down the left, but Custer had the lead. Custer got close enough to the river to fire into and over the tepees. It looked like the soldiers would go right into the village, but the Indians drove them back.

In the latter stages of the battle Good Voiced Elk saw dismounted soldiers break from the end of the ridge and try to run away by going toward the river. "There was a deep gully without any water in it. I saw many jump over the steep bank into this gully in their effort to escape, but these were all killed. There were probably 25 or 30 of them."[131]

Good Voiced Elk's story is fairly certain. There were 25 or 30 men who jumped over a steep bank into a deep gully. The description points to Deep Ravine.

5. Red Horse *Minneconjou Lakota*

In June 1876, Red Horse was a head chief in the council lodge, but Custer's attack was so unexpected that he had no time to stop and give instructions for the coming battle. He had to grab his horse and gun and go. Red Horse found himself in the same situation in September, at Slim Buttes, when a cavalry charge by General Crook's troops caught him similarly unprepared.[132] He surrendered in 1877.

Red Horse gave his version of the Little Bighorn fight to Army Assistant Surgeon Charles McChesney in 1881. The soldiers charged the Sioux camp about noon. They drove Reno's men into the hills and then charged the "different soldiers" (Custer's men) and drove them back in confusion. Many of the soldiers were foolish, throwing away their guns and raising their hands and saying, "Sioux pity us, take us prisoners." They did not take a single prisoner.

The Indians surrounded the soldiers, but Custer's men made five brave stands. Once the Sioux charged right in among the soldiers, fighting them hand to hand. One band of soldiers charged and the Sioux fell back. Then they stood there facing each other for a time. Then the Sioux became brave and again charged the soldiers.

*Red Horse,
Minneconjou Lakota.
Photo by D. F. Barry,
c. 1890.* —Little Bighorn
Battlefield National
Monument

Red Horse could see the officers riding in front and shouting commands to their men. It was now the Sioux that lost many men. The soldiers killed 136 and wounded 160, but the Sioux were still able to kill all these soldiers in the ravine.[133]

Red Horse does not provide enough specific information to enable us to identify which ravine all these soldiers were killed in. The troopers did make some brave stands, however, which indicated organized fighting and no panic rout. The one charge Red Horse mentioned does sound like other accounts that indicated soldiers came down from the ridge and drove back the warriors for a temporary respite, only to be driven back and overwhelmed themselves in turn. Yet, we cannot definitely categorize the ravine Red Horse spoke of.

6. Flying By (Keya Heyi) *Minneconjou Lakota*

Flying By was the son of Lamedeer, a leader of the Minneconjou who was killed by Col. Nelson Miles's soldiers in 1877. Flying By was 26 at the time of the Little Bighorn fight. He was interviewed by researcher Walter Mason Camp in 1907.

Flying By saw the soldiers attack the Hunkpapa camp first. This fight only lasted a short time, and his horse was shot. He went back for another horse when Custer's men appeared, carrying four or five flags. It looked like Custer would attack the village, but he did not cross the river. The soldiers did not charge after Flying By got there. The Indians crossed the river at all points and soon had Custer surrounded. The soldiers let go of some of their horses and the Indians captured many. Flying By took some horses back to the village and then headed back to the fight.

When he returned, many soldiers were already killed. They kept together all the time and were killed while moving along toward the Indian camp. Some of the soldiers still had their horses at this time. During the fight the gray horses were much mixed up with the others. The soldiers did not make any stand except in the place where Custer was killed at the end of a long ridge. The Indians closed in, and at the end of the battle the soldiers were running through the Indian lines trying to get away. "Only four soldiers got into [a] gully toward [the] river." The battle lasted about half the afternoon.[134]

From Flying By's story we see the gray horses standing out, even when mixed with the other mounts. They did not appear to be off on a separate detachment, but, at least for a time, were with the other companies on Custer Hill or along Battle Ridge. Flying By saw only one stand, at the Custer Hill position. From there, some soldiers tried to escape, but only four got into a gully toward the river.

Which gully? If we combine Flying By's story with other accounts that spoke of up to 40 men running for the river, we can see that the great majority of soldiers were killed before they ever got to the gully. This supports the stories that placed the Indians in the ravines. Only a few isolated soldiers managed to break away from their ridge positions and live long enough to make it to a very temporary refuge in Deep Ravine. The majority fell before they got that far, along the banks of Cemetery Ravine.

7. Black Elk *Oglala Lakota*

Black Elk was born in 1863 and was 13 at the time of the battle. He told his story to author John Neihardt in 1931. Black Elk was out the morning of June 25, grazing the horses until the sun was straight above and it grew very hot. He was swimming in the Little Bighorn when the attack began, raising a big dust beyond the Hunkpapa camp. Black Elk

Black Elk, Oglala Lakota. Photo by D. R. Sweetland, c. 1950. —Little
Bighorn Battlefield National Monument

was in the fight with Reno's men in the timber and got his first scalp. He
went back to his tepee to show his mother and saw the battle going on
with Custer's men. While riding toward the river he saw gray horses with
empty saddles stampeding to the water. "We rode over across the Greasy
Grass [Little Bighorn] to the mouth of a gulch that led up through the
bluff to where the fighting was."

Before Black Elk could get into the final battle, all the *wasichus* (whites)
were down, dead, or wounded. At the top of the hill there were gray horses
lying dead, soldiers scattered around and in between them. Black Elk found
his cousin, who was wounded badly by a bullet that went down through

his right shoulder. Black Elk's father and uncle "were so angry over this, that they went and butchered a Wasichu and cut him open. The Wasichu was fat, and his meat looked good to eat, but we did not eat any."[135]

What can Black Elk tell us of the fight? Gray horses were seen stampeding to the river and found dead up on the ridge. Black Elk went up Deep Ravine "to where the fighting was," indicating there was little or no conflict with the soldiers in the gulch. If any soldiers made it to the deep gullies, there were not enough of them to make any impression on Black Elk. Still, the account is not definitive enough to place the Gray Horse Troopers in any specific ravine.

8. Mrs. Spotted Horn Bull (Tatanka-he-gle-ska) *Hunkpapa Lakota*

A cousin of Sitting Bull called "Mrs. Tatanka" by the reporter who wrote her story, Mrs. Spotted Horn Bull had her eyewitness account printed in the St. Paul *Pioneer Press* on May 19, 1883. Her warrior husband, who was in the battle, sat beside her and aided in the narration. William A. Graham called hers one of the most interesting, graphic, and eloquent accounts of the battle ever recorded. Later, in 1886, she repeated her story to Edward Godfrey, which corroborated much of Gall's narrative and formed a basis for much of Godfrey's own articles on the fight.

When Custer was seen approaching, the Indians were ready for him, for they had already disposed of Reno, whose flight disgusted Mrs. Tatanka. The Indians quickly crossed the river and galloped to Custer's rear, out of range at first, going along the coulees and soon hemming him in narrowing circles. Mrs. Tatanka mounted her pony and went to where she could get a good view of the hills.

The troops came up, dismounted, and every fourth man held the horses. The rest deployed and advanced on the run toward the river. They were greeted with a withering fire from the Indians hidden in the willows on her side of the river. Mrs. Tatanka trotted north along the outskirts of the encampment and noted the Indians getting closer to the troops. The soldiers still alive retreated to their horses. By the time she got to the extreme left, not an hour's ride away, no white soldiers were visible on the field. There were many soldier horses captured. They were fat and good looking, but could not run as fast as the Indian ponies.[136]

Mrs. Spotted Horn Bull retold her story to Standing Rock Indian agent James McLaughlin in 1908. At that time, however, she was not carried on the agency rolls by that name. After the death of her husband, someone more imaginative than the agent had given her the name Pte-San-Waste-Win, or Beautiful White Cow. The name was not given in jest. She was still a fine, sturdy, upstanding woman of about 65 years.

The Great Spirit was watching over His red children that day, she said, for He allowed Reno to strike too soon and the braves ran over his soldiers like corn before the hail. Long Hair (Custer) was still three miles away when Reno escaped across the river. It was over so quickly that the shadow of the sun had not moved the width of a tepee pole.

Across from the camps of the Cheyenne and Sans Arc was an easy crossing of the Greasy Grass, and the Indians knew Custer had planned to strike at that point. From a hill and later from the riverbank, Mrs. Spotted Horn Bull watched the fight. The column of soldiers turned left and marched downriver. The warriors in the village rushed down the ravine, and the women went to gather the ponies.

The Indians rode to the end of the village opposite of the hill where the monument now stands. Between that hill and the soldiers was a ravine that started from the river by the Sans Arc camp and went all the way around the butte. To get to the butte, Custer had to cross the ravine, but from where he was marching he could not see into the ravine or down to the river. The warriors had joined opposite the opening into the ravine. Soon many Cheyennes rode into the river. Then there were hundreds running up the ravine. The others who were left moved back from the river and waited for the attack. She knew hundreds of Sioux were hidden in the ravine behind the hill where Custer was marching, and he would be attacked from both sides.

When Gall got to the fight, he and many of his men frightened the soldiers' horses, which were being held in small bunches. With shouts that could be heard across the river, they stampeded the horses and the women captured them. Mrs. Spotted Horn Bull saw Crazy Horse lead warriors across the river and up a ravine, followed by Crow King and then Gall, who rode along the bench by the river where Custer had once stopped with his men.

The war whoop of the Sioux sounded from the river bottom and the ravine surrounding the hill at the end of the ridge where Long Hair made his stand. The men of the Sioux nation, led by Crow King, Hump, Crazy Horse, and others, rose up on all sides of the hill, "and the last we could see from our side of the river was a great number of gray horses." The smoke and dust obscured the sight of the hill. The women crossed the river, and when they came to the hill there were no soldiers left alive.[137]

The substance of Mrs. Spotted Horn Bull's story is much the same as those told by other participants in the fight. The first ravine she spoke of, leading from the Sans Arc camp and around a butte, appears to be North Medicine Tail, or Deep Coulee. Many Indians, including Gall when he rode along the bench by the river where Custer's men stopped for a time, used the Deep Coulee to approach the main battlefield. This is essentially what Gall and Godfrey had to say. Meanwhile, the other Indians had waited to see where the soldiers intended to go. Hundreds then went up Deep

Ravine, where they "were hidden in the ravine behind the hill upon which Long Hair was marching."

We can see that in the final stages of the fight, the troops were on the hill, the Indians were in the gulches, and the gray horses ran loose amid the chaos. There was no mention of any close fighting or many soldiers dying in any deep ravine.

9. Foolish Elk   *Oglala Lakota*

Foolish Elk was 22 years old at the time of the Custer battle. He had a reputation for honesty and reliability and later was chief of police at the Rosebud Agency. Walter Camp thought him straightforward and a man of above-average intelligence when he interviewed him in 1908.

Foolish Elk was in the fight against General Crook at the Battle of the Rosebud, and he had only arrived at the camp on the Little Bighorn on June 24. The next day soldiers attacked the Hunkpapa tepees at the south end of the village, but they were beaten back. Before the Indians could decide what to do with those soldiers, another force (Custer's) was seen coming from the east. Those troops sat on their horses and fired into the village without going into it.

The Indians now got all their horses rounded up and arrived in large numbers. Some crossed there and others went downstream to cross. They were between Custer and the river and also going around east of him, front and rear. Custer followed the ridges while the warriors kept abreast of him by taking the hollows and ravines. Foolish Elk was with Crazy Horse that day, fighting mostly on the east side. The soldiers charged twice but could not drive the Indians away and the battle became furious.

Foolish Elk fought on the side of the hill where Keogh's men were killed as they went toward the high ground at the end of the ridge. There was not much of a stand made anywhere except at the monument. There was no stand in the Keogh area—the soldiers were all going toward the high ground. "The gray horses went up in a body; then came bay horses and men on foot all mixed together." The men on horseback didn't stop to fight, but went along as fast as they could. The men on foot were shooting as they passed. When the horses got to the top of the ridge, the grays and bays became mixed and all were in confusion. The soldiers must have known now that they were all going to die.

Camp asked Foolish Elk if any soldiers were taken to the village for torture. Foolish Elk just laughed and said that if Camp had seen the amount of firing done on the battlefield that day he would never suppose any soldiers came out alive. Camp asked him how he might account for some 18 bodies that were never found. Foolish Elk could give no explanation, but was sure they could all have been found if the searchers had just looked far enough.[138]

Foolish Elk did not see the grays go down to the river because he was fighting with Crazy Horse. This matches other accounts that placed Crazy Horse and his followers generally on the north and east sides of Battle Ridge and would preclude observation of occurrences to the south and west on the Cemetery Ravine side. Foolish Elk did see the grays going west on Battle Ridge, leading bays (Yates's F Troop had bays) and other men on foot. Other accounts described what subsequently happened to the Gray Horse Troop after it reached the monument area. Foolish Elk could give no further accounting of its fate.

There is another interesting point made by Foolish Elk in response to Camp's question of missing bodies. The death spots of Custer's men were no mystery to Foolish Elk. If the whites had searched well enough they would have found them.

10. White Bull (Pte-san-hunka) *Minneconjou Lakota*

A nephew of Sitting Bull, White Bull was born in 1849 and was 26 at the time of the Little Bighorn battle. He lived to be 98 years old and gloried in recounting stories of his coups and war deeds. Historian Stanley Vestal (Walter S. Campbell) interviewed him in 1930 and 1932. Vestal's technique was much different from that of researcher Walter Camp. Vestal let the Indian tell the story as he wished, uninterrupted and unorchestrated.

When the battle began about midday, White Bull was north of the camp, watering the horses. He got into the Reno fight briefly. Then he heard Indians yelling about other soldiers (Custer's) coming from the east toward the north end of the camp. White Bull crossed to the east side of the river near Reno Hill and went downstream.

Custer was trotting along the bluffs parallel to the river. The Indians streamed northeast up the ravine (Deep Coulee). Custer's troops had passed the head of that ravine by the time White Bull got near enough to shoot. The soldiers seemed to be in four groups of mounted men. White Bull fired at the group in the rear (Calhoun's).

The soldier fire there was effective, and White Bull and the other Indians had to fall back to the south. He then worked his way over to the east and joined some warriors under Crazy Horse. White Bull, in a feat of bravado, dashed between Calhoun's and Keogh's commands. Calhoun's men had begun to fall back into Keogh's, and then all of them went northwestward along the ridge.

The remnants of those troops joined around Custer Hill. The other mass of men (the commands of Yates, Tom Custer, and Smith) were below these, down the hill toward the river. White Bull fought hand to hand with one soldier and counted many coups. For a time, all the soldiers stood together on the hill where the monument now is, dying one by one. The

White Bull, Minneconjou Lakota. Photographed in 1926 at the 50th anniversary of the battle by G. J. McMurry. —Little Bighorn Battlefield National Monument

Cheyenne Bearded-Man (Lame White Man) charged these soldiers and died among them.

White Bull was now between those soldiers and the river, firing into the remaining ones on the hilltop. About ten of them jumped up and came down the ravine toward White Bull, shooting all the time. Two were killed, but the other eight forced White Bull to retreat. He was then hit in the leg

FIGURE 6: WHITE BULL'S MAP

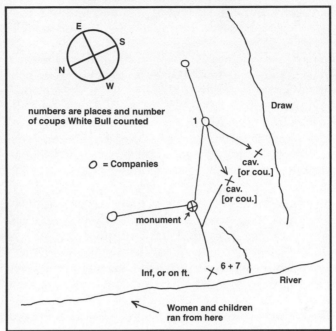

Adapted from a Stanley Vestal map illustrating troop movements and White Bull's coups.
The original map is in the W. S. Campbell Collection at the University of Oklahoma.

by a spent bullet and rolled into a shallow ditch, where he stayed until all the soldiers were killed.[139]

The actual notes that Vestal used to write the White Bull story are located in the Walter Stanley Campbell Collection at the University of Oklahoma. Two researchers, Wayne Wells and Richard G. Hardorff, have made Vestal's notes available to the public in recent years. They have left us, however, with some confusion as to which interview took place in which year. The interview noted by Hardorff in *Lakota Recollections* as being conducted by Vestal in 1930 is cited by Wells in his article "Little Big Horn Notes" as taking place in 1932. Conversely, the interview of 1930 cited by Wells is referenced by Hardorff as occurring in 1932. White Bull's map (fig. 6) is reproduced in both accounts and is also dated differently.[140]

Whatever actual dates the interviews were conducted, they provided details that were not included in White Bull's biography, *Warpath*. One interview indicates the troops were in four companies and Custer was in the second from the north. White Bull was on the east side, did a "center run," and returned. Then he charged right through the last company. The other Indians followed and the last company ran to the second, the second ran to the third, and so on. "The fourth company went to the third company in the draw, and they didn't go any farther. . . . The fourth company had lost their horses. They had white horses—that was the grey horse troop."[141]

White men from the first and second companies were on horseback. They still had their horses when they got to the fourth company. They ran from the third company and were all killed down in the draw. The fourth company started to run toward the hill. Most didn't get to the top, but they laid down and started shooting.

White Bull rode across to the west side of the ridge and counted more coups, the last of which were on the remaining few soldiers left in the draw. As he was going back uphill White Bull was hit in the leg, and he laid in a ditch until the battle ended.

The other interview with White Bull indicates he was on the east side of the river fighting Reno when he saw Custer moving from east to north. He rode north along the east bank and went up a draw to where Custer was. The Indians were met with a heavy fire and had to retreat south. The soldiers "made four companies, and one company was shooting at them in the draw" (Deep Coulee). White Bull worked his way to the east. Many Indians from the south and west charged at one company and drove them back to where the monument now is. White Bull jerked one soldier off his horse and counted several coups.[142]

White Bull's references to all the "companies" is confusing, and it is not easy to follow his story sequence. At least we can determine that the fourth company was the Gray Horse Troop. They were at the Last Stand portion of the ridge. Other companies ran toward them. We also note the fourth company ran to the third company in the draw. Was the draw Deep Ravine or Cemetery Ravine? On White Bull's map, the draw appears to be Deep Coulee. Later, the fourth company (the grays) ran toward the hill but didn't get to the top. Was this the retreat after forming the South Skirmish Line or a retreat from somewhere farther north, as seems to be indicated on the map (assuming the fourth company was the one farthest north)? None of the accounts are conclusive.

However, it may be the map itself that gives us the answer to the Deep Ravine-Cemetery Ravine question. White Bull drew it to show all of the coups he counted that day. Unfortunately, his map only shows three of the coups, and even then it is unclear whether two of the Xs read "cav" for cavalry or "cou" for coup (Wells and Hardorff differ on that also).

The significant point on the map is at numbers 6 and 7. White Bull had charged through the soldiers and went downhill on the western slopes. Vestal then recorded White Bull as saying that at 6 and 7 a bunch of soldiers on foot came in the draw. White Bull and another Indian got off their horses to fire at them. They jumped in the draw and took the soldiers' guns. More soldiers came. The two Indians rolled out of the draw and got away, after counting coup twice.[143]

Without the map all we can understand is that White Bull fought soldiers in a draw on the western slopes of the ridge. Seeing it on the map, the location of the action becomes plain. The soldiers came down from the ridge and monument area, but not down Deep Ravine. Their line of movement is significantly north of the axis of Deep Ravine—by the map's apparent scale, perhaps a few hundred yards north. Their line of movement is along Cemetery Ravine. The last soldiers attempted their escape down Cemetery Ravine and they were fought and killed by White Bull and other warriors in Cemetery Ravine.

11. Turtle Rib *Minneconjou Lakota*

Born in 1848, Turtle Rib was 28 years old at the Little Bighorn and fought there under Lamedeer. He was interviewed by Walter Camp in 1908. Turtle Rib said that Reno started the fight against the Hunkpapa camp. Turtle Rib was asleep at that time, but soon was aroused and managed to get into the fight. He killed a Ree Indian before Reno was forced back to the bluffs.

Turtle Rib did not see any fighting at Medicine Tail ford when he passed back through the village. The soldiers had already been driven back to the high ground east of the river. When he got up there he saw a running fight with the soldiers on foot. Those who kept their horses seemed to be stampeded. Some were going toward where the monument now is, and some were trying to ride back the way they came. Those on foot seemed the coolest and fought the hardest. No stand was made except at the end of the long ridge, "and here the bay and gray horses were all mixed together." There was a big dust and much running and excitement. One soldier rode across a hollow to try to get away. Turtle Rib was one who chased him, but the soldier killed himself. When he returned to the battlefield the fight was about over.[144]

Turtle Rib appears to have arrived at the Custer fight a little late to see the gray horse sortie downhill from the ridge. His is another corroborating account to locate the gray horses on Custer Hill.

12. Feather Earring *Minneconjou Lakota*

Feather Earring's story was given to Gen. Hugh L. Scott in 1919. He told Scott that he participated in the Reno fight, being one of the first to pass word from the scouts that the soldiers were coming. Feather Earring's brother was killed in the battle with Reno. They drove Reno into the hills by surrounding him in the bottomland and cutting him off from support.

When Reno reached the hill, word came that more soldiers below were attacking the village. When he got to the Custer fight it was almost over. Custer did not cross the river, but did fire on the village. The Indians crossed the Greasy Grass between Custer and Reno in great numbers and cut them off. They also got behind, east of Custer. The soldiers made their main stand on the ridge where the monument is now.

Feather Earring laid his brother's body in the bushes, then he got to the battle area in time to capture five gray horses. He drove them across the river. They were all wounded and trembling, so he let them go and went back toward monument ridge. He saw a white body about 200 yards from the river, and it appeared that the man's heart was still beating. He called to another Sioux. The warrior came up and put an arrow into him. The man jumped up and the warrior put another arrow into him. He had only been playing dead the first time. Feather Earring was asked what time Custer was killed. The women had just returned from picking berries, he thought, so it must have been about noon.[145]

Feather Earring was late in arriving for the latter stages of the battle and missed seeing the initial troop movements. He did capture five gray horses that had been stampeded from the main battle area, but we cannot determine Company E's fate from Feather Earring's story.

13. Flying Hawk *Oglala Lakota*

Flying Hawk was born in 1852 near what is now Rapid City, South Dakota. He was the brother of Kicking Bear and was also reported to be a nephew of Sitting Bull and cousin of Crazy Horse. He was interviewed by Eli S. Ricker at the Pine Ridge Reservation in 1907.

Custer, Flying Hawk said, came toward the camp from the second ridge back from the river and then stopped on a high hill (Nye-Cartwright) above the Indians. Flying Hawk was riding with Crazy Horse and other leaders and could see all of this. They crossed the river above Calhoun Hill before Custer left that second ridge. The soldiers saw the Indians down in the creek (Deep Coulee) leading to the river, then Custer came down off the second ridge and went up onto Calhoun Hill. Custer did not try to go to the river by the creek, and there was no fighting on that creek. He left a detachment there on Calhoun Hill and went over to Custer Hill.

On Calhoun Hill some soldiers stood and gave battle. Custer was already on his hill. The line on Calhoun was broken and the soldiers fell back, fighting as they went. A stand was made on the northeast side of the ridge (Keogh). Most of those soldiers were killed, but the rest continued to fall back toward Custer.

Flying Hawk was in the fighting from Calhoun Hill all along the ridge toward Custer. All the men on Custer Hill ran toward the river and were killed by the Indians who were on both sides of the retreating men. Custer and his men were killed before these soldiers ran for the river.[146]

Flying Hawk also told of his participation in the Little Bighorn fight to M. I. McCreight, in an ambitious little volume published in 1947, in which the Sioux chief interpreted American history. After leaving the Reno fight, Flying Hawk, while finishing chasing Reno up the bluffs, noted the Indians got in the battle with Custer's men, charging the ones "in the east and north on top of the hill. Custer was farther north than these soldiers were then." It looked like Custer would attack the lower end of the village. The Indians drove the soldiers down the hill along the ridge, where more soldiers were making a stand.

Flying Hawk said that he and Crazy Horse left the Reno fight to make a circuit along the river, then went up a gulch to the rear of the place where the soldiers were making a stand on the hill. Crazy Horse killed soldiers as fast as he could shoot. The soldiers broke and ran farther along the ridge toward Custer. They made a third stand but broke again and finally got with Custer's men. By then there were only a few left.

When Custer got nearly to the lower end of the camp, he started to go down a gulch, but the Indians surrounded him. The soldiers dismounted and made a stand, but it was no use. Their horses ran down the ravine right to the village, where the squaws caught them. After they were surrounded, the fight was over in about an hour.[147]

Flying Hawk was with Crazy Horse, and much of their battle activity was confined to the eastern and northern portions of the field along the upper reaches of Deep Coulee, Calhoun Hill, the Keogh ravine, and Custer Hill. Flying Hawk's narratives are important in that they mention troops occupying the high ridges in the Nye-Cartwright area and the fact that those troops left that position only after the other battalion (with E Troop) had left the river and nearly reached Calhoun Hill. There is only a brief mention made of the Custer Hill survivors making for the river, and no mention at all of them dying in any deep ravine.

14. Standing Bear *Minneconjou Lakota*

Standing Bear was interviewed by Walter Camp in 1910. He said the Indians saw the smoke from Custer's camp early in the morning of June 25 and knew the soldiers were coming. Custer's men advanced nearly to the river, but were engaged by the Indians and forced back to the ridge where the main battle took place. Some Indians crossed the river when they first saw Custer, but they weren't strong enough to stop him.

The Indians first prepared to fight were the ones camped farthest from the river. They were able to get ready while Reno's fight was going on. Standing Bear was up on the bluffs and could see Custer go down a coulee, into Medicine Tail, and then cross over to Custer Ridge while in full view of the village. The soldiers did not fire into the village.

"Custer's men did not fight by companies but were all together all the time." Camp tried to make Standing Bear change his mind on this point, but could not make him change his story. Standing Bear was clear. The gray horses were mixed in with the rest, but few horses got beyond the Keogh area. Nearly all were killed or captured. Keogh's area is the first place where the soldiers stopped to fight. "Between Calhoun and [the] monument there were Indians [on] both sides of the river as [the] soldiers went along. The soldiers killed between Custer and [the] river were men on foot trying to make the river, and they were killed in the deep ravine."[148]

In 1931, Standing Bear was interviewed by John Neihardt, as were Black Elk and Iron Hawk, whose contributions all appeared in *Black Elk Speaks*. Neihardt's original source notes were edited by Raymond J. DeMallie, and from them another battle description can be gleaned.

When Standing Bear crossed the Little Bighorn at the mouth of Muskrat Creek (Medicine Tail), the Indians were already swarming on Custer. His party was west of Custer at the time. When he got close enough, he could see the soldiers were off their horses and holding them by the bridles. They were ready for the Indians, but the Indians crept up and the bullets went over them.

Custer was on the ridge and Standing Bear could see the soldiers sitting with their hats off on the hill, shooting. The Indians fired back, and after a time he heard some men shout, "They have gone!" Standing Bear saw the cavalrymen's horses had broken loose and were running away. After the stampede there were fewer soldiers living. They began to retreat downhill, and the Indians went up after them.

Warriors were charging all around Standing Bear. Indians and soldiers were all mixed up, and many guns were going off. Some soldiers went toward the river and "went into the side of a hill into a draw and there was tall grass in here. We were right on top of the soldiers and there was no use in their hiding from us." The Indians killed every soldier and some of their own men by accident. The women came over after the fight, and it was quite a sight with the horses and men on top of each other and mixed up together.[149]

Standing Bear indicated that the grays were mixed in with the other horses up on the ridge and the soldiers fought for a time on the hilltops. Some troops came downhill to fight but soon lost their horses, and the battle accelerated to its conclusion. He didn't specify which troop or how many men came downhill to die between the ridge and the river, but some apparently made it to a deep ravine before they were killed.

15. Red Hawk *Oglala Lakota*

This account is listed under Red Hawk's name for ease of recording only. It is really the combined statement of Red Hawk, Shot in the Face, Big Road, and Iron Bull as they told it to Nicholas Ruleau, onetime fur trader and interpreter at Pine Ridge Reservation for 30 years. Ruleau in turn told their story to lawyer-historian Eli S. Ricker in 1906.

These Indians agreed that the battle with Reno started as early as nine in the morning. Reno could not hold against the great numbers of warriors and retreated. When they had him corralled on the bluffs, word came that soldiers were coming at the other end of the camp.

These other soldiers came down the ridge in three divisions, but they did not come down to the river. The first came to about one-half or three-quarters of a mile from the river. The Indians fighting Reno fell back down the river bottom through the village, then crossed the Little Bighorn and

FIGURE 7: RED HAWK'S MAP

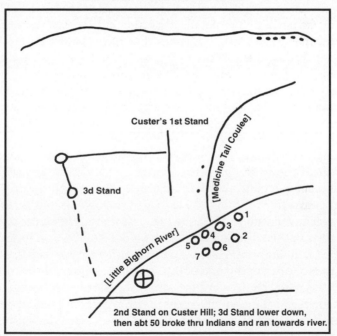

Custer's 1st Stand

[Medicine Tail Coulee]

3d Stand

[Little Bighorn River]

1
3
4
5
6
2
7

2nd Stand on Custer Hill; 3d Stand lower down, then abt 50 broke thru Indians and ran towards river.

Adapted from a map prepared for Nicholas Ruleau and Eli Ricker by Austin Red Hawk, 1906. The original map includes the following explanations:

1. Uncpapas	5. Cheyennes	⊕ This is the point to which
2. Oglalas	6. Yankton	the camps—old men,
3. Minneconjous	7. Santees	women, and children—
4. Uses Bows		fled and collected.

(The Nicholas Ruleau interview and map are found in the Eli S. Ricker Collection of the Nebraska State Historical Society.)

went up the high hill (Weir Point). Red Hawk said they went down from there to attack the first division of soldiers. They drove this group into the second division, and so on into the third, until the troops were forced back to where the first real stand was made on Calhoun Hill. There the soldiers stood in line and made a good fight.

Then the troopers divided and retreated on each side of the ridge, falling back to Custer Hill, where another stand was made. There the soldiers made a desperate fight. What was left of them retreated to a spot where they made a third stand. "These were surrounded and the Indians rushed on the soldiers. Some of the soldiers broke through the Indians and ran for the ravine, but all were killed without getting into it."[150]

Red Hawk drew a map for Nicholas Ruleau (fig. 7). It showed the Indian campsites, the Little Bighorn, Medicine Tail Coulee, and the three areas where the stands were made. The first stand was represented by a line drawn along Calhoun Hill and a bit down Greasy Grass Ridge. The second was a circle drawn on Custer Hill. The third was another circle just to the river side of the Custer Hill circle. The map was labeled "3d Stand lower down, then abt 50 broke thru Indians and ran towards river." The scale of the Red Hawk map indicates the third stand took place a few hundred yards down from Custer Hill, square in Cemetery Ravine. From there some soldiers ran for the ravine but were killed *without* getting into it. Red Hawk's map and story are clear. The majority of the troopers that made a stand down from Custer Hill fought and died in Cemetery Ravine.

16. He Dog (Sunka-Bloka) *Oglala Lakota*

He Dog was born in 1840 near Bear Butte, South Dakota, and was 36 at the time of the battle. He surrendered in May 1877. His high moral standards and leadership skills earned him a position as judge to the Court of Indian Offenses in the 1890s. He Dog was 70 years old when Walter Camp interviewed him in 1910. He was in many fights with the whites, including the battle with General Crook on the Rosebud on June 17, 1876.

At the Little Bighorn, He Dog was about to charge into Reno's men when they broke out of the timber on their horses and rode as fast as they could up the river. He Dog went back to the Hunkpapa camp and saw Custer's men coming on the big hill to the east. They went down Medicine Tail Coulee and went onto a little rise. Here the soldiers were scattered all along parallel to the river. Near the ford Custer moved as though trying to reach the lower end of the camp. There was no fighting down near the river except for a few shots. There were about 15 or 20 Indians along the banks east of the river firing at the soldiers, but not much shooting from either side. He Dog didn't hear Custer fire any volleys.

Before the fight started, the Indians drove Keogh up a slope to a ridge and over to the other side. The soldiers were mounted and kept going right along. They were all together all the time and did not fight by companies. The Indians were all along Custer Ridge and Custer went down along the hollow by Keogh. At first the gray horses were all together, but after they got on the hill they mixed with the other horses. The Keogh area is where Crazy Horse charged, broke through the soldiers, and split them in two bunches. The horses stampeded to the river.

"When the men rushed from Custer's last stand toward [the] river, the dismounted ones took to the gully, and the mounted ones tried to get away to [the] south."[151] At this point in the interview, Camp must have asked He Dog if he knew of 28 men going into a ravine, because Camp's next comment reads: "(Corroborates twenty-eight dead men in gully.)".

Apparently He Dog did not volunteer any information about a specific number of men going into a gully, and only responded when Camp supplied him with a number. Unfortunately, this happened more than once in an interview. The Indian may or may not have known exactly what the interviewer meant, but responded affirmatively only because the questioner seemed to want it that way. Camp did this many times, setting the scenario for the Indian to respond to instead of simply letting the Indian volunteer his own information. Whether or not He Dog even mentioned the gully without the leading question being posed first cannot be known. However, we have that number 28 again, the men coming down the ridge and making for the river. Which gully they went into is not specified.

Nine years later, in 1919, He Dog again told his story, this time to Gen. Hugh L. Scott. Scott was a skillful interviewer, had an abiding interest in the Indians, and had mastered the sign language.

He Dog told Scott he first attacked Custer near the dry creek (Medicine Tail) and Custer never got near the river. The troops were in lines of six companies. They stopped on a side of the ridge away from the river, and the Indians were on the opposite side of the same ridge. Along this ridge (where the monument is now) is a small gap where Crazy Horse broke through. Now and then some soldiers' horses would run down toward the river. Part of the cut-off men fought their way to the others at the end of the ridge. Some soldiers got away toward the river, but all were killed.

He Dog mentioned a soldier on a stocking-legged horse escaping a long way to the north and almost getting away before inexplicably shooting himself. He thought the battle lasted about two hours and believed the soldiers they fought were part of General Crook's men. He did not know anything about Custer being in the country. Custer's men "never got any nearer to the river than the monument. Only a few soldiers who broke away were killed below toward the river."[152]

In the latter interview, He Dog had no Walter Camp to ply him with leading questions. He volunteered no information at all about 28 men going into a gully. Instead, he was certain that only a few soldiers got away to be killed toward the river. Which of the two interviews is the most accurate cannot be determined. Either 28 got away to be killed in an undetermined ravine or only a few made their way downhill to be killed in an unspecified location. The testimony is equivocal.

17. Two Eagles *Brule Lakota*

Two Eagles was born in 1858 and was 18 at the Little Bighorn fight. He told his story to Sewell B. Weston in 1908 while living on the Rosebud

Reservation. Weston based his interview on a questionnaire and map provided by Walter Camp.

By referring to Camp's map, Two Eagles pointed out that some of Custer's men went from the high hills in the east to the ford and were driven back to Greasy Grass Ridge, while others went from the hills directly to the Calhoun Hill position. Those that went toward the river remained mounted, but they did not get all the way to the water and they remained there for a short fight only. There was more fighting with the troops as they pulled back from the ford to Greasy Grass Ridge.

Camp indicated the next part of his questionnaire was important and that the interviewer, Weston, was to get a definite answer about the troop movements at this point. Did the soldiers go from Greasy Grass Ridge to Calhoun Hill in a body or did they split up and part of them go from Greasy Grass Ridge down to Deep Ravine? All the soldiers went from Greasy Grass Ridge to Calhoun Hill, Two Eagles answered.

The fight was a moving one. Between Greasy Grass Ridge and Calhoun Hill the soldiers fired as they went along. Some were mounted, some dismounted. A slight stand was made in the Keogh area. The Indians were in the draws below the crown of the ridge. The only firm stand was made at Custer Hill. The gray horses were mixed with other horses of different colors. The last of the soldiers at Custer Hill were killed going down toward the ravine. They were dismounted. Two Eagles knew of no soldiers that reached the river. The battle ended about five o'clock.[153]

Two Eagles indicated that Custer's men were divided into two battalions. One did go near the river and one stayed back on the eastern hills. The troops did not go from the Greasy Grass Ridge area down toward Deep Ravine, but all traveled along Calhoun Hill and Battle Ridge to Custer Hill. The last survivors made their way down from there toward the river. No one made it. Which ravine they might have died in, if any, is unknown.

18. Lights (Cragre) *Minneconjou Lakota*

Lights, which may have been a nickname for Chases Red Clouds, was born about 1853. He was interviewed in 1909 by Sewell B. Weston, using a Walter Camp questionnaire similar to the one used for the Two Eagles interview.

Lights was in the fights with Crook and Reno. He got to the Custer fight in time to see the soldiers coming along Nye-Cartwright Ridge. They only got to within a quarter mile of the river, then they went from there to Greasy Grass Ridge in company formation and in good order.

As in the Two Eagles interview, Camp indicated that Weston should treat the next question as important and get a definite answer. When the troops were at Greasy Grass Ridge, did the men go in a body to Calhoun Hill or split up and part of them go down to Deep Ravine? All of the men went from Greasy Grass Ridge to Calhoun Hill, Lights said. He was just northeast of Calhoun Hill himself and could see them very well.

The Indians were on both sides of Custer at Calhoun Hill. At Greasy Grass Ridge and Calhoun Hill the fight was a moving one, and there might have been a short stand made in the Keogh area. There was only one firm stand, and that was at Custer Hill. On the way to that position, the soldiers fought mostly mounted. They were not running, but were giving up ground because of the superior numbers of Indians. One company had gray horses. They were fighting in the front up to the Keogh position, then they became mixed with the other horses, as one company then the next would alternate in covering the retreat.

Lights was asked if the men killed between Custer Hill and Deep Ravine were killed fighting their way up from the ravine toward the hill at the start of the fight, or killed running from Custer Hill toward the river at the end of the fight? They were killed "fighting," Lights answered, from Custer Hill toward the river at the last of the fight.

At the end of the fight, Lights was stationed just west of Last Stand Hill, about on the present cemetery grounds. He saw some of the last soldiers break away from the hill and try to get away by jumping over high banks at places "between" Custer Hill and Deep Ravine. None of the soldiers escaped to the river.

Near the end of the interview Lights was asked if any men were killed in the deep gully. How many, a few or a good many? Quite a number were killed in the gully, Lights said, but not so many as at Custer Hill.[154]

What can we learn from Lights? Although the questionnaire method is helpful in bringing out certain points that may not be spoken of by a narrator free to be his own guide, it raises other problems. Camp's questionnaire was loaded with misleading dichotomous interrogatives. All the situations he framed were not necessarily either/or scenarios. Did the soldiers do *a* or *b*? Did they move to *c* or *d*? Maybe both events occurred. Maybe neither. Maybe a third possibility happened that wasn't even suggested. In many cases the Indian might be trapped into answering a question when the situation as presented wasn't even in the Indian's frame of reference.

Weston asked if the troops went from Greasy Grass Ridge to Calhoun Hill in a body, or did they split up and part of them go down to the Deep Ravine? But what if they did not split up? What if all of them went in a body down to the Deep Ravine? The possibility was not accounted for in the dichotomous questions Camp provided.

Weston asked if the men killed between Custer Hill and the Deep Ravine were killed fighting their way up from the ravine to Custer Hill at the start of the fight, or if were they killed running from Custer Hill to the river at the end of the fight? It did not have to be one of these two possibilities. What if they had died moving in both directions at different times of the battle? What if they had been killed running uphill at the end, or fighting downhill at the start?

In at least a few instances, Lights did not let himself be entrapped by Camp's questions. Were the men killed fighting up, or running down? Neither. Lights said they were killed fighting down the hill from Custer. It is a significant difference. It indicates organized resistance in Cemetery Ravine.

On other occasions, Lights was ensnared. He indicated Custer only got to within a quarter mile of the ford at the mouth of Medicine Tail Coulee. He was then asked if Custer went from the ford to Greasy Grass Ridge in a body or in two divisions? How could Lights answer? He already said the soldiers weren't at the ford, and if they were, what if they were in three or four divisions? He answered that they were in company formation and in good order—probably about the best he could answer. Next, Lights was asked about the fighting between the ford and Greasy Grass Ridge. How could there have been fighting between the two points if the soldiers never went between the two points, as Lights already indicated? At this juncture, Lights probably just gave up and answered those persistent, presumptive, confusing questions. Yes, there was a continual fight! he said.

Lights was also asked if men were killed in the deep gully—just a few or many? Quite a number, he said, but not so many as at Custer Hill. Was this just another answer to please a questioner who always seemed to want an either/or answer? Remember, Lights had already said the soldiers *fought* below Custer Hill, and those that tried to escape did so by jumping over banks *between* Custer Hill and the Deep Ravine. These actions would seem to rule out a great number of running escapees being killed in Deep Ravine. Still, without knowing for sure if this was one of the times Lights escaped the dichotomy trap or was ensnared by it, we must take his word as it was reported. The decision is tenuous, but we will place the men Lights saw killed in the Deep Ravine column.

19. Lone Bear *Oglala Lakota*

Lone Bear was born about 1847. After surrendering in 1877 he enlisted as an Indian scout and later became a member of the Pine Ridge Reservation's Indian police. Sewell B. Weston interviewed him in 1909. Like the Two Eagles and Lights interviews, Lone Bear's was conducted using one of Walter Camp's questionnaires.

Lone Bear thought the Reno fight lasted from about nine to eleven in the morning. Custer's battle lasted from noon until four in the afternoon. Custer's men were first seen coming from the northeast down Nye-Cartwright Ridge. They went toward the river but never got to it.

No soldiers went from the Greasy Grass Ridge area to the Deep Ravine. They all went to Calhoun Hill. Lone Bear was very emphatic about that point.

The hardest fighting was done in the Keogh area, Lone Bear thought, although there was a shorter stand made at Custer Hill. Custer Hill "was the first and only place where the soldiers tried to get away, and only a few there." These men were killed in the last stages of the fight going from Custer Hill toward the ravine. Lone Bear did not go into the Deep Ravine to see if any soldiers were killed there, but as far as he knew no soldier ever got to the river.[155]

Lone Bear's story is not specific enough to pinpoint which ravine the Gray Horse Troopers might have died in. He did believe, however, that only a few men ran from Custer Hill at the end of the fight and none of them made it to the river.

20. Iron Hawk *Hunkpapa Lakota*

Iron Hawk was a big 14-year-old boy when he participated in the Little Bighorn fight in 1876. He, like Black Elk and Standing Bear, told his story to John Neihardt in 1931. Iron Hawk had slept late the day of the battle, and the sun was already overhead. He was eating his first meal when a crier yelled, "The chargers are coming." He ran to where the horses were grazing, roped one, and helped round up the others that had stampeded off toward the Minneconjou camp. By the time he returned to his tepee and prepared himself for battle the Reno fight had ended, and so he joined the warriors going to fight the soldiers who were coming to the other end of the village.

Iron Hawk and many other Hunkpapas gathered on the east bank of the river at the foot of a gulch that led back up the hill where Custer's men were. They followed a very brave Shyela (Cheyenne) who went uphill alone against the soldiers. The soldiers on the ridge were on foot and holding their horses. The Shyela circled near the soldiers several times, but their bullets did not hit him. He rode back to where Iron Hawk was at the head of the gulch.

They stayed there awhile, then Iron Hawk heard a voice cry, "Now they are going, they are going!" The cavalry horses were stampeding. "They were all gray horses." A big cry went up and it got dark from the dust and smoke. The soldiers started running downhill. They were nearly all afoot and looked so scared that they didn't know what they were doing. The Indians charged them in the twilight that had fallen on the field. Iron Hawk killed one soldier by shooting an arrow through his ribs so it stuck out the other side. He saw another Lakota riding along the edge of the gulch, yelling to look out because there was a soldier hiding in there. The Lakota charged in and killed the soldier with his knife.

Iron Hawk started back down toward the river. The dust began to lift, and the women and children started coming uphill to strip the soldiers. Then Iron Hawk saw something funny. Two fat old women were stripping a soldier who was wounded and playing dead. They had him naked and "began to cut something off that he had," when he jumped up and began fighting them. He was swinging one around while the other tried to stab him with her knife. In a while, another woman rushed up and stabbed him until he was really dead. Iron Hawk thought it was funny to see a naked *wasichu* fighting with the fat women.[156]

A more detailed picture of the fight can be gained from reading Neihardt's unabridged notes. Iron Hawk and other Hunkpapas gathered at the foot of the gulch that led up to Custer's Hill. He watched a very brave Cheyenne ride in circles in front of the soldiers and return unharmed. Iron Hawk said they had stood there a long time when he heard a voice call out. He looked up and saw the gray horses stampeding. After several more acts of bravado by Iron Hawk's companions, they looked again to see the soldiers coming downhill on foot.

The Hunkpapas charged. Iron Hawk had only a bow and arrows but got right in among the soldiers and shot one straight through under his ribs. He then saw two soldiers fleeing alone and went after them. "There was a little creek going up there and one of the soldiers got killed by Brings Plenty. There are headstones all over there and the furthest headstone shows where the second man that I killed lies." Iron Hawk hit the soldier with his bow across his back and head. The man fell off his horse, and Iron Hawk beat him several times on the head. He was very mad. "Probably this was the last of Custer's men to be killed and I killed him."[157]

Iron Hawk's story is much like other Indian impressions of this portion of the Custer fight. There were soldiers with gray horses on the ridge. The soldiers came downhill mostly on foot, holding their horses. The gray horses stampeded. They were killed by the Indians who had been hiding in the gulches.

There are significant finer points, however. Iron Hawk saw a Lakota riding along the edge of the gulch. The Lakota had found *one* soldier sneaking along in the ravine and killed him. The majority of the Gray Horse Troopers died before they got to Deep Ravine. This is well borne out by Iron Hawk. He was perhaps the only Indian to specifically reference one of his kills with a stone marker now on the field. He thought he killed one of the last of Custer's men. There are headstones all along the line, he said, "and the furthest headstone shows where the second man that I killed lies." Iron Hawk had no problem whatsoever with the markers. They were not phony. They obviously represented places where the soldiers fell, one in particular being a small monument to his own handiwork. And this soldier, perhaps the last killed, was struck down by Iron Hawk before he got into the Deep Ravine.

21. Waterman *Arapaho*

Waterman was one of a party of five Arapahoes that left the agency and were hunting near the Little Bighorn when they were made prisoners by the Sioux, who were under the impression the Arapahoes were scouting for the white soldiers. They remained in the Sioux camp for two days and were freed by the intercession of the Cheyenne Two Moon. To show their good faith, they went into battle with the Sioux and Cheyenne. Waterman was 22 in 1876. He and Left Hand were the only survivors of the five when Col. Tim McCoy questioned them in 1920.

Waterman indicated the fight began at the upper end of the village as early as nine in the morning. There was only one Indian killed there, and the soldiers were driven back across the river to a ridge where they dug some pits in the ground. The Indians kept them pinned down there.

After awhile there was shooting at the lower end of the village. The troops there tried to cross the river and attack the camp, but the Indians drove them back. The soldiers could have forded the river at that point, because the Indians easily crossed there and forced them back up the hill. On top of the hill they left their horses and the Indians took them. Some horses got away and came down to the river, where they were caught by the Indians. "There were gray horses and some sorrels. This left the soldiers on foot completely surrounded by the Indians."

The soldiers were on the high ground, Waterman said. In one of the first charges against them a Cheyenne chief named White Man Cripple (Lame White Man) was killed. Two Moon then took command of the Cheyennes and led them through the fight. "I was with some Indians in a small gulch below the hill where the soldiers were, but later we moved up the hill and closed in on the soldiers."

There was much noise, smoke, and confusion. "A few soldiers tried to get away and reach the river, but they were all killed. A few did get down to the river, but were killed by some Indians there." Waterman knew of only one soldier that he killed, but he did not scalp him because the soldier had short hair.[158]

Waterman's account shows that after the soldiers were driven back from Medicine Tail ford they took position along the high ground on Battle Ridge. Waterman and other Indians were in the gulches. They caught gray and sorrel horses that got away from the troops. Some soldiers tried to get away to the river but were killed. We cannot determine if these soldiers were killed in Cemetery Ravine or Deep Ravine, but as the warriors filled the deep gulches, the possibility that many troopers met their demise in the Deep Ravine is not likely.

22. Yellow Nose *Ute*

Born into the Ute tribe about 1849, Yellow Nose was captured by the Southern Cheyennes when he was about nine years old and remained affiliated with them the rest of his life. Early in the spring of 1876 he left the Indian Territory (Oklahoma) to visit the Northern Cheyennes, among whom his wife had relatives. Yellow Nose appeared in several Indian narratives of the Custer battle, including accounts by informants of George Bird Grinnell, Father Peter Powell, and John Stands In Timber, primarily because of his noted deed of capturing a soldier guidon. Yellow Nose's story appeared in the *Chicago Record-Herald* in September 1905 and in *The Indian School Journal* of November 1905.

Custer's attack, Yellow Nose said, was a surprise to the Indians, for they had kept their eyes on Crook's defeated forces to the south and did not expect Custer to come out of the east. Yellow Nose was bathing in the river about noon on the 25th when the attack began. Because his pony was not readily at hand, he did not participate in the Reno fight. By the time he had mounted, other soldiers were coming down from the eastern hills, and many of the Cheyennes went after that party.

Yellow Nose crossed at Medicine Tail ford and closed with the troopers coming toward the river. Early in the action a color bearer advanced at him with flagstaff held out like a spear. Seeing its brass ferrule shining and thinking it was a rifle, Yellow Nose wrested the guidon from him. The trumpeters blowing their calls at this time also made the Ute liken the scene to that of a regimental band playing.

Very soon, however, the soldier advance turned into a stand, then into a retreat. Yellow Nose said that the soldiers made three stands while they fell back to the final hill, all the while stubbornly holding the ground to their advantage and giving it up grudgingly. As the fight progressed to its final phase, Yellow Nose engaged in combat with a soldier that he later thought might have been Custer himself.

Yellow Nose gave us no information about the Gray Horse Troop, yet his close involvement in the final action sheds light on the issue of the number of men who attempted to escape. He estimated "that there were about thirty men with Custer, all on foot, when the last stand was made at a small mound on the ridge." As the Indians pressed closer, Yellow Nose said "several soldiers lost courage and ran to lower ground, close to the base of the mound."[159] That was all. There was no mass exodus, and they only went as far as the base of the hill.

23. Two Moon (Ishe-heyu-nishis) *Northern Cheyenne*

Two Moon was born in western Wyoming in 1842, the son of a captive Arikara married into the Northern Cheyenne tribe. Hamlin Garland was given Two Moon's story in 1898 at his little cabin near the Rosebud on the

Cheyenne Reservation. The story appeared later that same year in *McClure's Magazine*. Two Moon was a chief in the Fox Warrior Society and fought in many engagements with the whites.

The first warning of the fight on June 25 was a great dust rising like a whirlwind in the direction of Sitting Bull's camp. When Two Moon rode there, he saw Reno's men fighting in line, covering the flat land. The Indians were too many and chased them across the river and up the hill. Then messengers came and said more soldiers were coming.

Two Moon rode back to his camp. While sitting on his horse he saw flags come over the hill to the east. The soldiers rose all at once, mounted in columns of fours. They formed in three bunches with a little space in between. Then they dismounted and some soldiers led the horses back over the hill.

The Sioux rode up all around the soldiers. The Cheyennes went up farther to the left. The shooting was very quick and there was a great cloud of smoke. Some soldiers stood and some kneeled. One soldier on a sorrel with white face and white forelegs rode up and down the line shouting orders. He was very brave.

The Indians swirled around and many soldiers fell. All but five of the soldiers' horses were killed. "Once in a while some man would break out and run toward the river, but he would fall." At the end there were about one hundred men and five horsemen left on the hill all bunched together.

> Then a chief was killed. I hear it was Long Hair, I don't know; and then the five horsemen and the bunch of men, may be so forty [*sic*], started toward the river. The man on the sorrel horse led them, shouting all the time. He wore a buckskin shirt and had long black hair and a mustache. He fought hard with a big knife. His men were all covered with white dust. I couldn't tell whether they were officers or not. One man all alone ran down toward the river, then round up over the hill. I thought he was going to escape, but a Sioux fired and hit him in the head. He was the last man.[160]

Two Moon told his story again to Dr. Joseph K. Dixon at a great Indian council that convened on the battlefield in September 1909. Custer, Two Moon said, came up and along the ridge from the right of where the monument now stands. He deployed his soldiers along the entire length of the ridge, then they rode beyond the monument down in the valley where they couldn't be seen. The Cheyennes and Sioux came up from the valley of the Little Bighorn. Custer placed his men in groups along the ridge. They dismounted and seemed to have let their horses go down the other side of the ridge.

Two Moon stood at the monument in 1909 and indicated that the gray horses stood right on that very spot, all out in the open. The Indians swarmed like ants toward the bunch of gray horses where Long Hair

Two Moon,
Cheyenne.
Photo by L. A.
Huffman, 1878.
—Little Bighorn
Battlefield
National
Monument

stood. Two Moon said he led the Cheyennes up the long line of ridge from the valley, blocking the soldiers. They broke the soldiers' line and went over the ridge. Another band of Sioux attacked from over beyond the ridge. Two Moon's warriors advanced, yelling and firing. "I could not break the line at the bunch of gray horses and I wheeled and went to the left down the valley with the line of soldiers facing me as I went, firing at me, and all my men firing at the soldiers. Then I rode on up the ridge to the left." There Two Moon met the Cheyenne Black Bear. They killed and scalped a wounded soldier and took the clothes and guns from a few other dead ones. When Two Moon rode back down the ridge, the soldiers and Indians were all mixed up together and almost all the soldiers were killed. Along the ridge where Custer's troops had been killed he saw one man running away to the high hills beyond, but he was overtaken and killed.[161]

Two Moon also granted an interview to Richard Throssel in 1909, which was printed in the Billings *Daily Gazette* in 1911. Two Moon was preparing to fight Reno when he saw another bunch of soldiers coming down a draw toward the camp. It was Custer. The Indians hurriedly crossed the river, some up and some down, to get on each side of the soldiers. They came to the edge and stopped, and then the guns began to roar like thunder. Custer's men dismounted and slowly moved back up the ridge with their horses on the inside and the soldiers around them.

The Indians surrounded them. The first big charge swept in all together, and nearly one whole band of soldiers was killed. At the next big charge the Indians all went in together, and the fighting was done in a little bit. "The grey bunch were the last killed." Two Moon said Custer must have been brave and gave him credit for attacking when so badly outnumbered. Yet, Two Moon thought Custer's men did not fight as they should have, by taking more evasive action. "They did not run nor seek shelter, but stayed right out in the open where it was easy to shoot them down. Any ordinary bunch of men would have dropped into a watercourse, or a draw, where they could have fought for a long time."[162]

In 1913, Eli S. Ricker conducted two interviews, one with interpreter Henry Leeds and the other with Willis T. Rowland. Two Moon told his story for what he said was the fifth time. There are a few significant points to be gained from the interviews. Custer marched in as if he was going to cross the river. When he got within a few yards of the Little Bighorn the Indians turned him "so that his course was thrown about ½ a mile away from the river."

When Custer got "up on top where the stones are," the troops dismounted and led their horses into the gulch. The Gray Horse Company held their horses, and not a shot was fired by the soldiers while preparations were being made. Two Moon and his men charged up the slope three times and then turned and swept to the right and north of the ridge. The horses in the gulch were turned loose and fled toward the river. Specifically naming Company E, Two Moon said, "The White Horse Troops fought with signal desperation. If the others had not given up, but had fought with equal stubbornness of the White Horse Troop, Custer would have driven the Indians from the field."[163]

From Two Moon's accounts we can definitely see the grays were intact along the ridge on Last Stand Hill, and they were a tough nut to crack. In fact, it was exceptional to Two Moon that men would stand and fight on open ground in such a determined manner when they could have sought gullies to hide in. Once in a while a man would break out and run toward the river but would be killed.

About 40 men in one group also attempted a maneuver down the hill from Custer's knoll. They too were killed before reaching any deep ravine. They were led by a man in buckskin with black hair and a large knife. Two Moon may have been describing the scout Mitch Bouyer. His body was identified during the archaeological dig of 1984-85, resting along the South Skirmish Line on the Cemetery Ravine side of the divide, only halfway down from the monument to Deep Ravine.

In only one of his several accounts did Two Moon mention a large-scale, end-of-battle sortie down from Custer Hill. The other times he emphasized that the soldiers stayed in the open and fought hard, few men ran or sought shelter, and only one man reached the river. If 40 men did head down from Custer Hill, it looks like they met their end in Cemetery Ravine.

24. White Shield *Northern Cheyenne*

White Shield's story was given to George Bird Grinnell while the naturalist/historian was compiling his notes and interviews in the late 1800s. Grinnell got all of his information for the Custer fight from Northern Cheyenne accounts that consisted of a number of individual observations, none of which, by itself, could give a general idea of the fight.[164] This account is listed under White Shield's name for convenience only. It consists of contributions from many, including White Shield, Bobtail Horse, White Bull (Ice), Roan Bear, and Brave Wolf. Their composite observations allowed Grinnell to tell the story of the Custer battle.

After Reno's men retreated from the valley, the Indians did little pursuing, instead turning back to see to their own wounded and to plunder. Then they heard the shouts that other soldiers were attacking the lower end of the village. The women who had fled east of the Little Bighorn to escape Reno's charge soon discovered Custer's men coming and had to run back across the river and to the bluffs on the west side of the valley.

A part of Custer's troops went down a dry creek and were "right down close to the stream," according to Brave Wolf. There the fighting began. White Shield saw Custer's men in seven groups approaching the river. He, along with Roan Bear, Bobtail Horse, Buffalo Calf, and Mad Wolf were at the river. Mad Wolf said they should not charge the soldiers just then, for they were too many. The Indians crossed the river toward the troops and circled away from them, but the soldiers kept going on down toward the ford about a half mile above the main battlefield. White Shield thought Custer would cross and get into the camp, but suddenly, before they reached the river, the Gray Horse Company halted and dismounted, and all who were following them stopped and dismounted.

White Shield rode left and down the river while Bobtail Horse, Buffalo Calf, and others stopped close to the river and, under cover of a low ridge, began to shoot at the soldiers. One soldier was killed about the time the Gray Horse Company halted. More Indians began to gather and cross the river and string up the gulch like swarming ants. The two troops of cavalry that had come nearest to Bobtail Horse and his party fell back to a little knoll. They remained there only a few moments, then crossed a gulch and climbed the hill on the other side. They "held their line of battle," Brave Wolf said, "and kept fighting and falling from their horses—fighting and falling, all the way up nearly to where the monument now stands." The Gray Horse Company stopped on that ground and opened such a heavy fire that the Indians fell back.

Some Cheyennes charged up close to the soldiers, especially Yellow Nose, Contrary Belly, and Comes In Sight. Yellow Nose even snatched and carried off a company guidon. The charges frightened many of the soldier horses and they stampeded. It looked like the soldiers were running, but that was not true.[165]

The Gray Horse Company stood its ground at the place where the monument now is. However, said Brave Wolf, "A part of those who had reached the top of the hill went on over and tried to go to the river, but they killed them all going down the hill, before any of them got to the creek." Different groups of soldiers moved about on the higher ground, some going toward the river and some away from it, but drew closer together when the Indians closed in. By that time most of the soldiers had lost their horses. One company lost theirs near where the road goes now. They tried to make their way on foot toward the Gray Horse Company on the hill a half-mile away. The firing became close, within six-shooter range, as they went up the hill.

They did not make it. Every ravine running down from the ridge and every bit of brush was occupied by Indians. White Shield said the Gray Horse Company held their horses to the last and most all were killed, but Bobtail Horse declared that some gray horses got away and charged through the Indians, for he got two of them himself.

The great majority of the troops were not killed by charging into them, but from long-range firing. The final charge was made after most of the troops in the main body had fallen, though many soldiers were still on foot scattered down toward the river. "When all the troops on the hill had fallen, the Indians gave a loud shout and charged up the ridge. The soldiers toward the river backed away, and after that the fight did not last long enough to light a pipe."[166]

White Shield and other Northern Cheyennes were very definite in stating that the Gray Horse Troop came near the river. There was an engagement for some time, and the grays eventually retreated from the water and along the ridge to Last Stand Hill. They put up a very good fight. Much of the firing was done at long range between the Indians in the gulches and the troops on the ridges. No mention was made of grays going down into any deep ravine. In fact, as Two Moon also indicated, they put up a stubborn resistance on the open hilltops and slopes. There was a viable line from the hill toward the river, for they seem to have put up a notable resistance there also. That line was not ambushed and overwhelmed in a deep ravine, shot down en masse. They were organized and fought hard until "backed away" by the last charge. They backed away and died along Cemetery Ravine.

25. Tall Bull (Hotuya-kostache) *Northern Cheyenne*

Tall Bull was born in 1853 and was 22 years old at the time of the Little Bighorn fight. He was a brother-in-law of the Southern Cheyenne Lame White Man. Walter Camp interviewed him in 1910.

Like some of Grinnell's informants, Tall Bull indicated that women who were escaping from Reno's charge went east of the river and discovered Custer approaching. Custer got on the flat near Medicine Tail ford before the Indians drove him back. The troops were back on the first rise above the river and going up the ridge when Tall Bull got into the fight.

The warriors who did not get to their horses quick enough to get into the Reno fight were the first ones to meet Custer. The soldiers made no charges against the Indians and were driven back from the river, some mounted and some on foot, and not in very good order. Tall Bull heard the soldiers fire volleys. One was at the start of the fight at "C" (which on Camp's map in the publication where the Tall Bull interview is reproduced is in Cedar Coulee, see fig. 8). The last was at "G" (near the mouth of Medicine Tail Coulee).

Tall Bull said the gray horses were mixed with the bays. He was standing near "H" (which appears to be on Greasy Grass Ridge per Camp's map, fig. 8) when he heard a big war whoop. "Soldiers came on foot and ran right through us into a deep gully, and this was the last of the fight, and the men were killed in this gully." The men who ran from the edge of the ridge to the gully were firing their guns at random.[167]

Tall Bull said the gray horses were mixed with the bays, which could have been from any one or all of Companies F, I, or L, who rode the bays. Tall Bull saw soldiers on foot that ran "through" them into a deep gully. Using the Camp map that accompanied the interview, the visualization of Tall Bull's story becomes cloudy. Was Tall Bull really observing from somewhere on Greasy Grass Ridge? Warriors' accounts and relic finds show that the ridge was an Indian position. Did Tall Bull see the soldiers charge from Custer Hill, all the way to Greasy Grass Ridge, go "through" them, and into a deep gully? If so, then the gully they went into could not have

FIGURE 8: WALTER CAMP'S MAP OF CUSTER'S POSITIONS

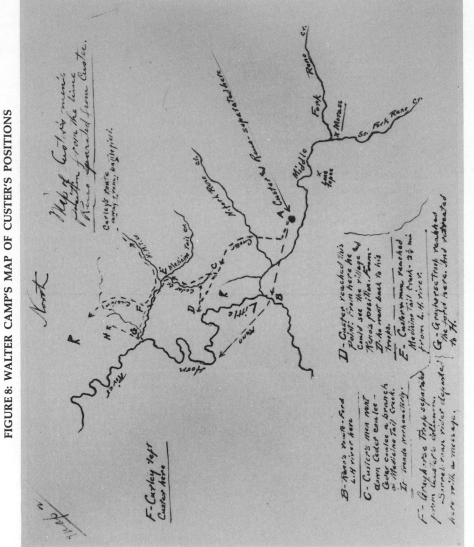

been Deep Ravine, for the soldiers would have passed by Deep Ravine several hundred yards before coming to Tall Bull's position at "H." Another possibility is that Tall Bull really was on Greasy Grass Ridge and the soldiers he described were making a dash down Calhoun Coulee from the Calhoun-Keogh area.

Was Tall Bull not at "H" at all, or was Camp's map erroneous in scale and location? It may be that the editor of Tall Bull's account, Kenneth Hammer, included the wrong map to illustrate Camp's interviews (fig. 8). Another of Camp's maps, which we will reference again in a later chapter (fig. 13), does have a point "H" placed right near Deep Ravine. This most likely was the actual map that Camp had Tall Bull refer to. In addition, Tall Bull's referrals to volley firing make no sense when referenced to "C" and "G" on the map Hammer used. We should give Tall Bull the benefit of the doubt. Camp's map should have conformed to his story. We should not assume the story is wrong because it does not conform to the map. Tall Bull's position was at "H" on the figure 13 map, not at "H" on the figure 8 map. In that case the charge could have gone "through" the Indians and into Deep Ravine.

Unlike other accounts, which indicated the Indians were in the ravines and the soldiers were stopped and forced back, Tall Bull said the soldiers went "through" them. This is a significant change from "toward" them. Tall Bull indicated some soldiers did get through and into a deep gully. The number of men was not specified, but it was quite likely not very large, for those men had to run a gauntlet of over six football fields in length just to get from Custer Hill to the nearest reaches of Deep Ravine, and double that distance if they managed to get as far as Greasy Grass Ridge. This would be one hell of a dash in a football game for a sprinting running back with only eleven defenders trying to stop him; it would be nigh impossible for an exhausted soldier surrounded by several hundred Indians. The number of men that reached any gully must have been small indeed. The decision is tentative, yet we will place the charge Tall Bull witnessed as terminating in Deep Ravine.

26. Wooden Leg (Kum mok quiv vi ok ta) *Northern Cheyenne*

Wooden Leg was born in 1858 near the Cheyenne River, close to the Black Hills, and lived his entire life between the Yellowstone River, the Black Hills, and the Bighorn Mountains. The boy Eats From His Hand became Wooden Leg when he proved he could travel all day long on foot without tiring. He was a warrior of the Elkhorn Scrapers Society, and at 18 years of age he was one of the biggest men in the tribe. Author Thomas B. Marquis measured him at six feet two inches and 235 pounds when recording his story in the late 1920s.

Wooden Leg fought against Reno and counted coup against one of the Indian scouts by crashing his rifle into the man's head. He found a gun and cartridges and felt very brave when word came of Custer's attack. The soldiers had come along a high ridge about two miles east of the Cheyenne camp, but went on past and swerved off of the high ridge to a lower ridge where they were later killed.

The Indians flocked from the camps and from the direction of where Reno's men had been halted. Wooden Leg was late and didn't get into the fight that took place nearer the river. He heard that Bobtail Horse, Roan Bear, and Buffalo Calf, along with some Sioux, were the first to cross the river and go to meet the soldiers. They exchanged some long-range shots with them while the soldiers were on a far-off ridge.

The soldiers spread themselves into lines along a ridge. Some Indians went to the lower ground in front of them, between them and the river, while others moved up and around a long coulee to get behind them. Wooden Leg swerved up a gulch to the left. The Indians were working themselves around the ridge occupied by the soldiers. They hid in the gullies and behind the sagebrush, and the shooting was from a distance at first, but it got closer as they crept in. Much of the Indian shooting was from high-arcing arrows and was kept up for maybe an hour and a half. The soldiers and their horses were on the ridge and could be seen more easily than the Indians.

After a long time of slow fighting, about 40 soldiers came galloping down the ridge toward the river where most of the Cheyennes and Oglalas were hidden. The Indians ran back into a deep gulch, and the soldiers stopped and got off their horses when they arrived at a low ridge where the Indians had been. When the Southern Cheyenne chief Lame White Man saw them do this he called out, "Come. We can kill all of them." The Indians charged. Wooden Leg saw many white men go crazy, turning their own guns upon themselves. The Indians took many of the soldiers' guns and used them against the troops remaining on the high ridge.

Wooden Leg next went to the east end of the ridge, but by then the soldiers there were dead. He made his way to a gulch on the north side of the west end of the soldier ridge. By that time most of the troopers there were dead also, for the shooting had almost stopped. Suddenly, seven of these last soldiers broke out and ran down the coulee sloping toward the river from the west end of the ridge. Wooden Leg was on the opposite side of the ridge at the time and did not see them run, but he heard of it later. They did not get far.

By this time the sun was just past the middle of the sky. Wooden Leg went with other Indians across the Last Stand Hill. He got himself a new kind of scalp when he skinned off one man's enormous sideburns (Lieutenant Cooke). He found the Cheyenne Noisy Walking badly

Wooden Leg, Cheyenne. Photo by Thomas B. Marquis, 1928. —Little Bighorn Battlefield National Monument

wounded down in a gulch nearer the river. Moving eastward up the gulch, he also saw the body of Lame White Man, apparently killed by mistake by the Sioux.

Summarizing the fight, Wooden Leg told Dr. Marquis:

> None of the Custer soldiers came any closer to the river than they were at the time they died. When the first Indians went out and met them, and exchanged shots with them, these soldiers were riding along the ridge far out north-eastward. They kept moving westward along its crest until they spread out on the ridge lower down, the ridge where most of the battle took place. After about an hour and a half of the slow fighting at long distances, the group of forty soldiers who rode down from the ridge along a broad coulee and toward the river were charged upon by Lame White Man, followed at once by many Cheyennes and Sioux. The place of the first Indian charge and the first sudden great victory is inside of the present fence around the battlefield and at its lower side.[168]

Wooden Leg's story of the battle is one of the most lucid accounts available, Indian or white. The soldiers moved toward the Cheyenne camp along a high eastern ridge (Nye-Cartwright) and then down a long lower ridge (Battle). After an hour of long-distance firing, about 40 soldiers came down the coulee to the low ridge above the deep gully. If there was any doubt as to which "low ridge" Wooden Leg spoke of, it was clarified by Dr. Marquis himself in his book *Keep the Last Bullet for Yourself.* The doctor spent many hours walking the field with Cheyenne battle survivors in the 1920s. They pointed out the location of this action. It was on "a low ridge about 500 yards down the gulch slope from the present monument."[169] Lame White Man then rallied the Indians, they charged, and the action was over quickly. Later, seven soldiers from the west end of the ridge ran for the river but were killed. None of the soldiers got closer to the river than they were at the time they died. Whether any of the soldiers committed suicide or not is a moot question. One way or another, they died. Where? The Indians went back into the deep gullies. The soldiers died in the coulee below the west end of the ridge and as they came down to the low ridge above the deep gully. They died in Cemetery Ravine.

27. Kate Bighead *Southern Cheyenne*

Kate Bighead was born while her village was in camp near the North Platte River in 1847. She was at the Washita River when Custer attacked there in 1868 and came in to the agency at Fort Sill when Custer again found her village in March 1869. Kate saw Custer several times and thought him handsome. Her cousin, Me-o-tzi, was said to have been Custer's lover. Kate Bighead went to live with the Northern Cheyennes in 1870 while they were in the Black Hills country. She was 29 at the time of the Battle of the Little Bighorn. Her story was given to Dr. Thomas B. Marquis in 1927. Kate Bighead's story was used, with some

Lt. William W. Cooke, 7th Cavalry Adjutant. He scribed Custer's last message, and his sideburns provided Wooden Leg with a new kind of scalp.
—Monroe County, Michigan, Library

embellishment, as the narrative for the Indian point of view in the 1991 movie *Son of the Morning Star.*

On June 25, sometime past the middle of the forenoon, Kate was visiting some friends in the Minneconjou camp when she heard the shouts that the soldiers were coming. The Indians all rushed south to beat back Reno's men. By the time she got to her lodge, the warriors were racing back to the north to fight the other soldiers (Custer's battalion).

107

She saw them coming on a ridge far out east of the Cheyenne camp. Some Indians were already in the hills, exchanging shots with the soldiers at long distance. Others crossed the river and made their way up the coulees toward the high ridge. Kate got a horse from her brother, White Bull (aka Ice, not the Minneconjou White Bull whose story we examined earlier), and went to watch the fight. She had no son of her own, so she went to sing strongheart songs for her nephew, Noisy Walking.

Kate Bighead crossed the river and went up the broad coulee, which the warriors were still going up. The soldiers had lined themselves out on a long ridge nearer the river and a little lower down than the ridge where they had first been seen. Most of the Indians hid their ponies in the gulches and crawled forward along the little gullies. When the soldiers dismounted, both sides could shoot more accurately.

Kate rode right, going around the soldiers and to the north of them. All she could see on that side were Sioux. She kept riding around, searching the north, then the west, and finally the south side. "At the south side, in the deep gulches and behind the ridges between the soldiers and the river, I found none but Cheyenne and Oglala Sioux." She still did not see Noisy Walking.

The Indians were using the bow and arrow more than the gun, firing constantly and creeping closer, following the gullies or dodging from knoll to knoll. "On the southern side, where I stopped to watch the fight, almost all of the Cheyennes and Oglala Sioux had crawled across a deep gulch at the bottom of a broad coulee south of the ridge where were the soldiers, and about halfway between them and the river." They fought there for a long time, maybe an hour and a half, without much harm done to either side.

> Then a band of soldiers on the ridge mounted their horses and came riding in a gallop down the broad coulee toward the river, toward where were the Cheyennes and Oglalas. The Indians hidden there got back quickly into the deepest parts of the gulch or kept on going away from it until they got over the ridge just south of it, the ridge where I was watching. The soldiers who had come galloping stopped and got off their horses along another ridge, a low one just north of the deep gulch.

Kate Bighead had a clear view of the soldiers and their saddled horses standing nearby. She heard Lame White Man and the Oglala chiefs call out to their young men to be brave. On all sides the warriors jumped up. The soldiers' horses were frightened and broke away toward the river, where they were captured. The Indians rushed forward and soon all the white men were dead.

The last of the soldiers collected in a group at the west end of the ridge, where there now is the big stone with the iron fence (the monument). The shots quit coming and it looked like they were all dead when seven white men sprang to their feet and went running toward the river. There was such a crowd and so much dust and smoke that she did not see what happened to them.

Kate Bighead went back down in the deep gulch halfway to the river where the Cheyennes and Oglalas had been earlier in the fight and found her nephew, Noisy Walking. He had been shot and stabbed. She and some other relatives came and carried him back to the camp. He died that night.[170]

Kate Bighead's narrative is one of the clearest, most comprehensible Indian accounts recorded, perhaps more so than Wooden Leg's. Her circumnavigation of the battlefield and her observations allow us to pinpoint many of the locations she described. At the time the soldiers came down from the ridge, Kate was probably watching from the northwest end of Greasy Grass Ridge. In front of her, Deep Ravine was filled with Cheyennes and Oglalas sniping at long range at the soldiers on the ridge. Then the soldiers came down as far as the low ridge north of Deep Ravine, where they dismounted and formed a line. This low divide is still 200 or more yards short of Deep Ravine. It was then that Lame White Man charged and was supported by other Cheyennes and Oglalas in the ravine who circled around the troopers' left and rear. Company E was shattered. Survivors may have fled uphill. At the battle's end, seven soldiers from the west end of the ridge ran toward the river. They may have made it as far as the gulch; they may not have.

Kate Bighead's story corroborates Wooden Leg's and leaves little doubt that the troopers died in and along Cemetery Ravine.

28. Little Face *Southern Cheyenne*

Little Face is credited with this narrative for ease of recording. His was only one of a score of contributions given by men such as Wolf Necklace and John Stands In Timber to Peter J. Powell. The influence of Stands In Timber is evident in the narrative, for many similarities will be found in Stands In Timber's own story, which follows.

Little Face, son of Roman Nose, was born in 1864 and was only 12 at the time of the battle. He was a source for much of the Cheyenne traditions and was able to pass on a significant amount of the oral history of his tribe before his death in 1961.

On the night of June 24, the Suicide Warriors' Dance, or the Dying Dance, took place in the village. Participants were young men, "suicide boys," who pledged to fight to the death in the next battle. Some of those who danced were Noisy Walking, Cut Belly, Fist, and Limber Bones. It was customary to hold a parade for those boys the next morning. When the marching and singing was done, the warriors returned to their lodges.

Lame White Man was in a sweat lodge when Custer struck. He was about to head away from the fight when he decided that he must not leave, that he must follow his boys into battle. With only his blanket, moccasins, belt, and gun, he rode off.

The soldiers were going down toward the river. A band of warriors in the far east, including the Cheyennes Wolf Tooth and Big Foot, followed the soldiers, one group on the north and one on the south of the divide. The soldiers fired and the Indians moved back, allowing the troopers to go closer to the river. Then the Indians followed the soldiers into a dry gulch above the head of Medicine Tail (the north fork of Medicine Tail, or Deep Coulee) and close to the present monument.

Custer's men followed the ridge down to a level place near the present cemetery site. Indians, including Yellow Nose and Low Dog, fired at them. The soldiers continued down toward the river across from the Cheyenne camp, but Indians concealed along the river turned them back toward the cemetery ground, where they halted for a time.

Wolf Tooth, Big Foot, and others fired down at the soldiers from the ridge. Custer rode toward a dry gulch and followed it "up to the center of the basin, below where the monument now stands." The Indians covered the ridge so that the soldiers could not retreat in that direction. Custer moved toward the lower bank of the basin and dismounted. "The soldiers of the Gray Horse Company got off their mounts and began to move up on foot. Some soldiers lay down on the ground, firing from that position. Others advanced for a distance, running, covered by the rifles of the men already hugging the earth." Some soldiers fired from behind dead horses. The Indian fire was heavy from both sides.

"The soldiers were grouped near the monument site, with a number of them in the ravine." The suicide boys galloped up to the level area where the cemetery now stands. Some of them stampeded the horses of the soldiers, some charged right into the midst of the troopers. More followed after the horses were stampeded. "Some of the soldiers jumped on their horses and attempted to ride farther up, toward the site of the monument." The suicide boys cut them off. Other Indians on the ridge swarmed in from the other side. The soldiers had no time to reload or aim. Yellow Nose fought well, capturing a soldier guidon. "Hand to hand fighting was going on everywhere—all along the ridge, down toward the river— filling the basin with struggling men."[171]

The Little Face narrative is clear. There is no reference to Deep Ravine, but there are several references to the basin below the present monument and cemetery grounds. The ravine spoken of in the same breath as the monument is the ravine slightly downslope of it. Troops went into that basin, they dismounted, and fought from it. They were attacked there, they struggled there, and they died there. The basin where all this occurred is Cemetery Ravine.

29. John Stands In Timber   *Cheyenne*

Born in 1884, the grandson of Lame White Man, John Stands In Timber spent much of his life collecting and studying the Cheyennes' reminiscences and lore. Their acknowledged historian, he was one of the last men to hear and record the Cheyenne tribal story from those who lived it. John died in 1967, the year the book he had worked on all his life was published.

The day before the fight with Custer there was a dance, the "dying dancing." It was arranged by other villagers to honor those Sioux and Cheyenne boys who had taken the suicide vow. In the next battle they would fight until they were killed. Some of the Cheyennes who took the vow were Little Whirlwind, Cut Belly, Closed Hand (Fist), and Noisy Walking. The Sioux who danced were mostly Oglala.

The next morning there was a parade going on for the boys who had been in the suicide dance when riders came into camp hollering that the soldiers were attacking. Lame White Man was in a sweat lodge and did not have time to dress properly for battle; he just wrapped a blanket around his waist and got his moccasins and gun. Wolf Tooth and Big Foot were among some Cheyennes who had crossed the river north of the Indian camp and circled around to the north and east. They took part in a long-distance fight with the soldiers on what is now called Nye-Cartwright Ridge. It was the first fighting with Custer's troops.

The Indians then fell back into the hills and the soldiers crossed to the south end of the ridge where the monument now stands. They followed the ridge down to the present cemetery site and headed down toward the river. Warriors in the brush at the river fired at the soldiers and made them turn back in the direction they had come from. One soldier was shot off his horse, but the others carried him back with them. They stopped at the cemetery site and waited 20 minutes or more.

The delay was too long. Many warriors had a chance to get across the river and behind the ridge where the monument now is, too many for the soldiers to get away in that direction. "Custer went into the center of a big basin below the monument, and the soldiers of the gray horse company got off their horses and moved up afoot."[172]

Before long the criers went along the line calling out to get ready to watch for the suicide boys. They were the last to get into the fight. They charged up from the river to the level ground where the museum now is. Some of them turned and stampeded the gray horses. The rest charged right in where the soldiers were making their stand, and the other Indians followed them. The suicide boys started the hand-to-hand fighting. Some soldiers ran along the edge under the top of the ridge for a distance but were scattered. They were all killed before they got very far. The battle lasted maybe another half an hour.[173]

Stands In Timber's is one of the more complete, chronological render-ings of the Little Bighorn fight. As the Cheyenne historian, he did not focus on the limited perspective of one participant, but used the tales of men such as his step-grandfather, Wolf Tooth, Frank Lightning, Hanging Wolf, Black Horse, Old Bull, and his grandmother, Twin Woman, to draw the larger picture. Their stories were similar to the account Wooden Leg gave to Marquis; however, Wooden Leg recanted a few statements when Stands In Timber talked with him years later. The soldiers were not drunk and they did not commit suicide, he said.[174]

There is, however, a substantially different interpretation in Stands In Timber's story that relates how Custer went beyond the present cemetery area to a ford northwest of the final battlefield. This perspective also shows up to a lesser extent in the Little Face/Powell rendition. Custer was re-pulsed at this northern ford and returned to the cemetery grounds, where he halted for a fatal 20 minutes. He waited either for his other troops to catch up with him or, according to Beaver Heart, he was deciding which Sioux girl he was going to take as his next squaw.[175]

Though the locations of these encounters, per Stands In Timber, differ from other accounts, the stories are very similar and would be almost exactly the same if a few key words were changed. The repulse of the troops and the killing of one soldier at a ford to the northwest of the final battlefield could be a misinterpretation of almost the exact same events that may have taken place at Medicine Tail ford. The delay at the cemetery site could be a misinterpretation of a similar hesitation that may have oc-curred on Nye-Cartwright or Luce Ridge. Then again, the possibility exists that Custer did make a second move toward the river, for a few other Indians—Two Moon, White Bull, and the Blackfoot Lakota Kill Eagle, for instance—intimated a move beyond the Last Stand area.[176] More corrobo-rating evidence for a movement of this magnitude would be helpful, and the issue of whether or not there was a sortie to the river northwest of the cemetery merits further investigation.

For our purposes, we must return to the fact that whether or not Custer made it all the way to the river a second time, he still ended up with at least one troop, Company E, at Last Stand Hill and in the basin below. The suicide boys came up from the river to the present museum area and stampeded the grays. It was the beginning of the end for Custer's battal-ion. The locale is nowhere near Deep Ravine. Stands In Timber's informants described the death of the Gray Horse Troopers in Cemetery Ravine.

30. Curley (Shuh shee ohsh) *Crow*

Only 17 years old at the time of the Little Bighorn fight, Curley was one of six Crow scouts who were detached from Lt. James H. Bradley's 7th Infantry command and turned over to the 7th Cavalry on June 21,

Curley,
Crow scout
with Custer.
—Little Bighorn
Battlefield National
Monument

1876. He, along with Hairy Moccasin, Goes Ahead, and White Man Runs Him, accompanied Custer's battalion after it split with Reno. Apparently Curley remained on the bluffs with half-breed scout Mitch Bouyer after the other Crows turned back. He and Bouyer then rejoined Custer after witnessing Reno's repulse in the valley. Curley and Bouyer rode with Custer to the Calhoun Hill position where Curley finally made his escape from the doomed battalion.[177] Curley was the only allied Indian to stay with Custer through the first stages of the battle, and thus he was able to describe the troop movements.

Lt. James Bradley, with the help of interpreter Thomas H. LeForge, got Curley's story during the scout's debriefing on July 3. Bradley used it in his account of the battle printed in the Helena *Herald* on July 15, 1876.

Custer, Curley said, moved from the bluffs around the base of a high hill and down a ravine just wide enough to admit his column of fours. They rounded the hill and came in sight of the village. When they got nearer, the Indians concealed in the undergrowth of the river opened fire. A portion of the command dismounted and went forward toward the river. Curley said he saw two of Custer's men killed and then fall into the stream. After a few moments of fighting, the head of the column turned right and bore diagonally into the hills, downstream. The Indians began crossing the river and appearing on Custer's right flank and in the rear. After a time it was necessary to renew the fight, and the troops deployed right and left, forming a crude circle. The horses were taken to the rear and the men fought on foot. At this point Curley left the field and concealed himself in a ravine some distance to the east. He thought the fight lasted from two-thirty or three o'clock until almost sunset.[178]

Curley accompanied Capt. Michael V. Sheridan to the battlefield in July 1877, but the captain thought too little of the scout's story of the fight to record it.[179] Curley was next interviewed by Lt. Charles F. Roe at Fort Custer in March 1881, the interpreter again being Thomas LeForge. Roe included Curley's story in his *Army and Navy Journal* article of March 25, 1882.

Curley rode with Mitch Bouyer. Mitch told him that the two men leading the column down the coulee were brothers. The white horses, Curley explained, were the first company coming down the ravine to its mouth. One man with stripes on his arm rode a gray horse very fast across the river and right into the village. He acted like a man who wanted to die. The soldiers remained mounted. The front part of the line did the firing because the line was stretched up the coulee and back on the side of a ridge. The troops then turned away from the mouth of the coulee.

The lead men motioned with their hands to go northeast, and the companies broke from the main column as if to meet on the main ridge again. The Indians crossed at the coulee and farther below, about opposite Custer point. They rode up to the command. The troops fought all the while they moved up from the mouth of the coulee and up onto the ridge.

Curley gauged the time Reno retreated from the valley to be about the same time Custer's command turned from the mouth of Deep Coulee toward Calhoun Hill. He then left the command and went back to the pack train. After a time he returned to the hills east of where Custer was fighting, the total trip taking about two hours. He could no longer see any fighting because it had shifted to the far sides of the ridges. There was no more moving or firing on Custer's field. Curley saw Reno's sortie to Weir Point when he was on the hill east of Custer's field.[180]

Walter Mason Camp interviewed Curley several times, first in 1908. Curley told Camp that Custer went along the bluffs, fully in view of Reno, for three-fourths of a mile. He went north down a tributary and into the bed of Reno Creek (Medicine Tail Coulee) about one mile from its mouth. Bouyer and the Crow scouts kept to Custer's left on the high ridges, where they could see the river bottom and Custer's men. Three Crows stayed back to watch the Indian camp, and Curley and Bouyer continued alone on a course parallel with Custer, north, until they came to the bed of the creek and met Custer about one half of a mile from its mouth.

The command continued rapidly down to the ford, where there was much shooting. The troops did not dismount, and some even rode into the river before turning back. One soldier galloped across the river and into the Sioux beyond the ford. The soldiers withdrew from the ford and went directly to where the markers are now at the southeast part of the battlefield. They drove any Indians in front of them and were in turn being driven by the Indians in their rear. At the Calhoun position, Custer stopped briefly and conferred. Bouyer told Curley that they thought if they could make a stand somewhere, the rest of the regiment would soon come up. It developed that the men could not make a stand for very long and most joined in the general retreat toward the west, headed for the highest ground.

Those able to do so followed the line of retreat diagonally up the slope toward the monument. "In this the men with the gray horses appeared to be keeping well together," but the other companies seemed to be getting mixed up. Bouyer was wounded and thought that they would all be killed. He told Curley to try to save himself. Curley rode down into a ravine, out of sight. Back to the east, maybe half an hour later, Curley looked back and saw the soldiers still fighting.[181]

Camp interviewed Curley in 1909 with the assistance of Russell White Bear. Curley said that the four Crows and Bouyer were on the cutbank about 1,500 feet south of the mouth of Medicine Tail ford. Custer's command came in sight, galloping down the coulee. Bouyer and Curley went down the bluffs to meet them while Hairy Moccasin, Goes Ahead, and White Man Runs Him returned upriver.

Curley said that Custer left Dry Creek (Medicine Tail) about 900 feet east of its mouth and struck the river 1,000 feet downstream from its mouth. A good many soldiers got near the river, but only one, a noncommissioned officer, rode across to be killed in the village. The hot fire made Curley believe it would be necessary for Custer to retreat, and he did so, going downstream and quartering back up on the ridge. The troops didn't stop, but fired at Indians to the left and right until they reached just west of the present Calhoun marker. There they dismounted and were twice ordered to load and fire together. Curley thought it was a signal. Curley left the field from the area of Calhoun Hill on the suggestion of Tom Custer and Mitch Bouyer.[182]

In 1910, this time with Fred Old Horn as interpreter, Curley again gave his story to Camp. Custer did not see Reno's fight, Curley said, because he was down in the coulee. Curley and Bouyer saw the fight, and Bouyer signaled to Custer by waving his hat. They rode down to Custer, and Bouyer did much talking to Custer while they rode side by side.

Camp asked Curley (when he was on the hill with Bouyer) if Custer's command was standing still or coming down the coulee? "Coming," Curley answered. When he and Bouyer went down to meet Custer, did Custer remain there any length of time? "No, kept going right on." Did Custer stop in Medicine Tail Coulee? What was he doing? Did he wait? "Did not stop." When they retreated from the river, were they in column or skirmish formation? What officer did he see there? What was Custer doing at the river and how long did he wait there? "No time at all."

The command then went up to the Finley area (at the Greasy Grass Ridge-Calhoun Hill junction) and fired the volleys. Bouyer had been talking with General Custer and his brother Tom. Then Bouyer came over and told Curley he should leave. Curley rode out through a coulee to the east.[183]

Curley's 1913 interview, with Thomas LeForge as interpreter, brought out no significant new insights. Curley had repeated much of the same information to Walter Camp. He and Bouyer saw Reno defeated in the valley and rode down to tell Custer. They joined him while he was advancing down the coulee toward the village. Custer did not halt after they joined him. On the battlefield near the Calhoun marker, Bouyer talked with the general, then Mitch came over and told Curley they would all very likely be killed and that the scouts should get out while they could. Curley went to a lookout point, where he remained until about sundown.[184]

In 1919, Gen. Hugh L. Scott visited the battlefield with White Man Runs Him and Curley. Frustrated by the bickering and interruptions between the two ex-scouts, Scott was nevertheless able to piece together another Curley interview.

Bouyer and the four Crow scouts went to the bluffs to look into the valley. Reno had crossed the river. Custer and his brother went to their right as they were standing on the hill. On the ridge top Custer turned and waved his hat, and his men at the bottom of the hill cheered. Custer and his men kept on going and were about 100 yards ahead of the scouts. Custer then followed a coulee (Cedar) down in a northerly direction.

Bouyer and the scouts stayed on the ridge, traveling north. Closer to the village, they fired some shots into the camp. Custer reached the river when they got to this point on the bluffs. They could see Reno retreating, and Bouyer said he would go down to Custer. He told the rest of the scouts to go back to the pack train.

At this point in what was originally labeled as Curley's story, the tale continues as if all of the scouts had left Bouyer. They saw some of Custer's Ree scouts capturing Sioux ponies below the ridge; they saw some soldier stragglers around where Reno later made his stand; they saw Reno retreating; and then they all headed east toward the Rosebud and the pack train. There is no further mention of Custer's battalion. This is so radically different from Curley's other narratives that one wonders if it really was Curley doing the talking. In fact, Scott then interjected a note made by the stenographer: "While White Man Runs Him was talking, Curley often interrupted him and laughed and said he was telling many lies. . . . General Scott told them to talk one at a time."[185]

It may be that Curley started the story and White Man Runs Him cut in and finished it off. It was headlined and quoted as if Curley did the speaking, but it finished up with Curley interrupting while White Man Runs Him was talking. It appears that Curley's actual telling ended about where Bouyer suggested going down to meet Custer, since the latter half of the story differs so much from four out of five of Curley's previous accounts. The only other time Curley indicated going to the pack train was to Lieutenant Roe in 1881. In Curley's next interview he returned to the old story, if indeed he had ever left it in the first place.

Crow Indian and interpreter Russell White Bear visited the old scout in 1923, shortly before Curley's death. He asked him to tell his story for the last time, to clear up any points that might still be uncertain.

Curley said that Custer's troops were moving at a walk when they went up the grade east of Reno Hill. When the scouts reached the ridge the soldiers kept on going down the west side of the ridge, down a ravine running north. Custer, Bouyer, Curley, and two other soldiers rode over to a high point to look into the valley; they could see Reno riding toward the Indians. Custer turned and rode to his command. They went down a ravine that went away from the valley. They came out at Medicine Tail Creek, and Custer turned left and rode down the coulee.

After riding awhile, Custer halted the command and the Gray Horse Troop left them and went down the creek. Curley and the rest of the command turned north, crossed Medicine Tail Creek, and went to the hills north of the creek. There they halted again and a messenger on a sorrel-roan horse left the command. Bouyer called to Curley and told him he had better leave, pointing to the ridge east of Custer Hill. Curley did so. From the ridge he watched the battle awhile, then rode away.[186]

Curley cannot tell us anything about the phase of the battle pertaining to the Cemetery Ravine-Deep Ravine question. He left too soon, and his vantage point from a ridge to the east did not allow him to see to the river slope of Battle Ridge. On the other hand, had he not left when he did, he probably would not have lived to give us the accounts of Custer's tactics prior to the battle's final phases.

One other allied Indian left a record of what he had seen on Custer's field. The Arikara scout Young Hawk had been sent off with others one-half mile to the east to keep a watch for the Dakotas (Sioux) while the burials were taking place. They received the signal to return when the sun was near the horizon. On his way back to camp, Young Hawk noted he could see no bodies of soldiers, but there was "evidence of fighting from the Custer Hill clear to the river by the dead horses."[187]

Historians and researchers have had divided opinions concerning the veracity of the Indian accounts of the battle, particularly in Curley's case. It appears that Camp believed him implicitly, while Colonel Graham argued for caution. Dr. Charles Kuhlman used Curley's accounts, but only so far as they served to support his ideas. More recently, historian Richard G. Hardorff, author of several fine monographs on the Custer battle, has discounted Curley's stories completely, questioning both his honesty and intelligence. At the same time, historian John S. Gray, also a Custer scholar, has reevaluated Curley's accounts and found them to be honest, conscientious, and reliable.[188]

Should we be cautious before accepting all of Curley's stories? Charles Kuhlman, who did not believe that any of Custer's men went to the river, assailed Camp's interviewing techniques because Camp believed Custer did go to the river and framed many of his questions with that assumption in mind. The 1910 Curley interview was particularly bothersome to Kuhlman, especially where Camp framed the whole scene and only allowed Curley what were, in effect, "yes" or "no" answers. But that was Camp's interviewing technique in many instances, as we have seen in the Two Eagles, Lone Bear, and Lights examples. Did Custer stand still or was he coming down the coulee? "Coming," said Curley. When they met Custer, did he remain there for any time? "No, kept going." Did Custer stop in Medicine Tail? What was he doing? Why was he waiting? "Did not stop." Did they retreat from the river in column? What officer did he see? What was Custer doing there? How long did he wait there? "No time at all."

Kuhlman imagined he could see Curley sitting there perplexed, answering to things that never happened, all because Camp assumed certain events to be true and framed his questions in a way that Curley could only ignore parts of them in his replies. This resulted in Camp understanding Curley's responses in an entirely different manner than they were intended to be understood. Kuhlman then rhetorically asked himself why he (Kuhlman) would ignore the majority of Curley's statements and select only the exceptions to prove his (Kuhlman's) contentions? The answer: because the exceptions were the only statements not the result of

Camp's leading questions![189] Far from a statement of vindication, Kuhlman's distorted reasoning is more of a rationalization of a questionable technique. He used only the evidence he wanted, and he helped no one who wished to find out what really occurred.

Apparently Camp conducted his interviews with certain preconceptions about the events of the fight and framed many of his questions in such a manner that those preconceptions nullified an accurate answer. However, Kuhlman also had his preconceived notions as to what occurred. He threw out the answers he didn't like as being overly solicited and used others that fit his notions better.

In the hope of avoiding the traps that these men may have fallen into, would it not be better to simply accept Curley's stories? His honor was not at stake. There was nothing self-serving, nothing to be gained in misrepresenting the troop movements. Tom LeForge, who interpreted for Curley to Lieutenant Bradley a week after the fight, said the Crow never made any exaggerated claims for any recognition. "I was not in the fight," Curley stated frankly. "I did nothing wonderful; I was not in it."[190] That was not the statement of a glory seeker.

We should therefore be able to read Curley's accounts and get a reasonably accurate appraisal of Custer's movements. Custer's five troops went along the bluffs in the area to which Reno later retreated. Curley, Bouyer, and for a time the other Crow scouts were also on the bluffs. They could see Reno advancing across the valley. Custer himself went at least once to the bluff's edge to witness the action in the valley. His battalion then passed the scouts and went down what was probably Cedar Coulee to the north to its junction with Medicine Tail Coulee. They turned left toward the river. About this time Bouyer could see Reno being repulsed in the bottoms. He signaled to Custer, announced his intention of going down to meet Custer, and suggested to the Crows that it was time for them to leave. Three of them left. Curley and Bouyer rode down to intercept Custer while he was still a mile or so from the river. There was a short halt to further divide the battalion. The grays and one other company continued on toward the river. Custer, Bouyer, Curley, and three companies went north across the high ground of Luce and Nye-Cartwright Ridges. After making a demonstration near the river, the detached two-company battalion (under Yates) made its way back uphill in a northeasterly direction away from the river. Custer's battalion continued north, and a meeting was effected on or near Calhoun Hill. The action became heavier. Volleys were fired. Somewhere along the route from Nye-Cartwright Ridge to Calhoun Hill it was again suggested that Curley leave, and this time he did so, traveling east. He stopped on a high ridge where he could see some of the soldiers still fighting. He could not testify to events in the Cemetery Ravine-Deep Ravine locale because he was too far east and on the opposite side of the ridge to witness that action. From that point on, it was the Cheyenne and Lakota who supplied a glimpse of the final chapter.

After a brief study of the Indian accounts that mentioned the Gray Horse Troop we are able to gain several insights. First, it is quite obvious that some white researchers and writers were not correct in their negative assessments of the Indian stories. The belief that they were contradictory, irreconcilable, or fanciful does not stand up to examination. Historian Robert M. Utley's assessment of Indian stories as "a disconcerting jumble of ephemeral non-chronological impressions" that "skipped indiscriminately from one incident to another without regard to time or place" is not a rule but an exception.[191] In fact, the very consistency of the Indian accounts is outstanding. The accusation that their views were parochial, limited to personal deeds and observations, and lacking in a white man's supposed better grasp of overall strategy and tactics should not be taken as derogatory at all. What else can a witness be expected to testify about but that which he experienced or saw with his own eyes? No court of law would expect a witness to testify on hearsay or speculate as to what might have occurred out of sight or hearing distance. Such conjecture would not be allowed in the record at all. There is no reason to criticize Indian accounts if they lack generalizations on a broad spectrum.

What the Indians recalled was what they had seen in their own comparatively limited field of vision. When enough of these separate accounts are collected, a meaningful whole emerges. This is nothing but plain inductive reasoning, the dictionary definition being the act or process of deeming general principles from particular facts or instances. From specific to general, the Indian stories *do* paint a very reliable, consistent picture.

It must appear by now that we are belaboring a point, but the very subject of the route taken by Custer's battalion has engendered almost as many stories as there are storytellers. The Indian accounts show that Custer's five companies came down from the high ridges to the east in the area of Medicine Tail Coulee. Some troops made a move toward the camp near Medicine Tail ford. Indian pressure forced them back. Other companies continued north along another ridge back from the river. The Indians swarmed up the gulches and took positions on all sides of the troops. Many warriors took a defensive stance in Deep Ravine, where they were concealed yet able to fire at long range at the troopers on the high ground. The gray horses went along the ridge and were at the west end of that ridge as a recognizable unit. They had not been destroyed near the ford, nor on their way up any ravine toward Custer Hill. They fought for a time on the ridge as an organized force. After a time, they came down from their position toward the gulches in the direction of the river. They were attacked and scattered, some dying along their line, others making it back to Custer Hill. At the battle's end, more soldiers broke for the river. They were all killed. Some may have made it as far as the steep-walled course of Deep Ravine. The great majority died along Cemetery Ravine and to a lesser extent in the upper Deep Ravine watershed.

The congruity of the Indian stories is remarkable. If there is any confusion, it may be in the accounts relating to the gray horses coming near the Little Bighorn at the mouth of Medicine Tail Coulee. Some of the earlier Cheyenne stories, particularly those as told by George Grinnell and David Miller, indicate that the soldiers came right down near the water and were fired at by Indians on the west bank. Other Indians, such as Gall and Wooden Leg, said the soldiers came nowhere near the river, but passed by in a northerly direction far to the east. For many years these seemingly irreconcilable differences made many a historian, as Colonel Graham said, throw his hands up in frustration.

However, does this have to be an either/or situation? Must we respond within that framework? Limiting ourselves to those two choices is tantamount to being trapped in the "fallacy of false dichotomous questions," as explained by David Hackett Fischer. A dichotomy is a division into two parts where the parts are mutually exclusive and there is no overlap and no middle ground. The law of the excluded middle may demand attention in formal logic, but it does not work in history. The false dichotomous question demands a choice between two answers that are in fact not exclusive or exhaustive.[192]

We have already seen where the use of the either/or interview technique by Walter Camp caused confusion in several Indian accounts, including those of Two Eagles, Lights, and Curley. The very existence of a preformulated choice may not only persuade, "it may artificially produce a previously unformed answer or an unformulated opinion—whereby the observation does not only influence the character, it falsifies the essence of the object."[193]

According to author-researcher Bruce A. Trinque, if Wooden Leg or Kate Bighead had answered Camp's questionnaire, the "fighting up" or "running down" conflict below Custer Hill would have been correctly answered as "None of the above." Trinque's previous training in military intelligence led him to believe that Camp's technique was "practically guaranteed to get you exactly the answer you're expecting—without telling you anything about whether that answer is actually true or false."[194]

Likewise, the route of Custer's battalion was not an "all or nothing" movement. Why couldn't he be far back on the eastern ridges and near the river? When the Indians spoke of Custer, they only did it after the battle and after they were told who it was they had fought. When they said "Custer," they didn't necessarily mean the lieutenant colonel himself, but only the portion of the troops they happened to see. Some could have seen "Custer" on the ridges, while others just as legitimately could have seen "Custer" near the river. To the Indians, "Custer" was almost always a generic term.[195]

For some reason, early chroniclers of the battle were also shackled with the assumption that Custer's battalion stayed together in a tight, five-company unit, believing that if one company went to the river, they all must have gone to the river. Such a theory has since proven inoperable. Participants themselves, such as Lt. Winfield S. Edgerly, Capt. Myles Moylan, and Sgt. Daniel Knipe, said that Custer's battalion was also subdivided into two units.[196] It is thought that these battalions were under Capts. Myles Keogh and George Yates, but exactly which companies went with which commanders is still hotly debated.[197]

Today, it is not fashionable to espouse simplistic explanations for historical events. Some years ago, one might have said that the single cause of the Civil War was slavery and no one would have raised an eyebrow. Today, that statement would likely cause a heated argument, for historians, with their own values and preconceptions, semantics and logics, have made explanation a self-created puzzle more than a solution.[198] Likewise, we retain the problem of who went to the river and who stayed on the ridge: either Yates's battalion or Keogh's, either Companies F and E, or I and C, or E, F, and C, or almost any other possible combination, depending on whose interpretation is being used.

About the only thing we can be reasonably certain of is that one of the units that did approach the river was the ubiquitous Gray Horse Troop, the one David Miller said "galloped ghostlike" through so many Indian accounts. The grays made a demonstration toward the river at Medicine Tail ford. How near the water? "Near," used as an adverb or adjective, is a relative word, its substance depending on the context and the individual witness. A young Indian boy in his first battle, seeing the soldiers and hearing their carbines from a half mile away, might report that the troops were right on top of him. Another warrior, experienced in killing, might have fired at a trooper from a distance only as wide as the Little Bighorn and reported that the soldier was far away because he did not close to hand-to-hand combat range. The gray horses did come "near" the river.

Why did warriors such as Wooden Leg and Gall insist that the soldiers did not come to the river? The question is not so very mysterious. Those Indians were not in a position of time and terrain to see events at the mouth of the Medicine Tail at that time. Wooden Leg was a long while at the Reno fight and just returning from that action, and Gall was in his camp mourning his slain family. They appeared at the ford only after Company E had pulled back.

Did the grays cross the river? No. With the possible exception of an uncontrollable horse stampeding one unfortunate trooper into the massing Indians, they did not cross. Because of Indian resistance, because they had been recalled, because there was a change of plans, because they had seen all they wanted to see, because their move had only been a feint, for whatever reasons, Company E pulled back. They went up along Deep Coulee to meet the other companies near Calhoun Hill. The slight confusion of "Custer" and his "nearness" to the Little Bighorn notwithstanding, the Indian accounts of the Gray Horse Troop are very consistent.

Did Lieutenant Smith's men move down along the river until they reached Deep Ravine, then travel up its meandering floor only to be massacred by warriors waiting in ambush? No. The grays were seen time and time again moving along Battle Ridge, well beyond Deep Ravine, either on their own or mixed with the bays. They fought as a unit on the ridge tops. It was the Indians who used the ravines as avenues of approach to the final battlefield or as temporary defensive positions. None of their accounts indicated setting up an ambush in the Deep Ravine. Only one, Good Voiced Elk, indicated a large number of troopers were killed in a deep gully, and that was the result of a retreat from the hilltop, not during a pullback from the river. The great majority of Indian accounts tell of no large numbers of troopers seeking escape in any deep gully. Wooden Leg's 40 soldiers came down to fight early in the battle, and they stopped before reaching Deep Ravine. Two Moon had the 40 soldiers coming down late in the battle, but taken in context with his other renditions, those men appeared to succumb in Cemetery Ravine. In fact, the numbers of men that might have reached Deep Ravine were small; there were "ten of them" breaking from the hill, or there were "seven whites," or "only four," or "several," or "some," or "only a few," or "one," or none mentioned at all. E Troop did not get caught and slaughtered en masse in any deep gulch.

The Indian accounts do provide us with a traceable itinerary of Custer's movements, particularly those of Lieutenant Smith's Company E. The Indians were eyewitnesses. Their accounts establish the flow of the battle. However, they were obviously not concerned with the exact positions that the dead soldiers lay in. Three days after the battle the majority of the 7th Cavalry came upon the field to do the burying. It was the soldiers' interpretations of Custer's battle tactics that were speculative, not the Indians'. The soldiers were eyewitnesses only to the locations of the dead. The Indian accounts of where the Gray Horse Troopers went while alive, combined with the white accounts of where the Gray Horse Troopers were found dead, provide a very accurate picture of what actually happened to Company E that afternoon in the hills above the valley of the Little Bighorn.

SUMMARY OF INDIAN ACCOUNTS

	Year of Interview or Publication	Ravine Indicated: (C) Cemetery, (D) Deep, (?) Uncertain
Sioux		
1. Gall	1886	?
2. Crow King	1881	?
3. Runs The Enemy	1909	?
4. Good Voiced Elk	1909	D
5. Red Horse	1881	?
6. Flying By	1907	C
7. Black Elk	1931	?
8. Mrs. Spotted Horn Bull	1883, 1908	?
9. Foolish Elk	1908	?
10. White Bull	1930, 1932	C
11. Turtle Rib	1908	?
12. Feather Earring	1919	?
13. Flying Hawk	1907	?
14. Standing Bear	1910, 1931	D
15. Red Hawk	1906	C
16. He Dog	1910	?
17. Two Eagles	1908	?
18. Lights	1909	D
19. Lone Bear	1909	?
20. Iron Hawk	1931	C
Arapaho		
21. Waterman	1920	?
Ute		
22. Yellow Nose	1905	?
Cheyenne		
23. Two Moon	1898, 1909	C
24. White Shield	c. 1895	C
25. Tall Bull	1910	D
26. Wooden Leg	c. 1925	C
27. Kate Bighead	1927	C
28. Little Face	c. 1960	C
29. John Stands In Timber	1967	C
Crow		
30. Curley	1876, 1881, 1908, 1909, 1910, 1913, 1919, 1923	?

Totals Cemetery: 10, Deep: 4, Uncertain: 16

Capt. Frederick W. Benteen, Company H, 7th Cavalry. His tardiness in reaching the battlefield may have led to Custer's demise. Photo by D. F. Barry, c. 1874. —Little Bighorn Battlefield National Monument

4. White Accounts

In this chapter we will detail and analyze those accounts of white observers that mentioned Company E or Gray Horse Troopers meeting their deaths in a ravine. Other accounts that may not specifically mention a ravine can also be useful in determining the death spot of E Troop when taken in context with other contemporary observations. There are dozens of accounts in this category. There are also numerous accounts describing the battlefield after the fight that made no mention of the ravines in question here. Many of those that paid no notice to the Deep Ravine-Cemetery Ravine areas did focus on Last Stand Hill and Custer's burial site. Indeed, perhaps every one of the thousands of visitors to the field in the decades after 1876 made a pilgrimage to the death spot of the field's star attraction. Some described only Custer's purported grave. Others visited various parts of the battlefield but left records too vague to pinpoint the exact locale they had been describing. We will not be concerned with those.

Of those that alluded to the ravines in question, we will first examine accounts of the 7th Cavalrymen who came to Custer's field on the 27th or 28th of June to identify or bury the dead. They will be considered eyewitness accounts.

THE 7TH CAVALRY

1. Frederick W. Benteen *Captain, Co. H*

Frederick William Benteen was born in Petersburg, Virginia, in 1834. When his mother died in 1841, the family moved to Missouri. Benteen was out of school at age 16 and worked for several years as a sign painter. He entered the army as a 1st lieutenant in 1861 and served with distinction through most of the Civil War in the 10th Missouri Cavalry, being promoted to lieutenant colonel in 1864. Benteen always resented not being given a general's star in 1865, yet he did remain highly regarded by his superiors. Benteen was a complex person, capable of maintaining a calm outward appearance while seething with hatreds within. He disliked as a fool or incompetent almost every man he met, including George Armstrong Custer. Although Benteen regretted his entire army career while philosophizing about it late in his life, he was a welcome, experienced addition when he accepted a captain's commission in the 7th Cavalry in 1866.[199]

After meeting units of Colonel Gibbon's command at midday on June 27, Benteen, who expressed skepticism of Lieutenant Bradley's report of finding 197 bodies, followed the latter back to the battlefield with the unenviable task of attempting to identify the dead. With elements of his Company H, Benteen trailed Custer's tracks behind Reno's position on the bluffs down a canyonlike ravine. He went down a gorge toward the river but became convinced that Custer did not go as far as the river, so he too turned north and "went to the right of the second divide." The nearest body he found to the middle ford was six to eight hundred yards from it. Benteen could find no evidence of organized lines, the bodies making no other patterns than would a handful of scattered corn. The only evidence of a line was in the Calhoun area and behind Battle Ridge, where men had been killed while apparently trying to get to Custer. Custer Hill showed the only evidence of a slight stand. Benteen testified at the 1879 Reno Court of Inquiry[200] that he thought there were about 22 bodies found in a ravine down near the river. "There was a trail leading to a crossing about a hundred yards above that ravine, but I could cross that river almost anywhere."[201]

Benteen's dislike of Custer probably colored his perceptions of any evidence of organized resistance. The more the battle looked like a rout, the more it appeared to be over in a matter of minutes, the less import would be attached to Benteen's dawdling in the face of Custer's "Be quick" order.[202] What of the ravine Benteen spoke of? Can it be identified? He went along Battle Ridge to the Custer area, then down toward the river. He found a ravine with 22 bodies.

> Q. Did the bodies of those men give any indication of what they had been killed with?
> A. I did not examine them at all. I rode along the ravine and looked down. The bodies had been counted by others. I made no personal examination of them.
> Q. Was there a ford at the mouth of that ravine crossing to the village?
> A. I could cross that river almost anywhere.
> Q. Was there an Indian trail leading across there with the appearance of having been used by the Indians as a crossing?
> A. There was a trail; I think probably a hundred yards or so above that ravine. I crossed and recrossed that river at so many places that I am of the opinion you could cross it most anywhere.[203]

There was another ravine *above* the one where Benteen saw the 22 bodies. This second ravine had the trail and crossing to the Indian camp. It was Deep Ravine that had the trail crossing at its mouth. Benteen's ravine with the bodies was downstream about 100 yards. It was Cemetery Ravine.

Benteen also had some additional commentary on deep ravines and their suitability for armed action. It is perhaps opportune to insert them here, for related thoughts will appear again in subsequent accounts. Benteen thought the men the Indians killed in the ravine were the wounded "that had gone into that ravine possibly to hide."[204] Why else would they go down there? It was useless, Benteen intimated, to attempt fighting in such a place. "They could not shoot out of the ravine, and they certainly did not go into it to shoot out of it."[205]

The skirmish line was the formation of necessity and choice in the Indian-fighting army from the high plains of Montana to the deserts along the Rio Grande. Said Col. Edward Hatch, commanding the 9th Cavalry in many actions with the Apaches, "We always fight in extended skirmish line."[206]

A deep gully was a hell of a place to shoot from, to defend, or to form a skirmish line in, especially a gully that was three or four times deeper than a man was tall. No one in his right mind would form a line in such a place, yet time and again we will find references to skirmish lines formed in a ravine. It will become clearer that the Deep Ravine could not be the place that many accounts have depicted. It may have been a refuge place of last resort for a few, but it was not the chosen place for a skirmish line for the many.

2. George W. Glenn   *Private, Co. H*

Accompanying Benteen to Custer's field on June 27 was George W. Glenn. Company rosters show his third enlistment in 1875 under the assumed name of George W. Glease. He was known as Glease at the Little Bighorn. He deserted in 1877, was apprehended, and was dishonorably discharged in 1880. Walter Mason Camp interviewed him in 1914.

Glenn told Camp he went up to Custer Hill via "Crazy Horse Gully." He reported seeing the bodies of chief trumpeter Henry Voss and correspondent Mark Kellogg near the river. In Crazy Horse Gully the bodies were thick, and someone commented that it looked like the whole command was lying there. Custer was found just below the end of the ridge, and fifty yards down from it was the body of Tom Tweed of L Company, once Glenn's "bunky."[207]

Which ravine was Glenn speaking of? There has been confusion about the location of Crazy Horse Gully. Some have used the term when speaking of Deep Ravine. However, since Crazy Horse did not attack from that direction, but rather from the east across the gully on the back slope of Battle Ridge in the Keogh area, it is this latter ravine that is more properly termed Crazy Horse Gully.[208]

The sequence of Glenn's approach is important in determining which gully he spoke of. Glenn marched with Benteen and the men of H Company. In the Reno Court record Benteen said he approached Custer Hill by way of Calhoun Hill and Battle Ridge. Sgt. Daniel Knipe of Company C also rode with Benteen and H Company to the Calhoun area. He was inspecting the dead around Keogh while Benteen's men filed past in ranks.[209] Since Glenn accompanied this detachment on its route from Calhoun Hill to Keogh and to Custer, it is most probable that Glenn saw the bodies in Keogh's Ravine to the east of Battle Ridge.

Glenn was interviewed in 1914. After all those years, perhaps he had the day confused. Maybe it was June 28, the day of all the burying, that he saw that ravine where the bodies were thick. But Benteen reported that his Company H buried the men of Company L on June 28—and nearly all of Company L fell on Calhoun Hill and in the ravine east of Custer Ridge.[210] It appears that Glenn spoke of neither Cemetery Ravine nor Deep Ravine, but rather of Keogh's Ravine. Those who have always assumed that Glenn saw bodies "lying thick" in Deep Ravine must reassess their convictions.

3. John Martin   *Trumpeter, Co. H*

John Martin, or Giovanni Martini, was born in Italy in 1853. He came to the United States and enlisted in 1873. He was promoted from trumpeter to sergeant in 1900 and retired in 1904. On the day of the battle he was Custer's orderly. He carried the lieutenant colonel's last message back to Benteen, an act that most assuredly saved his life.

In an interview in 1908, Martin mentioned seeing a "heap of dead men in a deep gully between Custer and the river." Nearby he saw one of the first sergeants, who had held some of the men's pay for safekeeping, and about $500, which was torn up and scattered around his remains. Martin mentioned there were not half as many dead horses as dead men on the field, indicating the Indians ran off with a significant number of live mounts.[211]

Which ravine did Martin speak of? His account of a heap of dead men in a gully is not detailed enough to make a distinction between Cemetery Ravine or Deep Ravine.

4. Charles Windolph   *Private, Co. H*

Born in Bergen, Germany, in 1851, Charles Windolph became a nineteenth-century draft dodger when he fled to Sweden in 1870 to escape compulsory military service and the Franco-Prussian War. He was slated to be taken by a dragoon unit. Instead, Windolph ended up in the United States, where he couldn't find a job and therefore enlisted in the 2nd Infantry. It was a situation that Windolph claimed hundreds of German boys like himself had faced.

But Windolph deserted. Then he enlisted again, this time in the 7th Cavalry under the name of Charles Wrangell. He was apprehended in 1873, sent back to the infantry for a time, and then transferred back to the 7th Cavalry, where he spent the next 12 years in a unit much like the one he had escaped from in Germany. Later in his life, Windolph thought the whole affair "always struck me as being funny." He told his story to Frazier and Robert Hunt in 1946. Windolph died in 1950, the last white survivor of those who had fought at the Little Bighorn.[212]

According to Windolph, on June 27 Reno ordered Benteen to take a few officers and 14 men of H Company and ride to Custer's battlefield. They rode north, crossing the coulee that Custer might have used to attempt his attack on the village. Ahead they caught glimpses of white objects lying along a ridge. "From the way the men lay, it was clear that first one troop had been ordered to dismount and fight as a skirmish line. Then a second troop had been posted a little farther on and to the east. Then a third and fourth troop." Windolph stood six feet away holding Benteen's horse while the latter identified the general and staked the spot. They left the knoll and went back to the land of the living.[213]

Windolph didn't give any account of finding bodies in a ravine. He did indicate, however, that the bodies he saw clearly showed the troopers had fought and died in skirmish lines.

5. Charles C. DeRudio *1st Lieutenant, Company E*

Charles DeRudio was born in Belluno, Italy, in 1832. He already had a colorful career before coming to America in 1864, including serving on the staff of General Garibaldi in Italy and escaping the guillotine in France after a failed attempt on the life of Napoleon III. He fought in the Civil War and was assigned to the 7th Cavalry in 1869. DeRudio was made 1st lieutenant in 1875 to occupy the vacancy created by the promotion of Thomas McDougall. DeRudio was on temporary duty with Company A on the day of the battle. He was a double survivor: the temporary duty out of E Company probably saved him from dying with Custer, and he was lucky enough to survive by hiding in the timber along the river for a day and a half after being left behind when Reno fled the valley.

In an interview with Walter Camp in 1910, DeRudio said that he had asked for and was granted permission to go along with Benteen on his ride to Custer's field on June 27. They followed the trail down Medicine Tail Coulee to the river. Shod tracks showed clearly in the blue clay where Custer's men turned away from the water. The first dead man was found about 150 yards from the river. On the battlefield DeRudio counted 214 bodies. Custer was found on a conical knoll, and the horses shot down as if to form a barricade were sorrels from Company C. DeRudio was not sure about the location of Company E's men, but he "saw a heap of men in a gully" and said the dead horses nearest the river were grays.[214]

In 1879 at the Reno Court of Inquiry, DeRudio provided a bit more detail. At the top of the knoll with Custer were several other bodies along with horses that had been killed to form barricades. There was other high ground nearby, and the men could not defend both front and rear. Part of the Gray Horse Troop was in a ravine 40 or 50 yards from the bank of the river. In another ravine nearer Custer's body, toward the river and about 150 to 200 yards from it, there seemed to have been some resistance. The men found in the ravine were in a position to have made a stand. They may have been separated from the main command, but they made a stand by themselves.[215]

The direct testimony from the official record is as follows:

Q. Did you examine the ravine where several dead bodies were found?

A. Yes, sir.

Q. How many bodies were found there?

A. I don't remember. I remember it was a part of the gray horse company.

Q. How near the river was that?

A. The ravine was forty or fifty yards from the river bank.

Q. Near the position of Gen. Custer's body is a straight line to the river—did you notice any ravine there with dead bodies in it?

A. Yes, sir.

Q. How near was that to the river?

A. From a hundred and fifty to two hundred yards from the river.

Q. What were the evidences of fighting there?

A. There seemed to have been a resistance there. Their position was lower than that of the Indians and they had to defend themselves from the enemy in front and rear.[216]

What ravine did DeRudio depict? His 1910 account of a heap of men in a gully does not allow for differentiation, and the 1879 testimony can be confusing. He saw where part of the Gray Horse Troop died. Were the bodies 40 or 50 yards from the river, or did the ravine begin that far from the riverbank? From the position of Custer's body was a straight line to the river, down which could be seen a ravine with bodies in it. They were 150 to 200 yards from the river and the men appeared to have made a stand. Does this tell us which ravine DeRudio is talking about? The "headcut" of Deep Ravine, where some accounts place the missing Company E troopers, lies about 700 yards below Custer Hill and 700 yards above the river at the mouth of Deep Ravine. The lieutenant's estimates do not match. In addition, the steep-walled portion of Deep Ravine from the "headcut" to the "bend" (fig. 5) cannot be seen in a direct line down from the position of Custer's body. However, there is another ravine that can be seen.

Looking down Cemetery Ravine from the Custer position one sees a broad valley that opens out on the horizon at the river. The more level landscape in the background can lead to a foreshortening of perspective. Perhaps objects in the middle distance will appear nearer or farther away than their actual location, for the gravestone clusters down Cemetery Ravine are about as far from the river along its axis as the "headcut" and "bend" areas are from the river along Deep Ravine's axis. DeRudio's yardage doesn't seem to match well with either ravine. However, we keep hitting up against the hard reality of three points: (1) one cannot see down Deep Ravine in a straight line to the river from Custer Hill, as DeRudio indicated he could do; (2) one could not stand in Deep Ravine anywhere in the vicinity of the headcut or bend and give a 150- or 200-yard distance estimate to the river because the ravine's many twists would preclude any visual sighting to the river; and (3) Benteen pointed out the ludicrousness of attempting a stand in a hole in the ground with banks possibly 10 feet over one's head. The very visibility of bodies from DeRudio's position and the physical ability to make a stand in accommodating terrain point to Cemetery Ravine. DeRudio saw the majority of Company E men in Cemetery Ravine.

6. Stanislas Roy *Sergeant, Co. A*

A native of France, Roy enlisted in the 7th Cavalry in 1869 at the age of 22. After his first enlistment, Roy signed up again six more times, serving with Capt. Myles Moylan's Company A for 30 years.[217] He corresponded with Walter Camp between 1909 and 1912. Roy accompanied the main burial parties that went to Custer's field on the 28th of June.

Roy didn't follow any trail down to the river along Dry Creek (Medicine Tail Coulee), but cut straight across to the battlefield. On the way he first passed the body of Cpl. John Foley of C Company, who he recognized easily because of his black hair and bald pate. He came across Sgt. James Butler next, about 200 yards from Foley. From there to the next group of dead near Calhoun Hill was a considerable distance. Roy told Camp that there were a number of dead cavalry horses among the men that his Company A buried "between Custer and the ravine." Roy said, "I helped to bury the bodies on the west slope of the ridge, and we wound up with E troop men over near the gully. I then took sick to my stomach from the stench and went to the river to get a drink."[218]

Can we determine which ravine Roy spoke of? There were dead cavalry horses among the men he buried "between Custer and the ravine," and he buried Company E men, but not in any deep ravine, just "over near the gully." The burials were not in Deep Ravine. Roy's description points to E Company burials in Cemetery Ravine and/or the upper Deep Ravine watershed.

Capt. Myles Moylan, Company A, 7th Cavalry. His testimony led people to believe a number of soldiers perished in Deep Ravine. Photo c. 1875. —Little Bighorn Battlefield National Monument

7. Myles Moylan *Captain, Co. A*

Moylan was the 7th Cavalry's adjutant from 1867 to 1870 and captain of Company A for two decades. He was born in Massachusetts in 1838 and joined the regular army in 1857. In February 1863 he was commissioned as a 2nd lieutenant in the 5th Cavalry, a unit whose 1st lieutenant was George A. Custer. After the Civil War, Moylan joined the 7th Cavalry as a private. Custer tried to get him a commission, but Moylan failed the test. After Custer entered a plea to the examining board, Moylan was given a second chance and this time passed. Although somewhat ostracized by some fellow officers because he had not gone to West Point, Custer took him into his mess and Moylan became part of the Custer "clique." He married the sister of Lt. James Calhoun, the latter being the husband of Custer's half-sister Margaret.[219]

In a July 6, 1876, letter to James Calhoun's brother, Lt. Fred Calhoun, Moylan attempted to describe the battle. There was little mentioned that had direct bearing on the ravine question; however, some of the body locations were given. Moylan saw the general, Tom, Cooke, and Smith on the hill where the last stand was made. "Bos Custer and the General's nephew were killed some little distance from the General. Both were recognized." About 206 bodies were found. Some might have been killed farther off, but there couldn't have been many because 206 nearly made up the number of the whole command.[220]

In 1879 at the Reno Court, Moylan had more to offer. On June 28 he placed his company with its left near the river and moved a skirmish line north, sweeping for bodies. He found little evidence of fighting close to the river. While his men were in the ravine areas, Moylan was called to a more easterly hill to identify an officer believed to be Lt. James Calhoun, Moylan's brother-in-law. Returning to his company he traveled along Battle Ridge to where Custer was found. Back down in the ravine "we found 20 odd bodies of E company; they were undoubtedly fighting and retreating. The marks were plain where they went down and where they tried to scramble up the other side, but these marks only extended half way up the bank. This was a half or three quarters of a mile from the river. Custer's body was not so far."[221]

Moylan thought 3 officers and 18 men were never found but probably were buried with the others, disfigured so much that they were unidentifiable. Moylan said he had known these men for 12 to 15 years and still some were unrecognizable. Other bodies were still missing and not accounted for, but some bodies that he thought were found a considerable distance from the field might make up for the deficiencies.

Let us again go to direct testimony. Moylan was questioned on how far the bodies were from the river.

> A. That must have been half or three-quarters of a mile.
> Q. Did you go up to the point where Gen. Custer's body was found?
> A. Yes, that was not so far I think.[222]

Which ravine was Moylan speaking of? At first glance his comments about scramble marks extending halfway up the banks would point to Deep Ravine. But what of his locations? The 20-odd bodies were one-half or three-quarters of a mile from the river, and Custer's body "was not so far." Not so far from what, the river or from the 20-odd bodies? If Moylan meant that the bodies were not as close to the river as was Custer's, then the corpses he viewed were farther east of Battle Ridge somewhere, maybe in Keogh's valley. He would not be speaking of either Cemetery Ravine or Deep Ravine. If he meant Custer's body was not so far from the 20 bodies as the bodies were from the river, then the locale shifts back to the west side of Battle Ridge, where it probably should be. Moylan meant the 20 bodies he saw were closer to Custer than to the river.

Let's examine Moylan's distance estimates next. The bodies were one-half to three-quarters of a mile from the river. Using the U.S. Geological Survey Crow Agency quadrangle for measurements, we find a line stretched from the water at the mouth of Deep Ravine toward the monument has the half-mile point touching the low divide between Cemetery and Deep Ravines near the cluster of graves around Mitch Bouyer's marker (fig. 15). Three-quarters of a mile reaches almost exactly to the monument. Surely Moylan couldn't have meant three-fourths, but even his half-mile estimate places the 20 bodies about 1,000 feet out of the "bend" and "headcut" area of Deep Ravine and over onto the slopes of Cemetery Ravine.

Perhaps his mileage judgments were simply inaccurate. However, we also established that he thought Custer's body was closer to the 20 bodies than the latter were to the river. The "bend" of Deep Ravine occurs about 1,800 feet from the river. The "headcut" is about 2,100 feet from the river.[223] It is about 2,100 feet from the "headcut" to the monument. Custer's body would have been farther from the 20 bodies than the latter were to the river had Deep Ravine been their resting place, but Moylan said they were closer. Using the Cemetery Ravine axis, it is about 3,200 feet from the monument to the river. There are also 20 or more bodies clustered in the upper reaches of Cemetery Ravine. Those bodies are about 1,400 feet down from Custer's and 1,800 feet from the river at Cemetery Ravine's mouth.

These measurements may be confusing if one does not possess an intimate knowledge of the terrain, but their essence can be easily summarized. It is only in Cemetery Ravine near the Bouyer cluster that Moylan's statement about the bodies being closer to Custer than to the river would have been correct. In Cemetery Ravine the locations, relative body positions, and distances to the river match Moylan's descriptions.

Still inconsistent, though, is the "scramble mark" reference. This statement is one that has led investigators to opt for a Deep Ravine locale. Perhaps Moylan did see marks in a deep bank, but they may have been made by only a few individuals. The majority might have fallen on the Cemetery Ravine side, but the graphic sensory impact of fingerprints in the dirt left in him a memory all out of proportion to the number of individuals that might have caused them. Another researcher has commented on this possibility. Seeing signs where a soldier might have clawed his way up a ravine, "It would not be surprising if such horrifying visions lingered longer than the sight of more bodies to bury on the ridge above."[224]

Capt. Thomas M. McDougall, Company B, 7th Cavalry. Recently transferred out of Company E, McDougall was in charge of the pack-train escort during the Little Bighorn fight. Photo by D. F. Barry.
—Montana Historical Society

An account that has been accepted for years as an argument proving a Deep Ravine location of the missing bodies is not so airtight upon examination. Which ravine? Moylan probably saw bodies in both. The cursory historical answer would be Deep Ravine. Closer study of distances, locations, and relative body positions would indicate Cemetery Ravine. Moylan's account is really too ambiguous to categorize, yet those scramble-mark references indicate he did see at least some bodies in the steep gully of Deep Ravine.

8. Thomas M. McDougall   *Captain, Co. B*

Thomas McDougall was in charge of Company B, which was the pack-train escort during the Little Bighorn fight. He was born in Wisconsin in 1845, fought in the Civil War at the age of 18, and was assigned to the 7th Cavalry in 1870. McDougall went to Custer's field on June 28.

At the Reno Court of Inquiry McDougall testified that he only went to where he presumed Company E's skirmish line was. Major Reno then ordered him to go to the abandoned Indian village and look for implements with which to bury the dead. Upon his return, Reno ordered him to bury Company E, since McDougall had commanded it for the previous five years and would likely be most able to identify the dead. "I found most of them in a ravine," McDougall testified. Using "H" on Lt. Edward A. Maguire's map as a reference point (fig. 10), McDougall said, "That is where the most of Company E were found . . . about half were in the ravine and the other half on a line outside." They "were lying on their faces and appeared to have been shot mostly in the side." McDougall thought they "probably were attacked from both sides."[225]

From McDougall's letter of May 18, 1909, to Gen. Edward Godfrey, just a few months before the former's death, we find that he altered his story. He wrote that he found most of E Troop in a ravine. The troopers apparently used the sides for a kind of breastwork, and fell to the bottom as they were shot. The stench was very great and the men of the burial party began to vomit. They piled chunks of earth from the sides of the ravine onto the bodies. Only a few men were found on the ground from the extension of the ravine. McDougall recognized Sgt. Frederick Hohmeyer of Company E by a sock on his left foot with his name on it.[226]

Apparently Walter Camp interviewed McDougall in the late spring of 1909, sometime between the May letter to Godfrey and McDougall's death on July 3. The essence of the interview was the same as the letter. The story was different from what McDougall had testified to at Reno's Court in 1879, perhaps because of a failing memory, or perhaps because events 33 years prior did not have such import to one facing his own imminent demise. In 1879, McDougall said the Company E men were half in and half out of the ravine. Thirty years later, responding to leading questions from Camp, he thought they were mostly in the ravine. There were only a few bodies between the gully and where Custer lay. Camp asked if he was sure there were less than a dozen? Yes, and maybe not more than half a dozen, McDougall acknowledged. Camp referenced the May 18 letter to Godfrey, in which McDougall said most of E Troop was in the ravine. Did he mean in the deep gully? Camp probed. "Were there as many as 28?" "Yes," McDougall replied. "All the bodies in the deep gully were buried in the gully—none was carried out. Hohmeyer was in there and Hughes."[227]

Which account is more accurate? The value of testimony is greater the nearer in time and space the witness is to the event described.[228] Thus, one would tend to more readily accept testimony given within three years of the fact rather than answers to questions asked more than three decades later. Whether Company E was all in the gully or half in and half out may not be as important as McDougall's 1879 description of finding them in a line. Would the men be ordered to form a line in the twisting Deep Ravine when all they would be able to skirmish with would be the sky above their heads? The less meandering, more open Cemetery Ravine is a more likely candidate for a skirmish line. What of McDougall's statement that there were less than a dozen bodies from the ravine to where Custer lay? There *were* less than a dozen, provided the ravine McDougall spoke of was Cemetery Ravine. As in Moylan's testimony, it is likely that McDougall saw bodies in a ravine and on a line outside. The accounts are ambiguous, but we will cautiously place them in the Deep Ravine column.

9. Winfield S. Edgerly   *2nd Lieutenant, Co. D*

Winfield Scott Edgerly was born in New Hampshire in 1846 and graduated from West Point in 1866. He was with the 7th Cavalry from 1870 to 1890. He retired from the army as a brigadier general in 1909. Edgerly testified at Reno's Court of Inquiry in 1879. He spoke of the men forming skirmish lines to sweep the field and find all the bodies they could. He corroborates being with Reno on Calhoun Hill when the major sent for Moylan. He went along the line where Keogh's men fell and ended up on Custer Hill. Bodies were lying around and there didn't seem to be any organization. Edgerly said that there were bodies between General Custer and the river, but "I did not go there."[229]

Edgerly found bodies in regular order from the Calhoun and Keogh positions to Last Stand Hill. There was evidence of a severe struggle on Custer Hill. It looked like that was where the men rallied. However, "The principal number of bodies were between General Custer and the river, and between General Custer and where we were." It looked like the men stopped to fight and that they fought very desperately.[230]

Edgerly didn't go over the entire field, but he did see a great number of bodies toward the river from his position on Custer Hill. In another account, this one in *The Leavenworth Times* in 1881, he was a bit more specific. Custer's trail, he reported, went near the river, because dead bodies were found all along the way from the ford to Custer's knoll. On that knoll he also found Tom Custer, Lieutenant Reily, and Captain Yates. General Custer's brother Boston and his nephew, Armstrong Reed, were found about 100 yards down from the general's body.[231]

Edgerly's accounts indicate there were bodies down toward the river from Custer Hill. He said he did not go down any farther than perhaps the spot where he saw Boston and "Autie" Reed, but he saw evidence of fighting down toward the river. Given his location on the field, he would not have been able to see down into Deep Ravine at all. Yet he saw a great number of bodies and evidence of a desperate fight down there.

The only "down there" Edgerly could see from his viewpoint was in Cemetery Ravine.

10. John M. Ryan   *1st Sergeant, Co. M*

John M. Ryan is mentioned in several accounts for playing a conspicuous part in the defense of Reno Hill. He had served 10 years in the 7th Cavalry, but took his discharge shortly after the battle because he felt Benteen held a grudge against him and wouldn't recommend him for the Medal of Honor. Apparently Ryan had strung up a man by his wrists for some minor infraction several months prior to the Little Bighorn fight, and Benteen had him court-martialed and reduced in rank; Custer reinstated him. That was sufficient, Ryan believed, to earn Benteen's undying enmity, a misfortune that was serious enough for him never to advance in the regiment again.[232]

Ryan's story was published in the *Billings Gazette* and the Hardin *Tribune* on June 25, 1923, the 47th anniversary of the battle. Ryan wrote that the bodies were scattered over the battlefield, which was probably one and a half miles square. There were two or three bodies together, then maybe a dozen, then other scattered ones. They were there so long that they had already turned black and were very hard to recognize. The companies made stands at different places. Burials didn't amount to much (mostly some dirt and wild sage thrown over the corpses), sometimes leaving arms and legs still protruding. Ryan saw where 18 or 20 men belonging to Smith's Gray Horse Troop got into a ravine. It looked like they traveled into it for a distance until it got so steep they couldn't get out. He saw marks where they tried to get out but were shot by the Indians and fell back into the ravine.[233]

Ryan's account came 47 years after the event. Though some details might be cloudy after all those years, he seems certain that Smith's men went down in a deep gully. His account goes in the Deep Ravine column.

11. William C. Slaper   *Private, Co. M*

Slaper was born in Cincinnati, Ohio, in 1855. Out of a job and with no other prospects, at the age of 20 he joined the army and served a five-year stint. As a new recruit at Jefferson Barracks late in 1875, he was assigned to Company M along with young Lt. James Garland Sturgis, fresh out of West Point and son of Col. Samuel Sturgis, the commander of the 7th Cavalry. Before they marched for Fort Abraham Lincoln, Sturgis asked the new recruits to take good care of his son. Slaper promised he would.[234]

Slaper related his story to Earl Brininstool in 1920. On June 28 his company was ordered to the spot where Custer fell to bury the bodies. They had few implements, and all they could possibly do was move a little dirt in a low place, roll a body in, and cover it. The stench was strong and not all the bodies were covered well. Slaper did not have time to go over the field and make notes, but he saw Capt. Tom Custer and thought he was the worst mutilated of all. He saw Lt. William W. Cooke with his magnificent sideburns scalped. He thought Boston Custer was near the bodies of his brothers, and correspondent Mark Kellogg was also close by. "These bodies were on the line nearest to the river, making it appear that they were halted by an overwhelming force, which closed in on them so rapidly and in such superior numbers that they were given but little chance to put up a fight."[235]

Can we determine which ravine, if any, Slaper may have hinted at? He was burying bodies on Custer Hill. His comments about Tom Custer and Cooke are borne out by other accounts.[236] However, both Edgerly and Godfrey saw Boston farther down the slope, and Kellogg was reported as being found much closer to the river.[237] Yet from Custer Hill Slaper saw bodies in line toward the river. One cannot see into the Deep Ravine gulch from Slaper's position on the hill, but one can easily see down Cemetery Ravine. Yet Slaper's confusion in identifying the location of the some of the bodies makes his testimony a bit tenuous. We will categorize his account as uncertain.

12. George D. Wallace   *2nd Lieutenant, Co. G*

George Wallace was the engineering officer during Custer's final march; he kept the records and drew the maps. It was his clock time that most official accounts of the battle follow. He was in Reno's valley fight and was left in command of Company G after the death of Lt. Donald McIntosh. Wallace was the second witness at Reno's Court of Inquiry. Early on the 28th of June, he testified, they moved out to bury the dead following what they assumed was Custer's route to the river.

> There or near there was a gray horse, then back almost on a line perpendicular to the creek, two or three hundred yards, was a dead man on top of a hill his body filled with arrows. Then to the left, or rather down the creek from that point, there were found some of the men. Further on they became thicker till we crossed over two ravines, then we found more men and horses till we came apparently to where the last stand had been made, there were the killed in a kind of circle, the bodies lying around thick.

At this point the court recorder, Lt. Jesse M. Lee, posed some questions about distances, elevations, and the topography of the area, then asked Wallace to tell of following Custer's route from the first evidences of fighting to the last. Wallace repeated his story in slightly different words, starting back with the horse near Medicine Tail ford.

> Where we found the first horse was a ravine making a little valley running into the river. On a knoll was the first man and then another

ravine running into the first ravine, then on a ridge and over to a second ridge. It was on this second ridge the last stand was made. There was one ravine running in a southeastern direction, the side of it forming a ridge in one direction, then striking another in front of the position. There was a second ravine running into the river; back of that another ravine running in another direction, making General Custer's last stand on a T-shaped ridge. It was not the highest point, there was a higher point between it and the river and back of that about 200 yards was a still higher ridge.[238]

Testimony concluded for the day. On Thursday, January 16, 1879, the fourth day of the proceedings, the court decided to lift their "no pencils" order. Heretofore reporters had to rely on their memory, albeit prodigious memories in the case of the *Chicago Times* men, several of whom rotated in and out of the courtroom, writing notes in the hall and returning as the next man stepped outside to record his portion. Now, all in attendance could produce pencil and paper to record all that had transpired.[239]

Wallace returned to the stand. Under cross-examination by Reno's counsel, Lyman D. Gilbert, Wallace stated that the men of the burial party were formed in parallel columns of fours. They swept the field to bury the dead and total up the numbers. Gilbert asked where the men of Captain Calhoun were found and if they had been drawn up in order of battle.

> A. There was some indications of a skirmish line.
> Q. Had you seen before you reached that point any indication of a skirmish line?
> A. None, I afterward saw in the ravine some men lying in skirmish order, but they were at the bottom of a deep ravine, and I don't know how it was.
> Q. What company were they members of?
> A. Of "E" company—Lieut. Smith.[240]

Can we determine Wallace's route? He was at the river near Medicine Tail ford heading north. Nearby was a gray horse in a little valley running toward the river (Deep Coulee?). They went uphill and back from the creek to a dead man on a knoll (one of the Finckle-Finley cluster near the battlefield's southern gate?). There they turned left down a creek and found more of the men (in the south fork of Deep Ravine?). Then another ravine ran into the first (the junction of the north and south forks of Deep Ravine?). They crossed two ravines and went over two ridges (across the south fork, sometimes called Calhoun Coulee, over the first ridge dividing the north and south forks, across the north fork in the vicinity of the "headcut," and over the second ridge dividing Deep Ravine from Cemetery Ravine?). The bodies became thickest over the second ridge, and it looked like a stand was made (the Bouyer cluster just north of the divide between Deep and Cemetery Ravine?). It was not the highest point, because there were higher spots between it and the river and back of it about 200 yards (the high divide between the north and south forks toward the river and the present cemetery ground to the rear?).

Wallace's descriptions appear to show his route as we have conjectured, yet later in his testimony he seems to say that he went from Greasy Grass Ridge to Calhoun Hill to Custer Hill. It is difficult to accept the stand he described as being Custer's, for there are no higher hills between it and the river, nor back of it by 200 yards; certainly no higher point that could command Custer's knoll with direct gunfire. On the contrary, it was Custer's knoll that was the dominant position. One can understand that fact simply by standing today near the monument or by noting some historical accounts. Trooper Ami Frank Mulford of M Company, visiting the field in 1877, recorded that the elevation of Custer's knoll is a little above the divide of which it is a terminus and that the knoll is a commanding position.[241]

We have already mentioned the great improbability of forming a skirmish line in Deep Ravine, yet Wallace saw E Company men in skirmish line and in a ravine. His conjectural route had him climbing out of that second ravine and over that second ridge. It was only then that he saw evidence of organized resistance and was in terrain more conducive to forming a skirmish line. The stand Wallace spoke of seems to have taken place in Cemetery Ravine, yet his testimony remains too confusing to categorize.

13. **William G. Hardy** *Trumpeter, Co. A*

William Hardy did not leave much in the way of reminiscences of the Little Bighorn fight. He was interviewed by Walter Camp in 1910. All he had to say that remotely pertains to our analysis follows: "Parker and Driscoll [Co. I] lay on the river side of the hogback on ground a little higher up than Cooke. . . . Says only a few men between Custer and the gully. In the gully men were lying on top of one another. Could see where they ran down one side and tried to scramble up the other side."[242]

Which gully? Hardy saw only a few men between a gully and Custer Hill, but in the gully men were lying on top of each other and he could see scramble marks where they tried to get up. Bodies may well have rested on top of each other in Cemetery Ravine also, but the reference to scramble marks leads us to believe the steep-walled portion of Deep Ravine was the place Hardy spoke of. He did not specify a number, unfortunately. Were there 28 bodies, or a dozen, or only a handful?

14. **Edward S. Godfrey** *1st Lieutenant, Co. K*

Edward Godfrey was born in Kalida, Ohio, in 1843. He served in the Civil War and graduated from the U.S. Military Academy at West Point

Lt. Edward S. Godfrey, Company K, 7th Cavalry. His writings and correspondence contributed to a greater understanding of the battle. Photo c. 1877.
—Little Bighorn Battlefield National Monument

in 1867. He took part in every major action of the 7th Cavalry from 1867 through Wounded Knee in 1890. He received a Medal of Honor for his part in the Nez Perce Campaign in 1877 and was promoted to brigadier general in 1907. Godfrey may have put more of his thoughts about the Little Bighorn fight on paper than any other participant. At Reno's Court in 1879 he testified that he did not find any bodies nearer than one-half to three-quarters of a mile from Medicine Tail ford. He did help his company bury the dead on June 28. Its line of march as it swept north searching for bodies was far from the river, only one or two companies being farther to the right. He found many .45 carbine shells. "The bodies that I found where I found the shells were some distance from where General Custer's body was found. I think they had attempted to make a stand there. There were some 15 to 20 bodies buried in one place by my company. All the troops I found there appeared to have made a stand."[243]

In 1892, Godfrey published his story of Custer's last battle in *Century Magazine*. The article was enhanced by a dozen more years of study, his attendance at the 1886 battlefield reunion, and his incorporation of battle accounts from Indians such as Gall and Mrs. Spotted Horn Bull. The Indians insisted Custer's route was some distance back from the river. Finally it flashed to Godfrey that, indeed, he had seen Custer's trail himself that day he left the burial detail and went back east on a high ridge to look for escapees. He wondered whose heavily shod tracks they could have been, but dismissed the thought that they might have been made by Custer's column because it did not fit the current theory that Custer had attempted to cross at the ford. Listening to the Indian accounts and seeing the evidence in a different light, he then became convinced that Custer did not go to the river.[244]

Also in that *Century* article was a map (fig. 9) in which Godfrey depicted Custer's route trailing up to a mile and a half back from the river. At Calhoun Hill it began to angle toward the river to Custer Hill, then it turned sharply and headed down for the Little Bighorn. This was the route of Smith's Gray Horse Troop. They had disappeared from the ridge, leaving their dead to mark their line. About 28 bodies of men from E Company and other organizations were found in one ravine nearer the river.

Tenth anniversary reunion, 1886. Left to right: Corporal Hall, Sergeant Horn, Capt. Thomas McDougall, Mrs. Mann, Capt. Frederick Benteen, Capt. Edward Godfrey, Mrs. Benteen, Dr. Henry Porter, Mrs. Garity, Capt. Winfield Edgerly, Trumpeter Penwell, White Swan.
—Little Bighorn Battlefield National Monument

145

FIGURE 9: EDWARD GODFREY'S MAP

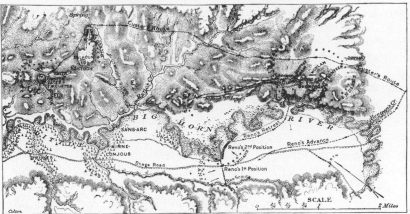

Godfrey's original map, which first appeared in Century Magazine, *January 1892.*

A redrawing of the portion of Godfrey's map showing the main battlefield area.

B. *Where Keogh's and Calhoun's troops dismounted and advanced along the ridge.*

C. *A few bodies were found here, mostly from Yates's and T. W. Custer's units.*

D. *The ravine where many of Smith's troop were found.*

E. *The hill where Sergeant Butler's body was found.*

Boston Custer. He left the pack-train to join up with his older brothers in time to die with them on Last Stand Hill.
—Little Bighorn Battlefield National Monument

The Indians had defensive forces along the river and in the ravines to destroy any who left Custer's lines and came their way. The place of E Company's demise is marked as point "D" on Godfrey's map.[245]

For the burials on June 28, Godfrey said the regiment was deployed by troop so as to cover the entire battleground, each troop to bury the dead on its own front. The ground covered by his Company K took him two or three hundred yards below the monument. There he identified and supervised the burial of Boston Custer, the general's brother.[246]

In an 1896 letter to Montana artist Edgar S. Paxson, who was about to paint a scene of Custer's fight, Godfrey described Boston Custer as being dressed similarly to his brothers. His body was found about 200 yards from Custer Hill, toward the Little Bighorn and at the foot of a ridge that runs up from the river and forms a lower boundary of the battlefield.[247]

In 1909, Walter Camp wrote to Godfrey for some information about the slain in the Deep Ravine. Camp had "overheard a conversation" between the battlefield custodian and "some man who professed to have been present" when the dead were buried in 1876. Camp thought this unknown man said something about only a few bodies lying between the general and Deep Ravine, a distance of some 600 or 700 yards. Camp wondered if Godfrey could shed any light on the matter. Unfortunately,

Godfrey did not have personal knowledge of the situation and had to write to Thomas McDougall for confirmation, which resulted in McDougall's May 18, 1909, letter to Godfrey.[248]

Godfrey could not shed much more light on the subject when he was interviewed by Walter Camp in 1918. He buried "Boss" Custer, who lay down on a side hill some distance below the general. He found Tom Custer on the ridge and identified him by the "T. W. C." tattoo on his arm. He said there were only a few bodies between that ridge and the deep ravine.[249]

In 1908, Godfrey rewrote his *Century* article, and in 1921, Elizabeth Custer reprinted it for the 45th anniversary of the fight. In this version Godfrey said Smith's men formed a skirmish line below Custer Hill and held their gray horses in groups of fours. Twenty-eight bodies of this troop were found in a big gully near the river. These were men, Godfrey believed, that belonged to a platoon under Lt. James Sturgis, who had been ordered to locate a ford for crossing the river.[250]

What can we determine from Godfrey's statements? First, he accepted the prevailing theory that Custer attempted a river crossing at Medicine Tail ford. Later, after revisiting the battlefield and talking with the Indians, he came to believe that Custer did not go near the river on his trek downstream. The route took Smith's troop to a point near Last Stand Hill and, either under Smith or Sturgis, down toward the river. E Company died along that route and in a gully, stopped by Indians defending in the ravines. Godfrey's men buried 15 to 20 bodies that appeared to have made a stand. Since he made no reference to burying bodies on any other parts of the field and did make several references to burying Boston Custer and all the other bodies two to three hundred yards down from Custer Hill, the burial of the 15 to 20 could not have been south of the Cemetery Ravine-Deep Ravine divide, which is over 400 yards below Custer Hill. In fact, using the present gravemarker map as a reference (fig. 15), we can see that Boston's position would be near the beginning of what has been termed the "South Skirmish Line." Only a little farther down the gravestones become more numerous and reach their largest concentration in the Bouyer cluster on the divide south of Cemetery Ravine. The stones along this line number about 20. It appears that Godfrey buried Boston Custer and a number of Smith's Gray Horse Troop in and along the line of Cemetery Ravine.

Godfrey's map in his *Century* article also bears this out. Smith's men are clearly shown going down from Custer Hill (fig. 9) to die in a ravine just below the bodies of Tom Custer and George Yates, who died on Custer Hill. Deep Ravine shows much more prominently, with its mouth across from the Sans-Arc camp and its fingers pointing to Calhoun Hill, but it is not marked as being the location of any body finds. Many of Godfrey's narratives and his map show that Cemetery Ravine was the final resting place for the majority of the Gray Horse Company. Then again, many years after the fact and after coming in contact with Walter Camp, Godfrey made some statements of finding only a few bodies between Custer Hill and the deep gully and that perhaps some of the markers along the line should have been placed in the ravine. Is it possible that Godfrey, like McDougall and several Indians, were influenced by Camp's preconceptions? After all of Godfrey's publications, correspondence, and interviews, there is still too much ambiguity to enable us to pinpoint the location of Smith's men.

15. Luther R. Hare   *2nd Lieutenant, Co. K*

Luther Rector Hare was born in Indiana in 1851 but became a Texan when his family moved there in 1853. He graduated from West Point in 1874. At the Little Bighorn he had command of the Crow scouts. Hare fought at Wounded Knee and in the Philippines during the Spanish-American War. He retired for disability in 1903.

Hare mentioned only a few items concerning the burials and bodies on Custer's field to Walter Mason Camp in 1910. He helped bury some men near Calhoun and noticed that an arrow had been shot into Lieutenant Crittenden's eye. He saw dead horses on Custer Hill, but they did not seem to have been shot down to form a barricade.[251]

At the Reno Court of Inquiry, Hare's commentary was more thorough and pertinent to our examination, though portions of Hare's testimony show significant differences as set down by the court stenographer versus the *Chicago Times* reporters. Since the fourth day of the proceedings, when the pencil ban was lifted, both parties had equal opportunities to record the witnesses' actual words, yet there were variations. The stenographer, H. C. Hollister, inscribed more of the questions posed by Recorder Lee and Counselor Gilbert, while the *Times* men included fewer questions and let the answers run on into more unbroken paragraphs. There were times, however, when Hollister would fall behind in his shorthand and revert to the *Times* columns to modify his own notes.[252] Occasionally, the accounts were in complete opposition. For example, Hare said he went to Medicine Tail ford, where the left bank was boggy and the right gravelly and easily fordable. He said there was no evidence of a fight between that ford and *Reno's* stand, per the court stenographer; no fight between the ford and *Custer's* stand, per the *Times* reporter.[253]

Variations are also found in the following passages; from the official record:

> I saw what was supposed to be General Custer's trail that went down on the left bank. The first evidences of that fight was a dead man of E Company probably 300 yards from where the final stand was made. There were 28 men of E Company, I assisted in burying the men of E Company and remember more about them.

Lt. Luther R. Hare, Company K, 7th Cavalry. He helped bury the men of Company E in Cemetery Ravine. Photo by O. S. Goff, c. 1877.
—Little Bighorn Battlefield National Monument

and from the *Chicago Times:*

His fight must have opened about where that first dead man was found, and it must have continued from there to where the final stand was made. The bulk of "E" company was probably killed 300 or 400 yards from the hill where Gen. Custer made his final stand. There were 28 men of "E" company killed there. I am not certain about the rest of the companies. I assisted in burying the men of "E" company and a number more about that coulee where they were found. I didn't see any dead officers there.[254]

Even more substantial differences appear. From the official record:

Q. How far from the point "B" [Medicine Tail ford on Maguire's map, fig. 10] were the first dead bodies found?
A. I think about half a mile, or a little less.

Q. What evidence did the position of the dead men present to your mind of a prolonged struggle?

A. I don't know anything about that. I can't say anything in particular about the appearance.

Q. State whether you found any men in skirmish line except those about Captain Calhoun?

A. I did not see his company. Lieutenant Smith's was the only one I saw and 28 of his men were in a coulee.

Q. Did the position of those men indicate a prolonged resistance?

A. It indicated a skirmish order. They were about at skirmish intervals.

Responding to the same initial question, the *Times* wrote that Hare said:

I think the first dead body was found about half a mile from that watering place up in a coulee. I saw a great many of the dead men and noticed the position in which they laid. A great many of them were shot in the back. Evidently the Indians shot them from behind. Several of those 28 men of company E were shot in the back. From the position they were in it was very easy for the Indians to crawl up behind them while they were resisting in front, and kill them. I didn't see Calhoun's company. Lieut. Smith was in command of the company that I saw dead there. The position of the bodies of those men indicated a regular skirmish order. They lay about at skirmish intervals.[255]

Why did those comments about Smith's men being shot in the back appear in the *Times* and not in the official record? Those doing the recording heard enough testimony to keep their minds and fingers working at full speed. It seems unlikely the *Times* men would have the luxury to invent extra details, and we have already seen where Captain McDougall made an observation similar to Hare's. Perhaps we have discovered the court stenographer in the embarrassing moment of a snapped pencil point.

In any case, the substance of Hare's accounts is clear. Coming up from the ford he saw no bodies in Deep Ravine, because the first evidence of a fight was not noted until he came upon a skirmish line of 28 men of Company E about 300 to 400 yards below Custer Hill. Hare's description places Smith's dead directly in Cemetery Ravine, square within the confines of the 25 to 30 gravestones that presently mark this portion of the line.

Hare's observation that a number of Smith's men were shot in the back while resisting in front is very informative. It reinforces the Cheyenne accounts that the Indians had taken position in the Deep Ravine. While Company E was formed along the South Skirmish Line facing the threat of warriors approaching over the present-day cemetery grounds and up Cemetery Ravine, other Indians could use the upper reaches of Deep Ravine, particularly the small northward branching fork that points to Custer Hill, as a perfect concealed avenue to circle Company E's left and rear. While some Indians assailed the Gray Horse Troopers from the northwest to southwest quarter, other warriors trailing up Deep Ravine's upper forks could hit them from the rear, just as Hare surmised. It was over in a flash, and it is no wonder that Smith's men died as if frozen along their skirmish line.

Lieutenant Hare's account is definite. Cemetery Ravine is the place the majority of E Troop fought in, died in, and was found in.

16. Theodore W. Goldin *Private, Co. G*

Goldin was born as John Stilwell in Wisconsin in 1858. He enlisted in April 1876 and was a raw recruit at the Little Bighorn fight. He was discharged in November 1877 when it was found that he had lied about his age at enlistment. He did not receive the Medal of Honor with the other water carriers on Reno Hill, but managed to have one awarded to him in 1895 upon his own application. Goldin's character has been questioned by more than one student of the Custer fight, including W. J. Ghent and William A. Graham. Goldin's unverifiable stories and his convenient amnesias and contradictions make his accounts untrustworthy.[256] History Professor James T. King, in the introduction to Cyrus T. Brady's *Indian Fights and Fighters*, praised Brady's collection of stories, except for the chapter by Theodore Goldin. John M. Carroll, editor of the *Benteen-Goldin Letters*, did not believe Goldin's correspondence to be historic truth.[257]

Theodore Goldin, however, left voluminous writings for later researchers to consider. In a series of letters with one Albert W. Johnson of Marine-on-St. Croix, Minnesota, Goldin commented in October 1928, "We found the bodies of a number of men and horses of 'E' Troop. To all appearance they had angled off across the hillside, finally entering a narrow coulee . . . which proved to be a veritable cul-de-sac, ending with a high bank in front and on both sides of them." The men and horses were shot down there. The burial party shoveled dirt down from the banks to cover them.[258]

In a letter to Johnson in December 1929, Goldin said that he had visited Custer's field with Benteen on June 27. They followed a well-marked trail down the bluffs north of the Reno entrenchment area, then picked up a faint trail leading left along the bluffs. The main trail led north toward where Calhoun's troop was found.

In February 1930, Goldin wrote that the bodies were poorly buried because of a lack of picks, shovels, and axes, and because the ground was so hard it couldn't even be loosened with shovel or spade—a pick was required to make an impression in it. The bodies were in such a state of mortification that some men taking hold of an arm often saw it come loose from the body. They just heaped dirt or sagebrush over them and left them to the mercy of the coyotes, wolves, and vultures.

In October 1931, Goldin wrote to Johnson that it was his recollection that there was no evidence that the White Horse Troop approached the river much nearer the point where they entered the valley. The trail seemed to lead diagonally along the hillside until it ended in a dead-end ravine.[259]

Which ravine did Goldin write of? His references to cul-de-sacs and dead ends don't match either Cemetery Ravine or Deep Ravine. The high banks point to Deep Ravine, but even Deep Ravine has no dead-end or high banks that would have confronted men on three sides, leaving them no exit but the same way they had come in. There are points of entrance and egress at almost any spot along its length. Even the steepest banks near the present "slump" and "headcut" would allow egress simply by moving left or right 20 feet or so, a movement that would have taken a running trooper only a few seconds. Though there are inconsistencies with Deep Ravine, Goldin's description matches Cemetery Ravine even less. We will place Goldin's account in the Deep Ravine column.

17. Jacob Adams *Private, Co. H*

Born in Ohio in 1852, Jacob Adams enlisted when he turned 21 years of age. He was five feet eight inches tall, with brown eyes and brown hair, and listed his occupation as a farmer. Adams warned to "Never enlist in the regular army and give your occupation as a farmer." He spent most of his time in the quartermaster department driving mule teams, and didn't care for the business. He served his five-year enlistment and decided the army wasn't for him. Adams printed his reminiscences in a little booklet that he sold for two dollars from his home in Vincennes, Indiana.

Adams described the place where the Reno-Benteen contingent made its stand as being in a shallow basin. When he was able to get over to Custer's field after the fight, he had a similar description for the site where Custer had his battle: "Where General Custer made his stand was also a basin, but a larger basin than we had." The Indians must have gotten on the hills around them. The dead were "all laid about the center of the basin," except for Custer, Cooke, and Capt. Tom Custer. They were lying away from the other men, killed over on a little yellow hill with five or six dead white horses.

Later in Adams's narrative he returned to the scene of Custer's demise. The general, he said, saw he was trapped. "They ran back until they came to a basin and before they had time to do anything these Indians had the basin surrounded . . . the men were all lying about the center of the basin." Near the end of the pamphlet, Adams reiterated the same theme. Curley, he thought, got away from the battlefield because "He never got into the basin with the other men."[260]

Adams's comparisons of the terrain on Reno's and Custer's fields allow for a fairly positive identification of the place many of Custer's men made their stand. His "basin" defensive area on Reno Hill was the gentle, saucerlike depression in the center of the perimeter where the "hospital" was established for the wounded. On Custer's field, the larger version was the "basin" below the monument area. In no stretch of the imagination do either of these locales resemble Deep Ravine. The basin Custer's troopers fought in and died in was Cemetery Ravine.

18. Thomas W. Coleman   *Private, Co. B*

Thomas Coleman was born in 1849 in Troy, New York. At the start of the Civil War, Coleman, only 12 years old, attached himself to the 5th Michigan Volunteers as an assistant to the surgeon. By 1864 he had seen enough of wounds and death, and he left the regiment while it was in Virginia to join the navy. At this time he was four feet seven with hazel eyes and brown hair. He was discharged in 1865 and stayed a civilian for seven years. In 1875, Coleman joined the army again and was assigned to Company B while they were stationed in South Carolina chasing moonshiners and keeping an eye on the Ku Klux Klan. In 1877 he was discharged again as "a private of good character" after five more years of service. His military career was over at age 27.

Coleman kept a diary of his experiences in the campaign of 1876. As a member of Company B he was part of the escort for the pack train. Coleman's time estimates for the start of the Little Bighorn battle are earlier than Lt. Wallace's "official" watch. He said Reno struck the village at half past twelve and Company B got to the bluffs at two o'clock, leaving plenty of time for a move to assist Custer. Coleman said he buried Lt. Hodgson on June 27 east of the Little Bighorn under a cedar tree on a knoll overlooking the river. On the 28th they went to Custer's field. The "Bravest General" died with his brothers and brother-in-law about five yards away. Coleman thought most of the 42 surrounding bodies were men of Company E, though most were mutilated and hardly recognizable. His company buried about 30 bodies from Company E that were lying "in line not 10 feet apart."[261]

Coleman did not write anything about Company E being found or buried in any deep gully. His thought that most of the dead on Custer Hill were from Company E may be incorrect, as it appears that most of the bodies on that knoll were from Company F, with a scattering of Company C and E men. Yet he spoke definitely of burying 30 E Troopers in a line at 10-foot intervals. The cluster of bodies on Last Stand Hill in no way approximated a skirmish line of 10-foot intervals. Coleman most assuredly saw this line extending downhill from the knoll, a sighting well reinforced by dozens of similar accounts. Seeing bodies of E Troop on Custer Hill and stringing down with 10-foot spacings from there definitely rules out Deep Ravine as the death spot for Smith's men. The sighting does place them in the upper reaches of Cemetery Ravine.

In a corroborating narrative, another private burying the dead that day spoke of seeing men of Company E in definite skirmish order, much as did Private Coleman. John Dolan of Company M said, "Where Custer made his last stand, there were about 40 men lying around amid their horses just as you might have knocked them down with an axe. The men of companies E and L fell as straight as if they were on a skirmish line."[262]

19. Frank Berwald   *Private, Co. E*

Frank Berwald was born in Poland in 1851. He came to America and enlisted in the army in 1873. His civilian occupation was listed as blacksmith. He had gray eyes, brown hair, a florid complexion, and stood just under five feet six inches in height. He was discharged in 1878 as a sergeant of good character.[263]

Berwald accompanied the pack train during the battle of June 25. In an interview with Walter Mason Camp in 1912, Berwald indicated that others of his company assigned to the packs were Sgt. James T. Riley and Pvts. Herod T. Liddiard, John James, and probably John G. Kimm. Being with the packs was not necessarily a saving grace: Sergeant Riley was wounded and Private Liddiard was killed while helping to defend Reno Hill.

After the fight Berwald said that survivors of the Gray Horse Troop helped bury their comrades, and he and Kimm engaged in that task for certain. Berwald identified four E Troopers in a gully: Cpl. Albert H. Meyer, 1st Sgt. Frederick Hohmeyer, Pvt. Richard Farrell, and Pvt. William Huber. They were "all in [a] bunch in [a] deep gully."[264]

Which ravine did Berwald speak of? He identified Sergeant Hohmeyer in a deep gully, as did Captain McDougall. We have determined that McDougall probably saw bodies in both ravines, but we placed his account in the Deep Ravine column. It is likely that since he and Berwald saw the same body in a gully they must be speaking of the same gully. Although Berwald did not specify further, we will mark the dead he saw as lying in Deep Ravine.

20. Dennis Lynch   *Private, Co. F*

Dennis Lynch was born in Maryland in 1848. He served in the 8th Illinois Cavalry in the Civil War, and at the Battle of Brandy Station in June 1863 he came under the command of Capt. George A. Custer.[265] Lynch also fought at Cedar Creek, Winchester, and Yellow Tavern, the latter fight resulting in the death of Confederate Gen. J. E. B. Stuart at the hands of Custer's Michigan Cavalry Brigade. By the time of Lynch's enlistment in the 7th Cavalry in August 1866, he was among the minority who actually had a war full of cavalry experience under his belt. Dennis Lynch was with the pack train at the Little Bighorn, probably a lifesaving assignment.

Lynch was interviewed by Walter Camp in 1908 and 1909. Lynch said he dressed the wounds of Comanche, Capt. Myles W. Keogh's horse and one of the very few surviving creatures on Custer's field. The men detailed to the pack train remained with the mules, but they did help in the burials. At some point north of Calhoun's final position, Lynch observed what he thought might have been men of the 7th Infantry carrying the dead out of a deep gully. Lynch remembered someone saying that they ought to go down there and see what the "dough boys" were doing. He found them, including one he knew, Sgt. Dave Heaton (Company K, 7th Infantry), carrying dead bodies up the south side of the gully. They already had seven bodies laid out on the bank. Some of these were carried up and buried on the ridge.[266]

William R. Logan, the son of Capt. William A. Logan of Company A, 7th Infantry, wrote to Walter Camp in 1909 about Lynch's statements. As a courier and guide, Logan claimed he was the first white man on the battlefield after the fight, a statement that contradicts Lt. James Bradley's more accurate journal. Logan said a squadron of men under Sergeant Heaton did not carry bodies out of the coulee. The bodies were buried where they were found. The men were killed in bunches, generally by company and sometimes in skirmish formation. The burial party had no picks or shovels, and graves were dug with knives and broken plates. The dead were covered with a little dirt and sage.[267]

Logan's protest has been adequately answered by Francis B. Taunton. What Logan wrote to Camp sounds like a misunderstanding on the former's part, Taunton argued. If Logan thought Camp may have believed that all the bodies of Custer's men were buried in a coulee, then he was correct in trying to remove that misconception. But it is not clear that Logan saw the burial of Smith's men, whereas Lynch did categorically state he saw it. Since Colonel Gibbon's men predominantly buried Reno's dead in the valley, and Logan took part in those burials, it is very likely that Logan simply confused burials on one part of the field with those on another. There was no reason for Lynch to invent his story, and it is hardly possible for Logan to have witnessed the burial of the entire command, since no one else did. Lynch's statements should stand as accurate.[268] He did see infantrymen carrying at least a few bodies out of a gully below Custer Hill and laying them out on the bank.

Other witnesses attested to this likelihood. Sgt. Riley R. Lane of Company D, 7th Infantry, wrote that he had been up on Custer Hill. Pvt. John Mahoney of Company C, 7th Cavalry, told Walter Camp that he thought he saw Company C of the 7th Infantry help bury bodies on Custer's field. Arthur F. Ward told judge/editor/historian Eli S. Ricker that men of his 2nd Cavalry and the 7th Infantry were involved in the burials. Lt. Alfred B. Johnson of Company I, 7th Infantry, was on Custer's knoll and said that the ground the soldiers on the hill fell on was only about two or three times larger than his father's yard. One of Johnson's men, Pvt. John Lanahan, wrote that he was one of the party that buried Custer and 12 other officers.[269] The 7th Infantry did participate in the burials on Custer's field.

What of Lynch's ravine? He saw soldiers carrying bodies out of a ravine and placing up to seven of them on the south bank. Some were carried to a ridge for burial. It matters not so much which unit did the carrying, but that the action did take place. Could this have been in Deep Ravine? How could decomposing bodies, with skin sloughed off and arms pulled out of the sockets, have been carried up the precipitous south bank of Deep Ravine? Could men have carried rotting bodies out of a ravine that has been depicted as being too steep for men to scramble out of under their own power while very much alive? What ridge would the soldiers have carried the bodies up to? Battle Ridge? Custer Hill? Would they have hauled those corpses the length of seven football fields to the north after they laid them out on the south bank? Preposterous.

What if the bodies Lynch saw were in Cemetery Ravine? It is a much more likely site. It has easily negotiable sides and a gentle, sloping south bank that would serve nicely as a temporary repository for bodies. Continuing a short way up the south bank it becomes a ridge—the low divide between Cemetery and Deep Ravines. It is this ridge that was to become the burial place of some of the men that fell nearby, as we shall see in the next account. It is in Cemetery Ravine that Lynch saw the bodies of the Gray Horse Troopers.

21. Daniel A. Knipe   *Sergeant, Co. C*

Knipe was born in North Carolina in 1853. He indicated to Walter Camp that his name was spelled "Kanipe," but it is under the former spelling that he enlisted in 1872. Knipe was in the Yellowstone Expedition of 1873 and the Black Hills Expedition in 1874. On June 25 he was sent back as a messenger to hurry Captain McDougall with the pack train and thus was almost certainly spared from the fate that awaited the remainder of C Troop. Knipe was discharged from the 7th Cavalry in 1877.

In 1924, Daniel Knipe told his story in the Greensboro, North Carolina, *Daily Record*. However, it contains only a few items that are pertinent to our examination. He rode near Tom Custer, the captain of C Troop. Riding with them for a time was the half-Sioux, half-French scout Mitch Bouyer and the Crow scout Curley. Knipe saw Sgt. August Finckle's horse play out and drop back out of column. After the fight, on June 27, Knipe

Sgt. Daniel A. Knipe,
Company C, 7th
Cavalry. He identified
Mitch Bouyer's body
in a ravine after the
battle. Photo c. 1875.
—Little Bighorn Battlefield
National Monument

was allowed to go with Benteen to Custer's field and look around wherever he wanted. He recognized Finckle's body. He saw where Custer and his brother Tom fell. He understood that there were 14 enlisted men and two officers, Lieutenants Harrington and Sturgis, that were never found.[270]

Knipe left a record much more relevant to our problem in his interviews with Walter Camp in 1908. Down by Medicine Tail ford, he saw a dead horse and a dead trooper on the west bank, practically in the Indian camp. This led him to the opinion that Custer did try to ford and charge the camp at this point. It was sometime after three or four o'clock on the 27th that Knipe continued along the line of dead. The first body he found was that of Sgt. Jeremiah Finley of C Troop, stuck full of arrows. The dead lay in plain sight, all stripped. Next he found the body of Sergeant Finckle on the way to Calhoun Hill. There he turned left in the direction of where the monument now stands. Near where Keogh fell he saw the horse of 1st Sgt. Edwin Bobo of his own company. It was evidently going along the ridge close to the gully when it was shot and slid down the bank into the gully where it died. Sergeant Bobo himself was found in a pile of men lying around Captain Keogh. As Benteen's men were kept in ranks and passed by him, Knipe was able to examine the field at his own pace. He traveled to the end of the ridge, where he found Custer, Cooke, Smith, and others.

"I next went along the line of dead bodies toward the river, and riding along the edge of the deep gully about 2,000 feet from where the monu-

Mitch Bouyer.
The half-Lakota,
half-French guide
and interpreter
was the only
scout to die with
Custer's battalion.
Photo c. 1875. —Little
Bighorn Battlefield
National Monument

ment now stands, I counted 28 bodies in this gulch. The only one I thought I recognized at the time was Mitch Bouyer. . . . I was then well enough satisfied that the corpse was that of Bouyer."[271]

We may be sure Knipe's perceptions were sharp that day. Certainly he noticed the demise of Sergeant Bobo and his horse. We may wonder what thoughts were going through his mind at that time, for he married Bobo's widow less than a year later.[272] Knipe also saw Bouyer's body in a deep gulch. Which gulch? For years it has been assumed that Knipe spoke of Deep Ravine. A deep gulch about 2,000 feet from the monument would very likely be identified as the Deep Ravine, but more than one soldier made erroneous distance estimations that day. Knipe was sure he recognized Bouyer with his distinctive features and attire, the pipe-smoking scout of mixed Sioux and French ancestry that the Indians called "the man with the calf-skin vest."

Did Knipe see Bouyer in Deep Ravine? No! We know he did not, because Bouyer's remains have been found. Archaeological excavations in 1985 have enabled positive identification and location of the remains of the scout. Bouyer's body was found at gravemarkers 33-34, near the middle of the South Skirmish Line, up the gentle south slope of Cemetery Ravine proper and about 60 feet below the crest of the "ridge," the low divide between Cemetery and Deep Ravines.[273] Bouyer's stone, now newly marked as number 34, sits amid a small cluster of seven, numbers 33 through 39, and is centrally located in a larger grouping of seventeen markers, numbers 29 through 45 (fig. 15).

Was Bouyer's body, seen by Knipe in Cemetery Ravine on the 27th, among the seven that Lynch saw being laid out on the south bank the next day? The descriptions match almost perfectly. We cannot say so with absolute certainty, but we have found another indication that the deep ravine many people spoke of was not today's Deep Ravine. Cemetery Ravine *was the deep ravine* to Knipe.

THE MONTANA AND DAKOTA COLUMNS

Soldiers of the 7th Cavalry were not the only ones to leave records of the aftermath of the Little Bighorn fight. In addition to the 12 companies of the 7th Cavalry under Custer, the Dakota Column included Company B of the 6th Infantry, Companies C and G of the 17th Infantry, and a gatling gun detachment from the 20th Infantry. The entire command was led by Brig. Gen. Alfred H. Terry.

Another organization, the Montana Column, left Fort Ellis on April 1 to attempt to coordinate with the Dakota troops in crushing the Indians between them. The Montana troops were under Col. John Gibbon, leading six companies of his own 7th Infantry and four companies of the 2nd Cavalry under Maj. James S. Brisbin. The Montana men were in the field one and a half months before Terry left Fort Abraham Lincoln on May 17. Although possibly not strong enough to defeat a large number of Indians by itself, Gibbon's column was to police the Yellowstone and prevent the hostiles from crossing to the north side of that river. Just how that was to be accomplished was not explained, for the Indians proved time and again that they could cross the river at will, while the soldiers found themselves at the mercy of the Yellowstone's currents.

However, on the day the Dakota Column left their base, 1st Lt. James H. Bradley of Company B, leading a mounted detachment of the 7th Infantry along with some Crow scouts, brought back a report to Gibbon of a large Indian village about 30 miles distant on the Tongue River. Gibbon decided to attack. A company of men reached the south shore, but the swift current caused only panic, chaos, and drowned horses.[274] The attack was canceled. Gibbon settled back to await Terry and Custer.

The two forces met on June 9. They moved up the Yellowstone and finalized plans. On June 22, Custer's 7th Cavalry headed south up the valley of the Rosebud. Gibbon's men, now joined by Terry and the rest of his troops minus the 7th Cavalry, moved west up the Yellowstone. The next day Gibbon was struck with a debilitating stomach illness. In effect, Terry was now in command of all the units.

Terry's and Gibbon's troops moved up past Pease Bottom and crossed to the south bank of the Yellowstone in the vicinity of Tullock's Fork with the assistance of the steamer *Far West*. It was understood that they should be at the mouth of the Little Bighorn on June 26. In a series of miscues, dawdlings, and poor judgments, the Terry-Gibbon troops stumbled into the Little Bighorn Valley and reached the field two days after Custer's fight. Given all their abortive exertions, they were rather lucky after all, for it is not entirely certain that they scared off the Indians by their mere presence. Though some Indian accounts credit Gibbon with their vacating the field, others stated that the Indians had simply had their fight, were tired, and decided to go off on their own separate business.[275]

Late on the 26th, 2nd Lt. Charles F. Roe of Company F of the 2nd Cavalry spotted some "buffalo" far off in the hills east of the Little Bighorn. The next morning, Lieutenant Bradley took his scouts there to inspect the sighting. He returned to Gibbon and Terry with the news that he had just counted 197 bodies lying in the hills. "White men?" was the first question. "Yes, white men," Bradley answered.[276]

About that same time others made contact with Lieutenants Wallace and Hare, who had just come down from Reno Hill. "Where's Custer?" was the question the 7th Cavalry officers asked. Apparently he and his men were all dead up on the ridge. Then came the shocked silence. It was the first realization for all of the enormous calamity that had occurred.

The next morning the main burials began. While the men of the 7th Infantry and 2nd Cavalry assisted mostly in helping Reno's wounded, in constructing litters, and in helping bury the dead in the valley, some had the dubious luxury of visiting Custer's field.

The following accounts were given by other members of Gibbon's and Terry's units. They walked the fields from June 27 through the 29th, viewing the same scenes the 7th Cavalrymen did. Their records will also be considered eyewitness accounts.

22. Walter Clifford   *Captain, Co. E, 7th Infantry*

Captain Clifford had led his company with Colonel Gibbon's troops for the past several months, logging in hundreds of marching miles up and down the Yellowstone, seeking to engage the hostiles. As yet, they had not fought an Indian and rarely ever saw one. What was to be the climax of the campaign on the banks of the Little Bighorn turned out to be a nightmare of gravedigging for Clifford and his men.

The captain recorded his thoughts in his diary. It flows with Victorian verbiage as he quotes lines of poetry from "The Bivouac of the Dead" and waxes eloquent with woes unto those who had fallen to the "pitiless enemies." Custer was their "dauntless chief," news came "like a clap of thunder," the round moon was "as bright as burnished silver," and the bodies were "like polished white marble." He also spoke of ghastly butchery, brooding sorrow, sickening stench, and repulsive green flies.

Clifford found the bloodstained underclothes of Lt. James Sturgis in a tepee in the abandoned Indian village. He was shown a coat with bullet holes in it and the name of Lieutenant Porter in the lining. That night Clifford speculated that some of Custer's command were missing. On June 28 his diary indicated that many of the 7th Infantrymen helped with Reno's wounded and buried dead in the valley "and on Custer's field," the latter notation tending to corroborate Dennis Lynch's statements concerning 7th Infantrymen burying men in the Deep Ravine and Cemetery Ravine areas.

Clifford commented on the condition of the dead on Custer's field, where almost all but George Custer and Keogh appeared to have been mutilated. Keogh was spared, he believed, because of a papal medal suspended from his neck. Clifford said nothing about the Gray Horse Troop being found in any ravine, but he did contribute something for our purposes. An examination of the ground showed that Custer's five companies had perished in skirmish lines, and inside the lines it appeared they fell in groups of fours.[277]

Men of the 7th Infantry helped bury the dead on Custer's field, which buttresses Lynch's observations, and all of Custer's companies were in skirmish lines, which tends to rule out Deep Ravine. Yet the account is not specific enough to categorize. We will list Clifford's account as uncertain.

23. Holmes O. Paulding   *1st Lieutenant, Asst. Surgeon, U. S. A.*

Born in 1852 in Washington, D.C., of a distinguished family of ranking naval officers, Paulding later studied medicine in the Columbian University in Washington. In 1874 he received his appointment in the army as an assistant surgeon. Paulding became acquainted with Custer at Fort Lincoln, but was transferred to Fort Ellis in 1875 and thus accompanied Colonel Gibbon's men during the campaign of 1876.

In a series of letters Paulding wrote to his mother, he was critical of Gibbon and the whole campaign, calling the march nothing more than "purposelessly fooling around in the sage brush bottoms all summer." Gibbon's attempts at fighting Indians accomplished nothing more than drowning horses and men; Gibbon would have had to part the Yellowstone like "Bvt Gen Moses" to get across. The whole trip was "a miserable farce and everything has been as disagreeable as idiotic, pig headed stupidity could make it."[278]

When Paulding got into the Indian village on June 27, he entered a lodge and found a buckskin jacket with Lieutenant Porter's name on it, a pair of Captain Yates's gloves, and some underclothes of Lieutenant Sturgis. Paulding did not go directly to Custer's field because he was too busy with Reno's wounded. He could only speculate on the battle from descriptions provided by some of the surviving officers. He saw nothing but a few bodies and some heads evidently dragged from a distance. The bodies were probably tortured. The scouts returning from east of the Little Bighorn sent word that they "found 28 white men (soldiers) lying dead in a ravine crossing the bluffs opposite & a mile or two behind, where we then were." They reported 196, then 204 dead, all of them found along the summit of the bluff except for the first 28.[279]

There is the "28 men in a ravine" story again. From Paulding's letters, however, the exact location of the ravine is impossible to determine.

24. Richard E. Thompson   *2nd Lieutenant, Co. K, 6th Infantry*

Thompson was acting commissary of subsistence, in charge of the rations for the men of the Dakota Column. He spent much of the campaign on the supply steamer *Far West*, but on June 27 he accompanied Benteen to Custer Hill along with Capt. Robert P. Hughes, Capt. Otho E. Michaelis, and Lt. Henry J. Nowlan.

In 1911, Thompson told Walter Camp that the dead horses looked as if they formed a barricade on Custer Hill. He saw Tom Custer, his face hacked with a hatchet and only identifiable by the initials tattooed on his arm. He and others identified Dr. George E. Lord's body just 20 feet southeast of Custer's. He saw Mark Kellogg's body, a reporter for the *Bismarck Tribune* and *New York Herald,* down about 100 yards from the river. Thompson thought there were only about nine or ten men between the gully and Custer. In the gully there were many bodies—maybe thirty-four.[280]

Thompson's story increases the usual twenty-eight up to thirty-four, but he still saw them in a gully; he saw only nine or ten between the gully and Custer. This could very well be true—if the gully was Cemetery Ravine. Were the bodies Thompson saw those of the Bouyer cluster? Today there are 11 stones running north from the Bouyer cluster to the southern fringe of Custer Hill, numbers 46 through 56. Remove Lieutenant Sturgis's spurious marker, grave number 48, which was not there when Thompson was observing, and there are ten remaining, the same nine or ten he specified. Coincidence? Maybe not. But Thompson did not give enough detail. The specific ravine he referred to remains unknown.

25. Edward A. Maguire *1st Lieutenant, Engineers*

Edward Maguire was the chief of engineers for the Dakota Column. He accompanied Terry and was under his orders, but his reports were sent directly back to Washington. Maguire was a more disinterested observer than any other member of the 7th Cavalry, and his accounts were more dispassionate and objective. Maguire completed two reports, a preliminary one, sent to Gen. A. A. Humphreys from camp at the mouth of the Bighorn July 2, 1876, and an official one, sent to Humphreys from camp on the Yellowstone and dated July 10, 1876.

The preliminary report details entering the Indian village, being met by members of the 7th Cavalry, ascending almost perpendicular bluffs to where Reno was besieged, and there being greeted by the hysterical shouts and cheers of the survivors. Maguire listened to the men's stories and wrote down what he surmised had happened. His theory had Custer attempting to cross at ford "B" (Medicine Tail), being repulsed, and retreating in two lines. One stand was made at "D" (Calhoun Hill) and another on crest "E" (Custer Hill). "Leading from this crest to the ravine marked 'H' was a regular line of bodies, there evidently having been a line of skirmishers on this line, as the men fell at skirmish distance from each other. The ravine marked 'H' contained 28 bodies, as if in retreat the men had taken to it for shelter."[281]

Maguire's official report was very similar to his preliminary report. Again he admitted his account was conjecture and said that one must be content with knowledge gained from the appearance of the field.

Custer attempted to cross at "B", the second report read, but was met by an overpowering force. The troops retreated to the hills in two lines to concentrate at "E". Calhoun made a stand at "D". "The column which retreated along the line 'BHE' must have been dismounted and fighting along the whole distance. A portion of its men taking to the ravine 'H' for shelter must have been surrounded by the Indians. There were 28 bodies found in this ravine. From 'H' to 'E' stretched a line of dead men with skirmish intervals."[282]

Maguire had maps drawn to accompany his reports. The first report spoke of two lines of retreat from ford "B", but its map only showed one—the Calhoun Hill to Custer Hill route. The trail then went down from Custer Hill to a ravine marked "H". The second report also spoke of two retreat routes from the ford, and this time the map showed two—one by way of Calhoun Hill to Custer Hill and the other by way of ravine "H" to Custer Hill. Sometime between the 2nd and 10th of July, Maguire either changed his mind or had mistakenly omitted one trail from the first map and added it onto the second. Of course, it makes a great difference in one's conception of the battle, for the first map would have the troops moving down from Custer Hill to the ravine and the second out of the ravine and up to Custer Hill.

At the Reno Court of Inquiry another of Maguire's maps was entered into evidence (fig. 10). It included more details and refinements, but kept the same lettering reference: Medicine Tail ford was "B", Calhoun Hill was "D", Custer Hill was "E", and the ravine was "H". This map, like the others, was actually drawn under Maguire's supervision by Sgt. Charles Becker of Company D, Battalion of Engineers, an experienced cartographer who had also tallied the miles on Custer's Black Hills Expedition in 1874. The map served as reference for the witnesses' testimony.

The Reno Court convened in Chicago on January 13, 1879, and Maguire was the first witness called. He gave his own map faint praise, saying it was only a sketch made to illustrate a report and did not purport to be anything more than that. Every other witness whose testimony involved Maguire's map severely criticized it, but the main difficulties were centered in Reno's sphere of conflict: the coulee the Indians hid in, the skirmish line in the valley, and the course of the river. On Custer's field the situation was otherwise. One can accept the map and the measurements as a satisfactory representation of the terrain.[283]

Had Edward Maguire known what minute examination his work would be subjected to a few years after the fight, he would, no doubt, have made sure every cottonwood and cutbank was in its exact place. As it was, the map used at the court of inquiry had already gone through several revisions, the last version leaving out scores of red Xs that marked where individual bodies had fallen—Xs that traced out neat little skirmish lines in the ravine down from Custer Hill. Researcher W. Kent King argued that the alteration was done at the instigation of the authorities in a sinister plot to discredit Custer, save the reputations of other 7th Cavalry members, and even protect President Grant, "with all the breathless

FIGURE 10: EDWARD MAGUIRE'S MAP

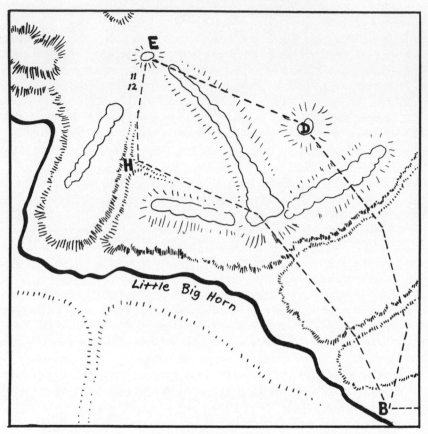

A redrawing of a portion of the Maguire-Becker map used at the Reno Court of Inquiry, 1879.

B. *Medicine Tail ford*
D. *Calhoun Hill*
E. *Custer Hill*
H. *Ravine where Smith's men took shelter and where 28 bodies were found*

Numbers 11 and 12 represent where Boston Custer and Armstrong Reed fell, respectively. Their bodies were found just below Custer Hill and in the upper reaches of Cemetery Ravine. Maguire placed the location of the 28 bodies farther down that same ravine.

prose, insinuations, rhetorical questions, and heavy handed ironies characteristic of conspiracy theories."[284]

On the battlefield, Maguire and Becker did the best they could under the circumstances. The map, Maguire said, "is a mere sketch; it is not like a survey made with a transit and chain. The dotted lines on the map are lines I put on to illustrate the report I sent to the Chief of Engineers. They are what I suppose to be the trail of the troops in marching." An odometer cart was used, some views were taken with a prismatic compass, "and the map filled in by eye on the field." The distance between Reno's position and where Custer's body lay was accurate, Maguire stated, and "The location of the ravine and the general direction of the battlefield are correct."[285] His *perception and viewpoint* were more important than exact values.

Maguire's testimony concerning the ravine is very similar to what he had previously stated in his reports to Humphreys. Near ford "B" there were empty shells and marks of horses. The first dead soldier found was six-tenths of a mile up from "B". There were more shells up the hill and bodies all the way from "D" to "E". In ravine "H" 28 bodies were found.

Under cross-examination by Reno's counsel, Lyman Gilbert, Maguire admitted his dotted route lines were conjecture only. On at least three separate occasions, to questions concerning the trails, he responded that he was not over it, did not go between the points, or was not there at all. In fact, Benteen was over the trail first and the tracks Maguire saw might have been his.[286]

There are discrepancies between the Reno Court record and the *Chicago Times* versions of Maguire's testimony, much as we witnessed with Lieutenant Hare's testimony. From the *Times:*

> Q. Do the dotted lines represent the paths the troops took in reaching point "B"?
> A. They represent simply my idea of the paths.

In the court record, point "B" became point "E":

> Q. I see dotted lines on the right side of the river, do they represent the paths taken in reaching "E"?
> A. They represent my idea of the paths taken on looking at the ground. . . .

Did Maguire travel over any of those paths or not? He didn't examine between the bluffs on the right (east) bank of the river and the trail he drew there. He did not go over the heavy trail he drew leading to "B". He did not go over the ground represented by many of the dotted lines. The only trail, in both records, that Maguire stated he had gone over was the path from "B" to "D" to "E". In the court record he added that he had also gone over the "B" to "H" to "E" portion. In any case, Maguire said, the ground was all cut up by hoofs and it was only a theory on his part that the troops separated into two bodies and took those routes.[287] We may never know which trails Maguire actually saw and which were pure conjecture.

Will we have any more success in discovering whether Maguire's ravine "H" was Cemetery Ravine or Deep Ravine? He was very definite concerning the skirmish lines he had seen between the ravine and Custer Hill. But when were the skirmish lines formed? Maguire's hypothesized route would mean E Troop was repulsed at the ford; they continued over to a ravine where they were surprised and assaulted, with 28 or more men slaughtered. The survivors then scrambled out and managed to form a skirmish line between that ravine and Custer's position. The scenario offends logic. It is a movie played backwards. It would be much more reasonable to come down from the ridge, form a skirmish line, face a shattering attack that resulted in a score of casualties, and then perhaps have a few fugitives run and hide in a deep ravine.

There is also another problem with the "B" to "H" to "E" scenario. Company E could not have been "jumped" by an overwhelming force of Indians while they trailed up Deep Ravine because the Indians simply were not there yet. It was still too early in that segment of the battle for a great number of Indians to take position around the Deep Ravine. And why would they have done so if they had had the time? Would the warriors, in their wildest dreams, believe that the soldiers would oblige them by trailing along in the bottom of a gully while they sat along the top, picking them off at their leisure? The Indians did go into and along Deep Ravine, but only in pursuit of the soldiers who had already passed beyond Greasy Grass Ridge, Calhoun Hill, and Battle Ridge, a sequence that we have seen was borne out by the Indians themselves.

Regardless of Maguire's faulty speculations on the route taken by the troopers, what is more important here are his observations rather than his surmisings. Maguire saw skirmish lines. One cannot form a viable skirmish line in Deep Ravine. Reexamine Maguire's map. He said it was not a survey with transit and chain. It was a sketch. His perception and viewpoint were more important than exact values, and the terrain was *filled in by eye* on the field. Like so many others, Maguire and/or Sergeant Becker stood on Last Stand Hill and looked toward the river. They could only see down the length of one ravine from that viewpoint. Maguire's map was drawn with but one ravine. The men who testified had but one ravine to point to. Deep Ravine's main upper branches point *away* from Custer Hill, its lower end barely visible as a small notch on the left horizon to an observer on Custer Hill. While the very presence of Deep Ravine is barely

Lt. Charles F. Roe, Company F, 2nd Cavalry. In 1881 he placed the granite monument that still stands today on Custer Hill. Photo by D. F. Barry, c. 1880. —Little Bighorn Battlefield National Monument

noticeable to one viewing or sketching from Custer Hill, Maguire's ravine is overwhelmingly obvious.

Stressing perception, viewpoint, and filling in by eye, Maguire's map depicts a ravine that arrowheads from its point right at Custer Hill and cuts like a hunting knife directly down to the Little Bighorn. There is only one ravine that resembles Maguire's rendition. It is Cemetery Ravine.

26. Charles F. Roe *2nd Lieutenant, Co. F, 2nd Cavalry*

Riding with his company of 2nd Cavalrymen up the Little Bighorn Valley late on June 26, Roe observed what he thought were dead buffalo on the hills east of the river. It was at his suggestion that Lieutenant Bradley took his scouts to inspect the area the next morning, thus finding the first of Custer's dead.

Roe spent many years of distinguished service in the army. He returned to the Little Bighorn in 1881 to rebury Custer's dead and place the monument now poised atop Last Stand Hill. He resigned from the army in 1888, but became a brigadier general of volunteers in the Spanish-American War. In 1904 he told his story in an address delivered to the Albany Convention of the New York State National Guard, of which he was then commanding major general. The address was printed in the Guard's *Annual Records*, again in 1910 in *The Castle*, by the Army Corps of Engineers, and again in 1927 by Robert Bruce.[288]

Roe's story of Custer's movements could only be told, he stated, "in a general way," the information being gathered from the Crow scout Curley and from his own visits to the field. Roe spoke of Curley and Mitch Bouyer watching Custer move down Medicine Tail Coulee, which he called "Green Grass Creek." The head of the column reached the river, and a man with stripes on his arm (a sergeant) rode into the water, testing the ford. The Indians opened fire and the troops turned away. Some went farther back up the ridge, but others went along the bank to see if they could locate another ford downstream. The troops along the river met heavy fire from Indians in the timber on the opposite bank and could not cross. They "went along the bank until they came to a deep ravine which ran back about a hundred yards. They were unable to cross, so undertook to go around it; at the head of this ravine we found several dead soldiers and horses." Dead men and horses were strung along toward the high ridge. Custer and nine of his men were at the point of the ridge, and just downslope from them "were twenty-five dead men and horses in a small space, and mixed in together."[289]

Roe's speculations on the troop movements, like Maguire's, suffer from flaws in the sequencing. It makes no sense to be attacked by an overwhelming force, routed, then somehow maintain the organization and discipline to string out in a skirmish line with the shocked survivors to face an assault that already occurred. Hence, as with Maguire's comments, what Roe saw outweighs what he surmised. He found *several* dead at the head of a deep ravine, and dead men were strung out along a line from there to the high ridge. Roe drew no map to pinpoint his ravine; regardless, it only contained "several" bodies, not 28, and from there they strung out in a line to Custer Hill. This supports the likelihood that a line was formed along Cemetery Ravine and in the upper Deep Ravine watershed—the 25 bodies he saw in a small place were just downslope from Custer, not out in Deep Ravine. If the line subsequently was overwhelmed, only a few men managed to escape to a temporary respite in Deep Ravine.

27. Henry B. Freeman *Captain, Co. H, 7th Infantry*

Henry Blanchard Freeman was born in Ohio in 1837. He enlisted in the 18th Infantry at the outbreak of the Civil War, receiving two brevets for gallantry and the Medal of Honor. He was captured at Chickamauga

FIGURE 11: HENRY FREEMAN'S MAP

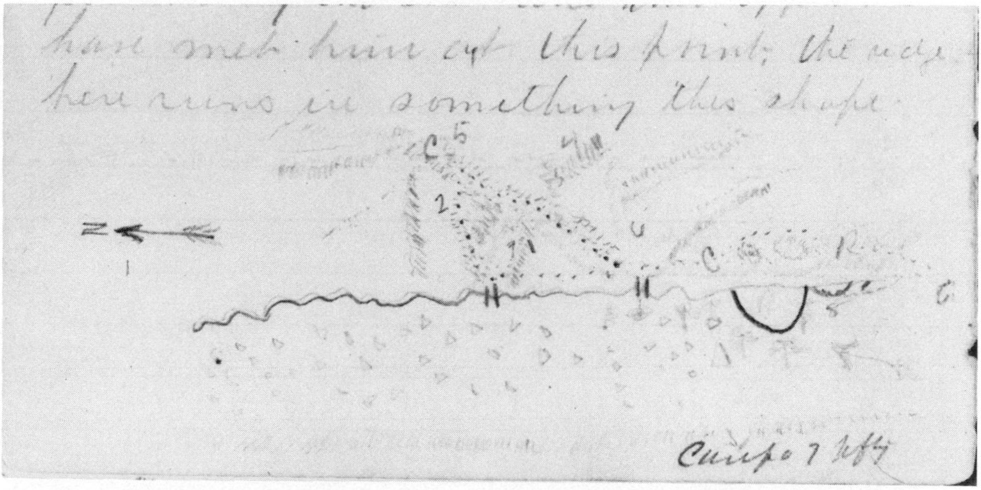

Freeman's journal included the following map explanations:

C at upper end is the point where Reno crossed the [creek or coulee].

The dotted lines along the bluff to the ford, Custer's trail.

At 6 the first bodies were found.

At 1 & 4 there were indications that they had dismounted and made a stand, and again at 2.

At 5, the highest point on the ridge, Custer was killed with what remained to him of his 5 cos.

From the upper ford ╫ *to 5 is about ¾ of a mile; from the same point to the upper C is 3½ miles; from lower R to upper R, by the trail, 2 mi.*

The Indians, Crows, say that there were more Sioux killed from Custer's point than in all the rest of the fighting below the ford.

7 is a ravine which toward the upper end is very steep and forms a pocket in which 28 bodies were found.

Reproduced by permission of the Yale Collection of Western Americana, Beinecke Rare Book and Manuscript Library, Yale University.

and spent one and a half years in prison, successfully escaping on his fourth attempt in February 1865. He served in the Indian Wars and the Spanish-American War and retired as a brigadier general in 1901.

Freeman's observations were recorded in a journal that owed its existence to his being placed in command of five companies of the 7th Infantry with the temporary absence of Colonel Gibbon and the incapacity of Capt. Charles Rawn. The entries record the march of the Montana Column from March to October 1876.

On June 27, Freeman wrote that the troops entered the Indian village after a march of three miles from their morning camp. After they inspected it, they continued another half mile and met some of Reno's men. Lieutenant Bradley came in with news of finding bodies across the river. They camped near the site of Reno's valley fight and spent the day making litters and getting the wounded down from Reno Hill. The June 28 entry continued with notes on making arrangements for the wounded and moving back north five miles before stopping for the night. On June 29, Freeman voiced more concern for the wounded and talked of making horse litters. They marched back along the old trail that they had approached the battlefield on. Freeman took the initiative in lighting fires to guide the men along the trail in the darkness. In the short entry of June 30, Freeman said General Terry liked his idea about the fires the previous night. Then they began the trip back home.[290]

The journal appears interrupted between the June 29 and June 30 entries. There Freeman inserted several pages that he titled "Incidents of Custer's March from mouth of Rosebud and the battle." It is clear at this point he was speaking of events he had no firsthand knowledge of, but had garnered his information from other witnesses. He speculated about several causes and events in Custer's approach, including worn-out horses and divided forces, and made an incorrect assumption that the regimental colors were captured. Freeman heard other officers say that Custer crossed the river, but he didn't think so. He thought Custer turned right at the ford, pushed hard by the Indians. Freeman ended his journal "extra" with a map of the field (fig. 11). He included a key, which clarified the numbers and letters on the map. The "6" was where the first bodies were found. The "5" was where Custer was killed. At "1", "2", and "4" were indications that dismounted men had made a stand. A steep ravine at "7" showed where 28 bodies were found. The dotted lines were Custer's trail.

It isn't clear whether or not Freeman actually traversed the field. His journal entries made no mention of it, yet his map is informative. Did he draw it from his own observations? Did he draw it after seeing the preliminary sketchings of Maguire's map or after talking to the other officers? Was this a case of one person passing information on to another, the next person passing it on in turn, perhaps slightly altered, and so on down the line until the last telling little resembled the original?

Compare Freeman's depiction of events with Maguire's and Roe's. Maguire's first report told of two battalions moving from the ford to Custer Hill, but his first map had only one trail along Battle Ridge. The second map accompanying his official report depicted two trails, one along Battle Ridge, the other to the *head* of a ravine. Roe, on the other hand, would have his audience understand that one battalion went along Battle Ridge and the other along the river to the *mouth* of a deep ravine, couldn't cross, and then had to go up and around it. Freeman drew one trail along Battle Ridge and one along the river to the mouth of a ravine where it *did cross* the mouth and moved up the divide between Cemetery Ravine and Deep Ravine to Custer Hill. Three men, three different depictions.

Freeman's map does show the wide, prominent valley of Cemetery Ravine cutting straight down from Custer Hill to the river. One-third of the way down, at "2", he indicated that a stand was made. This corresponds nicely with the 17 present-day gravemarkers of the Bouyer group, numbers 29 to 45 (fig. 15). However, at number "7" on Freeman's map, he noted 28 bodies found in a steep ravine. Did he see any of these locations with his own eyes? Did he hear others talking about 28 men in a gully and construct it from their stories? Freeman's men were concentrated in the valley, and his journal does not indicate that he crossed the river to inspect Custer's field; yet he drew a stand in Cemetery Ravine and also marked 28 men in a steep (not deep) ravine. A categorization is tentative, and while we will place the missing bodies in Deep Ravine, we will note Freeman's verification of a stand made in Cemetery Ravine.

28. Charles A. Woodruff *2nd Lieutenant, Co. K, 7th Infantry*

Lieutenant Woodruff marched with Colonel Gibbon until their junction with General Terry. Then, as part of Captain Freeman's battalion accompanying Terry, Woodruff was made battalion adjutant and placed in command of the gatling gun.[291] In 1912, it was General Woodruff who gave a speech pertaining to the Sioux War of 1876 at a Commonwealth Club meeting at the Palace Hotel in San Francisco.

Woodruff commented on the considerable hardships suffered by the troops during that campaign, which included the weather. A soldier, with no change of clothing, had to contend with temperatures that went from 40 below zero in March to 111 above in August—a range of 151 degrees. There were no roads and no supplies, nothing but buffalo and Indians.

Woodruff was on the battlefield a few days after the Little Bighorn fight. He returned in 1908, accompanied by three Crow participants, and spent a week examining the terrain between the Crow's Nest and Custer's field. Woodruff was of the opinion that Custer halted for a time in Medicine Tail Coulee, waiting specifically to hit the fleeing Indians that would surely be driven across his front by Reno's attack. But there was no mass panic to his front for Custer to exploit. Instead, he went closer to the river and found the Indians prepared for him.

They exchanged shots and Custer moved north. Woodruff could define the line of march by the dead bodies and expended cartridges that he found. Custer must have first deployed Calhoun, then Keogh, Woodruff speculated. The bodies of Keogh's men appeared to be lying in skirmish order. Evidently, Custer pushed hard for the bluff area where the monument now is. "He had two troops with him in skirmish line. I think eventually those two troops struck for the river. But they did not get far. They were all killed along the ravine." Custer and about 58 others were found around the point where the monument now stands.[292]

Woodruff came tantalizingly close to pinpointing the site of E Troop's demise, but he did not quite give us enough information. The troops fought with Custer on or near Last Stand Hill. They were in skirmish line. They eventually struck for the river. They didn't get far and all died along the ravine. Had Woodruff said, "some died in a deep ravine," a case could be made for a Deep Ravine location. Since they were all in a ravine that wasn't deep, since the men were in skirmish line, and since they didn't get far, the description tends to support a Cemetery Ravine location—but we will still have to leave it as uncertain.

29. Edward J. McClernand   *2nd Lieutenant, Co. G, 2nd Cavalry*

McClernand was born in 1849 in Jacksonville, Illinois, the son of John A. McClernand, a major general in the Civil War who served for a time under Ulysses Grant but later became an anti-Grant Democrat. Edward graduated from West Point in 1870 and was assigned to the 2nd Cavalry. He received a Medal of Honor for services against the Nez Perce in 1877. In 1879, McClernand was ordered to West Point as an instructor of tactics. He served in the Spanish-American War in Cuba and in the Philippines and retired as a brigadier general in 1912.

There has been much made of the story that Custer entertained presidential ambitions and the Democrats were waiting at their 1876 National Convention in St. Louis for news of a great victory that would assure Custer a nomination as a dark-horse candidate for president.[293] On the most important day of the convention, Wednesday, June 28, former Gen. John McClernand, chairman of the Democratic Committee, presided over the nominations. Names placed in contention were Sen. Thomas F. Bayard of Delaware, Gov. Thomas A. Hendricks of Indiana, William Allen of Ohio, Winfield Scott Hancock of Pennsylvania, and Gov. Samuel J. Tilden of New York. George Custer's name was never mentioned. In fact, on the very same day and possibly at the very same moment that Chairman John

McClernand pounded his gavel in an attempt to keep order during the voting, his son Edward was gazing upon Custer's dead body 1,500 miles away on a now-tranquil field of battle.²⁹⁴

In Edward McClernand's later years he wrote a manuscript about his experiences on the plains titled "With the Indian and Buffalo in Montana." The narrative appeared in *The Cavalry Journal* in 1926. The part that concerns us covers his time spent as a young 2nd lieutenant serving as engineering officer for the Montana Column. In this respect, McClernand acted in the same capacity as did Maguire for the Dakota troops. In fact, McClernand said he superintended the making of a considerable portion of what has come to be called the "Maguire Map." Sgt. Charles Becker, mentioned before in conjunction with the Maguire map, was actually McClernand's assistant. The two had begun mapping the field immediately after their short ride with Lieutenants Wallace and Hare to Reno Hill. McClernand said one-third of the map was complete when his superior, Lieutenant Maguire, told General Terry that the mapping ought to be under his supervision. Terry assented, and McClernand was verbally released as assistant engineering officer. McClernand had a bit of a hard feeling about the action, for he knew that some distinction would accrue from making the map. However, since the duties of an engineering officer were not very much to his liking anyway, he was rather glad to relinquish them. McClernand stated that "With the exception of one slight error [unspecified] the Maguire map is good." It was, he thought, perhaps the best map made of the field.²⁹⁵

McClernand also went over the field with other officers of the Montana Column. It appeared to him that Custer did enter the coulee (Medicine Tail) and turn toward the river, as could be shown by the positions of the dead. The Indians appeared in numbers near the ford and pushed the soldiers downstream along the coulee used by Gall (Deep Coulee). Calhoun's men dismounted to hold the Indians in check, and Keogh's dead showed he did the same farther on. Custer proceeded on to the knoll on which he died. Then he had skirmishers dismount along the ridge running from the knoll toward the river and possibly placed some of Smith's troop on the higher ground toward Keogh. The skirmishers toward the river were evidently told to turn their horses loose, for there were no dead animals along that portion of the line. The position Custer established was the best obtainable. The line along the ridge from his position down to the river showed more care taken in placing the men than on any other part of the field, including Reno's positions.

It appeared that Calhoun's men died almost entirely as placed on the left of the line and almost all of Keogh's men died where they were placed in the middle, but Smith's may have broken from their position when the end was near and tried to escape in the deep coulee. The intervals of the dead skirmishers on the line toward the river were remarkably regular, indicating their deployment must have been closely supervised by an officer. "At the lower end of the line—toward the river—in a deep coulee, slightly to the front and right of the line of skirmishers a number of bodies, 28 I believe, were found."[296]

Although McClernand's speculation of Custer's route cannot be given more weight by itself than Maguire's, Roe's, or Freeman's, his suggested route is more sequentially logical, and it does match the eyewitness Indian accounts of Two Eagles, Lights, Hollow Horn Bear, Lone Bear, and others. The troops moved up from Medicine Tail ford to Calhoun Hill and along Battle Ridge to Custer Hill. The remainder were deployed down the ridge—the "low divide" between Cemetery Ravine and Deep Ravine—from Custer's knoll toward the river. They were attacked and died along the skirmish line at remarkably regular intervals. They died in a deep coulee.

Which coulee? McClernand was specific. From his viewpoint on or near Custer Hill he looked to the river. In front of him stretched bodies in skirmish order from the lower left on the Cemetery Ravine-Deep Ravine divide, diagonally across his field of vision, and to the nearer right under the slopes of Cemetery Hill. Where were the 28? "In a deep coulee, slightly to the front and right of the line of skirmishers."

To the *front and right!* Cemetery Ravine is to the front and right of this line. The slump and headcut area where Deep Ravine advocates would place the 28 bodies is to the left and even the rear of this line, not at all to the front and right. McClernand's description leaves no doubt. The 28 bodies were in a deep coulee, but to McClernand the deep coulee was Cemetery Ravine.

30. John Gibbon *Colonel, 7th Infantry*

Born in 1827 in Pennsylvania, John Gibbon was an experienced soldier by the time of the Sioux Campaign of 1876, having a distinguished Civil War record that included commanding the famous Iron Brigade as a brigadier general of volunteers and later commanding a division and a corps as a major general. Wounds he received at Fredericksburg and Gettysburg left him with a limp, causing the Indians to name him "No Hip Bone." In 1876 he lead the Montana Column and recorded many of his experiences in a diary. His narrative was first published by *The American Catholic Quarterly Review* in 1877. Although the diary has been lost, his account has been reprinted and is considered one of the most authoritative and reliable.[297]

When the wounded were gathered and the burials completed late on June 28, the combined columns moved north. They had only progressed about four and a half miles when the lateness of the hour and the inad-

Col. John Gibbon, 7th Infantry. His soldiers came to the
relief of the 7th Cavalry survivors. U. S. Signal Corps
photo, c. 1875. —Little Bighorn Battlefield National Monument

equacies of the transport for the wounded forced a halt just below the
north end of the abandoned Indian camp.

Being engaged in numerous duties while the command was encamped
below Reno Hill, Gibbon did not have the opportunity to visit Custer's
field. Since the combined units were finally in motion and the new camp
was closer to the Custer area, Gibbon took the morning of the 29th to pay
it a visit. However, the exact route of Gibbon's approach is uncertain. He
spoke of two fords being near the camp. He crossed one and moved up
the right bank of the river, which there ran nearly due south. On his left
the valley opened into a grassy prairie. He rode upstream and came to a
point where the river cut the bluffs, skirted it on the north, and then
abruptly turned south. He found sloping hills separated by little valleys,

177

one of which before joining the river valley was cut into a gulch eight or ten feet deep and filled with brushwood. It seemed to be a natural outlet from the scene of the fight. Gibbon thought it was possible that men might have sought shelter in the gulch on their way to the river. He closely examined the gulch for bodies but found none at all.

Continuing up the valley, which then became an open grassy slope, he found one body, which was identified as correspondent Mark Kellogg. Beyond that point the ground rose more rapidly and was broken into several smaller valleys. Following one, he came to a rolling, not very broken space, still rising until it reached the culminating knoll now commonly called Custer Hill. There were numerous bodies and dead horses scattered along the southwestern slope. Gibbon continued up, bearing to the left or westward, until he reached the top.

Let us leave Gibbon's narrative at this point and attempt to determine his route. By which ravine did he make his way up to Custer Hill? The gulch, cutbanks, brush, general direction of travel, rising valley opening out into grassy slopes, and the left turn seem to indicate he crossed the river at the Deep Ravine ford. Also, other accounts report that Mark Kellogg was found near the junction of the north and south forks of Deep Ravine.[298]

Confusion comes in the early stages when Gibbon mentions crossing the ford and moving up the right bank where the river runs nearly due south. There are and were some hairpin turns in the Little Bighorn near the Deep Ravine crossing that could have fit Gibbon's description, but they would have called for a longer, tortuous approach to the ford.

In a recent study by Michael Moore and Michael Donahue using the same account, it has been argued just as convincingly that Gibbon's approach to the field was more direct. He crossed at a ford farther north, downstream of the Deep Ravine ford, in a loop of the river near some present Park Service buildings at the northwest corner of the monument grounds. His northern crossing may have used the same ford that Custer possibly searched for, had he followed the route credited to him by some Indian witnesses.[299] Gibbon crossed at that northern ford, said Moore and Donahue, where he would have been at a point on the right bank where the river ran nearly due south. He then went up a cutbank in the bluffs and found Kellogg's body in a ravine just west of the present cemetery grounds. He continued to an open, grassy spot (probably near today's cemetery and museum area), then turned left or west to Custer Hill.[300]

Which ford did Gibbon use? Assuming a Deep Ravine approach, we have a problem with the statement that he moved up the right bank where the river flowed south. Assuming a northern ford crossing, we can eliminate the right-bank, south-flow inconsistency, but we create a new problem. If Gibbon approached up a ravine west of the present cemetery, turning left or west upon nearing Custer Hill would send him back in the same direction he had just come from. There are inconsistencies in both interpretations. Yet for our study, there is very much insight to be gained.

Whether Gibbon crossed at the mouth of Deep Ravine and ascended it to Custer Hill, or whether he made a crossing at the northern ford and ascended a ravine that cut into the cemetery ground from the west, there is one salient point that emerges: he *did not see any* number of bodies or graves on either approach! Besides the probable identification of Mark Kellogg, there were no 28 bodies, no dozen bodies, no handful of bodies. Were they already buried and covered up? No—Gibbon had seen them easily enough on the southwest slope of Custer Hill. They were "thickly lying in all conceivable positions, and dotted about on the ground in all directions . . . little mounds of freshly turned earth." But there was no significant number of bodies or graves in the northern ravine or in Deep Ravine. Where were they?

Let us return to Gibbon's narrative. However he got there, he stood atop Custer Hill. Before leaving that prominent point he would look around. He looked down a long, level ridge (Battle Ridge) and noted both graves and dead horses along the slopes, stretching into the distance. Far

Aerial view of Deep Ravine, c. 1990. —Don Schwarck Collection, S. Lyon, Michigan

beyond the end of this ridge rose a peak (Weir Point) that hid from his sight the bluffs where Reno was besieged.

> Turning now to the right and facing the river, the ground is seen to be broken up into rolling hills and valleys, the sides formed of gentle slopes, but now and then where these valleys approach the river their bottoms are washed into gulches sometimes ten or fifteen feet deep. One is especially noted, to the right and front, running in a direction nearly perpendicular to the river, and at the bottom of this one were found some forty or fifty bodies. The general surface of the ground does not slope off toward the river, but continues high up to the bank and above it; here and there the eye catches sight of the tops of the trees bordering the stream, and, beyond, the site of the Indian village.[301]

Gibbon's description is a perfect illustration of Cemetery Ravine! The valley with gentle slopes to the right and front, perpendicular to the river, the general ground surface continuing high up to its abrupt edge at the river, and the treetops visible above the high bank all fit flawlessly. It appears almost certain which ravine Gibbon saw 40 or 50 bodies in. Deep Ravine does not match what Gibbon described from Custer Hill. It is to the left, it reaches the river in three or four major turns, it does not have gentle slopes, and it does not continue to a high, abrupt edge at the river. Gibbon's description of Cemetery Ravine shows he truly observed and accurately noted its character, including its western edge, the resemblance being not unlike a wooden cutting board with errant, irregular knife gouges along the outer edge. There is little doubt. Gibbon saw the bodies in Cemetery Ravine.

THE REBURIALS AND POST-BATTLE ACCOUNTS

In the 14 years between the 1876 battle and the placing of the marble tombstones in 1890, Custer's field was seen by hundreds of people. During the summer of 1877, an expedition headed by Lt. Col. Michael V. Sheridan visited the grounds to exhume the officers' bodies and remove them to stateside cemeteries. Soon after, Gen. Philip Sheridan paid the place a visit while on an inspection tour. In 1878, Col. Nelson A. Miles and a battalion of mounted 5th Infantry rode to the field. In 1879, Capt. George K. Sanderson of the 11th Infantry went to the field for more reburials and tidying up. In 1881, Lt. Charles Roe with his 2nd Cavalrymen went to the field to collect all the remaining unburied bones and place them in one pit at the base of the granite monument he had erected. In 1890, Capt. Owen J. Sweet of the 25th Infantry took marble headstones to the field to place at the position of every fallen soldier. In between, many more visits occurred, official and otherwise. Many of those people left accounts of their observations. Though they walked the field after the soldiers' bodies were nothing but bleaching bones, what they had to say is revealing in our search for the actual valley of death for the Gray Horse Troop.

31. Michael V. Sheridan   *Lieutenant Colonel, Co. L, 7th Cavalry*

Brother and aide-de-camp of Gen. Philip Henry Sheridan, Michael Sheridan was instructed to go to the Little Bighorn battlefield and take care of two orders of business. Distressing reports about the shocking condition of Custer's field had been circulating in eastern newspapers for some months after the fight. Michael Sheridan was to collect and return to civilization the remains of all the fallen officers and to tidy up and rebury the bodies of the enlisted men.

Sheridan moved up the Yellowstone and Bighorn to Post Number Two, then under construction by soldiers of the 11th Infantry under Lt. Col. George P. Buell and soon to be renamed Fort Custer.[302] There, at the junction of the Bighorn and Little Bighorn Rivers, pine coffins for Custer and his officers were built. The little expedition included Capt. Henry J. Nowlan, Lt. Hugh L. Scott, and 88 men of the rejuvenated Company I of the 7th Cavalry. The guides were George Herendeen, who had been at the Little Bighorn fight, and John Baronette. The interpreter was Thomas H. LeForge, with a detachment of eight Crow scouts including Curley, Half Yellow Face, and White Man Runs Him, also battle participants. No reporters were allowed with the column to cover the delicate operation. Sheridan reached the field on July 2, 1877.

In his report back to his brother the general on July 20, 1877, Sheridan said that he, Nowlan, and a small detachment of Crows had made an examination of the field by crossing to the east bank of the Little Bighorn at a ford where he assumed Custer had tried to cross (Medicine Tail), and that they followed the route shown on Maguire's map. About one-quarter mile back from the ford and upslope, they began finding graves all the way from there to Custer Hill. On that last knoll were the remains of about 60 men. From that hill they pursued the route shown on the map in the direction of the river, a path "still plainly marked by the line of dead."[303]

Sheridan had heard rumors that some men had escaped from the battlefield the previous year only to be killed some three or four miles away. He sent the scouts and Indians in a ten-mile circuit in the hope of finding their remains. The search was followed up the next day by a more comprehensive one, and on the third day another was sent under Captain Nowlan with most of his company and all the Crows and scouts. One writer questioned Sheridan's motives in sending out these parties to search for possible escapees. He believed it was a wild goose chase, done for no other reason than to be rid of too many inquisitive minds that might question the rather impossible task Sheridan had of actually identifying and placing the correct officers' bones in the correct pine boxes.

What was the result of the three-day search? There was no indication to show that any men had escaped from the battlefield. Sheridan had gathered his bones with the men of brawn while the men of brains were hunting nonexistent bodies.[304]

The officers had been found. All were removed with the exception of Lt. John J. Crittenden, whose family wished him to remain buried on the field of his death. The remains of Custer, Keogh, Yates, Smith, and the rest were identified with ease by Captain Nowlan, Sheridan claimed, because Nowlan assisted in the original burials, had a distinct recollection of the ground, and found all the numbered stakes at the head of each grave, which corresponded to the numbers on Maguire's map.

Meanwhile, other troopers of Company I skirmished the field to find all the graves of the enlisted men. They were all found, they were all recovered, and they were all marked with cedar stakes. After completion of the work, the command again thoroughly searched the area for any missing bodies. None were found. Late on July 4 they returned to Post Number Two.[305]

Sheridan was interviewed by the *Chicago Times* when he returned to that city. The story appeared in the July 15, 1877, edition of the paper. On July 2, Sheridan said, 50 men crossed the field looking for graves. Each carried willow sticks to mark the sites as they came upon them. "All the graves of both men and officers were discovered without difficulty." In the evening the men made three-foot cedar stakes, and on July 3 a fatigue party exhumed or reinterred all the officers and soldiers, marking every grave with a stake driven two feet into the ground. "There were large and small trenches. Some contained but few remains. Others contained long rows of separate sets of bones, indicating that as many as a dozen had been buried together. Where a little band had fought together, and had fallen side by side or in a heap, they had received burial in about the same order in which they fell." After a few hours' work the dirt had been removed from 200 graves "and the remains re-interred in the same trenches," but more decently this time, with three feet of earth mounded and packed on each and the head marked by a cedar stake.[306]

Appearing at the Palmer House in Chicago for the Reno Court of Inquiry in 1879, Michael Sheridan made some comments about Medicine Tail being a good ford and that perhaps 25 men positioned above its banks could have covered the ford from a fairly large force of advancing Indians. He acknowledged that troops killed in a charge would be more scattered than those killed while resisting (a point to be considered in assessing the validity of the South Skirmish Line with its regularity of bodies). Sheridan produced a sketched map of Custer's field that he said was made by Captain Nowlan. It showed positions where some of the officers' bodies were found. He testified that the positions the bodies were found in were the positions they were buried in.[307]

Do any of Sheridan's statements give an indication of bodies being in Cemetery Ravine or Deep Ravine? In his official report he said there was a line, plainly marked by the dead, from Custer Hill down toward the river, and all graves were found and marked with cedar stakes. In the *Times* account Sheridan said there were some large trenches with up to a dozen men buried together, some side by side, some in a heap. They were all buried about where they fell, in the same trenches they were found in, and they were all marked with a cedar stake. Men in trenches, by the dozen, some in heaps, plainly visible in a line toward the river, and marked! Of course, we have heard the story of a dozen or more men heaped together before. Are these men buried side by side the missing 28?

Sheridan said he found all the graves. He said he re-covered all the graves in the *same places* they were found. He said he marked all the graves with three-foot cedar stakes. But Sheridan pounded no cedar stakes in Deep Ravine. Had there been bodies there, they too would have been reburied and marked. No subsequent visitors to the field ever found cedar stakes in Deep Ravine. The plain line of graves, in trenches large and small, were found and staked. They were staked on Calhoun Hill, on Keogh's ridge, on Custer Hill, and in Cemetery Ravine. There was no necessity for stakes in Deep Ravine.

32. Philetus W. Norris

Fifty-six-year-old "Colonel" Norris of Detroit, Michigan, was on his way west in June 1877 to assume his duties as the newly appointed superintendent of Yellowstone Park. Norris was also a friend of Custer's scout Charley Reynolds, who died in Reno's fight in the valley. When Norris learned of Michael Sheridan's expedition to exhume the officers' bodies, he decided he would do the same for his onetime civilian friend. Norris was also a correspondent for the *New York Herald*. It was an opportune chance to get the scoop on a hot story of the exhumations.

Norris got a late start and found himself in a stern chase trying to catch Sheridan's party. Traveling up the Yellowstone on the steamer *General Meade* was agonizingly slow because of low water. At the Tongue River, Norris switched to horseback, but then the streams became nearly unfordable because of heavy rainfall. He reached Post Number Two only to learn that Sheridan was already at the battlefield and that reporters had been strictly barred. Norris disguised himself, crossed the Bighorn in a dugout canoe fashioned from a hollow log, and continued his journey just in time to find Sheridan on his return march from the field.[308]

Undaunted, Norris saw another old friend, Jack Baronette, a scout with Sheridan, and persuaded Jack to take him back to the battlefield. On July 5, Norris located Reynolds's remains: several small bones, some tufts of his auburn hair, and fragments of clothing. These few mortal relics were taken away for Christian burial.[309]

The next day Norris was back at Post Number Two, where he drafted a dispatch for the *Herald* datelined July 6. He outbluffed an orderly who appeared with orders for his arrest and then rode north across the Bighorn until his pony went lame. Norris continued on foot, only to be buffeted by a most incredible hailstorm that fell in sheets eight inches square, bursting like bombs and cutting like knives. A nearby Crow village lost hundreds of ponies in the storm.[310]

Norris's story first appeared in the July 15, 1877, edition of the *Herald*. After all his exertions, his reconstruction of the Sheridan expedition was still predominantly a secondhand version of things seen by Jack Baronette. Norris had also heard about many soldiers who died in a ravine. He thought they were trapped "in one of those deep and impassable washout coulees and slaughtered like a flock of sheep." Norris saw partially unearthed bodies, "the remains of General Custer and most of his friends . . . disfigured by the coyotes . . . and many, if not the most of the skulls there and throughout all the fields were smashed to fragments, mangled or missing. . . ."

The landscape was still a horror even after Sheridan's efforts. Norris and Baronette were able to locate many of the graves with a map provided by Fred Gerard, one of Reno's scouts. There was "a rude inscription at the head . . . but most of the soldiers, either singly or in groups, have a stake driven where they rest. They are not in graves, but lie with a sprinkling of earth upon each or in groups as they fell last year."[311]

Norris's conjecture about a ravine where many soldiers died does not allow for differentiation. However, his account is important because it emphasizes the fact that the graves, although perhaps graves in name only, were marked with stakes or headposts, just as Sheridan claimed. The death spots were found by Norris and would be found by others.

33. Henry J. Nowlan *Captain, Co. I, 7th Cavalry*

Born in 1837 on the island of Corfu, Nowlan graduated from Sandhurst, England's military academy, and served as an officer in the Crimean War before coming to the United States in 1862. He served in the Civil War in the 14th and 18th New York Cavalry and joined the 7th U.S. Cavalry in 1866.[312] Nowlan was the acting quartermaster with the 7th Cavalry in 1876 and accompanied General Terry on the march to the Little Bighorn. Nowlan was a good friend of fellow Irishman Myles Keogh. After Keogh died, Nowlan was given command of the decimated Company I with the job of rebuilding it. He went to Custer's field on June 27 with Bradley, DeRudio, Benteen, and the H Company detachment.

Lt. Henry J. Nowlan, Regimental Quartermaster, 7th Cavalry. He helped identify and map the positions of the dead on Custer's field. Photo by O. S. Goff, c. 1873. —Little Bighorn Battlefield National Monument

Captain Nowlan left no official report of his participation in the Sheridan expedition. His observations have to be gleaned in a more round-about manner. In a letter written to author Joseph Mills Hanson, Edward Godfrey indicated that Nowlan had told him that he (Nowlan) marked the grave of every officer with a stake driven into the ground. The name of the officer was written on a slip of paper, the paper was put into an empty cartridge shell, and the shell was driven into the top of the stake.

Nowlan then made a sketch of the ground to show the location of every grave.[313]

Nowlan's reticence, if that is what it was, to produce official commentary on Sheridan's activities provides an illuminating sidelight on the whole issue of the reburials. He may very well have left his observations for posterity in another manner.

No reporters were allowed to accompany Sheridan, Nowlan, and their men. Philetus Norris was perturbed by the ban. He knew not the origin of the order, but thought it was not from Washington or personal to himself. More likely it was "a desire of some parties to be unquestioned chroniclers of an event historically important, especially as to the genuineness of at least some of the remains purporting to have been removed from [for] pompous burial elsewhere."[314]

Which party wanted to be exclusive chronicler? The army had banned reporters. Yet in July and August, with barely enough time for Sheridan to return to headquarters, stories began appearing in newspapers such as the *Bismarck Tribune, Chicago Times,* and New York *Daily Graphic* to counter the concern raised by the *New York Herald'*s claims of unkempt graves, scattered bones, and battlefield horrors. The latest columns would gladden the hearts at the Chicago headquarters of the Division of the Missouri. The exposed bones, mixed graves, and plunderings were downplayed. Instead, every officer's grave was said to have been unmistakably identified. Accounts to the contrary were called cruel and untrue fabrications, guilty of disrespect to Custer's dead and indifferent to the feelings of the relatives.[315]

In August, Mike Sheridan wrote directly to Custer's widow, Elizabeth. No reporter connected with the *New York Herald* went with his party, he claimed, and any stories coming off the *Herald'*s presses were untrue. He and Nowlan identified every grave of every officer without the slightest difficulty.[316]

Was it true that no reporter accompanied Sheridan? The July 28, 1877, copy of the *Army and Navy Journal* indicated that a correspondent of the Philadelphia *Telegraph,* a civilian not in the employ of the government, was allowed on the expedition. The correspondent was R. N. Price of Philadelphia, who had resigned from the army in 1872. He was allowed to go on behalf of the family of Lieutenant Hodgson, to take charge of his remains on their way back to Philadelphia. Price also wrote that the *Herald'*s claims of exposed bones and smashed skulls and the field appearing as a charnel house were erroneous. In fact, all the officers were found and their remains collected quite easily. The enlisted mens' remains were also carefully reburied in their graves. The country was scoured by Captain Nowlan east of the river and by Lieutenant Scott west of the river. No other remains were found.[317]

If Price countered the *Herald*'s story for the Philadelphia newspaper, who wrote the articles for the *Tribune, Times,* and *Daily Graphic*? The pen name "Wren" was affixed to only the *Daily Graphic* account, but the correspondent writing to counter Norris's battlefield descriptions also appeared to be an eyewitness. In each paper the writer used the same style, made the same claims, and the same errors. "Wren" argued that all the officers were found, unmistakably identified, and disinterred. All were carried out in pine coffins. The enlisted men were carefully reburied and their graves marked. Who had access to all that information? Apparently correspondent "Wren" was none other than Henry J. Nowlan.[318]

If, in fact, Captain Nowlan was dissuaded from producing official commentary on his activities with the Sheridan expedition, perhaps he still felt compelled to pass on information to the newspapers on his own initiative. Maybe Nowlan did talk to the press without the army's sanction. Yet since his views did closely echo those of Mike Sheridan, perhaps the army did surreptitiously bring along its own reporter.

What was seen by Price and Nowlan/"Wren"? The Sheridan party was to be congratulated on a job well done. Bodies were found, and officers were identified and exhumed for return to the States. Graves were remounded neatly. Cedar stakes or headboards were placed at every gravesite. There was no indication of finding, reburying, or marking graves in Deep Ravine.

34. Hugh L. Scott   *2nd Lieutenant, Co. I, 7th Cavalry*

In July 1877, Hugh Scott had been with the 7th Cavalry less than one year. He had missed the Battle of the Little Bighorn by a few months, being assigned shortly after his graduation from West Point. It was the beginning of a distinguished career that would span four decades and see him retire as a major general. Scott recorded in his memoirs, published in 1928, that he traveled to the field with Capt. Henry Nowlan and the rebuilt Company I. They were part of 11 companies of the 7th Cavalry that went west that spring on what Scott called "the annual expedition." Scott met Mike Sheridan near the confluence of the Bighorn and Little Bighorn Rivers. Nowlan was a very close friend of Capt. Myles Keogh, who was killed with Custer the previous year. Both men were most fond of the government horse Paddy, which was along on the expedition. Paddy, not Comanche, was Keogh's favorite horse. When Paddy became tangled in his lariat while swimming the Bighorn and was swept against a cutbank in water 20 feet deep, there was no one who could swim or would volunteer to extricate him. Scott had to go to the rescue.[319]

After continuing 15 miles to the battlefield, Scott said they arrived on June 25, exactly one year after the fight. Although he had not been at the battle, he reported that in 1876 the valley was thick with dust from a drought; in 1877, flowers were in abundance and luxurious grasses grew as high as the horses' stirrups. Scott said that Nowlan had a chart that he had made the year before (when he was quartermaster for General Terry) on which he had marked where each officer was buried. Five-foot pieces of lodgepole were staked at each grave and marked with numbers that allowed for easy identification. While Nowlan and Sheridan worked, Scott kept camp, but later he went out with his own detachment to bury any bodies he could find. He found little time to dig deep graves, so he covered the bodies as best he could, "but the soil was like sugar and I have no doubt the first rain liquefied it and exposed the bones later." They had neither the force nor the time to rebury the entire command in deep graves, so they packed up and left the next day.[320]

Scott's times were at variance with Sheridan's. He indicated spending June 25 and 26 on the field, while Sheridan claimed July 2 to 4. In any event, Scott made no mention of discovering or reburying bodies in any specific ravine. We do know the hasty reburials and the condition of the soil as Scott described it would set the stage for those ubiquitous bones to pop out again, and very soon.

35. Michael C. Caddle   *Sergeant, Co. I, 7th Cavalry*

Sergeant Caddle was a member of Keogh's ill-fated company but was spared by his assignment to remain with the 7th Cavalry's property at the Powder River camp and by his service on the steamer *Far West*. Company I was later reorganized with a few old survivors and many new recruits. Caddle was with Nowlan on the Michael Sheridan expedition and was of much assistance in identifying the dead in July 1877.

Caddle told his story in personal letters to his friend Capt. Grant Marsh, onetime skipper of the *Far West* and other riverboats plying the Missouri. Caddle said that he reached the area in July and "camped on the field for about ten days, interring the bones." He said all the officers, except two who were never found, were placed in coffins. Unfortunately, the grave marked "Number One" on the list, supposedly George Custer's, had some remains lying on a blouse marked with the name of a corporal on the inside pocket. It was disconcerting. They searched around and found another grave. "I think," Caddle said, "we got the right body the second time."

Caddle claimed he could identify most of his former comrades by their clothes or other distinguishing marks. All the men he saw were lying in skirmish order about nine feet apart. Each grave was marked with a wooden headboard on which was painted the name and rank of the dead, if known. A large marker was erected on the spot where Custer supposedly fell.[321]

Caddle did not specify whether he saw bodies or graves in Cemetery Ravine or Deep Ravine. However, he did see what apparently had been well-spaced skirmish orders, which leads one away from a Deep Ravine locale. Yet we cannot with certainty place his account in either category.

What is most instructive in Caddle's recollections is his statement that each grave, known and unknown, was marked with a wooden headboard. He did the burying and marking, and, unless seriously misinterpreted in his letters to Grant Marsh, his statements should be considered accurate. We also find Sheridan saying the graves were marked with three-foot cedar stakes and Scott mentioning using five-foot lodgepoles. Whichever method or combination of methods was used, we have a definite indication that *all of the graves* were marked, officers and enlisted men. Subsequent visitors should have been able to find these death spots easily enough, and they did. Yet, neither this expedition nor any to come was to comment on finding 20 to 30 graves, bodies, or markers specifically in Deep Ravine.

36. Thomas H. LeForge   *Scout, Private, 7th Infantry*

Tom LeForge was born in Portsmouth, Ohio, in 1850. His family moved to Missouri when he was two and then to the Montana goldfield region in 1864, where he spent most of the rest of his life. LeForge married into the Crow tribe and for many years lived with them, becoming, in effect, a "white Crow Indian." Dr. Thomas B. Marquis recorded LeForge's reminiscences in the early to mid-1920s and completed his story in 1928.

In 1876, LeForge was with Lt. James Bradley's Indian scout detachment as the Crow interpreter. When six Crow scouts and LeForge's friend Mitch Bouyer were transferred to Custer before the march up the Rosebud, LeForge was unable to accompany them. In a heavy downpour on June 9, LeForge's horse had thrown him and he had broken his collarbone.[322] Bradley refused his request to join the expedition. LeForge thought about the incident years later. Instead of joining Bouyer and Custer he went to the field hospital. "The remote result may be that I am alive instead of having been dead more than fifty years. Perhaps I should have been by the side of Mitch Bouyer when he was killed with Custer."[323]

LeForge went along as a guide for Sheridan and Nowlan in 1877. He had already been to Custer's field several times after the battle. The bones of Custer and his men were scattered about. Many ribs, limbs, and grinning skulls were on top of the ground or partially covered with dirt. A year of rain, drought, freezing, and thawing had combined to create a ghastly situation, and the mingled odors of decayed horses and humans still permeated the air.

Nowlan's soldiers brought with them seven pine boxes, LeForge declared. He watched not 10 feet away while they went through the disinterring and burial motions. LeForge was not impressed with the accuracy or completeness of collecting Custer's remains. They gathered nothing substantial except one thigh bone and a skull attached to part of the trunk. "Besides these, the quantity of cohering and transferable bodily substance was not enough to fill my hat."

On other visits to the battle area, LeForge spoke of finding soldiers' bodies and army articles scattered as far as 25 miles eastward on the Rosebud and many more within 10 to 15 miles of the field. They were the remains, LeForge thought, of what he understood to be 40 or 50 soldiers missing at the time of the original body counts on June 27 and 28, 1876.[324]

What can LeForge add to our examination of the Cemetery Ravine-Deep Ravine dichotomy? For one thing, he doesn't appear to be aware of any problems locating bodies in a ravine. They were found with ease. Somehow, however, the idea had taken shape that there were a number of soldiers that escaped from the fight, only to be killed miles from the field. Gibbon had made a similar statement in his *Catholic Quarterly* article. After describing 40 or 50 bodies in Cemetery Ravine, Gibbon turned his back to the river and looked east to the rough, broken badlands and speculated that there may have been 25 or 30 missing comrades lying dead in those far hills and gullies. Perhaps LeForge had been caught up in similar speculations. It must have been at a later date that LeForge found all those bodies he claimed to have found. If he knew of them in July of 1877, he certainly didn't show Sheridan where they were. In any case, the existence or nonexistence of soldiers' remains far from the field do not detract from LeForge's on-field observations. He watched Nowlan's men find, disinter, rebury, and mark all the remains. There were none missing or impossible to get to in any deep gully.

On the heels of Michael Sheridan's expedition to the Little Bighorn battlefield came his brother, Gen. Philip H. Sheridan. The general was accompanied by units of the 5th Cavalry. Included in the entourage was Gen. George Crook and his aides, Lt. Walter S. Schuyler and Lt. John G. Bourke of the 5th and 3rd Cavalry, respectively. James W. Forsyth, his brother George A. Forsyth, and Dr. Julius H. Patzki rode with the escort, Troop L of the 5th Cavalry under Lt. Charles Rockwell. The chief scout was Frank Grouard. They were later joined by companies A, B, and I of the 5th Cavalry under Maj. Verling K. Hart.

Phil Sheridan was disturbed by reports circulating in eastern newspapers about shoddy burials, exposed bones, and improper care of the dead. For these reasons he ordered his brother to the battlefield. While traveling through his department, Phil also decided to make a personal inspection of the battlefield. He traveled by rail to the Green River station of the Union Pacific, then his party struck north across the Wind River

Mountains, northeast along the Tongue River and through the Bighorn Mountains, then north along the Little Bighorn Valley. They reached the field on July 21, 1877.[325]

A few weeks before General Sheridan's arrival, the area was hit by one of the most terrific thunder and hailstorms ever seen in those parts. Tom LeForge remembered it as one of the most torturous experiences he had ever been through. The hail bludgeoned to death several horses, and LeForge only saved himself by using a horse as a shield.[326] It was the same storm that tormented Philetus Norris after his escape from arrest. The result of the storm was to thoroughly "liquefy" the battlefield soil, as Hugh Scott had predicted. The once freshly mounded graves Phil Sheridan's party saw now more resembled a charnel house. Phil Sheridan, in his report to the adjutant general of the army, was more sanguine. He said Maj. George Forsyth and a detail of 70 men had been sent to scout the country around the field to look for bodies and to bury them where found. On the main battlefield Phil found the graves relatively neat, and most, if not all, marked with headboards or stakes. He was inclined to think that most of the desecrations of the graves had been done by curiosity hunters in the shape of human coyotes.[327] He reported no specific information about Cemetery Ravine or Deep Ravine. Others did.

37. Christian Madsen   *Private, Co. K, 5th Cavalry*

Chris Madsen was a native of Denmark and a true soldier of fortune. He fought against the Prussians in the Schleswig-Holstein War of 1864, enlisted in the French Foreign Legion, and was taken prisoner at the Battle of Sedan during the Franco-Prussian War in 1870. Madsen came to the United States with the adventurous notion of wanting to fight Indians. He took part in the 5th Cavalry's fight at Warbonnet Creek in July 1876, seeing his first Indian up close when he witnessed "Buffalo Bill" Cody kill and scalp the Cheyenne Yellow Hand. Killing would later become a bit more routine to Madsen, as he went on to earn himself a place in the *Encyclopedia of Western Gunfighters* and become one of the celebrated marshalls of Oklahoma Territory with Bill Tilghman and Heck Thomas, together known as "the Three Guardsmen."[328]

The ways of frontier America were still relatively new to Madsen on August 5, 1876, when he visited the Little Bighorn battlefield. The place still smelled of death, and guns, bits of saddles, bridles, and war materials were still strewn about. Madsen found one body missed by Terry's and Gibbon's men and buried it. He had previously done some surveying and was approached by John F. Finerty of the *Chicago Times* to make a map of the field. It took three days to complete, but it somehow was lost.

Madsen returned to the field in July 1877, accompanying Phil Sheridan as an orderly. His story was recorded by Oklahoma historian Frederick S.

Barde in 1923. Corroborating Hugh Scott's observation, Madsen said the battle area was covered by grass so tall it was difficult to see a man riding in front of him. During their stay, however, a great storm struck, which Madsen called a tornado, that actually whipped the place "bare of vegetation." To his surprise the storm uncovered bodies in remote ravines, depressions, and sage thickets that had been overlooked by the previous burial party. He found skeletons still in faded uniforms that had been mauled and dragged about by the wolves. Insects that resembled winged ants half the length of a man's finger came out of the carcasses of the dead horses to torment them. Sheridan ordered them to rebury the bones.[329] Madsen did not specify the ravines he saw the exposed skeletons in. The storm was providential for our purposes, however: it laid bare the bones for others to see and make additional comment on.

38. Homer W. Wheeler   *2nd Lieutenant, Co. L, 5th Cavalry*

Homer Wheeler was born in Vermont in 1848. At the age of 10 he moved to Minnesota, where he saw his first Indian and became enthralled with frontier life. After spending some time back east, he moved to Kansas at age 19, getting a job at Fort Wallace in 1868. Wheeler was a sutler, a cattleman, and a volunteer scout. He gained such high regard among army officers and performed so well in the Sappa Creek fight in 1875 that he was offered a 2nd lieutenant's commission direct from civilian life. He accepted and joined Troop L of the 5th Cavalry in October 1875.

Wheeler served in the escort for Phil Sheridan on his trek across Wyoming to Fort Custer. In the Bighorn Mountains they managed to do a little relaxed hunting and fishing. Prior to reaching the Little Bighorn battlefield, Wheeler also experienced the severe hailstorm that devastated the whole valley, "washing out several of the bodies which had been buried near a ravine." Wheeler noted that the men had been buried where they fell and the graves were marked by stakes driven in at head and foot. They could be identified by empty cartridges containing a paper with the name of the fallen man placed at the head. Wheeler helped rebury all of the bodies that had been washed out.

Wheeler examined the field with Lt. John G. Bourke of the 3rd Cavalry. They saw no graves nearer than 50 to 75 yards to the river and concluded that Custer never crossed, but was driven back from there to where the last stand was made. There they located the spot where the Custers, Adjutant William W. Cooke, and Autie Reed were buried. Wheeler and Bourke cut off the hoofs of a dead horse they believed was George Custer's, a sorrel with three white fetlocks. Wheeler lost his set during the Nez Perce Campaign; Bourke had his pair made into inkstands. Wheeler said they went over the battlefield thoroughly.[330]

*George A. (Sandy) Forsyth. General Sheridan's aide-de-camp
when he visited the battlefield in 1877, he was already famous
for leading the defenders at the Beecher Island Battle in 1868.
Photo by D. F. Barry.* —Montana Historical Society

Wheeler found bodies washed out *near* a ravine. They were marked
with stakes. He reburied them. From his account alone we cannot single
out which particular ravine he spoke of. Yet, when read in conjunction
with the following accounts of George Forsyth and John Bourke, it will
become very evident which ravine Wheeler spoke of.

39. George A. Forsyth *Major, 9th Cavalry*

Born in 1837, "Sandy" Forsyth, aide-de-camp to Gen. Philip Sheridan, had already led an eventful life on the frontier. One of his exploits came from being selected by Sheridan to lead 50 frontiersmen on a scout against the hostile Cheyennes in September 1868. The resulting Battle of Beecher Island saw the death of Lt. Frederick H. Beecher and four others, the wounding of fifteen men, the near annihilation of the command, and the threatened amputation of one of Forsyth's bullet-shattered legs. After being besieged for nine days they were saved by a relief force from Fort Wallace. Among the rescue party was young Homer Wheeler.[331]

Forsyth recuperated and returned to service with the army. He accompanied Phil Sheridan's party to the Little Bighorn in 1877. His report was sent to the headquarters of the Military Division of the Missouri in April 1878.

With a detail of sixty men and three officers, Forsyth and Major Hart made a complete search of the battlefield on both sides of the river. They found the graves generally in good condition considering the extreme lightness of the soil and the absence of clay, gravel, or stones to give it substance. The soldiers' graves were grouped in four distinct clusters and were still reasonably well covered. However, "On the side of a ravine where a number of bodies had been buried, we found several skeletons that had been exposed by rains washing the side of the ravine, as it was as easily washed out as so much ashes." Seventeen skeletons were reburied, but Forsyth thought there would probably never be a time when the rains would not wash out and expose the bones.[332]

The four clusters of bodies Forsyth commented on are very likely the same four depicted by Dr. John S. Gray's modern map of the grave patterns on Custer's field drawn in the shape of a broad quadrilateral. The east side is Custer Ridge, the south side is Calhoun (Finley) Ridge, the west side is Greasy Grass Ridge, and the north side is the South Skirmish Line.[333]

Since three of these positions, all except the South Skirmish Line, are associated with ridgelines, we may be safe to assume that the ravine Forsyth saw skeletons in was in the South Skirmish Line cluster. But which ravine? The bodies were buried and washed out "on the side of a ravine." It was not indicated that this was a *deep* ravine, nor were the bodies buried in the *bottom* of it. They were buried in the *side* of a ravine. Can one seriously believe that the soldiers of 1876, exhausted, hurried, and without tools, turned the Deep Ravine into an outdoor mausoleum, with cryptlike excavations made in the sides and the bodies stacked and layered like those in the county morgue of a Hollywood movie? The soldiers admitted to no such exertions. In fact, they readily acknowledged just how cursory the burials were. The notion of side-burial excavations in the walls of Deep Ravine is, of course, preposterous.

Where could Forsyth have seen burials in the side of a ravine? The answer must be becoming obvious by now. Private Lynch saw bodies laid out on the sides of that ravine for burial. Forsyth saw the results that a great thunderstorm had on the bodies buried in that same ravine. It was a ravine that could accommodate a side burial on its gentle slopes without the horizontal tunneling that would be needed in Deep Ravine. It was Cemetery Ravine. The evidence will become abundantly clear with the next account.

40. John G. Bourke   *1st Lieutenant, Co. L, 3rd Cavalry*

John Gregory Bourke was born in Philadelphia, Pennsylvania, in 1846, the son of Irish immigrants. He attended a Jesuit school and a commercial college for a time, but the Civil War interrupted. He lied about his age and joined the 15th Pennsylvania Cavalry when he was only 16. Bourke won a Medal of Honor for gallantry at Stones River. After the war he attended West Point, graduated in 1869, and was commissioned in the 3rd Cavalry. He stood five feet ten and weighed 160 pounds. Bourke became aide-de-camp to General Crook in 1871, and for the next 15 years served with him as adviser, confidant, and press agent. Bourke was a well-known ethnologist and folklorist, one of the prominent American soldier-scientists of the waning years of the nineteenth century.[334]

As acting assistant adjutant general, Bourke accompanied Phil Sheridan and George Crook to the Little Bighorn battlefield in July 1877. On the 21st, while Maj. V. K. Hart's 5th Cavalry troops were reinterring exposed remains, Bourke had time to wander the field along with George Forsyth, Homer Wheeler, and others. Sheridan's comment that much of the battlefield owed its appearance to desecrations by human coyotes appears all too true, for his own people were engaged in souvenir hunting. We have already mentioned Lieutenants Bourke and Wheeler tramping around the Custer Hill area and cutting the hoofs off of a dead horse. Bourke and his confederates hunted all over the northern portion of the field, and Bourke recorded much with his prolific pen.

Lower down from Custer Hill, Bourke wrote, the graves were marked with stout saplings, the extremities cleft to hold fragments of paper with the names of the fallen. It appeared that after the butchery had nearly ended on the hill, about 30 or 40 men strove for the banks of the river, but were killed like wolves. Making their way along a ravine, Bourke and his companions stumbled on four skulls in one spot, a few farther on, more in some brush, and yet another beyond that. The corpses had been buried exactly where they fell the year before, but the rains had washed them out and it was hard to go 10 yards in any direction without stepping on skeletons. Pieces of coats, hats, and boots with human feet still sticking in them strewed the hill. Down the ravine from Capt. Tom Custer's grave was yet another, marked with a sapling. The paper in it, a leaf from a pocket diary, bore the name of Boston Custer. Also, "Sticking out from the ground in the ravine was the body of a man still clad in the rough garb of a scout, boots and bullet-ridden hat still by him; there was nothing to give the slightest idea as to who he might have been."[335]

Today, Bourke's ravine with 30 to 40 bodies down from Custer Hill can be identified. He, Madsen, Forsyth, Wheeler, and others saw the skeletons that had been washed out of its sides. Down from Tom Custer's grave they found Boston Custer's grave. Beyond that was the body of a man in the garb of a scout. Numerous accounts have placed Tom Custer's grave just down the southwest slope of Custer Hill. Lieutenants Godfrey and Edgerly established that Boston's body was found 100 to 200 yards down from there. Archaeological excavations have shown that the unidentified scout that Bourke examined down that same ravine from Boston was none other than Mitch Bouyer, the "man with the calf-skin vest." All along that ravine the bones of 30 or 40 bodies were strewn. All of Bourke's observations took place down a line in and along the sides of a ravine stretching about 350 yards down from Custer Hill. The Bouyer cluster represents the terminus of that line of bodies, now sometimes called the South Skirmish Line. The "headcut" area of Deep Ravine begins about 700 yards down from Custer Hill. Bourke never got that far. All of his recordings were of bodies he had seen in Cemetery Ravine.

41. Fred M. Hans *Scout*

Accompanying Gen. Philip Sheridan's party to the Little Bighorn battlefield was a young Nebraska farm boy, Fred Hans. Hans had come west to look for his younger brother, who was allegedly kidnapped, taken to the frontier, and sold to the Indians. Hans served from 1876 to 1879 as a courier and scout for General Crook and Col. Ranald S. Mackenzie. His employment gave him the opportunity to search the frontier for clues to the whereabouts of his brother. In fact, his appearance at the battlefield with Phil Sheridan was already his second visit of the season.

Hans set out from Red Cloud Agency in May 1877, worked his way northwest to the Belle Fourche and Powder Rivers, and eventually reached the site of old Fort Phil Kearny. He went down the Tongue, then west to the Rosebud, following it up and over the divide on much the same route as had the 7th Cavalry. On June 8, Hans reached the battlefield. He recorded his observations in his journal. The battleground

> is designated by a large rude monument, besides a great many graves of slaughtered soldiers. The graves seem to have been made quite shallow & have been dug out, by wolves, & Arms & Feet lay on the ground; some of the legs are still in the cavalry boots & contain some flesh, dried to the bones. Horses' bones are still thickly scattered over the little valley & hillside.

Looking over the posts that marked certain graves I found the names on the Head-Posts of Capts. G. W. Yates & T. W. Custer; First Lts. A. E. Smith; D. McIntosh & James Calhoun; besides the nicer headstone marked "Gen'l. Geo. A. Custer," & giving the date, June 25, 1876, of the great battle.[336]

Hans continued north to Post Number Two, traveled back southwest to the Yellowstone Park area, then southeast to Camp Brown, at the present site of Lander, Wyoming, where he met General Crook and the men gathering for Phil Sheridan's expedition.

On July 1, Hans began his return trip to the Little Bighorn. Of the second visit, he had less to say, recording, "July 19th. we left Tongue River going north down the Little Big Horn River; through Custer's Battle Ground & reached 'Post No. 2,' at Junction of the Big Horn, on July 22nd."[337]

Though recording nothing specific about the ravines, Hans noted the presence of a large, rude monument, indicating the 7th Cavalrymen left more than just a few haphazard stakes in the ground. Hans had no trouble finding the officer's graves, which were apparently well-marked and legible after one year's exposure. The misgivings of some researchers concerning Mike Sheridan's veracity in indicating the relative ease of identifying the graves is thus discounted by Hans.[338] He found them without any hint of a problem. Less than two months after Hans's first visit, both Sheridan expeditions had visited the field and continued the job the 7th Cavalry had begun by tidying up the graves and re-marking them with those ubiquitous cedar stakes that appear so often in the reburial narrations.

However, could those expeditions have specifically used cedar stakes? Probably not. Robert G. Rosenberg, a Wyoming historical consultant with a background in forestry and western history, indicates that true cedar trees simply do not grow in the Rocky Mountain West. What many people call cedars are in reality Rocky Mountain junipers, which are common throughout that region. They can grow 40 to 55 feet tall, but are more commonly 10 to 25 feet tall. This shrublike tree with blue berries and scaly leaves looks very much like cedar, and its wood is dull red and similar to cedar. Even today, Rosenberg declares, one can find juniper posts in abandoned and active fencerows throughout the area. The juniper posts are "ideal because they last forever and are readily available."[339]

That the Little Bighorn area is home to the juniper was attested to by Andrew Ward in an April 1992 article for *American Heritage* magazine. Ward walked Custer's approach route to the battlefield in a 1991 trek sponsored by the Custer Battlefield Historical & Museum Association, a jaunt that this writer also participated in. Ward, upon traversing the "Cedar Coulee" portion of the hike, commented that the tree-lined gully "is actually populated by junipers."[340]

If the "cedar stakes" used by the men marking the graves were really juniper stakes, they had chosen well. They used a tough, hardy wood that would last a very long time. Hans and the two Sheridan parties had no trouble finding the stakes, and subsequent visitors would also note their presence in identifying the graves.

42. Ami Frank Mulford   *Private, Co. M, 7th Cavalry*

A. F. Mulford was a "Custer Avenger," enlisting in September 1876, a few months after the news of the Little Bighorn disaster sent shock waves across the nation. Mulford was born in New York in 1854 and listed "clerk" as his occupation prior to enlistment. He stood five feet five and had blue eyes and light-brown hair. Mulford missed the Sioux Campaign of 1876, but he participated in the Nez Perce Campaign the next year. He was with the 7th Cavalry at the time of Chief Joseph's surrender. While on a scout, Mulford was thrown from the saddle and his horse fell on him, injuring his spine. A mere sore back at first, it soon turned into paralysis. He was discharged for disability in December 1877, at the age of 23.

Mulford's memoirs appeared a year later. He wrote that in August 1877, as a trumpeter in Company M, he went from the camp on Tongue River to the Little Bighorn on a combination scout and escort detail for some officers who wanted to see the battlefield. They camped on a depressed tableland near the ford about halfway through the abandoned Indian village. They were plagued by cold, wet, hunger, and hundreds of lizards that tried to share their wet blankets with them. The next morning they passed over Custer's field.

The bones, Mulford wrote, were still bleaching on the ground. Going upslope about one-quarter mile from the ford, a well-traveled trail led to the summit. At that point a ravine with gentle sides, one-half mile in length, could be seen trailing off. "Nearby are the uncovered remains of eighteen men, in six piles, with a piece of tepee pole sticking in the ground at each pile." On one pole hung a white sombrero with two bullet holes in it. A heavy trail ran along the crest of the divide that separated the river from the ravine, and it too was strewn with whitened bones. Three hundred yards up the trail they came to where Custer made his stand. The elevation at the terminus of the divide was a commanding position. There were only the skeletons of four horses and men on Custer Hill.[341]

Which ravine did Mulford speak of? It is evident from his description that he went up from Medicine Tail ford to Calhoun Hill, using a trail that had become well trod, then along the crest of Battle Ridge to Custer Hill. The ravine he saw was the gully on the north side of the Battle Ridge divide, Keogh's area. It doesn't appear that Mulford described either Cemetery Ravine or Deep Ravine.

Did Trumpeter Mulford, in fact, see any of the battlefield at all? It turns out that Mulford's narrative is almost a verbatim copy of a story that appeared in the *New York Sun* on August 21, 1877. The unidentified *Sun* reporter was on the field about the same time as Phil Sheridan, for he spoke of the four companies of cavalry under Major Hart encamped on the plains at his feet, apparently prior to their burial efforts. The correspondent complained they had done nothing but picnic in the vicinity for weeks, guarding only themselves and making no effort to cover up their comrades' bones.

The *Sun*'s man continued with a battlefield description, a near duplication of what Mulford was to say. However, where Mulford stopped his field description with the four skeletons on Custer Hill, the reporter continued. "Upon the slope toward the river I counted twenty-eight heaps of bones, and the skeletons of fourteen horses." The graves were huddled together without order and were located where the men fell. Back along the "canyon" were more heaps of bones, along with a pine cross for "Col. Keogh," a tablet for "Wild I Co. 7th," and at the head of the canyon a cross-shaped monument for "J. J. Crittenden, Lieut. 20th Inf." Scores of tepee poles marked the other graves.[342]

Who was the real surveyor of the scene? Most likely it was the *Sun* reporter.[343] The correspondent still saw bones all across the field. It would have been after the time Mike Sheridan's men covered them up and after they had been washed out again by the great storm of July 6, but before Hart and Forsyth policed the field. Mulford claimed he was on the field in August, which was after Phil Sheridan had left. The field would have been relatively "clean" again for Mulford's visit. And of course, the newspaper story came out one year before Mulford's memoirs.

Nevertheless, whoever walked the grounds that July or August easily found the graves well-marked with tepee poles or tablets or crosses. The *Sun*'s man even noted 28 heaps of bones downslope from Custer Hill toward the river. They weren't in any particularly deep gully in his perspective. The "canyon" where Keogh fell was apparently more prominent. Twenty-eight heaps of bones down the slope from Custer and not in any terrain worthy of the adjective "deep"—the description points to Cemetery Ravine, but is not definite enough to categorize.

43. Dr. William A. Allen

Dr. Allen was the leader of a wagon train that rolled past the Little Bighorn battlefield in August 1877. It left the Black Hills with 150 immigrants and prospectors, headed for the Bighorn Mountains and points west. Traveling up the Belle Fourche River, Allen's train crossed the divide to the Powder River near Pumpkin Buttes and then went up the Bozeman

Col. Nelson A.
Miles, 5th Infantry.
A colonel when he
visited the battlefield
in 1878, Miles was a
general when D. F.
Barry took this photo
in 1885.
—Little Bighorn
Battlefield National
Monument

Trail to the ruins of Fort Phil Kearny. Some wagons left to prospect in the Bighorns and the rest continued north to Post Number Two.[344]

Allen's adventures were published in 1903. He wrote that his party crossed the Little Bighorn to the battlefield on the morning of August 18. Each soldier was found where he had fallen, and Allen thought the troop movements could be read as from a page in an open book. The Indians must have poured across the river, filing up a gulch Allen called "Dry Creek" and up another nearby coulee to form a "deadline" surrounding the troops. The soldiers must have come downhill, where they were attacked. The survivors tried to regain the hill and escape by the route through which they had entered the "death valley." There lay the bodies of 50 or 60 men and horses. Allen walked to the hill where Custer met his death, the center of a fight where 40 more men and horses succumbed. He found a cross with Custer's name on a slip of paper. He also saw the graves of Keogh, Wild, Crittenden, and Boston Custer. Allen returned to the wagons sick at heart, but spent a restful night and decided to pass another day on the field to see all he might have missed.

Early on the 19th, Allen determined he would make a complete circuit of the "deadline" occupied by the Indians. Along the positions he called Dry Creek and the coulee, Allen and other members of the party "found thousands of cartridge shells lying in piles, each pile showing clearly where each warrior was situated." After they examined the Indian positions they returned to the soldiers' lines, which seemed to make a "triangle of dead men," showing the troops made three distinct movements before all being killed. The graves were built up with small amounts of earth, and sometimes the heads and feet protruded from the ends.[345]

What can be determined from Allen's story? He mentioned 50 or 60 men killed along the slopes as if trying to regain the position occupied by Custer. He found the Indian positions definitely demarcated by their cartridges in a dry creek and a coulee distinctly removed from the triangle of soldiers that they fired at. The triangular positions may very well be the South Skirmish Line and the lines on Battle Ridge and Calhoun Hill. Dry Creek and the coulee could very well be the Indian positions in Cemetery Ravine and Deep Ravine. The line of 50 to 60 men could be those stretched from Custer Hill across Cemetery Ravine and toward Deep Ravine. Allen's account, however, is still too ambiguous for definite categorization. One thing is certain: Allen saw no bodies in any deep ravine, for the ravines were the Indian positions.

44. Nelson A. Miles   *Colonel, 5th Infantry*

In 1878 an excursion to Custer's field was conducted to honor the wishes of Col. Samuel D. Sturgis, the commander of the 7th Cavalry. The colonel had lost his son, Lt. James Garland Sturgis, as he rode with E Troop in Custer's battalion two years earlier. The lieutenant's body was never found. The distraught Mrs. Sturgis firmly believed she could go to the field and learn more about the fate of her missing son. There was the possibility that young Jack had been captured, tortured, or maybe had been held captive. Out of respect for the family, Colonel Miles was authorized to take Mamie Sturgis to the battlefield, accompanied by a battalion of mounted 5th Infantry, scout William Jackson, Crow scout Curley, and about 25 prominent Sioux and Cheyenne Indians who had been at the

Lt. James Sturgis's bogus gravemarker set up in 1878 prior to his mother's visit. Photo by S. J. Morrow, 1879. —Little Bighorn Battlefield National Monument

fight and had surrendered to Miles in 1877. In June 1878 they proceeded from Cantonment Tongue up the Yellowstone and Bighorn to Fort Custer, and thence to the battlefield.

Many had been there before. Billy Jackson, a half-blood Blackfoot, had been in Reno's valley fight and was trapped in the timber when the soldiers retreated. He spent some anxious hours near Lieutenant DeRudio, hiding out from the searching Indians until he escaped to the hilltop. Early on June 27, Jackson claimed, he was given a message to take to General Terry. Riding north three miles from Reno's position, Jackson came upon Custer's field, and therefore affirmed he was the first man to look upon that horrible sight, ahead of Lieutenant Bradley by a few hours. The mutilations were too much for him, though, and he rode away to find Terry. Two years later he was back, he and the Indians doing their best to help Mrs. Sturgis (Jackson's recorder called her Mrs. Eustis) find her missing son.[346]

What Mrs. Sturgis found after a few days of searching amid the markers and bones was a cairn of stones with a board reading "Lt. Sturgis 7th Cav June 25, 76." It wasn't much, but perhaps she left finally convinced of the reality of her boy's death. In fact, just before she got to the field, a detail of soldiers had built and marked the cairn for her benefit. The cairn was supposedly torn down after she left, but the site with the mound and stake still visible was photographed by Stanley J. Morrow in 1879. In 1910 a marble marker for Lieutenant Sturgis was shipped to Oscar Wright, the battlefield superintendent. Wright, evidently using the terrain in the old photo as a reference point, set the marker where he thought it should be placed.[347] Today, Lieutenant Sturgis's gravestone, number 48, sits in Cemetery Ravine along the South Skirmish Line, an illegitimate marker. Although this may not be the exact spot Sturgis fell, it does not preclude the possibility that he may have fallen elsewhere on the line.

Miles visited Custer's field a second time that summer, while trying to establish a wagon and telegraph route west from Fort Keogh. Riding in Miles's entourage on that trip was his brother-in-law from Cleveland, Ohio, a 29-year-old budding capitalist and advisor to John D. Rockefeller, Colgate Hoyt. Hoyt's train arrived in Bismarck on August 1, and he reached Fort Keogh on the 14th. Six days after leaving the fort they camped on the site of the Indian village on the Little Bighorn. The next morning, Hoyt explored the battlefield. "It is a sad & lovely Spot and the bones of many a poor Soldier lie bleaching in the hot August sun (for they were never properly buried). . . . Glad to get away from a place bearing the works of so much suffering."[348]

Colonel Miles wrote his own recollections of the 1878 battlefield visits in a book published in 1897. He recorded that his party remained on the field for several days, examining the ground and trying to get an understanding of the Indian side of the fight. Miles measured the distance from Reno Hill to Custer Hill at four miles. He took cavalry horses between the two points and found the distance could be covered in 58 minutes at a walk and 15 minutes at a variable trot and gallop. The Indians were very cooperative and gave all the information they could about the battle of 1876.

From Miles's observations and the Indian reconstructions, he concluded that many Hunkpapa and Oglala that had crossed the river to chase Reno had come down to the Custer fight on the right (east) bank of the Little Bighorn. The Minneconjou, Sans Arc, and Cheyenne, who were camped lower downstream, went down the left (west) bank or crossed directly into the ravines leading up to Battle Ridge and Custer Hill. The former groups fought mostly with the soldiers on the left on Calhoun Hill, the latter mainly with the soldiers on the right on the Custer Hill side. The right flank let go of their horses, which included many grays, and the Cheyennes captured some of them. Other gray horses on the right side of the line were killed by the soldiers to form barricades. When the fight was nearly over, about 40 men from the extreme right rose up and made a rush for the river.

> The Indians state that as these men rushed toward the timber they first started in the direction of a small ravine, but as the fire was so hot from the position the Cheyennes had taken up, they swerved toward the head of a neighboring ravine. But the Indians killed the last one before he reached the timber. The graves of these men to-day confirm this account of that part of the tragedy, and the fact there were no horses found along this line of bodies indicates that their version of it is correct, and that Custer and his command never went down that ravine.[349]

What can Miles's narrative tell us about soldiers dying in a ravine? The Gray Horse Troop was on the right of the line at or near Custer Hill. The men came downhill from there, toward the river, and dismounted. They first started in the direction of a small ravine, but the Indians occupied that ravine and their fire was so hot the troops were diverted to the head of a neighboring ravine. The maneuver failed. All the soldiers were killed.

In the first place, there could be no hidden Indians in Cemetery Ravine that soldiers could not have seen from near the summit of Custer Hill before they started their descent. One can look clear down to the river along that open lane. More likely, they headed toward Deep Ravine, the head of which begins as a "small ravine," where Indians *could* and *did* hide, and were diverted from that objective. Second, Miles saw the graves, and the graves confirmed the sequence of action. Had these events occurred in Deep Ravine, Miles would have pointed out that the graves *did not* confirm the action. Since the burial sites validated the Indians' version and since there were many graves strung along Cemetery Ravine, it is logical and obvious that the troopers were killed in Cemetery Ravine. It was clear to Miles that Custer's command never went down Deep Ravine.

45. George K. Sanderson *Captain, 11th Infantry*

Captain Sanderson led another reburial and cleanup expedition to the Little Bighorn battlefield in 1879. For some time there was confusion about the date of Sanderson's visit. Researcher Fred Dustin insisted that the detail had gone there in July 1877, just after Nowlan left and before Phil Sheridan arrived, making three reburials in that month alone. Sanderson dated his report April 5, 1879, but Dustin argued that was an error. He based his assertion on pictures that were taken by Stanley J. Morrow, the photographer that accompanied Sanderson. The photos, Dustin said, were taken in 1877. Subsequent examination has proven that Sanderson's and Morrow's visit was in April 1879, just as the report indicated.[350]

Sanderson and a company of the 11th Infantry went on their mission as a result of an October 29, 1878, order from General Terry's headquarters in St. Paul to Lt. Col. George P. Buell, the commander at Fort Custer. The directive stated that because of persistent reports in the papers about the poor condition of the graves of Custer's men, at earliest opportunity an inspection must be made of the field. If any remains were exposed they should be collected at the highest point of the ridge in the rear of where Custer was found. There they should be buried in a high pyramid of loose stone to protect them from depredations. The graves of the officers were already marked and should not be disturbed unless to make them more secure by piling stones upon them. The area for five or six miles around should be searched again for traces of the remains of any missing men, which should all be collected and returned to the main grave.[351]

The October 29 order was not received until November 18, too late in the season for action, and was not complied with until the following spring. The new commander of the post, Lt. Col. Albert G. Brackett of the 2nd Cavalry, dispatched Sanderson in the first week of April. Sanderson's report stated that he went to the battlefield as directed but was unable to obtain rock within five miles of the field and so built a mound out of cordwood. The center was filled with all of the horse bones he could find. In the middle of that mound he dug a grave and interred all the human bones he could find, which only amounted to parts of four or five bodies. The entire structure was 10 feet square and 11 feet high. It was built just in the rear of where Custer's body was found.

Sanderson's men did not disturb any remains, but remounded all the graves. At each grave they drove a stake where any of those previously placed had fallen. There weren't many human remains to be seen. Sanderson thought the large number of horse bones lying around probably gave rise to the adverse newspaper commentary. The ground around the field was searched for six miles in every direction, and no other remains were found. The field now looked perfectly clean, with all graves mounded and all animal bones removed.

Sanderson understood that each grave that had previously been identified carried an empty cartridge containing the fallen man's name on a slip of paper. He saw that Lieutenant Crittenden's grave was still well marked but thought that eventually it ought to have a stone marker. Sanderson suggested that in the future a stone wall be built around the cordwood mound or stone headstones be placed at each grave. Either would be a more enduring monument.[352]

What information pertinent to our examination can be derived from Captain Sanderson's report? The number of human bones scattered about

"The Place Where Custer Fell," photographed by John H. Fouch. Taken in July 1877, this was probably the first photo of Custer's battlefield. —James Brust

were very small in number. Sanderson and his men found the graves, remounded some, and restaked a few others. It was a tidying-up operation. There was no report of finding bodies or remounding or restaking graves in a deep ravine.

Sanderson's expedition was significant in the line of continuity it was establishing. From the first burials in 1876 to the maintenance in 1879, the graves, if not constructed as well as they could have been, at least were being accounted for and maintained.

Sanderson's expedition was also significant because accompanying it was Stanley J. Morrow, a photographer who learned his trade under Mathew Brady while serving as a soldier in the Union Army. Morrow established a studio in Yankton, Dakota Territory, in the early 1870s. He was given permission to accompany the Dakota Column, but a supply of chemicals failed to arrive and the 7th marched out of Fort Abraham Lincoln without him.[353] The delay of the shipment from Chicago was probably very fortunate for Morrow. Three years later he was at the battlefield, but as a live photographer, not as a handful of bleached bones that Sanderson set under a cordwood mound.

There is a question of who actually took the first photos of Custer's field. Research reveals the honor might belong to John H. Fouch, the first post photographer at Fort Keogh, who rode for a time with Philetus Norris

Horse bones on Custer Hill, photographed by S. J. Morrow in 1879. The absence of horse's hair indicates this photo was taken some time later than Fouch's shot. Note three groups of men working along the South Skirmish Line. —Little Bighorn Battlefield National Monument

The cordwood monument built by Captain Sanderson, under which he placed the horse bones that had littered the field. Photo by S. J. Morrow, 1879. —Little Bighorn Battlefield National Monument

on his hurried ride to reach Mike Sheridan in July 1877. Fouch may actually have photographed the area later that same month.[354]

If Fouch was indeed the battlefield's first photographer, Morrow's pictures still received all the publicity. They depicted many aspects of the battle area, including the Reno crossing, the Medicine Tail crossing, the Keogh and Crittenden markers, Sturgis's mock grave, the bone piles on Custer Hill, and the cordwood mound built by Sanderson.[355] It is informative to note some of Morrow's photos, especially those viewing down Custer Hill toward the river picturing horse bones in the foreground and several groups of men standing by the graves along Cemetery Ravine's South Skirmish Line.

As a counter to those reports that say there were few or no bodies found on that line, we must pose the question, What are those men in Morrow's photos doing, standing in groups along the South Skirmish Line where today sit the clusters of white marble monuments? They are inspecting or reburying and tidying up the graves of all the men that fell along that line, of course.

Did Morrow take any photos of bodies, bones, or men working in Deep Ravine? No. Why not? Bodies, bones, and death are an attraction for human beings. For whatever peculiar attribute or idiosyncrasy we possess, innate or learned, death holds an attraction for all of us, if not consciously, then subconsciously. Throughout history, a major preoccupation of humans has been death. It underlies virtually all our social institutions and sleeps at the root of human behavior. A fascination for it is ensconced deep within our psyche. On a more mundane level, death, destruction, and human suffering have been emphasized by the media for years, hundreds of years, from pictures of battlefield skeletons that sell newspapers to artfully disguised skulls that sell cigarettes and whiskey. Simply stated, death is a big seller.[356]

Morrow knew the moneymaking potential in scenes of destruction and in piles of bones and bodies. Battlefield photographs of Civil War

Captain Sanderson, on right, stands by Myles Keogh's gravemarker. Photo by S. J. Morrow, 1879.
—Little Bighorn Battlefield National Monument

scenes had proven immensely popular. Had Morrow heard the story of 28 men slaughtered in a deep gully? The mental image was sure to evoke recollections of Alexander Gardner's famous shots of broken, twisted bodies in similar terrain—the sunken road, the "Bloody Lane" of Antietam. When Gardner's photos were exhibited in Mathew Brady's gallery in New York, a great crowd was attracted to his doorway. Hushed groups of potential buyers stared at the album cards and examined the details of death as if under a strange spell. A *New York Times* reporter commented in the October 20, 1862, edition:

> Crowds of people are constantly going up the stairs; follow them, and you find them bending over photographic views of that fearful battle-field, taken immediately after the action. Of all objects of horror one would think the battle-field should stand preeminent, that it should bear away the palm of repulsiveness. But, on the contrary, there is a terrible fascination about it that draws one near these pictures, and makes him loath to leave them.[357]

The *New York Herald* reported fascination with the photographs, the horrifyingly explicit tortures that could be seen in the faces of the dead when a magnifying glass was used on them, and *Harper's Weekly* applauded the detail, veracity, and value of pictures of the dead. There was a definite, widespread desire to witness the dying.[358] Nearly 30 years after Antietam, another correspondent commented for the Washington *Star* that the last people to leave the field at Wounded Knee were the photographers. They worked from dawn to dusk to "photograph the battlefields while the dead were still lying thereon. Such chances are not numerous . . . at this date. They are desirable for the money that is in them. . . . It was hard work to supply the local demand for the pictures they took and for quite a while impossible to fill the orders that tumbled in from all parts of the country."[359]

Morrow then, had a superb opportunity to sell pictures to a nation that hadn't had a good war in a dozen years. He was well aware of the money and recognition he could have received from a "Bloody Lane" type series of photos. Why on earth didn't he do any picture taking in Deep Ravine? Simple: there was nothing sensational down there for him to waste a wet plate on.

46. Charles F. Roe *Lieutenant, 2nd Cavalry*

We have met Lieutenant Roe before. In 1876 he traversed the Little Bighorn battlefield as part of Colonel Gibbon's column, and his observations of that field have already been examined. Roe was to return in 1881, however, because of the recommendations made for a more enduring monument. Two years earlier the secretary of war had finally called for the establishment of a cemetery, and Custer's last battlefield became a national cemetery of the fourth class in August of 1879.

The Custer Memorial obelisk erected by Lieutenant Roe, photo c. 1883.
—Little Bighorn Battlefield National Monument

More befitting of a national cemetery than a cordwood pyramid, a granite monument was ordered, a three-sectioned obelisk that would stand over 11 feet tall and weigh more than 36,000 pounds. In the winter of 1881 the blocks arrived at Fort Custer, where 1st Lieutenant and Adjutant of the 2nd Cavalry Charles Roe supervised the construction of sledges to transport them across the snow and ice to the battlefield.

In July of that year, Roe, now accompanied by Lt. Alvarado Fuller and Troop C of the 2nd Cavalry, built an ash derrick crane and capstan on the hill to set the stones in position. He located the monument within six feet of where the remains of Custer were found. Ten feet from the base of the obelisk and surrounding it on all four sides he had a trench dug. "I took great pains in gathering together all the remains from the Custer Battle Field, Reno's Hill and the valley, giving it my personal attention and scouting very thoroughly over the whole ground and miles back, so that I feel confident all the remains are gathered together and placed at [the] base of [the] monument."

Roe also indicated in the report he filed on August 6, 1881, that "Whenever I found the remains of a man, I planted a stake, well in the

211

Wooden stakes seen from near the monument on Custer Hill, looking down Cemetery Ravine. Photo probably by D. F. Barry, c. 1883. —Little Bighorn Battlefield National Monument

ground, so that future visitors can see where the men actually fell." A trooper with Roe that summer, John Lewis, also verified the operation to Walter Mason Camp. Lewis assisted in burying the men around the base of the monument. "As the remains of each body was taken up a stake or piece of board was driven to indicate where a body had lain."[360]

In a letter to Camp on October 6, 1908, Roe wrote that he had found the bodies of 267 officers and men, plus about half that number of horses. He personally conducted the search by skirmish line of the entire field from the river back to the mountains. All of the bodies of the dead on the Custer and Reno fields were found and buried at the base of the monument.[361]

Roe granted a short interview to Walter Camp in 1910. He claimed his men did not grade the area of the ridge where they placed the monument because it was already level enough for their purposes. The cavalry marched "all the way to the mountain" looking for any other men who might have gotten away from the battlefield, but found nothing. Roe said none of the enlisted men's remains were gathered up and buried on the ridge in trenches around the monument until his detail did it in 1881.[362]

What can we learn from Roe's activities? With the exception of Crittenden's, the bones of all the men—officers, enlisted men, and civilians—were finally removed from the field and placed in a mass grave around the monument. Counting the bones of the brain case and facial pieces, a human body consists of 206 bones. We shall later learn that Roe did not find all of them. Nevertheless, the majority were removed. In their place Roe left stakes to show future visitors where they once lay. Again we have continuity. The original body locations were preserved for the men who came later bearing the white marble gravestones. And Roe, like Sheridan, Nowlan, Forsyth, Hart, and Sanderson before him, planted no stakes in Deep Ravine.

47. Owen J. Sweet *Captain, 25th Infantry*

Official reburial expeditions to specifically gather up 7th Cavalry remains ceased after Roe's 1881 interments. However, there were still other visitors in the ensuing years. In 1882, Maj. W. W. Sanders inspected the field and recommended that iron posts be supplied to replace the wooden stakes then marking the graves.

In 1889, bodies from the post cemetery at old Fort Phil Kearny were moved to the Custer site and reburied on the ridge just southeast of the monument by Capt. John H. French of the 25th Infantry. Accompanying French was guide James Campbell. Campbell had been at Fort Custer since 1878, had been to the battlefield many times, and appears to have taken over as the fort's chief scout when Thomas LeForge left in 1886. While French's men interred the bones from Fort Phil Kearny, Campbell and another party of men went through the markers on Custer's field, locating, tidying up, and re-marking graves. They also reburied parts of four bodies that Roe had missed. Scout Campbell also conducted Senator Beck of Kentucky over the field in 1889. Beck later introduced and obtained support for a bill appropriating funds to have the wooden stakes replaced with marble headstones.[363]

All the parties to Custer's field in the previous decade included personnel, soldiers, and scouts, who had either witnessed the original burials or accompanied others who had, and received the knowledge of those eyewitnesses. The physical evidence of the locations of the gravesites was preserved and kept alive in fact and in memory.[364]

Capt. Owen J. Sweet led men of Company D, 25th Infantry, to the field on May 1, 1890. Preceding him to mark out the cemetery boundaries were Lt. Samuel J. Burkhardt Jr., guide James Campbell, and a few enlisted men. Gen. James S. Brisbin, who was on the field as a lieutenant colonel of the 2nd Cavalry in 1876, assisted Sweet in compiling his studies and reports. These men were another link in a continuous chain of men and

Photo of the South Skirmish Line, looking north to Custer Hill, taken from the divide south of Deep Ravine, c. 1894. —Little Bighorn Battlefield National Monument

memories that were able to locate and mark the positions of the 7th Cavalry's dead.

Sweet brought 249 marble markers with him. Obviously, this was going to create a problem, for the body counts as given by Reno, Benteen, Godfrey, Bradley, Roe, and others ranged from 197 to 267. Sweet either had too many if using Bradley's 197, or too few if using Roe's 267. Evidently the Quartermaster Department believed the best evidence indicated that 249 was the most accurate accounting of the dead. John S. Gray argued that since about 203 men fell on Custer's field, the extra stones were certainly meant for Reno's dead. However, he wrote, Sweet still faced a dilemma. He could not locate the graves of Reno's men. On Reno's hilltop the graves were obliterated to keep their presence hidden from prying Indians and were never marked later. In the valley the land was now under pasture and crops. Neither the Reno hilltop nor the valley area had been purchased by the government. The graves couldn't be found, and they couldn't be marked on private property if they could be found.[365]

Were these "extra" stones meant for Reno's field? Sweet's official report indicated, "As my instructions covered the setting of only two stones on this field, no search or investigation was made to develop these evident facts. On the 11th inst. I proceeded to the Reno Fields and set the head-stones on the places where Lieut. McIntosh and Asst. Surgeon J. M. DeWolf, U.S. Army are supposed to have fallen."[366]

Sweet spent 12 days in the area. Not until the eleventh day did he place his last stones on Reno's field. The first 10 days he spent in diligent search on Custer's field. He first marked all the identified, named gravesites he could find. Then he searched for the unnamed stakes. Apparently he didn't use the three stones sent for Lieutenants Porter, Harrington, and Sturgis, and no stone was sent for Lieutenant Hodgson. Sweet reported, "On examination of the field, it was found that the resting places of only 217 officers and men had been marked." Sweet had to do some extra-hard searching to find other gravesites. "I found it necessary," he reported, "to institute, systematize and persevere in a daily skirmish line search over an area of about 2 sq. miles of the battlefield. This was carried out persistently, and with the most scrutinizing care." His efforts were rewarded, and the last of the bodies were found, buried, and marked, making "a total of 246 officers and men, over whom headstones were erected on the Custer Field."[367]

In 1912 and 1913, Sweet corresponded with Walter Camp and provided more details of the care taken in locating the grave mounds:

> We repeatedly and daily crossed and recrossed the field in every direction . . . searching every foot of ground for remains or parts of remains. Every foot of ground was examined and dug into where there was the slightest indication of remains and all such spots examined by an officer or N.C. officer to prevent error. In erecting the markers each grave was dug into to see enough of the skeleton to determine which was the head to thus be sure in placing the headstone at the head. If the head was not found at all then the search was continued to find the shoulders, etc., thereby [to] avoid placing markers at the feet. In the case of the officers, I found board markers with all the officer's names on them as in the case of the civilians who fell with Custer.[368]

The bodies along the South Skirmish Line were very real. Sweet wrote in his official report:

> From the head of Big Deep Cut Ravine, left flank of Troop "E," to the top of slight ridge near the center of Smith's line, 25 men fell, including Asst. Surgeon G. E. Lord, U.S. Army, whose headstone is set in a group of four, near the Big Deep Cut Ravine and the extreme left of Smith's line. . . . From the top of the ridge—Smith's centre, to within about 200 yds. of the Custer group, the right of Smith's line, 26 men fell, some of whom were from the left flank of Troop "F."[369]

Fifty-one bodies on that line were found and marked by Sweet. While most of the soldier positions on the field were thin and weak, he wrote, "only three stubborn and decisive stands were made, viz: Keough, [sic] with perhaps sixty odd men, Troop 'E,' and Troop 'F' in a ravine, over 50 men and Custer's final stand with about 50 men."[370]

From Sweet's original find of 217 marked bodies, his "persistent and scrutinizing search" paid off with the locating of remains where he could place all 246 of his markers. How did he do it?

To show an extreme case, one is that of Asst. Surgin [*sic*] G. E. Lord, U.S.A., whose headstone is set in a group of four near the Big Deep Cut Ravine. I found no mark to indicate where he fell in digging into the remains at this spot I found pieces of clothing, a Staff officer's button or two which Dr. Lord was known to wear, hence his headstone was erected.

Sweet also told Camp that upon visiting the field "you may have noticed more than one marker at a grave. In that case two or more bodies were buried there."[371] Here Sweet may have stretched the truth, for the archaeological digs of the 1980s consistently found these paired markers to indicate the remains of but one individual more often than not. His tentative marking of Lord's site may have been "an extreme case," but what it illustrates is that Sweet needed bodies. He was insistent that he and his men searched every nook and cranny of Custer's field. He found the remains of 51 bodies along the South Skirmish Line, and he definitely was aware of the "Big Deep Cut Ravine." Had he found even the slightest trace of remains in that gulch he would have undoubtedly breathed a great sigh of relief and gladly planted the appropriate markers in that ravine, precluding the need for such legerdemain as Lord's. But the captain and his diligent searchers made no mention of finding bodies in Deep Ravine.

48. Samuel J. Burkhardt Jr.   *Lieutenant, 25th Infantry*

Although Captain Sweet had charge of the operation, the lieutenant that accompanied him to the field in April of 1890 did most of the actual work. Interviewed by Walter Camp in 1913, Burkhardt stated that, indeed, bones could be found and identifying markers still could be recognized in 1890. Gravesites were found by excavation marks, stakes, and bone fragments. And, Burkhardt said, "They put no markers in Crazy Horse Ravine."[372]

What ravine did Burkhardt refer to? We have already mentioned the confusion caused by the term "Crazy Horse Ravine." We have seen that Pvt. George Glenn called Keogh's ravine "Crazy Horse Ravine," or perhaps Walter Camp misinterpreted his remarks. Burkhardt obviously wasn't calling Keogh's ravine "Crazy Horse," because he placed many stones there, about 90 of them in fact. Burkhardt's Crazy Horse Ravine was today's Deep Ravine. Neither he nor Sweet placed headstones there. Like the expeditions that came before them, they were guided by evidence—evidence of bones, markers, and memories. Ten long days spent searching the battlefield could produce no evidence of any graves having been in Deep Ravine.

Two hundred and forty-six marble headstones were set on Custer's field, where most evidence indicates just over 200 men fell. Were there too many gravemarkers and were they erroneously placed? Writers have speculated on misplaced markers for years, John Gray, Francis Taunton, Douglas Scott, Richard Fox, Richard Hardorff, Henry and Don Weibert, Kent King, Charles Kuhlman, and Walter Camp among others. Their solutions would be to remove or reshuffle the stones along the South Skirmish Line, Custer Hill, and Battle Ridge. Assuredly, some do need to be removed and placed on Reno's field. But which ones? Captain Sweet said he found evidence of 51 bodies along the upper and lower portions of the line coming down from Custer Hill. Lieutenant Burkhardt said that he had extra gravemarkers and put them on "Custer's Ridge."[373] Did he mean the battlefield in general, as Camp seemed to record, or did he mean Custer's (Battle) Ridge specifically? Certainly Burkhardt said physical evidence led him to place the stones where he did.

Thirteen years after Burkhardt said he could still see enough of the graves to correctly place the headstones, Walter Camp walked the field to see for himself. Although Camp was probably the single individual most responsible for spreading the "28 in a gully" story, and although he believed there were too many markers on the field, he did provide his own firsthand account of the validity of those very same markers. Camp wrote of his 1903 visit:

> As late as 27 years after the battle, the distinctiveness of the empty graves, at which markers were located and where but few bodies had been buried in a place, was unmistakable. In nearly every one of these or scattered about there were bones of human fingers and toes, fragments of skulls and other bony parts; and at that time I witnessed the finding of several military brass buttons by scratching over the dirt thrown aside from these shallow graves. During the next five years, or previous to the fall of 1908, I noticed that the little hollows where bodies had lain had been filled up, the dirt had been carefully leveled down at these places and all trace of the burials had been obliterated.[374]

Camp also commented on Sergeant Roy's statements regarding the number of dead cavalry horses that the men of Company A buried between Custer and the ravine. "I myself also saw the bones of a good many," Camp wrote. "This contradicts what some have said to prove that the men who left the ridge were all dismounted."[375] Even Camp had to acknowledge the likelihood that a mounted troop came down from Custer Hill to do battle along the South Line.

Camp still saw horse bones, human bones, and grave hollows on the field 27 or more years after the fight. It was not until about 1908 that he witnessed the final obliteration of the gravesites. There is little doubt that Burkhardt and Sweet had plenty of evidence to guide them a decade and a half earlier.

There is no mystery here. There were no stones for Company E placed in Deep Ravine because those who marked the graves could never find any physical evidence of bodies being in Deep Ravine. Yet there may be too many stones on "Custer Ridge" because that is what is indicated by Burkhardt's testimony as recorded by Walter Camp. Very few of the 44 stones of the South Skirmish Line that today string down from Custer Hill and trail through Cemetery Ravine need to be altered. They were once set for the men of Company E, a few civilians, several refugees from other companies, and Assistant Surgeon George E. Lord. With the exception of Lieutenant Sturgis's marker and the probable exception of Dr. Lord's, they are not phantom stones. They mark a position that was once a tangible, viable line of flesh and blood—Gray Horse Troopers that existed for a brief moment in time that hot afternoon of June 25, 1876.

After examining the white accounts of the Little Bighorn fight and the subsequent burials, we must realize that they possess no special claim to truth and accuracy. The historians who would use only white accounts of the battle would have no better success in gaining a complete picture of events than those who would rely only on Indian accounts. In fact, there may be more inconsistencies in the white stories. The very complaint that has been made against the Indians, that they only told what they saw in their immediate sphere, turns out to be a blessing in disguise. Praise for the white men for their supposed greater ability to assume, assimilate, and generalize unseen occurrences, may, in fact, be a hindrance. Their propensity to speculate on Custer's movements has gotten them (or rather those who would try to draw conclusions from those speculations) in trouble. False impressions are their legacy. Had they simply reported only what they saw, the conclusions could have been drawn more easily by later researchers.

We have seen that suppositions of troop movements by McClernand, Roe, Maguire, and Freeman were all at odds with each other. All but McClernand had Company E traveling through one part or another of Deep Ravine *before* getting to Custer Hill, a scenario that we have shown offends logic and is contrary to every Indian account. By not giving credence to the Indian stories and by accepting soldier supposition as fact, we have gotten a reversed version of the gray horse movements entrenched in our literature, both fiction and history, and in our motion pictures. There have been over 45 movies made this century that concerned General Custer or the Battle of the Little Bighorn. The latest, *Son of the Morning Star,* aired as a TV mini-series in early 1991 and was praised as "by far the most accurate version of Little Bighorn ever filmed." It was said that even the purists would be enthralled by the attention to detail and the remarkable fidelity to the historical record.[376] Yet, in the final scenes, what did we see but the grays being repulsed at the river and then immediately going up a deep gulch, where they were ambushed and shot down as they scrambled up the sides. It is high time to correct this interpretation.

The only scenario to make sense naturally must be the one that the evidence points to. Company E came down from the ridge. They were attacked. Many were killed. Some fled back to Custer Hill. A few ran toward Deep Ravine and actually got there. The isolated refugee or two might expect to succeed in hiding amid the great confusion, the shouts, shooting, smoke, and chaos. Reno's three companies couldn't expect to hide in the timber on the bottoms and survive, but a few scattered individuals were able to do just that. Likewise, the deep ravine several hundred yards below Custer Hill must have appeared to be a place of refuge to the last desperate survivors.

What about the statements by soldiers such as Goldin, who saw bodies in a cul-de-sac, or Moylan and Ryan, who saw fingerprints and scramble marks in the side of a deep gulch, or Hardy, who saw men lying on top of each other? Is this not evidence? We faced a similar situation with the question of whether or not Custer went to the river. The solution did not necessitate an either/or answer. Likewise with Deep Ravine. Goldin, Moylan, Ryan, and Hardy could very well have seen bodies in Deep Ravine. We will not discount their word, but we will not weigh their word more heavily than we will Hare's, or McClernand's, or Bourke's, or the word of a dozen others. In fact, if all the testimony were assigned equal weights, we would find the Cemetery Ravine side of the scale weighing nearly three times more than the Deep Ravine side. Even if some readers would feel more comfortable shifting a few more accounts to the Deep Ravine column, there would still be a Cemetery Ravine preponderance. But Moylan and Ryan and McDougall did not lie (we are not so sure about Goldin). They saw bodies in a deep ravine. As Dr. Gray surmised, the sensory impact of a broken body, perhaps clutching the dirt just inches below its own fingerprints, would very likely remain impressed in one's memory longer than numerous other bodies reposing in a line on the grass above.

We cannot deny there must have been a few bodies in Deep Ravine, but we cannot escape the fact that there were many more bodies in Cemetery Ravine. Bodies being found in one ravine does not preclude the possibility that there were others found in another ravine. Yet, there are reasons for Morrow taking no photographs in Deep Ravine, for Sheridan and Sanderson and Roe driving no stakes there, and for Sweet and Burkhardt setting no gravemarkers there. There was no attempt to deceive, no dastardly cover-up, no conspiracy. There simply was no great number of bodies in Deep Ravine to be concerned with. There were, however, plenty of bones to rebury and mark along the grassy slopes above. The weight of the testimony on paper and the physical relics themselves show that the great majority of bodies fell along the South Skirmish Line, in the upper watershed of Deep Ravine and in Cemetery Ravine.

Let us leave the story of the troop movement to the Indians. They saw it, and they did not tell the story that we see in the movies or read in most of the histories. The soldiers found and buried the bodies. Let us read their accounts and hear what they have to say without preconceived notions and automatic assumptions that any ravine mentioned with bodies in it, was, ipso facto, today's Deep Ravine. We have reexamined the accounts. It is time to discard Deep Ravine as the assumed resting place of 28 troopers of the 7th Cavalry.

SUMMARY OF WHITE ACCOUNTS

	Year Visited Field	Year Account Told, Written, Published	Ravine Indicated: (C) Cemetery, (D) Deep, (?) Uncertain
1. F. Benteen	1876, 1886	1879	C
2. G. Glenn	1876	1914	?
3. J. Martin	1876	1908	?
4. C. Windolph	1876	1946	?
5. C. DeRudio	1876	1879, 1910	C
6. S. Roy	1876	1909-12	C
7. M. Moylan	1876	1879	D
8. T. McDougall	1876, 1886	1879, 1909	D
9. W. Edgerly	1876, 1886	1879, 1881	C
10. J. Ryan	1876	1923	D
11. W. Slaper	1876	1920	?
12. G. Wallace	1876	1879	?
13. W. Hardy	1876	1910	D
14. E. Godfrey	1876, 1886	1879, 1892, 1896, 1918, 1921	?
15. L. Hare	1876	1879, 1910	C
16. T. Goldin	1876	1928-31	D
17. J. Adams	1876	c.1890	C
18. T. Coleman	1876	1876	C
19. F. Berwald	1876	1912	D
20. D. Lynch	1876	1908-09	C
21. D. Knipe	1876	1908, 1924	C
22. W. Clifford	1876	1876	?
23. H. Paulding	1876	1876	?
24. R. Thompson	1876	1911	?
25. E. Maguire	1876	1876, 1879	C
26. C. Roe	1876	1910	C
27. H. Freeman	1876	1876	D
28. C. Woodruff	1876, 1908	1912	?
29. E. McClernand	1876	1926	C
30. J. Gibbon	1876	1876	C
31. M. Sheridan	1877	1877, 1879	C
32. P. Norris	1877	1877	?
33. H. Nowlan	1877	1877	?
34. H. Scott	1877	1928	?
35. M. Caddle	1877	1909	?
36. T. LeForge	1876, 1877	1928	?
37. C. Madsen	1876, 1877	1923	?
38. H. Wheeler	1877	1925	?
39. G. Forsyth	1877	1877	C
40. J. Bourke	1877	1877	C
41. F. Hans	1877	1877	?
42. A. Mulford	1877	1877, 1879	?
43. W. Allen	1877	1903	?
44. N. Miles	1878	1897	C
45. G. Sanderson	1879	1879	C
46. C. Roe	1881	1881	C
47. O. Sweet	1890	1890	C
48. S. Burkhardt	1890	1913	?

Totals Cemetery: 20, Deep: 7, Uncertain: 21

5. The 1989 Dig, a Few Maps, and the South Skirmish Line

New Discoveries

After an investigation of the historical accounts, it becomes obvious that we will have to reassess the idea that a significant number of men died in Deep Ravine. What was unearthed during the archaeological dig of 1984-85, or more accurately what *wasn't* unearthed, combined with the reports, narratives, diaries, and interviews, is very convincing. Yet, the archaeologists, anthropologists, historians, National Park Service employees, and volunteers weren't through. The 1984-85 dig was hardly over before plans were being formulated to complete some unfinished business.

Metal detector sweeps in 1985 had discovered an equipment dump site at the Reno-Benteen battlefield. Here was another potential opportunity to collect information on behavior patterns, dress, and equipage in the ongoing business of attempting to understand exactly what happened on the Little Bighorn that day in 1876. The main emphasis of the 1989 dig would be on the Reno-Benteen field, but no one could resist just one more attempt at solving the Deep Ravine mystery.

Although the Reno-Benteen dig is not directly related to this study, it did provide data useful for a better understanding of the geological processes that occurred in Deep Ravine. The dump site on Reno's field consisted of discarded equipment that was either damaged or unneeded after the Reno Hill position was abandoned. The unwanted articles were broken up and burned at a site downhill, west and south of Benteen's southern lines on June 25-26 and just above what came to be known as Water Carrier Ravine. The dump site was estimated at 300 to 400 square yards in area. A grid system was set up and horizontal block excavations were used, much as in the gravemarker digs on Custer's field.

This dig demonstrated that the dump site probably began as a single debris pile, with concentrations highest in the center and decreasing toward the outer edges. As such it would not be greatly dissimilar to the mass of 28 bodies that the historical record supposedly indicated were piled up in Deep Ravine.

The dump yielded 1,936 artifacts. Unlike on Custer's field, there were very few weapons-related relics. The majority were saddle and tack remnants, hardtack- and ammunition-box fragments, and many nails, screws, and rivets. Bioturbation, the settling of artifacts due to burrowing insects and animals, and pedogenesis, the grass-decay and soil-formation processes, had not been significant. With over 113 years to work, the vertical displacement due to these processes was only from one to four inches, with 92 percent of the artifacts still remaining within two inches of the surface.[377]

Besides the block excavations, three soil test pits were dug. From the floor of each pit, auger samplings were continued to bedrock, much as they were in Deep Ravine. The pits were placed in a north-south line, from the area of higher concentration at the dump proper in the south to the north where the surface dipped off more steeply approaching Water Carrier Ravine. Slope-wash strata were exposed, consisting of sands and silts in the same sequence as in Deep Ravine. On some of the northern slopes the grade approached 20 degrees. Such an angle would appear to encourage downslope migration of artifacts. Examination proved, however, that there was no evidence in the artifact pattern of slope-wash action, no preferred orientation even on relatively steep grades, and no abnormal concentrations in the drainages, as would be expected if slope washing had occurred. All indications were that, except for some bioturbation, the area has had a stable surface for 300 years.[378]

The dump site is a stable surface. Artifacts were still one to four inches below the buffalo grass, and they didn't scour away or erode off of a convex surface that approached a 20-degree grade. What chance would they have of washing out of Deep Ravine, with its one-degree, virtually flat bottom? The dump investigation provided more graphic evidence that artifacts have not been buried too deep or washed away on any parts of the battlefield.

The surprises of the 1989 dig were not over. When bad weather forced the cancellation of work on May 25, dig volunteer Monte Kloberdanz explored the west bank of the Little Bighorn at Reno's retreat crossing. In the muddy bank a few feet above the water he discovered a human skull, a clavicle (shoulder bone), and a humerus (arm bone). The find was turned over to the archaeologists and a forensic anthropologist. Their examination showed the man had been struck in the face with a heavy blunt object at the time of death. It was also determined that the bones belonged to a white male, about five feet eight inches tall, 30 to 40 years old. Further study narrowed the soldier's identity to two possible candidates—Sgt. Edward Botzer of Company G or Pvt. William Moody of Company A.[379]

Here was more evidence of the relative abundance of human bones still in the battlefield area. Bones could not be found in Deep Ravine, but they were found in the deepest ravine of them all—right above water's edge on the Little Bighorn itself. More remains were being found that hadn't been eroded away, disintegrated, washed out, or buried too deeply.

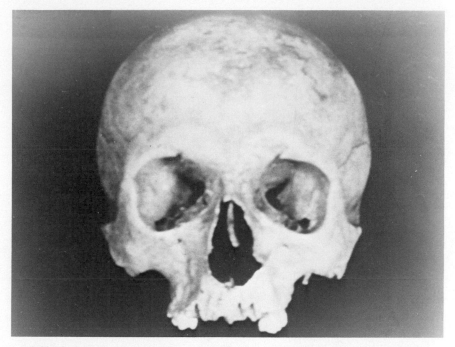

Soldier's skull discovered in 1989 on the banks of the Little Bighorn River, possibly that of Sgt. Edward Botzer or Pvt. William Moody. —Little Bighorn Battlefield National Monument

In 1989 the archaeological team, led by Dr. Haynes, went back down in Deep Ravine for another try. This time they were to specifically define the strata that might host the remains of the bodies. As determined the first time, the unit labeled "F" was the floor of Deep Ravine in 1876, and units below "F" were prehistoric and thus could not hold the bones. Remains had to be in unit "F" or a postulated unit "X", the fill from a buried headcut. It was possible unit "X" held the bodies. It was just downstream from trench 11, but was not excavated in 1985 because of the high water table.

In 1989 a hand auger was used to explore the untested locations. Line A was sunk about 27 yards below the lower Deep Ravine Trail crossing (fig. 5). It consisted of six holes dug to eight-foot depths through clay, silt, and gravel. The gravel, fragments of Fort Union sandstone, showed no rounding or abrasion caused by water transport. The postulated unit "X" was encountered and examined. There were no remains.

Auger-hole line B was placed 12 yards above line A and 15 yards below the lower trail crossing. Only one hole encountered unit "X". It was only

*Looking north from the lower trail crossing of Deep Ravine. Gravemaker
3 sits on the south bank in the foreground.*

one-third the width of the unit in line A. It contained no remains. Line C
was placed about 3 yards above the lower trail crossing. There was no
unit "X". There were no remains.

Two other single auger holes were sunk, one about 8 yards below
line C and another about 8 yards above it, right in the slump area that
was considered a prime suspect locale for the bodies in 1985. Nothing
was found.

What was concluded after this round of testing? There was a unit "X",
but it contained no remains. Dr. Haynes wrote that it appeared unlikely
that the remains would be found between lines A and C, but if they are
anywhere at all, they are probably even farther downstream of line A. But
then again, he thought, if they're not found downstream of A, maybe
they're upstream of trench 10 and the upper trail crossing.[380]

The "conclusions" of the 1989 dig were no different than those of 1984-
85. If the bodies are there, they are in a place no one has looked. The likely
sites, however, keep migrating downstream. That is, up to a certain point;
after that, they might really be upstream. This appears to be grasping at
straws. With each exploration, the steep-walled gulch of Deep Ravine

proves less and less likely to be the resting place of the 28 bodies. It is about time we raised our sights out of the ditch.

The South Skirmish Line Excavations

Above Deep Ravine, on the grassy slope of the upper watershed rolling north and east, stretches a line of gravestones trailing up and over a low divide and back up to Custer Hill. Some of the stones along this line were selected for excavation in 1984-85. The one closest to the testing done in Deep Ravine was gravemarker 7. It rests on the trail itself just a few yards above the lower trail crossing. A block excavation was dug on the south (ravine) side of the marker. Fourteen skull fragments, part of a neck vertebra, a nearly intact lumbar vertebra, a sternum fragment, a trouser button, and a horseshoe nail were found.

In 1989 the area was reexamined because visitor traffic along the trail was impacting and eroding the site. Perhaps more artifacts could be saved. This time the excavation was north of marker 7. More artifacts were found, all less than eight inches from the surface. There were 19 pieces of human bone, a canteen stopper top, a comb, an 1876 five-cent piece, and several bullets. The bone was from a soldier between 20 and 36 years old. The head appeared to have been severed from the body and crushed. Some time after its original placement the marker had been rotated about 35 degrees, perhaps to facilitate reading by visitors using the trail.[381]

The excavation was a repeat lesson. The artifacts were there. The more extensive the search, the more that were discovered. In a June 1992 con-

Looking north up Deep Ravine Trail. The first six stones right to left are numbers 13, 12, 17 (Lord), 16, 15, and 14.

Excavations underway at gravemarkers 9 and 10 on the South Skirmish Line.
—Little Bighorn Battlefield National Monument

versation, Richard Fox Jr. indicated that the metal detector sweeps at about 15-foot intervals probably missed three-fourths of the artifacts. However, the 20 or 25 percent of recorded "hits" were collected and provided a valid-enough sample to hypothesize about. Fox said that additional sweeps would also produce a proportional increase in finds.[382] This appeared to be exactly the case. Seven additional 100-meter sections had already been reinventoried, with each square yielding about twice the number of relics that had been uncovered in the initial sweeps.[383]

Gravemarker 7 represented a true death site. Its second excavation proved the rule that the more one looked, the more one found—except for down in Deep Ravine. What about other gravemarkers along the line?

There are about 44 stones associated with the "line" between Deep Ravine and upper Cemetery Ravine. Moving up the trail, about 27 yards north of marker 7, are markers 9 and 10. They represent one set of 43 pairs of stones scattered over the main battlefield. There have been several explanations offered for the pairings. They have been thought of as places where comrades, "bunkies," fought and died together. An alternative

Gravemarker 34. It reads, "Mitch Bouyer Scout . . . Fell Here June 25, 1876." Battle Ridge is in the background.

theory suggested that perhaps during the original burials a lone man may have been interred, but dirt was scooped up from both sides onto the body. Later details doing the marking saw two hollows, assumed they represented two graves, and planted two markers. Markers 9 and 10 yielded a fairly complete grouping of human remains. Fragments of skull, ribs, vertebrae, hands, both arms, and the right foot were found. The body lay face down. The head suffered a massive blunt-force blow. There were also bullets found in the head and chest area, an arrowhead, and several buttons. The man was between 30 and 40 years old and about five feet ten inches tall. The remains indicated that only one individual is buried there.[384]

The next markers excavated going north along the trail were at numbers 33 and 34, about 240 yards up from 9 and 10. These rest about 20 yards north on the Cemetery Ravine side of the low divide between the Cemetery Ravine and Deep Ravine watersheds. The area was selected for excavation because bones were found there on the initial

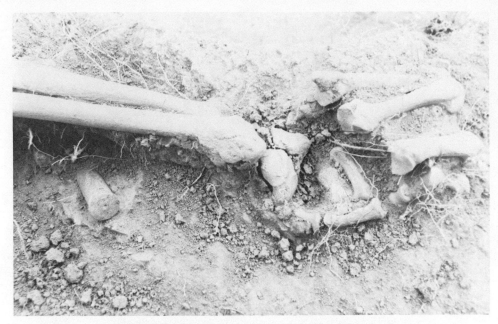

Human arm and hand bones with .45-.55 cartridge shell under the arm. Found at Lieutenant Smith's gravemarker, number 105, on Last Stand Hill. —Little Bighorn Battlefield National Monument

survey of the battlefield after the 1983 fire. Relics found included bullets, bootheels and bootnails, trouser buttons, a mother-of-pearl button, and a cedar stake fragment. The human bones included parts of a skull and facial fragments, cheek, eye orbit, teeth and nasal cavity, finger, and tailbone. The teeth showed a pattern of wear that is seen in pipe smokers. The man was between 35 and 40 years old, and his racial heritage was a Caucasian-Mongoloid mixture. "There is little doubt," wrote the archaeologists, "that the individual at Markers 33 and 34 is scout Mitch Boyer [sic]."[385]

About 25 yards northwest from markers 33 and 34 is marker 42. In 1984, a finger bone with a wedding band encircling it was found here. In 1985, only a jumble of river cobbles and additional hand bones were recovered.[386]

Another 125 yards north from marker 42, markers 52 and 53 are encountered. This is the head of the South Skirmish Line, about 165 yards from the visitor center. The 1984 excavation here recovered skull fragments, a trouser button, a cartridge primer, and a lead shot. The bones indicated the remains of just one individual, but there were too few to establish the man's identity.[387]

At the far south end of the "fugitive" line, gravemarker 2 was tested. The excavation recovered skull fragments, finger and toe bones, three trouser buttons, and six different types of bullets. The only battle-related injury that could be determined came from a heavy blow to the head.[388]

Two other markers along the Deep Ravine Trail were excavated, numbers 5 and 6. Unlike the others, however, these are located on the southern extension of the trail, across the ravine proper about 130 yards below the lower crossing, and are not considered part of the South Skirmish Line. These markers sit right above the ravine itself, just downstream from the angle in the channel called "the bend." Unfortunately, two inches below the surface sits the Fort Union bedrock. Nothing is buried there. The markers are spurious.[389]

Gravemarker 105 rests on Custer Hill. Although not part of the South Line, it is included here because it is named as the death site of Lt. Algernon Smith. The excavation uncovered an almost complete and articulated left lower arm and hand and many other bones of the hands, back, and feet. The remains represent an individual between 20 and 35 years old and approximately five feet three inches tall. There were trouser buttons, a cartridge and bullet, and cobbles scattered in the site. Although the stone is engraved with Lieutenant Smith's name and he was identified by several soldiers on Custer Hill, this does not appear to be his death site. The individual at gravemarker 105 is not tall enough to be Smith.[390]

Most of the excavations on Custer's field showed that the paired markers represented only one individual, so it is likely that the pairs were set up more in line with the "two hollow" suggestion than the "bunkie" theory. The excavations revealed that the soldiers charged with the burying and reburying certainly made no strenuous efforts to sink the remains in any substantial trenches, which is consistent with the historical record. They also indicated that the soldiers detailed to disinter the remains were not overly concerned about the thoroughness of the job they did. Apparently, displaying a good selection of the larger bones was enough to convince their superiors that they were completing their task sufficiently. The work was shoddy, but a blessing for the archaeologists, who could still find plenty to unearth 100 years later.

Stones 5 and 6, below the Deep Ravine Trail crossing, contained no artifacts, but no stones excavated along the South Skirmish Line proved spurious. Apparently there are 43 paired markers on the entire field, and about 10 of those sets are associated with the South Line. If the results obtained from the excavations over the entire Custer battlefield prove representative, in which paired markers really signify one body, we could expect the 10 pairs of markers in the South Line area to also contain the remains of but one individual each. The 51 markers along the South Line and its southeast branch thus may actually represent 41 men. The effective battle strength of Company E riding in Custer's battalion that day has been calculated at 38 to 40.[391] Lt. Algernon Smith's body was identified up on Custer Hill. The scout Mitch Bouyer was identified at markers 33 and 34, at the terminus of the formal South Skirmish Line. This still leaves about 41 legitimate graves. Lieutenant Sturgis's stone, number 48, is spurious, but his body, perhaps mutilated and unidentifiable, could still lie under one of the other markers on the line. In fact, Lieutenant Roe said that on June 27, Benteen claimed to have identified the bodies of all the officers except Lieutenant Harrington and Dr. Lord. By sunup the next morning, the additional 14 hours or more of exposure and decomposition added names to the unidentifiable or missing list that had not been there the day before.[392] Subtracting the possible illegitimate pairs, we are left with 41 markers, and there were 38 to 40 men in E Company. Is this an exact historical accounting or a fortuitous coincidence, or a little of both? Certainly the Gray Horse Troop can be adequately accounted for by the markers along the South Line. There are no bodies left over for piling in Deep Ravine.

What can we learn about the soldiers' positions from the artifact patterning? On a broad scale it can be determined that troopers deployed on Calhoun Hill in a 400-yard arc facing south and east. They deployed north of Battle Ridge in the Keogh area. They congregated on Last Stand Hill. They appeared to form a line down from Last Stand Hill toward Deep Ravine. The lines roughly formed a broad V with the point the farthest north on Custer Hill, a "classic offensive formation."[393]

The left, or west, arm of this inverted V is the South Skirmish Line. It runs south-southwest, down from Custer Hill to the divide between the Cemetery Ravine-Deep Ravine watershed. The "fugitive" stones continue an apparent line to the headcut area of Deep Ravine, with the farthest stones resting about 700 yards from Custer Hill. Under the South Line gravemarkers, with their attendant human remains, are scores and scores of battle-related artifacts. There is no complicated formula used to determine troop positions from artifact patterns. The soldiers were armed with .45-caliber Springfield carbines and Colt .45 handguns. The Indians had more of a variety of weapons besides the bow and arrow, including Sharps, Henry, and Winchester rifles. A trooper firing from any particular spot should have Springfield and/or Colt casings scattered near his position. If Indians fired at him there ought to be impacted bullets from a Henry, for example. Likewise, an Indian position should be able to be defined from the fallen Henry casings and an occasional impacted Springfield bullet. This is just what can be seen along the South Skirmish Line. Great numbers of soldiers' cartridge casings and Indian bullets or arrowheads were discovered there, making it very likely that soldiers died fighting from that position, not in a panic rout running through it.[394] Colt .45

handgun finds are likely to indicate close-in, hand-to-hand fighting, or possibly rounds fired into the bodies of the troopers after the positions had been overrun. Though there was not a large amount of Colt evidence found anywhere on Custer's field (about 40 bullets and casings), what was found was concentrated in the Keogh area and along the South Line.[395]

A *National Geographic* article summarized the archaeological findings by stating that the positions held by the soldiers had proven to be relatively stationary, while the Indians moved about freely as they overwhelmed one position after another. Another analysis indicated that the number and patterning of the artifacts found along the South Skirmish Line provided bountiful evidence "that the soldiers defended themselves in heroic fashion here." Neil C. Mangum, former Custer Battlefield Historian, thought the results proved conclusively that a major action did occur where the markers now stand and that the evidence supported the theory of the presence of a South Skirmish Line.[396]

The archaeologists themselves were impressed with the South Line's viability. Though they wouldn't go as far as definitely stating men fought there at skirmish intervals, they conceded it would be very appropriate to call the patterning a "South Defensive Area." Those that would discount the validity of the markers as representing true death spots were wrong, they stated. The evidence supported the South Line concept. It formed one projection of the V-shaped formation and was an integral part of the 7th Cavalry's defensive effort.[397]

The archaeological team appeared pretty well satisfied with their efforts. They had done a prodigious amount of work and met all their objectives. However, there was something that still stuck in the craw. Why were they unable to find any remains in Deep Ravine, and why did a disturbing amount of historical evidence not match the physical evidence? The wrench in the gearbox was Mitch Bouyer. Bouyer was identified by Sergeant Knipe as being in a deep ravine, but Colonel Gibbon mentioned seeing Bouyer lying slain in the midst of the troopers while he was describing the scenes below Battle Ridge, a spot nowhere near the river, where some accounts placed Bouyer's body.[398] Lieutenant Bourke unknowingly identified Bouyer by noting his scout's garb. We have seen in a previous chapter that Bourke and Gibbon were describing events in Cemetery Ravine—but Knipe too? Drs. Douglas Scott and Richard Fox were sure they had correctly identified the remains at gravemarkers 33 and 34 as Bouyer's. An Oklahoma pathologist even told Dr. Scott that he could prove in a court of law that the bones were Bouyer's.[399] Did this mean, Scott pondered, that Knipe's deep ravine was not today's Deep Ravine—that some of the South Skirmish Line could actually be a portion of the ravine that so many men spoke of? Archaeological data was contradicting some of the common interpretations of the historical accounts, and either the accounts or the interpretations were inaccurate. In either case, the documentary records would have to be reassessed.[400] Old assumptions were beginning to crumble.

Another historian, Dr. John S. Gray, also speculated about the same inconsistencies. Why was Bouyer found halfway down the South Line if he supposedly died in Deep Ravine? Why would the troopers enter such an apparent death trap as Deep Ravine? If they were there, why were all the buryings and restakings done on the ridges above?[401]

Perhaps a radically altered conceptualization of events may finally be entering the realm of possibility for at least a few scholars of the Little Bighorn fight. The apparent discrepancies between the physical evidence and the historical evidence may have finally taken their toll. Scott and Gray may have come to accept the possibility of historical misinterpretation—that we may have been probing all around the central problem without hitting the nail on the head because our perceptions have been distracted by an interpretive obstacle. They seem to be seeking a way out of the dilemma. It just may be the Cemetery Ravine explanation that proves to be the valid alternative that frees us from those nagging inconsistencies.

Mapping the South Line

Let us now raise our sights again and leave the excavations, bones, and bullets buried along the South Skirmish Line and focus on the line itself. The exact length of the line will vary with the number of gravemarkers one wishes to include in it. It is roughly 720 yards from the monument on Custer Hill to Deep Ravine following a line down from the monument to marker 54, then along the Deep Ravine Trail, which meanders a bit, touches near most of the remaining gravemarkers, and continues to its end at the lower trail crossing near gravemarker 7 (fig. 15). The trail continues down and across the ravine, but this is not considered part of the South Line.

The actual line begins about 200 yards down from Custer Hill at markers 52, 53, and 54 in the upper reaches of Cemetery Ravine. It wavers down the ravine and then climbs up obliquely across the ravine's south bank, following the gravemarkers in descending order. The Bouyer cluster, markers 33-39, is near the divide and about 180 yards from the start of the line. Markers 29-32 are the last stones on the Cemetery Ravine side of the divide and are about 200 yards from the head of the line. About 220 yards along the trail there is a soft crest where the trail begins to dip down into the upper Deep Ravine watershed. At 270 yards is another cluster, gravemarkers 24-28. The South Skirmish Line has been heading roughly north to south, but at this point a branch of markers diverges to the southeast. This branch consists of seven more or less isolated stones, numbers

Looking from the "low divide" through the Bouyer cluster of gravemarkers down Cemetery Ravine. Bouyer's marker is in left foreground.

20-23, 255, and 1-2. The latter two are down in the upper reaches of Deep Ravine, far above the headcut. Unless specified, we will not be speaking of this branch when mentioning the South Line.

The formal South Line terminates south of the Bouyer cluster on or just below the low divide, in the 24-28 group. Stones trailing off from there toward the upper reaches of Deep Ravine or to the headcut area are the "fugitive" stones, not part of the original line, but locations of the men who had fled when the original line was shattered or ran toward the river from Last Stand Hill at the end of the fight (fig. 3). Continuing down from markers 24-28 where the southeast branch splits off, the trail and fugitive lines follow the markers another 190 yards to stone 7 at the edge of Deep Ravine. The total length of the line—formal and fugitive, following the meanders of the markers and trail—is about 430 yards. By cutting across some of the twists in the trail and measuring less of the dips and bends, we find the line is about 400 yards long, with the low divide at 200 yards. Approximating 200 yards of formal South Skirmish Line to the north (Cemetery Ravine side) of the divide, and 200 yards of fugitive line to the

Gravemarkers 49, 50, and 51, looking down Cemetery Ravine.

south (upper Deep Ravine watershed side) of the divide, should provide a very workable visualization for our purposes. Today there are 44 stones along the main branch and 7 more on the southeast branch. Gravemarkers 3-6 are to the south across Deep Ravine and are not included in the count.

The exact number of gravemarkers along the line has also been open to interpretation over the years. In a previous chapter we have seen that Captain Sweet reported planting 246 markers on the entire field in 1890. In 1891, the United States Geological Survey sent topographer R. B. Marshall to map the field and locate the markers. His map depicted 244 markers, two short of what Sweet reported. Did Marshall miss two, or were the two merely the DeWolf and McIntosh markers that Sweet set on Reno's field? The South Skirmish Line portion of Marshall's map has 54 stones (fig. 12). Numbers 55 and 56 (possibly for Pvt. Gustave Klein and Cpl. William Teeman, both of F Company) are too close to Custer Hill to be part of the line. Omitting the 7 isolated markers of the southeast branch, this leaves 45 on the formal and main fugitive lines. Marshall's 1891 map still gives a reasonable approximation of the markers as they stand today, although the marker depicting the death spot of Surgeon Lord would today be above the "eu" in "Lieut. A.E. Smith's Command," and several other markers don't correlate well with present locations.

In 1896, the battlefield superintendent, A. N. Grover, reported that three more markers were set for Boston Custer, Harry Reed, and Mark Kellogg. In 1910, Superintendent Oscar Wright wrote that he placed four more stones on the field, those of Lieutenants Harrington, Sturgis, Porter, and Hodgson.[402] If this is true, then Sweet must not have placed Sturgis's marker in 1890, but neither did he report sending it back as he did Porter's. Perhaps he never brought one for Sturgis in the first place. If these reports are accurate, and Hodgson's stone was placed on Reno Hill, then the 246 markers Sweet set increased to 252 by 1910.

Probably in 1908, Walter Camp made maps of the field for his own research and as aids for his Indian interviews. Camp's map had 246 markers, which didn't account for any of the 6 supposedly placed on Custer's field by Grover and Wright. Camp must have mapped before Wright added his four stones, because by examining the enlarged South

FIGURE 12: R. B. MARSHALL'S MAP

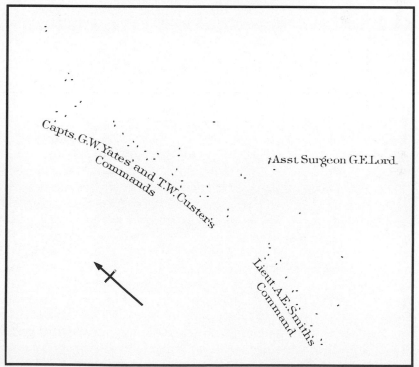

The South Skirmish Line portion of Marshall's 1891 U. S. Geological Survey map. Fifty-four stones shown.

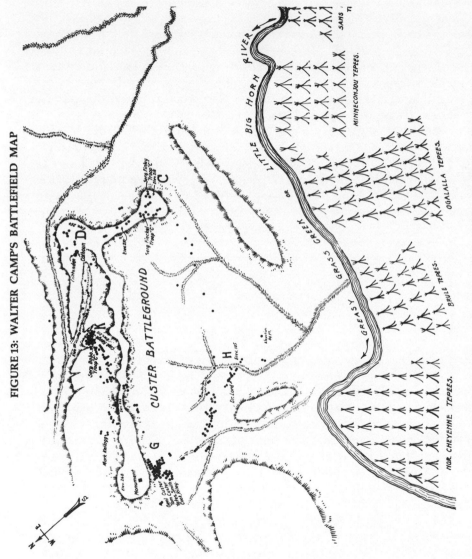

FIGURE 13: WALTER CAMP'S BATTLEFIELD MAP

Reproduced by permission of the Harold B. Lee Library, Brigham Young University.

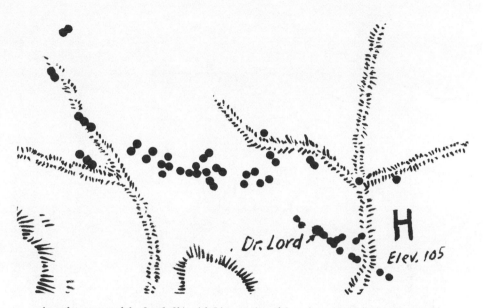

An enlargement of the South Skirmish Line portion of Camp's map. The "H" is where Tall
Bull witnessed the fight near Deep Ravine (see page 101).

Skirmish Line portion of Camp's map (fig. 13) one will notice there is no
dot as yet for Lieutenant Sturgis. Leaving out Teeman and Klein and the
7 isolated dots, we still can count 45 stones along the main South Line.
Surgeon Lord's marker was moved from its isolated spot on the 1891 map
to its present location as marker number 17 on the lower line. Camp's
map, at least as it pertains to the South Line portion, correlates better with
the present location of the stones than Marshall's 1891 map does. It is not
the best, but it is a good indication that the stones haven't been altered
much, if at all, since 1910. In 1935, Charles Kuhlman walked the field several
times. He too counted 246 stones.[403]

However, approximations won't suffice for credible historical and
archaeological study. It was obvious that a remapping of the field was
necessary. This was one of the 1984 archaeological survey's main tasks.
They produced a seemingly excellent, large, two-sided map that was
included in the 1987 publication *Archaeological Insights into the Custer Battle*.
One side of the map showed the locations of hundreds of army and Indian artifacts, and the other side depicted the numbered gravemarkers.

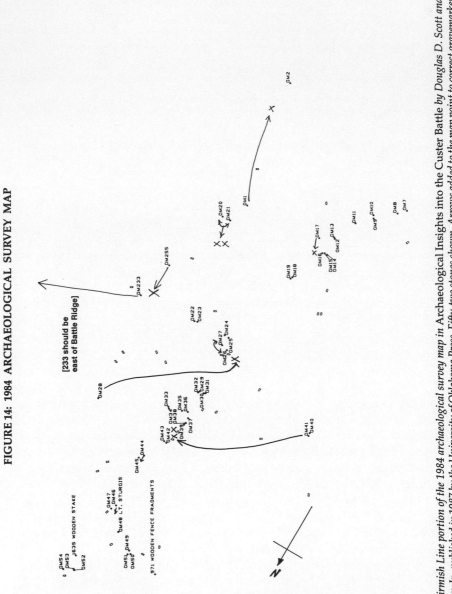

FIGURE 14: 1984 ARCHAEOLOGICAL SURVEY MAP

[233 should be east of Battle Ridge]

The South Skirmish Line portion of the 1984 archaeological survey map in Archaeological Insights into the Custer Battle by Douglas D. Scott and Richard A. Fox, Jr., published in 1987 by the University of Oklahoma Press. Fifty-two stones shown. Arrows added to the map point to correct gravemarker locations, based on the author's 1991 fieldwork (see fig. 15).

For any serious student of the battle, this was a tremendous aid. The South Skirmish Line portion of that map is reproduced here (fig. 14).

There were problems, unfortunately. The 1984 survey map showed 252 stones. No one had claimed planting any new ones since Kuhlman's tally of 246 in 1935. Perhaps Camp and Kuhlman miscounted. Another problem with the map was the lack of terrain that could have helped match artifacts and graves with the physical landscape, and it was a great nuisance to have to flip the sheet from front to back to try and correlate the features. A carefully scaled photocopy of the gravemarkers was made to enable the marker locations to be superimposed over the artifact locations. Now, new problems developed. Some of the gravemarkers just didn't match with certain artifact clusters. Some of the excavation sites didn't match with the gravestones. An excavation said to have been placed in Deep Ravine appeared to be 50 or more yards outside the ravine on the map. Several gravemarkers were plotted even farther from the main branch of the South Line than they were on Camp's map. From an examination of the new survey map, it appeared that Camp was much farther off in his mapping than had been imagined. And most frustrating, the new map's lack of contour intervals or terrain features still did not allow for precise placement. A trip to the field itself was necessary to match the gravemarkers to their physical settings.

Looking south down the Deep Ravine Trail. The five closest gravemarkers include numbers 40 and 41, misplaced on the 1984 survey map, and number 42, near where the finger bone and wedding ring were found.

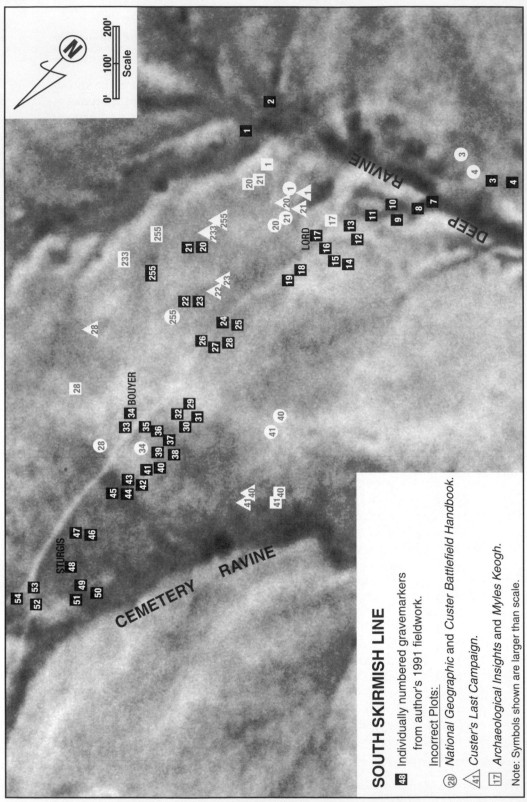

FIGURE 15: SOUTH SKIRMISH LINE 1991 CORRECTIONS

The trail along the South Line to Deep Ravine was closed in the spring of 1990. Excessive tourist traffic had broadened the one-lane footpath to a trampled expanse some 8 to 20 feet wide in places. Plants and grasses were being disturbed, and trash was being discarded along the length of the trail. The closing was done to let the area revegetate and recover. Because of the closure, I had to apply for permission to enter the area to complete my research. Battlefield Chief Historian Douglas McChristian granted access to the trail, and he and ranger John Doerner kindly assisted during the visit.

The day after Easter, April 1, 1991, was a bright sunny day with the afternoon temperature hovering in the mid-70s. Assisted by my son, Nathaniel, I walked the South Line with sketch pads, 100-foot tape measure, compass, camera, and the 1984 survey map. Not halfway into the mapping, however, we discovered that some of the gravemarkers on the 1984 map were not where they were plotted (fig. 14). Markers 28, 40, and 41 were nowhere near their indicated positions. Marker 233 could not be found. Perhaps 10 stones were not in the places where they had been surveyed just six years earlier. Stones along Battle Ridge and Calhoun Hill were moved to accommodate the road-building projects in the 1930s. One couldn't help but wonder if markers along the South Line were moved to accommodate tourist traffic. Our newly completed map of the line showed significant differences compared to the 1984 map (fig. 15).

I showed our map to a park ranger back at the visitor center. Gravemarker 28 was on the Deep Ravine Trail about 120 yards from its plotted position. Markers 40 and 41 were also on the trail, between 39 and 42, about 130 yards off their places on the 1984 map. Markers 26 and 27 were reversed, as were markers 20 and 21, and the latter two were 30 yards closer to markers 22 and 23 than plotted. Marker 17, Surgeon Lord's, was 15 yards closer to the trail. Marker 1 was not near 20 and 21 as shown, but about 100 yards farther on in the upper forks of Deep Ravine. Marker 233 was nowhere in the South Line area, but was duplicated on the northeast side of Battle Ridge in the Keogh area. The ranger couldn't account for the discrepancies.

A few weeks later, I sent a letter to Douglas Scott, an employee of the National Park Service and one of the authors of the book and map. I informed Scott of our experiences remapping along the South Line and that it appeared to us that the Park Service had been moving the gravemarkers around and ruining his fine survey. Not so, Dr. Scott replied. No one had moved the markers, rather, the map contained some errors. A printing deadline had left him unable to proofread the final copy. The markers were wrong because of a simple transposition of angles and distances (open squares on fig. 15). Dr. Scott also volunteered the information that marker 174 along the eastern fence boundary was actually about 100 meters north of its plotted position.[404]

Dr. Scott was extremely cooperative, and his candor was appreciated. The 1984 survey map had errors, but at least a corrected map of the South Line had been constructed. However, the erroneous version had been in print and circulating for the previous four years, and other publications had already made use of it.

Before *Archaeological Insights* had its first printing in 1987, a map based on the 1984 survey appeared in the December 1986 issue of *National Geographic*. Although it is a schematic map with a three-dimensional flavor, it was based on the 1984 survey and Dr. Scott was a consultant. The dead giveaways that *Geographic* used the erroneous survey are the very noticeable detachments of markers 40 and 41, and the lone dot representing marker 28 (see circles on fig. 15). A similar map based on the 1984 survey also appeared in the 1988 *Custer Battlefield Handbook*, distributed by the National Park Service itself and showing the same out-of-place gravemarkers.[405]

The use of an incorrect map in the above two instances may not seem to be of much import. After all, they were used mostly as an illustration to give the general reader an overall conception of troop configuration and were not to be taken as an exact replication. However, the same incorrect 1984 survey map was used by Dr. John S. Gray in his 1991 study *Custer's Last Campaign*, a volume historian Robert Utley hailed as "the most important book ever written about the Battle of the Little Bighorn."[406]

In this case the incorrectly plotted gravemarkers may have had more potential for damage, for Dr. Gray based much of his reasoning on their physical patterns. Gray used the 1984 survey and also commented on the deciphering problems encountered in studying a map without coordinates or geographical features. Gray believed that a higher authority had forbidden the archaeologists from locating the artifacts too precisely, perhaps to prevent future vandalism, but that the ban on publishing the locations only sabotaged the value of the project.[407] Gray was not to be denied the map's potential, however. He described how he measured the chart scale and, "Using all kinds of clues, I approximated the point on the chart that corresponds to the SE corner post of the reservation in order to anchor the system to the terrain. Its error is probably less than 15 meters, and since it is systematic, that is, identical for each marker, it cannot alter their pattern. . . . This procedure was adequate for displaying the pattern of markers and gives away no secrets."[408]

Gray believed he had solved the problem, and so he drew his own map from his calculations. He saw a broad quadrilateral pattern and formulated a counterclockwise troop motion hypothesis from his constructed map. He could do so, he believed, because the 1984 survey map was "systematic . . . identical for each marker . . . [and the map's errors] cannot alter their pattern."[409] There was the catch. The margin of error was not systematic, the relative positions of the markers were not identical, and their pattern was altered from reality.

The South Line portion of Gray's map contains nearly the same errors as in the *Geographic* and the *Battlefield Handbook*. Although Gray didn't try to reproduce every individual stone, one can still find the incorrect give-away clusters. In addition, Gray placed Dr. Lord's marker back where it was improperly located on Marshall's 1891 map (see triangles on fig. 15).

Our fieldwork on the South Skirmish Line uncovered gravemarker discrepancies. Doug Scott indicated that another stone in the Keogh area was incorrectly marked. It is not known if more might be mismarked on other portions of the field. Even so, since the patterning remains generally correct, perhaps Dr. Gray would still have postulated his quadrilateral, counterclockwise troop flow hypothesis. Yet, the simple transposing of angles and distances on the 1984 field survey map is certainly a cause for concern.

What may be even more disconcerting is the realization that a significant number of errors were made in plotting the positions of about 52 very visible gravemarkers. One cannot help but wonder what errors might have occurred in plotting the 2,000 artifacts on Custer's field, some of which may have been only a centimeter or two in size? Little Bighorn battle student Bruce Trinque pointed out that he would have hated to build up an elaborate theory about Indian movements based on cartridge-case distribution only to find critical pieces of evidence he thought were located on Greasy Grass Ridge, for example, were really found in Lincoln, Nebraska, and had been misplotted because of a data-entry error.[410]

The inaccuracies of the 1984 survey were being perpetuated. Richard A. Fox Jr. was coauthor with Douglas Scott of the *Archaeological Insights* book, which introduced the survey. Fox continued his examination of the relic finds and the historical record. In the 1991 publication *Myles Keogh*, he explained his understanding of events as they pertained to the demise of Company I. Included in his study, again, were maps based on the 1984 survey, but because it was thought that many of the adjacent markers actually represented one individual, he corrected the gravemarkers for pairing errors.[411] Whereas the 1984 map had a total of 52 stones, Fox's 1991 map showed the South Line's memorial twosomes represented as single stones, for a total of 35. The incorrectly plotted 40-41 pair, for example, became a single stone. However, there are still concerns with this setup. Should 17 markers have been removed? Ten of eleven randomly selected pairs on the entire field proved to have remains consistent with but one individual. Only three pairs along the South Line were actually excavated, markers 9-10, 33-34, and 52-53. They proved to be single—granted, but does it follow that the other pairs must be singles also, even though it is statistically legitimate to remove them? There is no way to tell without more digging.[412]

In 1993, Fox published a study that was to be a full synthesis of field-work and written documents, and a contribution to both culture history and anthropology. It was a new name for archaeology that Fox called "archeography."[413] Again, maps relating to the South Skirmish Line gravemarkers were included. One, corrected for pairing errors, was a near duplicate of that which appeared in his 1991 version. Another was apparently a map of the stones as they actually exist, with no pair removals (fig. 16). Again, it contains the same incorrect plottings as in the original 1984 survey (fig. 14).[414]

FIGURE 16: RICHARD FOX'S MAP

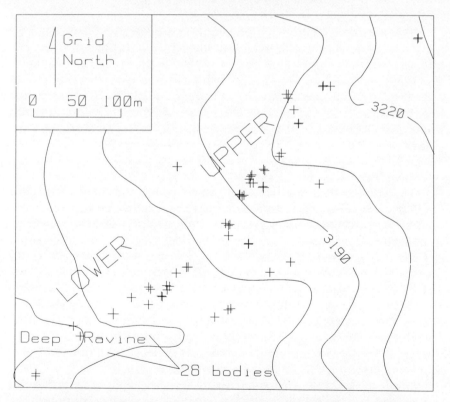

The South Skirmish Line map from Archaeology, History, and Custer's Last Battle: The Little Big Horn Reexamined, *by Richard Allan Fox, Jr. Copyright © 1993 by Richard Allan Fox, Jr. Published by the University of Oklahoma Press.*

Over nine years have passed since the first survey, and the gravestone placement has not improved. However, progress may be underway. Dr. Scott said the survey map in *Archaeological Insights* is in error because a printer's deadline left no time for proofreading, but since then he indicated corrections were made. The data was available on the computer, and Scott said he could print out almost any type of configuration or marker/artifact correlation that was desired. In addition, Dr. Fox indicated that he has included corrections for a second printing of his 1993 study. The press did have the changes for both works, prompted by these very queries.[415] We look forward to an accurate rendition of that 1984 survey, and sincerely hope that it will include the gravemarkers, the artifacts, and the terrain, to enable the reader to more fully comprehend what occurred during the battle. Surely, such a map would not compromise the security of the battlefield. In the meantime, we offer our rendition (fig. 17).

The South Skirmish Line Controversy

Of the many controversies surrounding the fight on the Little Bighorn, perhaps one of the most intense concerns the reality of this line of tombstones below Custer Hill. Do they really represent the death spots of the Gray Horse Troopers and possibly some men from Companies C and F? Do the stones designate positions that men fought from on a skirmish line? Are they markers showing where men died as they fled in panic from Custer Hill at the battle's end? Are they merely "phantom" stones, placed there for convenience, really representing men that died in Deep Ravine? Certainly there has been enough evidence presented here to lend credence to the existence of such a line.

What did some other researchers and historians have to say about the South Skirmish Line? Apparently, the conceptualization of a definable line of troopers south of Custer Hill was popularized by Dr. Charles Kuhlman in 1951. After he examined the gravemarkers and read the Indian accounts, *and* because he assumed all the white accounts spoke of Deep Ravine as the place where 28 men died, Kuhlman believed Company E made a stand farther south along the line than they actually did. For Kuhlman, E's center rested *in* Deep Ravine, with its left extending toward Greasy Grass Ridge and its right up the low divide to the north. In this precarious position, E would resemble a fat moth on an entomologist's pinning board, the body fit snug in the groove and the wings spread to dry in a shallow inclined V. It would not have been a very sound tactical stance.

Kuhlman theorized that Company C was to extend E's right at the divide back to Custer Hill. Lame White Man's attack split the seam between the companies and drove E's right wing back on its body in the ravine. It would have had to occur something like that to allow for 28 men

FIGURE 17: CEMETERY RAVINE - DEEP RAVINE GRAVEMARKERS AND ARTIFACTS

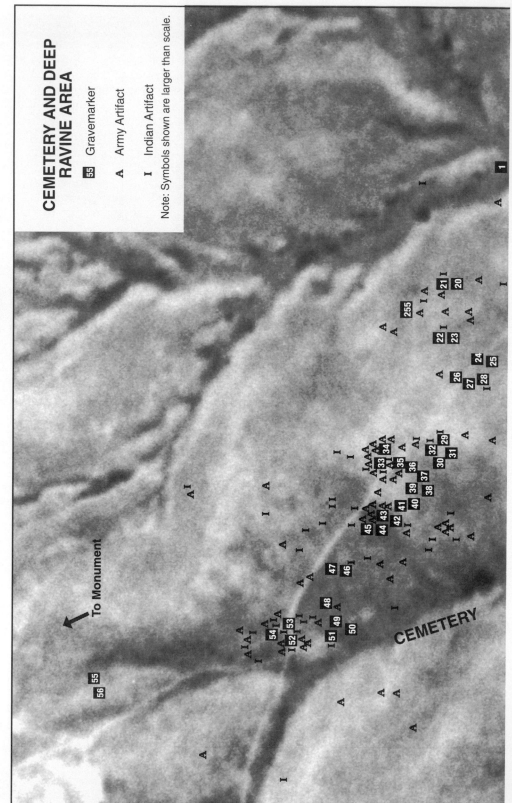

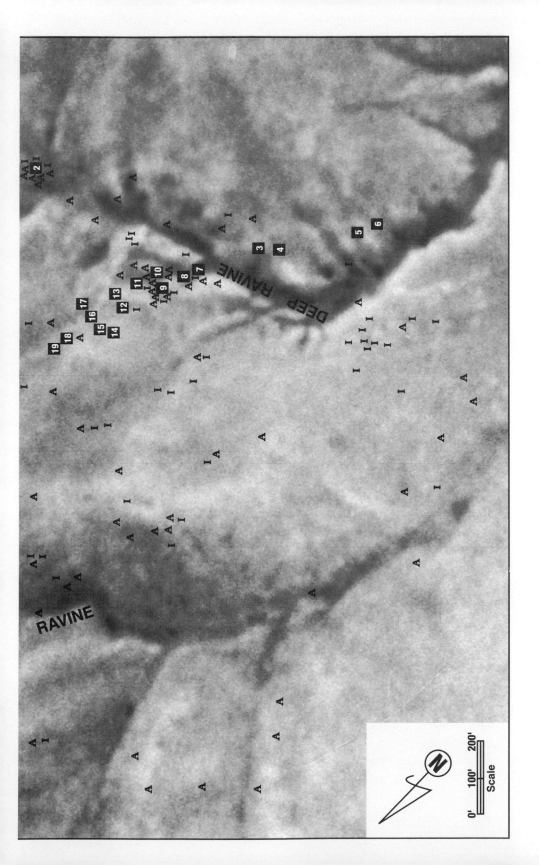

RAVINE

DEEP RAVINE

Scale
0'   100'   200'

N

dying in the middle of E's line. Kuhlman reconstructed that sequence of events from reading the accounts of participants such as Wooden Leg and Kate Bighead. One thing puzzled him, however: neither of those witnesses mentioned anything at all about the "ghastly mess found in the ravine behind the line."[416] The doctor couldn't conceive of an alternative possibility—that the Cheyennes mentioned no "ghastly mess" in the ravine simply because it was a case of there being no mess to see.

Kuhlman's peculiar use of evidence has been addressed in a previous chapter in reference to Curley's accounts. His theories have been assailed by more than one. Author Francis B. Taunton questioned Kuhlman's South Line thesis. Taunton declared, "None of the Seventh's officers suggested the existence of such a line," and then used the accounts of two officers to prove its nonexistence. One was Capt. Thomas McDougall, who said in one interview that there were no more than a dozen bodies between the gully and Custer. The other was Lt. Richard Thompson, who said there might have been 34 in a gully, but only 9 or 10 between the gully and Custer. Taunton thought a dozen or fewer men at the normal 15-foot skirmish interval would not successfully form a skirmish line between Custer Hill and the gray horse ravine.[417]

Of course, the comment that no 7th Cavalry officers suggested the existence of a skirmish line below Custer Hill does not match the historical record. McDougall himself even said at Reno's Court that he went to E Company's skirmish line and found them half in and half out of a ravine. Lieutenant Wallace mentioned seeing numbers of E troopers lying in skirmish order. Edward Godfrey, in his revision of the *Century Magazine* article, mentioned Lieutenant Smith's men in skirmish line. Lieutenant Hare said he saw Smith's men in skirmish order in a coulee. There were also several members of other army units who visited the field and commented on the South Skirmish Line. Taunton might be accused of no worse than honestly overlooking some of the evidence, except for the fact that three pages later, after saying no officer of the 7th suggested the existence of a skirmish line, he stated that Lieutenants Hare and Wallace *did* conclude that very fact: ". . . that E Company had died as skirmishers."[418] Taunton's doubt as to the existence of a South Line is itself open to question. Douglas Scott also thought Taunton's rejection of the South Skirmish Line was not an accurate assessment and did not stand the test of archaeological evidence.[419]

Taunton took exception to the comments in *Archaeological Insights.* He replied that he never intended to espouse any theories and only suggested that the small number of bodies indicated by the two cited accounts made the existence of a South Line "open to question." It was a simple statement, Taunton argued, not a thesis. He claimed to remain noncommittal. He believed there was little evidence to support the proposition of a South

Line, but there was no certainty that it did not exist at some point of time and in the general area.

In his rebuttal to the *Archaeological Insights* position, Taunton cited Lieutenant McClernand and Private Goldin as two men whose accounts would also cast doubt on the merits of a South Line theory. First of all, Taunton did not believe E Troop went to the ravine from Custer Hill. He thought they came from the east end of the ridge because Goldin had said, "The trail of the White Horse Troop left the main column and swung to the left."[420] The trail Taunton believed that Goldin saw swinging left at Greasy Grass Ridge or Calhoun Hill could have just as easily "swung to the left" from Custer Hill. In fact, some of the accounts said exactly that, and we have seen that Two Eagles, Lone Bear, and Lights were insistent in their statements that no troops swung left to Deep Ravine from the Greasy Grass Ridge-Calhoun Hill area. Secondly, trusting the veracity of one with the reputation of Theodore Goldin to comment on the movement of a troop that Goldin didn't even see would not be the surest thing to bet money on.

Taunton, in the preface to his 1990 edition of *Custer's Field*, also used McClernand's account to question the reality of a South Skirmish Line. This is puzzling, since McClernand made declarations that contradicted the statements of Thompson. Where the latter said there were only about 9 or 10 men between Custer and the gully, McClernand told Walter Camp that he couldn't recall any dead bodies in the cutbanks or near the river, but that "there were more than 10 men between the ridge and Crazy Horse Gully."[421] Taunton admitted there may have been a skirmish line of sorts, but he said McClernand indicated the skirmish line "faced east, not northwest." Of the scores of accounts available, McClernand's has to be one of those one would absolutely *not* choose to try to disprove the existence of a South Line. McClernand praised the apparent thought that went into the line's formation, how it was the best-established skirmish line he had seen on both fields, how much care appeared to be taken in placing it, and how regular the intervals were.[422]

I have had no success whatsoever in finding the account in which McClernand said the line faced east. The account cited by Taunton made no such claim. McClernand was describing one side of the broad V mentioned by Douglas Scott and Melissa Connor or one side of the quadrilateral as hypothesized by Gray. What utter confusion would have ensued had this portion of the line turned inward and faced east. One cannot help but visualize a British square on the crest of the ridge defending the road to Waterloo. Suddenly, appearing out of the valley below La Haie Saint are the charging French cuirassiers. What is the response of the infantry facing the attacking horsemen? Do they turn their backs to the charge and face to the inside of the square? Of course not. Yet this is what facing the

South Skirmish Line to the east would have been like. The men would not have gone down from the ridges to counter the Indian threat developing in that quarter and then turn their tails to the foe and face themselves to the east. Besides the reckless, lone warrior or two making a "center run" or showing his bravery with a suicidal dash through the soldier lines, there was no large, organized Indian force inside the box to cause one of the sides to face inward. When one is shackled with the assumption that many men died in Deep Ravine, the only way to make sense of McClernand's description of the 28 bodies being "to the front and right of the line of skirmishers" is to flip the line's facing 180 degrees and stand in the Indian position facing Battle Ridge. A preconception resulted in viewing the entire line backwards.

Company E moved down from the Custer Hill area to establish a position of more integrity. That they were temporarily successful is indicated by Cheyenne accounts that tell of Indians retreating from more exposed positions to the deepest part of the gulch or to the ridge south of it. For a short time, Custer's battalion was formed up in a rough box. Quickly enough, however, the Indians infiltrated up Deep Ravine, bypassed Company E's left, and swung around to their rear. Even after the threat to the left and rear developed, the company could not have turned away from several hundred warriors in its immediate front to counter the threat from some scores of Indians flanking its left. Its response was a slight refusal of the left flank resulting in a rough semicircle of defenders in the Bouyer cluster area.

However, the entire question of which way the line faced has absolutely no bearing on whether or not the South Skirmish Line existed. It is much more reasonable that the line faced west, but whether the men faced west or east, stood on their heads or spun in circles, it doesn't detract from the fact that they were physically present to face whichever way they wanted to. Gray Horse Troopers died in Cemetery Ravine. The way they faced when they received their death wounds is irrelevant. Their remains are still there to indicate a flesh-and-blood line once existed.

One of the oldest interpretations of this portion of the fight depicts a troop movement trailing uphill from the Deep Ravine area to Last Stand Hill. This idea, as we have seen, was fostered by inaccurate speculation by men such as Captain Freeman and Lieutenants Roe and Maguire. The latter, as noted from his testimony at the Reno Court, had a trail mapped through the Deep Ravine area even though he may never have been there himself to see if the drawing had any basis in fact. In addition, it appears Maguire was the first to write that "28 in a ravine" phrase, in his official report of July 2, 1876. Thus, the entire case of the missing 28 might have stemmed from the guesswork of a 2nd lieutenant who may never have actually examined the ravine or the bodies that he reported.

Maguire's illogical interpretation of a northward trail up out of Deep Ravine resurfaced again as late as 1985, in a publication by Henry and Don Weibert. Their interpretation differed from that of the above three soldiers however, in that it denied the idea that Custer's men went anywhere near Medicine Tail ford. Custer, according to the Weiberts, fought on and rode down from Nye-Cartwright Ridge, dropped off Calhoun on his hill, and continued on toward the river along the divide between the north (Deep Ravine) and south (Calhoun Coulee) forks of the ravine. The troops nearly reached the Little Bighorn before they realized they were no longer the hunters, but the hunted. At this point, according to the Weiberts, Mitch Bouyer rode up to Custer and shot him in the head. The leaderless troops headed back uphill. Company E separated from the rest and retreated up Deep Ravine, where they were trapped in the bottom. The Indians stood above them and dropped them from 10 to 15 feet away at point-blank range. The remaining companies reached Last Stand Hill with little loss. The fighting continued for a time. Troops were seen on Weir Point, and Keogh attempted a breakaway to the south, nearly getting back to the Calhoun area before succumbing.[423]

There is not much point in dissecting this interpretation. Besides the strong points made about the action on Nye-Cartwright Ridge, nearly the entire sequence of events on Custer's field has no correlation to the historical or archaeological record. This should be of no surprise. The Weiberts rejected Indian sources completely. They stated that the Indian information was always in conflict and unreliable. Not only were their stories untrustworthy, but the Indians outright lied through their teeth.[424] When an author refuses to utilize the only eyewitness sources available, it is no wonder the result is such an unsubstantiated interpretation. For the Weiberts, there was no South Skirmish Line at all, for they affirmed that all of Company E perished in Deep Ravine.[425]

Another writer, W. Kent King, constructed a slightly different scenario. His analysis was constricted by the need to place those Company E men in Deep Ravine also, and although he did not think highly of a South Skirmish Line, the evidence forced him to grudgingly acknowledge its existence. For testimony against a South Line he used the same McDougall and Thompson accounts as Taunton did, but also added one by Godfrey that claimed there were few bodies between Custer and the gully. However, to his credit, King did not stop there, but included evidence from McClernand, Maguire, Knipe, and Freeman that admitted to finding a significant number of dead between Custer and the gully. Thus, King tentatively accepted the South Line and said, "The indications are too strong: There must have been a line of sorts."[426]

King went on to say that the line was composed of only 37 men of Company E. Although he made no allowance for the horse holders, he said the men could have stretched out to cover the 400-odd yards of the line because the normal 15-foot skirmish interval could be changed at the discretion of the officer. Quoting a 1926 cavalry tactics manual, King said that a situation might dictate up to a 10-yard interval for skirmishers. It's rather strange that a twentieth-century tactics manual would be cited to make a point for nineteenth-century soldiers, but King's meaning is understood. The cavalrymen of the last century had their share of tactical manuals to study also, there being three systems used, Poinsett's, Cooke's, and Upton's, between the opening guns of the Civil War and the year of the Little Bighorn fight.[427] In fact, Cooke's *Cavalry Tactics* called for 10-pace (yard) intervals between files (men) on the skirmish line. He instructed, "If a less or greater interval is desired, the command would be given: '. . . files from right as skirmishers at (so many) paces. March.'"[428]

Variations were allowed. Lieutenant Maguire made some pertinent comments about skirmish lines at the Reno Court of Inquiry. He was asked by the defense counsel how many men it would take to man a skirmish line about a mile in length. Maguire thought for a few seconds and replied that he didn't have his "tactics" with him and couldn't tell exactly how far apart the men would be. The counsel, Mr. Gilbert, suggested that Maguire apparently did not wish to answer the question. No, Maguire protested, he was simply unable to do so. If he was told how far apart the men were placed he could tell how long the line would be.[429] The exchange between the attorney and the lieutenant is revealing. There was no standard interval for men on a skirmish line. The men's spacings determined the length of the line—they could be placed to respond to almost any contingency.

An officer could call for a skirmish line as long or as short as he believed would fit the situation. King thought the entire South Line extended about 1,900 feet. Even assuming officers could lengthen their skirmish line as they saw fit, would Smith or Sturgis have spread 37 men over that distance? One man every 50 feet would have made a very suspect formation with which to face a massing force of warriors. King, however, was committed to arguing for a line of this character, for he believed that when Lame White Man attacked, the lower 28 men of the line ran for Deep Ravine, where they were killed. That would still leave the 9 or 10 along the upper line that he believed Lieutenant Thompson described. Hence, King concluded, 28 stones along the lower South Line were "phantoms" and should really be placed in Deep Ravine.[430]

Of course, the bodies were not phantoms to the men who saw them there. King's analysis suffered because his assumptions were predicated on 28 bodies *having* to be in Deep Ravine. To even have the opportunity to die in Deep Ravine, the South Skirmish Line would need to have been manned at much thinner intervals and at double the distance than would be called for had those "28 in a deep ravine" accounts not kept forcing researchers to adjust evidence to fit its parameters.

Company E men did man the South Line, but they anchored their left on the divide of the Cemetery Ravine-Deep Ravine watershed near the Bouyer cluster. The line could have been formed by 38 to 40 of Smith's men in Cemetery Ravine only, 200 yards at intervals of one man every 15 feet, just as prescribed. Had every fourth man held horses, they would have been at eight-yard intervals. There was no need for King to quote tactics manuals that indicated officers could theoretically extend a line out to infinity. There was no need for such a long line. Forty men at five yards or 25 men at eight yards still fits the evidence quite nicely, and we can still allow for 20 or more of them to die in a ravine—Cemetery Ravine.

Jerome A. Greene, in a fine little volume, provided a map that showed Company E deployed in the center of Deep Ravine, much as Kuhlman had done. Greene, however, said it was Companies C and F that went down the hillside to establish lines to check the Indians approaching up the great ravine from the river. Company E remained behind, on the hill with Custer. Greene used Kate Bighead's and Wooden Leg's accounts to argue that it was C and F that formed the South Line. Why did he determine this? Because later, many of F Troop's men lay dead in the Last Stand area, proving that they had managed to get back to Custer Hill (while Company C disappears from Greene's narrative). Also, Company E was found dead in the ravine.[431] I may have missed something here, but I find it difficult to prove that Companies F and C came down from Custer Hill by finding bodies of their dead on Custer Hill. Likewise, how does one show that Company E stayed on Custer Hill by finding their bodies in a ravine?

We know E Troop fought on the hill for a time; a number of Indian accounts back that statement. Why Greene concluded Kate Bighead saw Companies C and F coming down the hill is unknown. She certainly made no reference to C or F (or sorrels or bays), while other Indians did indicate that grays were below the hill. It was some time later, said Greene, that Company E ran for the river, leaving Company F on the hill to face dangerous odds alone.[432]

Greene's scenario placed Company E on Custer Hill while C and F went south to form a line and check the Indians coming up the ravine. C and F were attacked by Lame White Man and/or other warrior bands. They retreated to Custer Hill. Then, apparently E left the hill and ran to their deaths in the ravine, while C and F were left on Custer Hill to die. Here is a perfect opportunity for one to harken to the wisdom of William of Ockham, the medieval English philosopher and iconoclast credited with initiating the common sense reasoning that the theory with the least amount of assumptions is the more useful, that the least complicated answer is the best. When applying "Ockham's razor" to Greene's various involved movements, we find that the same end result that Greene posited could have been achieved by E going down to form the skirmish line where their bodies were found, and F remaining on Custer Hill where their bodies were found. The simplest explanation makes the most sense—and it matches Indian accounts.

Greene also stated that a South Line was established to check Indians approaching up the great ravine. That may be partially correct, yet we must still wonder why a line established to check the advance of an enemy would be formed parallel with the axis of the enemy advance. They were likely more concerned with the Indians they could see out in the flats and along the river, and with linking up with Company F on what is now the cemetery grounds. An extension of the line down Cemetery Ravine was a tactical necessity to check those threats. The line was probably not expressly formed to counter Indians in Deep Ravine—if that was the case they would have formed facing south at a right angle to the line the bodies now delineate. Though the company may have eventually suffered because of a "hanging" left, they assuredly did not form up with knowledge of a grave danger to their flank. Neither did Company E form up in a Napoleonic column and charge down into the ravine to mix it up hand-to-hand with the Indians. Nor was the line formed, as Kuhlman said, to "facilitate the passage of Benteen either by holding back the warriors or closing in on their rear if they left to oppose Benteen."[433] The suggestion that Custer's downfall was caused by Benteen's men appearing on a bluff three miles away is unacceptable. There was no augmenting Benteen's potential three-mile passage by moving a company down a hill for 200 yards to a spot where it would be even more difficult to see.

The Indians, by the way, never made any reference to Deep Ravine being impassable. It was an avenue for them. There was no "headcut" with vertical banks to prevent their passage. Had there been an unscalable dead end or cul-de-sac, some mention of it surely would have been made by the eyewitnesses. Troopers would not be stopped cold by terrain that Indians could pass through freely.

The Gray Horse Troop deployed obliquely in and along Cemetery Ravine and anchored its left on the divide. They did not continue downslope and place themselves in the Deep Ravine watershed, cut off and out of sight of the headquarters guidon back on Custer Hill. Though they formed a broad V, it was not as a "classic offensive formation" at this point. The troops were now on a near-stationary defensive, not cohesive, without an adequate unobstructed field of fire, and reacting to the Indian initiative—all harbingers of doom.[434] Except for a possible small number in a refused perimeter on the left flank, the men of E Troop faced west and northwest, every fourth man holding horses. They covered about 200 yards, the 25 men on the front line spaced about one every 8 yards. Their right may have nearly connected with Company F on Cemetery Hill. Given the deteriorating situation, it may have been the best tactical response left for them (fig. 18).

However, Lame White Man and other warrior bands witnessed the troops string out in that manner and saw their opportunity. The attack was sudden and overwhelming. Not a man could be spared to hold the horses. The grays were released as a lifesaving necessity. It was nearly impossible to shoot accurately with a carbine in one arm and the reins of four horses in the other. Employment of a weapon became much more important than holding a rein. The near-simultaneous release prompted much of the Indian commentary made at this point regarding stampeded horses. The Indians caught many of the panicked mounts near the river. Only a small number of dead horses were discovered along the South Line after the battle, though there were bones enough to convince even Walter Camp that "a good many" were there to begin with.

A number of warriors may have traversed Deep Ravine's upper fork, circled around Company E's left flank behind the low divide, and hit them from the rear. Lieutenant Hare surmised this when he saw the soldiers' bodies in Cemetery Ravine and said that many had apparently been shot from behind. The few survivors, depending on their proximity to the nearest perceived refuge, either fled back to Custer Hill or toward Deep Ravine. It was during the last stages of the fight, after considerable time spent defending on Custer Hill, that the remnants of Company E and perhaps some men from Companies C and F, accompanied by Mitch Bouyer, made their move to the river. Some died along what had been the South Skirmish Line. Bouyer almost made it to the low divide. Others dropped along the downslope toward Deep Ravine, creating the impression that the original line extended down that far. Some, as Colonel Miles understood, went toward Deep Ravine first, only to be diverted back to the "neighboring" Cemetery Ravine side, possibly accounting for the southeast branch of gravemarkers. A few, not 28, made it to Deep Ravine.

A few days after the battle, survivors of the 7th Cavalry and men of the Montana Column reported seeing men lying dead down from Custer Hill in skirmish lines. They were honest-to-goodness corpses—mutilated, blackened, festering, and offensive. They were many horrible things, but they were not phantoms.

There were several troop movements down from the ridges. The first was the organized deployment of Company E to form the South Line. The second was the disorganized flight of the fugitives from Custer Hill late in the fight. There were also isolated instances of fleeing soldiers throughout the course of the battle. The numbers were described by the Indians, from upwards of 40 to only a few. It has been difficult for researchers to

reconcile the large variance and has led some to denigrate the Indian accounts. Of course, some Indians described the first deployment, some the major fugitive movement, others the isolated escape attempts, or any combination of the above. There is no enigma here. The Indians were not concocting fanciful tales, they were describing two or more troop sorties, and, depending on their position and arrival time, they described the movements as occurring early or late in the fight.

This scenario has its critics. One of the most outspoken contemporary opponents of the South Skirmish Line idea is Richard G. Hardorff, author of several fine monographs on the Battle of the Little Bighorn and western history. His thorough research has been appreciated and cited by this writer many times.

Hardorff did not think much of Kuhlman's South Line—or of his research techniques, saying that Kuhlman ignored contrary evidence and considered only data that favored his hypothesis. Hardorff said Kuhlman was oblivious to standards of integrity and his writings were based on an overly active imagination. He cited instances where Kuhlman used evidence to advance his ideas of a South Line, evidence that Hardorff affirmed was obviously not pertaining to a South Line. One of these examples is an extract from a letter by Col. J. W. Pope, who was on the field in 1877 as a lieutenant in the 5th Infantry, and is based on what Indians had told him about Custer's movements. "One troop was formed well forward," Pope wrote, "making an angle forward with the other troops along Custer Ridge." That troop apparently made a considerable fight and killed the majority of Indians that fell in the fight. However, the troop "was soon driven back to the position where it was overwhelmed with the whole command." When nearly all the command had been killed, a few men ran down to get shelter in the ravines.[435] Hardorff said Pope's letter obviously was not a reference to a South Line, as Kuhlman thought, but instead described a troop on Calhoun (Finley) Ridge.

In the first place, this is very equivocal evidence. There is nothing certain about it at all. It could very well be evidence of a South Line. One troop was formed well forward, making an angle forward of the troops already along Custer Ridge. Pope's statement made use of the word "forward" twice. Company E had been described many times by the Indians as being in the lead along Battle Ridge. On the other hand, Company L deployed along Calhoun Hill. Their position was in the rear of the other companies along the ridge. The troop in question was then driven back to the position where it was overwhelmed with the rest of the command. Then a few men ran down to the ravines. If anything, the episode seems to describe Company E almost exactly, their forward angle from Custer Hill and their demise at the battle's end. General Godfrey was aware of this letter, and he thought the troop Pope spoke of must have been either

Company E or Company I. Of the seven Cheyennes that Wooden Leg said died as a result of the battle, five of them fell in the fighting from Deep Ravine to the Custer Hill area, the very "angle forward" that Company E assumed.[436] Stating that this was obviously a reference to a troop on Calhoun Ridge appears to be more of a misinterpretation by Hardorff than Kuhlman.

Hardorff had some very definite answers to Kuhlman's hypothesis. It was invalid because it was an "absolute fact that a south line *never* existed, the command having been destroyed while moving *north* [Hardorff's emphasis] to Custer Hill."[437] This is a strong statement. Given the fact that much evidence is ambiguous, there is a tendency for some historians to hedge a bit on conclusions. We certainly cannot accuse Hardorff of hedging, and he must be congratulated for that; yet, in this case, it appears that he may have gone too far. Affirming there was no South Line because the command was destroyed before getting to Custer Hill denies nearly every Indian account we have previously cited. If anything can be learned from the Indians, it is that the grays successfully traversed Battle Ridge and fought on the hilltop as a definable unit. The command was not destroyed on its way north.[438]

Hardorff stated he had positive evidence that refuted "the deployment of any troop near the ravine south of Custer Hill."[439] He then cited numerous accounts that supposedly denied the existence of a South Skirmish Line. Benteen was cited. Of course, had Benteen disliked the Greek Leonidas as much as he did Custer, he probably would have called Thermopylae a panic rout also. Lieutenants Hare and Godfrey were quoted, as were Captains McDougall and Moylan. Also referenced were Lieutenant Thompson and troopers Knipe and Hardy. We have cautioned about taking the quick quote out of context. The accounts of the men in the following list were already examined in detail. Far from denying a South Line, they readily provide evidence for its existence. Was there sign of a skirmish line below Custer Hill?

Windolph: *It was clear the troops fought in "skirmish" lines.*

McDougall: *He went to E Company's "skirmish line." They were half in and half out of the ravine.*

Edgerly: *There were bodies "between General Custer and the river."*

Slaper: *Bodies were "on the line nearest to the river."*

Wallace: *He saw members of Company E in the ravine "lying in skirmish order."*

Hare: *The bulk of E were "killed 300 or 400 yards" below Custer. There were about 28 bodies in "a skirmish order."*

Coleman: *His company buried 30 of E Troop that were "in line not ten feet apart."*

Clifford: *Custer's five companies perished in "skirmish lines" and in groups of fours.*

Woodruff: *The two troops with Custer near the monument were "in skirmish line."*

Roe: *Dead men were strung along from the ravine "toward the high ridge."*

Freeman: *His map indicated men had "dismounted and made a stand" along the South Line.*

M. Sheridan: *A path, "still plainly marked by the line of dead," went from Custer Hill down toward the river.*

Mulford: *"Upon the slope toward the river I counted 28 heaps of bones."*

Maguire: *Leading from Custer Hill to the ravine was "a regular line of bodies." They "fell at skirmish distance from each other."*

Dolan: *The men of E fell "as straight as if they were on a skirmish line."*

McClernand: *"The line of skirmishers" was dismounted toward the river. The "line" from Custer down showed more care in placing than on any other part of the field.*

Even without the confirming archaeological evidence, these accounts alone make it clear that a significant number of dead were found below Custer Hill in formations that would support the concept of an organized line.

Perhaps a part of Hardorff's reluctance to acknowledge the South Skirmish Line lies in geographical considerations, for his conception of the location of Deep Ravine is suspect. There may be examples we have missed, but on at least four occasions, and in two books, he claimed the deep ravine was located 400 yards southwest of Custer Hill.[440] Of course, this was Cemetery Ravine, not Deep Ravine, that he described. It contains the line of gravemarkers and stretches to a distance of over 400 yards down from Custer Hill. Continuing that same line downhill, Deep Ravine begins over 700 yards below Custer Hill. Yet, Hardorff used Lieutenant Hare's testimony to argue for a Deep Ravine location of the 28 bodies of Company E men.[441]

Just as it is strange that Taunton would use the McClernand citations to argue against a South Skirmish Line, it is unjustifiable for Hardorff to cite Lieutenant Hare to prove Company E men fell in Deep Ravine. Hare's is one of the most concise accounts we have that indicates Smith's men fell in Cemetery Ravine. Hare buried E Company. He remembered them. They were in skirmish order. There were 28 of them in a coulee down 300 or 400 yards below Last Stand Hill. This is square on the South Line in Cemetery Ravine. It is unfathomable how one could use Hare's account to prove otherwise.

It is therefore possible that Hardorff may be employing the same techniques for which he faulted Kuhlman. Red Hawk indicated to interviewer Nicholas Ruleau that the soldiers made a third stand, down from Custer Hill. When some of the soldiers ran for the ravine, *all* were killed without getting into it. In a footnote to that statement, Hardorff flatly stated Ruleau was in error and accused him of mental editing. Ruleau was wrong, Hardorff thought, because he had said that Red Hawk told him the soldiers never got to Deep Ravine. But because Hardorff was certain 28 men died there, Ruleau must have been in error in interpreting Red Hawk and must have edited Red Hawk's story. Why? Hardorff suggested that Ruleau got an incorrect impression of the situation after viewing the gravemarkers that Hardorff claims are in faulty locations![442] You are not alone if you have trouble following that line of reasoning, and you may have already sharpened up "Ockham's razor" on your own volition.

Why is it so impossible to believe that Red Hawk truly told Ruleau that the soldiers didn't get into Deep Ravine? Hardorff may have accused Ruleau of an incorrect rendering of Red Hawk's tale because the Red Hawk/Ruleau account didn't fit his belief that 28 men went into Deep Ravine and died. Kuhlman was not the only one guilty of discrediting evidence that didn't fit his ideas.

There are further examples where Hardorff's analysis suffered because of his persistence in denying the existence of a South Line. In the Hugh Scott interview with He Dog, the Oglala said, "Custer never got any nearer to the river than the monument. Only a few soldiers who broke away were killed below toward the river." Again, in a footnote immediately following, Hardorff said, "He Dog's statement is incorrect." Then Hardorff went on to state that eight troopers may have held a position at the west end of Calhoun (Finley) Ridge on a cutbank above Deep Coulee.[443]

Why in the world is He Dog wrong? He saw it—not Hardorff. What do eight troopers on Calhoun Ridge have to do with He Dog's testimony about a few soldiers breaking away below the monument? The focus on testimony indicating an action below Custer Hill was ignored and reference was shifted to an event on another part of the field. The logical conclusion from He Dog's statement is that 28 men couldn't have died in Deep Ravine, which is in opposition to Hardorff's ideas. Hardorff transferred attention to eight men who went toward the river on Calhoun Ridge, a circumstance irrelevant to He Dog's statement concerning the paucity of fleeing troopers from Last Stand Hill.

The White Bull account did not emerge intact from Hardorff's editing either. The Indian couldn't have been much clearer when he said the "4th co... had white horses—that was the grey horse troop." However, Hardorff again attempted to "clarify" the statement in a footnote. He said there was sufficient evidence to prove that the third company consisted of Company E men, and that it was Company F that was the fourth company.[444] Company F had bays. White Bull made it clear that the fourth company rode grays. There is no need to continually "correct" the Indians' words. Perhaps the spirit of Dr. Kuhlman did not appreciate being accused of improprieties and returned to haunt and inflict the same curse on some of his detractors.

Hardorff did not care much for Wooden Leg's testimony either, especially when Wooden Leg described soldiers that moved down from Custer Hill as an organized force and deployed with a purpose. Hardorff called it "nonsense."[445] Poor Wooden Leg. He too, like Red Hawk, He Dog, and White Bull, had his fidelity questioned when it did not fit Hardorff's conception of events.

After the problems we have described with some of the above methodologies and the interpretations they have led to, it may be a surprise to find that there is one point we both agree on. Hardorff concluded, in *Markers, Artifacts and Indian Testimony*, that of the remains of 28 men in Deep Ravine, only two out of five have been identified as belonging to Company E, a ratio that possibly indicated only a few of the slain were from Smith's troop and Company E was probably never involved in a maneuver at that location.[446] Thus, "The alleged identification of E Troop in the ravine was based on misleading circumstantial evidence rather than fact, and E Troop as a unit was never near the ravine."[447]

In this case Hardorff is partially right—but for the wrong reasons. Company E wasn't in Deep Ravine as an organized unit, true—but not because it was destroyed on its way north along Battle Ridge, nor because it was there as a *dis*organized unit, nor because other companies might have had more dead in the ravine than did E. In fact, Company E wasn't in Deep Ravine as an organized unit because *it had already been destroyed as an organized unit on the South Skirmish Line in Cemetery Ravine.* Given Hardorff's reluctance to countenance Company E forming a South Skirmish Line, he would assuredly find this hypothesis anathema. When we can finally look beyond that roadblock of 28 men having to be in Deep Ravine, more than just Hardorff may be able to raise their sights out of that gully.

We must also reserve a comment for Drs. Scott, Fox, and other scribing contributors to *Archaeological Perspectives*, a book that, by the way, enthralled and inspired me to attempt this very study to seek a reason for their inability to find bodies in Deep Ravine. The authors of that fine work were also so entangled with the Deep Ravine scenario that it led them to an astonishing statement. They said that one thing was certain: soldiers died and were buried in Deep Ravine. "There is not a single convincing account to the contrary."[448] Now that is an eyebrow raiser!

Another interpretation of the South Line episode appears in Richard Fox's *Archaeology, History, and Custer's Last Battle*, a book likely to have a significant impact on future historical battle studies because its blend of archaeology and history portends more interaction between those disciplines.

Fox does not favorably view the idea of a South Skirmish Line. Though he agrees troopers were there, he argues they did not have much of an opportunity for resistance. His reconstruction of events in this sector depicted Companies E and F delaying low on Cemetery Ridge after their return from the north ford. They then traveled south to the flats and back north following the course of Deep Ravine until they reached the basin above upper Deep Ravine. Company F stayed as a reserve in the basin while E went up to Cemetery Ridge. Indians, including the "suicide boys," attacked from what is now the cemetery area and from the west. Company E went down into the basin with Company F, then they both went up to Custer Hill to form a defense, also rescuing survivors of the Calhoun Hill fight. Subsequently, Company E left the hill and went south, either to drive off the Indians or to assist horsemen in an attempt to ride for help. They were all killed. The 50 to 60 men still left on Custer Hill were being steadily whittled down by attrition. The last survivors fled to Deep Ravine. They died. The South Line never existed. Nearly all of the markers there are phony.[449]

As in Greene's example, perhaps Fox's reconstruction of events could be achieved more profitably with a bit less shuffling of troops. Additionally, there are some negative proofs employed to explain his scenario.[450] Fox states E Company formed a line on Cemetery Ridge. There is no direct archaeological evidence for it, so Fox assumes that the evidence must have been destroyed when the visitor center, cemetery, and road were built. He tells us he deduced E's location because of the lack of archaeological evidence.[451] A lack of artifacts does not prove that they once existed, only to be subsequently destroyed by construction crews, and it does not constitute a proof of E's presence. Company E may have been on Cemetery Ridge, but we must infer this from historical documents, not from an absence of artifacts.

Fox contends Company F was the reserve company for the left wing. He states that only Cheyenne traditional accounts refer to F Company in the basin. "This silence tends to validate the company's reserve status. . . . But the most compelling evidence is archaeological. The absence of physical evidence for organized fighting in the basin (i.e., the South Skirmish Line sector), or anywhere near it, is consistent with a reserve company, and that could have only been F."[452] Again, lack of physical evidence of fighting in the basin is not proof that the basin contained a reserve company that did not fight.

Fox maintains that Captain Freeman's map (fig. 11) depicted Company E in a fight on Cemetery Ridge. "Freeman remains silent about what he saw," writes Fox. There were few if any dead cavalrymen there, so "something else must have caught his eye." Because there were no alternatives, Fox states, "Quite likely, Freeman saw expended government cartridges at intervals suggesting pedestrian skirmishing." Freeman's silence about any specific evidence certainly does not demonstrate that he saw expended cartridges at skirmish intervals. Proofs of this sort will not sustain a serious historical argument.[453]

Fox said he changed his thinking in some ways during the preparation of his last few books, and certainly this is acceptable and healthy in the course of uncovering new evidence. Apparent inconsistencies, he added, between this and his earlier works might be the result of multiple authorship. He hoped the situation would not lead to confusion, but unfortunately, such is not the case.[454] In 1987, Fox and Scott appeared impressed with the viability of a South Line, partially because the presence of Colt .45 bullets and casings indicated the likelihood of close-in fighting. There were not a lot of these .45s found, but those found were located in the South Line and Keogh areas. In 1989, Scott and Fox and others wrote again that a tough fight must have occurred in the "South Defensive Area," that 29 Colt bullets and 11 cases were found in the South Line and Keogh area, that the South Skirmish Line was a valid historical concept, and that the memorial markers along the line were among the most accurate on the field.[455]

Conversely, in 1993 Fox argued that there was no sustained fight on the South Line, Colt cases were "entirely absent," and most markers there "are phony."[456] Although Fox kindly clarified to me that he has not accepted the existence of a South Skirmish Line since 1985, the two interpretations are in opposition and beg further clarification.[457] Both were based on the same archaeological data, yet the evidence is either pro or con, depending on whether the hypothesis calls for a valid defense or a quick disintegration. Which are we to believe? Perhaps we are witnessing the results of more of those data-entry errors, much as in the case of the gravemarkers. "Hard" proofs of this type are no improvement over ambiguous historical documents. We still remain in a quandary over how to assess the evidence as it pertains to the validity of a South Skirmish Line.

Though it is reasonable for Fox to say that troops did not defend along the South Line for very long, it does not appear as reasonable to contend that only 6 to 10 men died along the upper South Line.[458] Six gravemarker sites were excavated in the upper Deep Ravine watershed and in Cemetery Ravine—three in each. All six (100 percent) proved to contain human bones. As Scott and Fox stated in 1989, "Every single marker excavated represented a fallen soldier, every pair represented a fallen soldier. Other than the second marker in each pair, the placement of markers in these areas appears accurate."[459] Contrast this with Calhoun Hill, an area that appears strongly defended in the historical record, where only three

The upper South Skirmish Line from the "low divide," looking toward the national cemetery and visitor center.

out of five excavations (60 percent) proved to have remains. How is this anomaly explained?

A legitimate possibility is that roadwork in the Calhoun area disturbed the markers. Along the upper South Line, however, Fox states that "postburial disturbances" may have scattered the remains to make it appear that more men were buried there than in actuality. What is the essence of these "disturbances"? "On a subjective note," wrote Scott and Fox in *Archaeological Perspectives*, "the excavations on the South Skirmish Line and the Keogh area produced the feeling that there may be much bone scattered throughout the area."[460] Thus, there was not much substance to the disturbances on the upper South Line except the "feeling" that bones were scattered. It is believable that roadwork on Calhoun Hill would result in legitimate burial sites being unmarked by headstones, but it is not acceptable that the "feeling" of disturbances on the upper South Line would result in more headstones than legitimate burial sites. Road construction can disturb graves, but feelings cannot.

A reason that Fox must dismiss the legitimacy of the South Line gravemarkers is that he, like Hardorff, King, and others, must account for the 28 men he believes are buried in Deep Ravine. Fox has placed a great reliance on archaeology to provide the "skeleton" and history to supply the "clothes" for his story of Custer's last fight. In the great majority of instances, he has been able to adhere to this construction. This framework, however, does not solve the problem posed by the "missing 28." In this case, there is literally no "skeleton" to hang the "clothing" on. Fox maintains that the bodies are still there, near the modern "headwall" (headcut), where the 1876 surface is more than six feet below the present gulch floor.[461] Yet, the inability of the archaeological digs to provide any direct physical evidence of bodies means that one of the legs of the framework is missing. With no "skeleton," Fox is left only with historical documents to go by, and we have illustrated the likelihood that those documents have been misinterpreted.

We have come full circle. It is not proven that 28 men are buried in Deep Ravine, nor that the South Skirmish Line never existed. The hypothesis of this study, that 28 men cannot be found in Deep Ravine because the majority of them fell on the South Skirmish Line, still remains the most likely alternative.

A view from Calhoun Hill, looking down Calhoun Coulee. Greasy Grass Ridge runs from left to center in the background.

Lame White Man and the South Line

The belief that Deep Ravine holds 28 bodies is an obstacle to recognizing a South Skirmish Line. Another obstacle to cognizance stems from placing the Lame White Man attack in the Calhoun Coulee-Greasy Grass Ridge area.[462] Shifting of the attack site may, in turn, be a consequence of misreading the Wooden Leg narrative. Wooden Leg said, "about forty of the soldiers came galloping from the east part of the ridge down toward the river" where the Cheyennes and Oglalas were hidden. The Indians fell back to a deep gulch, but the soldiers stopped and dismounted on a low ridge. Lame White Man then led the counterattack. In only a few minutes the soldiers were overrun. The Indians got the soldiers' guns to use against the other troops on the high ridge. Wooden Leg went to the east end of the ridge, but by the time he got there, those soldiers had also been killed.[463]

After the fight, Wooden Leg heard that Noisy Walking had been wounded. He found him "down in the gulch where the band of soldiers nearest the river had been killed in the earlier part of the battle." He had been shot and stabbed, and his relatives were coming for him with a travois. Wooden Leg then "moved on eastward up the gulch coulee," where he discovered the body of the scalped Lame White Man. He knew the Cheyenne chief had gone with the young men in their charge against the soldiers, perhaps had gone farther than the others, and was killed on his way back. Wooden Leg helped remove Lame White Man and Noisy Walking from the field.[464]

By examining Wooden Leg's account we can deduce that Lame White Man's attack occurred along the low divide between Cemetery Ravine and the upper reaches of Deep Ravine. Misconceptions may stem from two statements. Wooden Leg said that the troop that Lame White Man attacked "came galloping from the east part of the ridge down toward the river." Later in his narrative he added that the "forty soldiers who rode down from the ridge along a broad coulee and toward the river were charged upon by Lame White Man." The place of this first charge and victory "is inside of the present fence around the battlefield and at its lower side."[465]

Of course, because one troop galloped down from the "east part" of the ridge does not mean they stayed in the east—Custer too came down from the east, only to die on the far western end. There are several solid reasons that lead us to reject the Greasy Grass Ridge-Calhoun Coulee scenario.

First, inside the fence at its lower side does not necessarily mean today's fence line along the southeast park boundary from Calhoun Hill to the river. In the context of the battlefield, lower means downstream or down valley, which is actually to the northwest, not the southeast. For example,

Lame White Man's marker from Battle Ridge. Upper Deep Ravine is in the background.

the lower village was north of the upper village. Lower may also mean in the lower elevations down in the flats southwest of Cemetery Ravine and the low divide. This too was "inside of the present fence" to Wooden Leg. Remember, he walked the field with Dr. Thomas B. Marquis in the 1920s, when there *still was* a fence line boxing in all four sides of the battlefield. The southwest side ran parallel to the river and crossed lower Cemetery Ravine and Deep Ravine about 900 to 1,000 yards down from the monument. The Indians told Dr. Marquis they were stationed there as "go-betweens," cutting the soldiers off from the camp. The old southwest fence line, no longer standing, is shown in R. B. Marshall's 1891 Geological Survey, copies of which can still be purchased at the battlefield. This latter "inside of the present fence," about midway along the southwest side, where the Indians ran back into the deep gulch, was the line Wooden Leg spoke of.[466]

Second, Wooden Leg said the 40 soldiers moved down from the ridge and stopped on a low ridge where the Indians had been. There is no similar terrain in the Greasy Grass Ridge-Calhoun Coulee area that fits this description. In fact, the extension of Calhoun Hill where the Finley-Finckle group of Company C were found forms some of the highest terrain on the

269

battlefield. Rising about 60 feet higher than the west end of Greasy Grass Ridge and 120 or more feet higher than the Deep (north fork of Medicine Tail) Coulee, this imposing ridgeline could be described as anything but "low."

Third, Wooden Leg said that *after* the Lame White Man attack ended he *went* to the east end of the field to catch the finish of that action. He was not already *at* the east end.[467]

Fourth, from Wooden Leg's narrative it is obvious that the troopers that came down from the east end of the ridge did not remain there. In fact, their bodies were found in the ravine where he found Noisy Walking—the upper Deep Ravine—the same "gulch where the band of soldiers nearest the river had been killed in the earlier part of the battle."

Fifth, after finding Noisy Walking in the same gulch where the soldiers died, Wooden Leg "moved on eastward up the gulch coulee," where he came upon the body of Lame White Man. We know that the Cheyenne leader was found about 300 yards south-southeast of Custer Hill—not 1,200 yards, where he would have to have been in order for the Greasy Grass Ridge-Calhoun Coulee scenario to make any sense. Or, from another tack, if it was Calhoun Coulee that Wooden Leg described walking up (which it was not because Noisy Walking was not found in Calhoun Coulee), he would have come out along the Calhoun-Greasy Grass crest, but he still would not have found Lame White Man's body, for it would have been a full half-mile away to the north and west.

Sixth, Thomas B. Marquis was the interpreter for Wooden Leg and a dozen other Cheyennes. He walked the battlefield with them on many occasions. If the Indians weren't sufficiently succinct to enable us to comprehend their meaning, then Marquis certainly was.

Marquis said that the attack by Lame White Man took place against the soldiers on a low ridge "about 500 yards down the gulch slope from the present monument." All these considerations clearly remove this event from the Greasy Grass-Calhoun area and place it in the Cemetery Ravine-Deep Ravine-South Skirmish Line sector.[468]

Other testimony that may contribute to the shift of the Lame White Man attack site is from the Cheyenne Red Bird, who later took the name of his prominent uncle, Little Wolf. In 1918 he told Walter Camp that he watched Custer's men pass the upper reaches of Medicine Tail Coulee and that the Indians followed after him. Camp's notes read, "Only line on Custer ridge was from C to D. I was there Lame White Man charged them here & chased them to Keogh where he (L.W.M.) was killed."[469]

We must remember, however, that in addition to being interviewed by Walter Camp, Red Bird/Little Wolf was also an informant of Thomas Marquis. The doctor would not have clearly written of Lame White

Man's attack 500 yards below the monument if Red Bird and other informants had told him that the attack was directed against a troop on Calhoun Hill or in Calhoun Coulee. Camp attributed a few sentences to Red Bird based on two letters on a paper map; Marquis received direct on-field input from Red Bird and other Cheyennes and was less likely to misconstrue their meaning.

Another factor that may lead one to an interpretation of an attack by Lame White Man on Calhoun Hill is from a map drawn, perhaps in 1930, by Young Two Moon. This map, apparently a representation of the ridge stretching from Calhoun Hill to Custer Hill, shows a "1" south of what appears to be the Calhoun Hill end where the "Walking White party" (Lame White Man's) apparently was located for a time. Other than that, the phrase "Walking White party first charge, side of hill," is our only other clue to his participation. Where that attack might have occurred is uncertain.

Nevertheless, we will not discount the word of Red Bird or the map of Young Two Moon, although when we compare their contributions with those of Wooden Leg, Kate Bighead, and a dozen informants of Marquis, Powell, and Stands In Timber, we find that the contention that Lame White Man attacked the Greasy Grass-Calhoun area is not supported by the bulk of the historical record. However, there is danger in selectively utilizing or discarding testimony. We do not wish to say any one of the above witnesses was untruthful, since it is more likely that the white chroniclers have misunderstood their meaning. And though Red Bird and Young Two Moon do not balance the other evidence, we will not ignore their word.

It may be that the Red Bird and Young Two Moon statements are not diametrically opposed to those of the other witnesses. What may need adjustment is simply the *axis* of the Lame White Man attack. In the past, the assault has been described as proceeding on a west to east line, from the flats to the South Skirmish Line. Perhaps the assault really developed from the south-southwest and headed in a north-northeast direction—which could very well be the essence of Red Bird's statement and Young Two Moon's map, since conception of the terrain's configuration depended on individual perceptions.[470]

Could the northwest end of Greasy Grass Ridge have been the starting point for Lame White Man's attack? Inspection of the field from this vantage point reveals its potential (fig. 19). The illustration was drawn from a series of photographs taken from a point on the ridge just south of the south (Calhoun Coulee) fork of Deep Ravine. This was the area the Cheyennes gravitated toward as they crossed Medicine Tail ford and began to follow the troops north as "go-betweens," a living roadblock protecting the village. From this point today, one can still see the marble markers rising a foot or so above the sere buffalo grass along the crest of the "low divide."

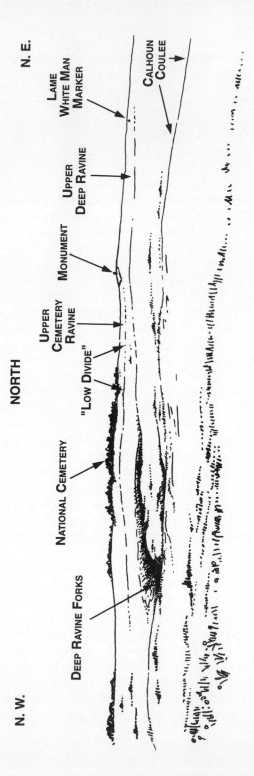

FIGURE 19: VIEW FROM GREASY GRASS RIDGE

Many of the Cheyenne informants may have been in this vicinity when they described Lame White Man's attack. The gray horses came down from the north and were forced back in the direction of the cemetery as per Stands In Timber. Custer's men came down toward the river but were pushed back to the cemetery and fought in the basin below the monument as per Powell. Both renditions had the "suicide boys" entering the fight in the national cemetery-Cemetery Ravine area. The 30 or 40 soldiers killed by Lame White Man were 500 yards below the monument, according to Marquis. Wooden Leg saw 40 men come down toward the river and dismount on a low ridge. That troop was destroyed in the upper reaches of Deep Ravine—where Wooden Leg found Noisy Walking. Kate Bighead may have watched the battle from south of the soldier position in the same locale. She saw a troop come down from the main ridge and dismount on a low divide north of the deep gulch. All of these actions could be seen while looking north from the western end of Greasy Grass Ridge. The descriptions make little sense if the witnesses were looking back to the east or southeast in the direction of Calhoun Hill.

Though Lame White Man may have started his assault from Greasy Grass Ridge, his destination was against what was probably Company E on the low divide between Cemetery Ravine and Deep Ravine. The weight of the historical record, coupled with terrain corroborations and physical evidence, makes this the most probable scenario. Thus, the only adjustment we may need is in the axis of Lame White Man's approach, rather than the object of his attack. When this affair is placed in its proper temporal and spatial setting, the South Skirmish Line episode becomes increasingly sustainable.

The Defense of Custer's Field

Of prime importance in any study of the Custer fight is the problem of sequence. When did events occur in one sector of the field in relation to events in another? Archaeologists Scott and Fox concluded that the action in the Greasy Grass-Calhoun sector ended before the South Skirmish Line action. They believed the Indians moved in two broad lines, generally south to north, one line from Calhoun Hill to Custer Hill and the other from Greasy Grass Ridge to the South Line and to Custer Hill. Through modern ballistics examinations of the cartridges and bullets, much as in criminal investigations, they discovered that at least 23 Indian weapons and at least one army carbine were used by the Indians in two or more sectors of the field. They concluded that the evidence showed Greasy Grass Ridge was overwhelmed prior to the South Line position.[471]

The same evidence offered by Scott and Fox was examined in an article by Bruce Trinque, but an entirely different conclusion was reached. Trinque stated that ballistics can prove a firearm was fired at point A and point B, but it cannot establish which came first. Trinque's examination of possible captured weapon cartridges showed very few were used against the South Line while a large number were used in the Greasy Grass Ridge and Calhoun Hill positions. This, combined with the fact that the region to the east (rear) of the South Line is virtually empty of cartridges, showed that the archaeologists' sequencing is out of order. The Indians did not leave Greasy Grass Ridge to attack the South Line, but rather the reverse was true. Trinque summarized his analysis by stating, "the South Skirmish Line soldier position fell first. . . . Some warriors undoubtedly turned towards Last Stand Hill, others—now partially armed with captured Army carbines—moved south towards Greasy Grass Ridge . . . the soldier positions furthest west along Greasy Grass Ridge were evacuated, the soldiers falling back to Calhoun Hill, itself already under attack from the south and east." Calhoun Hill fell next, as the Indians continued their counterclockwise circuit, then the survivors retreated toward Last Stand Hill.[472]

Where Scott and Fox saw two broad south to north movements, Trinque viewed the sequence from north to south, then west to east, then south to north. Gray saw a similar counterclockwise pattern, almost a circular flow, but his sequence began at Greasy Grass Ridge. Kuhlman thought the troops traveled north up Battle Ridge to Custer Hill, sent a branch down the South Line, then the main body retreated back down Battle Ridge. Greene and Hardorff basically saw a south to north pattern. Greene thought some troops moved south from Custer Hill to check the Indians in Deep Ravine. Hardorff wouldn't even acknowledge that much, but thought the troops were all but destroyed on their way north. The Weiberts viewed the sequence of events as a clockwise flow, the complete opposite of Gray's version. In the latest biography of Custer, by Robert M. Utley, the battle flow is south to north, with a troop advance toward Deep Ravine originating on Calhoun Hill. Lame White Man attacked and pushed the soldiers back south to Calhoun Hill before the retrograde movement was halted and the remaining troops continued north to Custer Hill.[473]

There are five more or less discernible soldier collapses in the Custer fight: at the South Line, on Greasy Grass Ridge (actually in the Finley-Finckle position midway between Greasy Grass and Calhoun Hill), on Calhoun Hill, in the Keogh area, and on Custer Hill. The beginning of the end commenced with the fall of the South Line.

An important point can be drawn from all the conflicting alternatives. The above descriptions of sequencing, battle flow, troop dispositions, and Indian movement, juxtaposed with the locations of the artifacts, amply illustrate one fact: After their offensive maneuvers were frustrated, Custer's troops did attempt to form up in a defensive perimeter. Though that defense was apparently short-lived, the perimeter did exist for a time *before* any of its sides collapsed. Indeed, Kate Bighead's ride around the troops verified the existence of a perimeter and clarified the sequence of events. Had there been no troops in a central defensive formation, Kate would have had no need to circumnavigate them in her search for her nephew.

The sequencing and significance of Kate Bighead's ride has been lost on more than one Little Bighorn battle researcher. William Hedley used Kate's account, among others, to attempt to show that Custer had spent well over an hour on Nye-Cartwright Ridge and that the move off the ridge was the catalyst causing the Indians to swarm to the attack. Hedley argued that the soldiers' movement from the ridge was a movement by C Troop down from Nye-Cartwright Ridge and onto Greasy Grass Ridge. After that move, the fight began in earnest and was over quickly.[474] There was little, if any, time for the soldiers to continue much farther north of Calhoun Hill.

Again, we simply have to examine the sequence of events to see how illogical Hedley's scenario is. Kate had *already circumnavigated* the battlefield before she described the troop movement coming down from the ridge. What reason would she have for making a several-mile circle around Custer's perimeter before his troops even got there? Obviously, the troops she described were not just making their first appearance on the battlefield from Nye-Cartwright Ridge, for she had already ridden around them. The troop she saw was Company E coming down from the Custer Hill area. Interpretations that place this movement and attack in the Calhoun Hill area simply do not follow the logical sequencing as evidenced in the historical record.

Kate Bighead's story provides further evidence that the troopers formed up in a defensive perimeter. This may not appear to be a statement of great significance at first, but consider the ramifications. The fight on Custer's field was not haphazard. It was not a helter-skelter free-for-all. It was not a rout. The troopers were not "scattered like corn" as Benteen would have us believe. The majority did not die in a panic flight for their lives. The skirmish lines that so many spoke of were real and not imagined patterns. The marble markers and the bodies they represent, the relic finds, the lack of bodies in Deep Ravine, and the lack of relics inside the "box" all support the likelihood of a definite defensive formation that survived intact before exploitation of its weak point caused the entire structure to topple.

Many Indians, albeit without the detail of Kate's account, spoke of the defense made by the soldiers. Gall said that Keogh and Calhoun never broke, but fought strong and desperately in a line along the ridge and were shot down in line where they stood. Two Moon said the troops were in place. They fought in the open and were dropped in line, along their various occupied positions. Low Dog said he never saw such a fearless band as the white warriors, who stood their ground bravely. Feather

Earring said the soldiers fought hard and made their main stand on the ridge. Lights said the soldiers were killed fighting and the Indians captured guns along the South Line to use against men who still resisted on the main ridge. Hollow Horn Bear indicated all the soldiers were brave and none rushed to get away. Moving Robe Woman claimed it was not a massacre, but a hotly fought battle. Wooden Leg said the soldiers occupied the ridges and the Indians kept up a long-range firing for up to an hour and a half. Yellow Horse said Custer's fighting was superb. He kept his ground clear to the last, fighting well enough to keep the Indians from mingling in hand-to-hand combat and keeping the warriors at bay until only a handful of soldiers were left standing.[475]

While a good number of Indians spoke of lines, established positions, and long, desultory firing, there were others who did say it was a moving fight that was over quickly. Again, it was a case of separate events. There was a moving fight—but only after the stalemate on the perimeter was broken. Although a broad box pattern is essentially correct, the sequencing impressions presented by some writers have led us to visualize fleeing troopers in constant motion, being overwhelmed at one position, falling back to the next, ad infinitum, resembling nothing more than mice scurrying in a cage from one wall to the next.

Once we inspect the evidence, allocate the events in proper sequence, and break through the pictures of chaos, the battle unfolds in a different light. Obviously, there were not enough troopers to adequately man the entire position, and the foe they faced could have been more profitably deterred with a tighter perimeter and a more uniform dispersion. Yet the idea of forming up in a defensive square is not so odd as it may sound at first. Many of the officers in the fight, commissioned and noncommissioned, were Civil War veterans. They were not metamorphosed creations of any new techniques or training, they were products of their past experience, and their primary past experience was the Civil War. Many were more interested in refighting Gettysburg or Five Forks than in formulating new strategies of unconventional warfare to meet a new type of foe. The period between 1865 and 1880 has been labeled the army's "dark ages" because of the long shadow cast by the Civil War. Traditionalism, a conservative reluctance to change tactics to meet new conditions, was the shackling characteristic that sapped the army and its officers of vitality and vision.[476]

Paddy Griffith, a British historian and senior lecturer at Sandhurst, has suggested that far from being the first "modern" war, or even a "transitional" war, the Civil War was a carryover from many Napoleonic fighting traditions in the persistent use of obsolete assault tactics, in the adherence to obsolete doctrine and training, and in the improper usage of new technology that effectively rendered those methods null. When Generals

Grant and Sherman adopted a strategy of "total war," it was nothing new, but rather a return to tactics similar to those already employed in the Thirty Years' War of the seventeenth century. Sherman never would have thought of himself as a prophet of modern war.[477] U.S. Army tactics in the late nineteenth century could have been implemented more comfortably by Frederick the Great, Clausewitz, or Jomini than by Haig, Foch, or Pershing. Forming a square as a defense against a mobile foe comprised a section of Gen. Winfield Scott's three-volume tactical manual that appeared in 1835 and was based on 35 years of French experience. By the time of the Civil War, Scott's work was superseded by Lt. Col. William J. Hardee's tactical manual. It too was based on French manuals and retained the sections on forming defensive squares; it was not a revolutionary document at all. In 1867, Maj. Gen. Emory Upton produced an updated tactics manual that was to be used for the next several decades. The defensive square was still there, as were the ideas of skirmish lines and fighting in formed ranks. This was a Napoleonic document that debarred Upton from his title as a champion of modern tactics.[478]

Though Griffith's depiction of the Civil War as Napoleonic may be debated, we must acknowledge that for hundreds, even thousands, of years forming square was a tried and true method of defending against a mobile enemy. It was used in the American Indian Wars: Brig. Gen. Alfred Sully formed up in a box more than a mile per side in length to fight about 1,600 Sioux at the Battle of Killdeer Mountain in 1864. It was used by Gen. Alfred Terry in the valley of the Little Bighorn two days after Custer was killed. Custer himself formed a "defensive triangle" at Trevilian Station in 1864 and squares in his battles with the Sioux along the Yellowstone River in 1873. It may have successfully been used by Custer on June 25, 1876, had he been in terrain where a field of fire extending 400 or 500 yards in every direction could have been established.[479] The square was much used in 1879, just three years after the Battle of the Little Bighorn, by the British in their wars with the Zulus—successfully at Khambula, Gingindlovu, and Ulundi, and unsuccessfully at Isandlwana, a battle that very much resembled Custer's fight at the Little Bighorn.[480] Squares were used at Abu Klea in 1885, at Omdurman in 1898, and in almost any number of countless actions across the breadth of Africa and Asia during the British Empire's "little wars" throughout the entire nineteenth century.[481]

Yet, perhaps the term "forming square" fosters too anachronistic a connotation. While we can easily conceptualize a square in Napoleonics, we have a harder time visualizing the same on the American steppe, and rightly so. There was no classic square at the Little Bighorn, but there was an expedient response to the situation. When one lacked the numbers, training, or time to form up shoulder to shoulder, a more informal response would suffice. The laager served the Boer at Blood River. Circled wagons worked for the trekking pioneers along the Oregon Trail. A log corral sufficed for the hay cutters near Fort C. F. Smith. A barricade of dead horses was enough for the defenders of Beecher's Island.

Did Custer not have enough troopers to man such a large perimeter? Companies were at least posted at the apexes of the box, perhaps spreading out to cover the intervening gaps as the battle progressed. Was this still too large for five troops? Maybe so, but maybe not if the response was formulated with the understanding that seven more companies under Reno and Benteen would soon arrive to help flesh out the formation. The perimeter that Custer's command died along measures about one and one-half miles long—two miles if we complete the rough rectangle by adding the unfinished river quarter where the north and south forks of Deep Ravine intrude. Could 12 companies defend a two-mile perimeter? Sully's command thought they were facing 6,000 warriors at Killdeer Mountain. They formed a square at over one mile per side with 20 companies. Thus, Sully had 5 companies to cover each mile of front—and he was successful. Had Reno and Benteen made it to Custer's position, he would have had 6 companies per mile.

Custer's tactics on the Little Bighorn were not out of line with contemporary battle theory. He was not "mad," as some twentieth-century authors and movie producers would depict him in their revisionist histories or attempts to produce "politically correct" social commentary. Custer's "mistakes" were precisely related to the fact that he was a product of his times, not because he was an aberration. His actions must be carefully weighed in a nineteenth-century framework. One of the most pernicious errors of modern commentators is that they allow themselves to be trapped in the fallacy of ethnomorphism, whereby behavior or morals, conceptualization of characteristics of another people in another time, are judged in terms of one's own.[482] Successful aggressive Civil War formulas practiced by Grant, Sherman, and Sheridan were imposed on the Indians. The policy entailed necessary risks and accepted losses as a matter of fact. At the Little Bighorn, Custer was fulfilling the role written for him by Sheridan, and essentially achieved the purpose of the campaign, which was to find and fight the enemy. The Sioux War was the most conventional war the army ever fought against the trans-Mississippi Indians, one that the Civil War veterans were used to, in which adversaries maneuvered for control of a battlefield. Custer was outmaneuvered and defeated in a conventional battle.[483] Neither Custer nor his tactics were asynchronous.

As in the case of the South Skirmish Line, where we found that the question of which way its soldiers actually faced did not negate its existence, so too with the entire battle line: because its defenders eventually perished does not mean they attempted no stand. Examination of the record indicates that, with the exception of the last desperate fugitives at battle's end, the conflict was not the panic rout theorized in recent publications. Custer, after realizing that there was to be no immediate charge through the village, withdrew to a new position to await Reno and Benteen before continuing offensive operations. The wait took longer than anticipated, and Custer's holding pattern in terrain poorly suited for defense left him vulnerable. Too late, he attempted to stabilize the situation by employing tactics for dealing with a more numerous, mobile enemy. After a significant time of stalemate, the collapse did come quickly.

It is beyond the scope of this work to analyze the viability of the other positions on the field. However, we have studied one segment of the line and presented a case that the men there attempted a defense. Though they may not have held their ground long, there was little bunching and little, if any, evidence of a panic rout. Twenty-eight men did not die clustered in Deep Ravine, evidence which, were it there, would have made a stronger case for a rout. The men died resisting in Cemetery Ravine.

The interpretations of events on Custer's field are almost as numerous as the number of interpreters, and the great quantity of seemingly ambiguous evidence allows for a myriad of conclusions. An anticipatory mind will produce its own cause and effect, and we would be superhuman to resist its dictates. If the chronicle fits, use it, but the hypothesis should be shaped to the evidence, not vice versa. In addition, one can only go so far with the primary evidence. Much of what has been written about the battle is "in fact and by necessity, a study of the *study* of the battle." If the truth is ever to be known, "previous analyses must be examined, evaluated and discussed. If errors of logic exist, if evidence is misinterpreted or distorted, then it is only right that this should be pointed out." One cannot worry about a little argument in a field that has, in the past, engendered such sharp tongues as those of Frederic Van de Water, Fred Dustin, and Mari Sandoz.[484]

We have been critical of some interpretations, but we are not trying to foster a negative impression of anyone's historical work. The nature of the Little Bighorn battle leaves the road open for anyone wishing to try their luck in sorting out the evidence, and any honest attempt at interpretation should be nearly as valid as the next. We have already mentioned our appreciation for the research done by the many scholars in this field. However, we must be aware of the danger of being overly attached to an idea, even though, as Dr. Kuhlman said, "A working thesis is an absolute necessity for the historian." This is nothing new to students of the Little Bighorn fight. All those who think historically make assumptions in their work, and those assumptions have logical consequences that must be respected.[485]

Nevertheless, those assumptions must not put a damper on our openness to alternatives. Facts do not contradict each other. Our theories are the source of contradictions. In the case of the troop dispositions and time sequencing, we may have to make future assessments with the understanding that there was no panic bunching in Deep Ravine, and therefore the fight may have been more organized and lasted longer than some current theory would allow. In the case of the memorial markers, we must admit that they closely represent the positions of the soldiers that fell, and that the army first, and the National Park Service later, did a commendable job in preserving their pattern for contemporary visitors to speculate about. In the case of the ravines, the assumption that all historical accounts must have been speaking of the "Deep Ravine" may have blinded us to other possibilities.

I may be accused of using the Cemetery Ravine idea as a working thesis and favoring it over others. If that be true, so be it; let the hypothesis be thrown into the ring as a counterweight to the many who espouse the consensus alternatives. If we are to be honest with ourselves, it is high time we admit that we have been misinterpreting evidence, and our search for 28 bodies does not have a solution buried beneath the soil in Deep Ravine.

6. Beyond the Historical Record

Time Warp

Thus far we have concentrated on the historical record of the Battle of the Little Bighorn and whether or not that record has been misinterpreted. That there was an apparent discrepancy between the written record provided by the soldiers and the physical record of the discovered relics has been noted by the archaeologists who participated in the battlefield excavations.[486] Yet there may be a way we can bridge the credibility gap between those records other than by contending we simply have not been perspicacious enough to grasp the nuance between what was said and what was meant. To accomplish this we may have to leave some of the customary sources behind and seek answers in psychological constructions.

If we have been shackled by long-accepted interpretations of the record and have found it difficult to shed our perceptions of events, we are not the only ones to experience such difficulty. It is not so strange that we have trouble assessing eyewitness accounts that purport to be describing similar scenes. After a century we lack the immediacy of the firsthand impact that the participants experienced. But the witnesses themselves—how could their statements differ to such a great extent?

Let us consider, for example, recording the time of the start of the battle. When did the fight begin? It seems like a simple enough question. Almost every officer, most noncommissioned officers, and some enlisted men carried a timepiece. All one had to do was look at his watch. Sunrise on June 25, 1876, was at 5:22 A.M. and sunset was at 9:04 P.M.[487] Lieutenant Wallace, the adjutant and "official" timekeeper, said they crossed the Little Bighorn and began the attack some time after half past 2 P.M.[488] Major Reno, in his report, stated he began the charge at 2 P.M. Assistant Surgeon Henry R. Porter testified at Reno's Court that the attack began about 1:30 P.M. Sergeant Knipe said Reno's attack began a little after noon. According to a letter written by Private Martin, the battle started before 11 in the morning. The Arikara scout Young Hawk estimated that it was still before noon when the Sioux were leaving Reno to go downstream and fight Custer. Scout George Herendeen thought they got to the battlefield around noon. Interpreter Fred Gerard insisted that he had a very good timepiece that had just been to the jewelers for cleaning and repairing, and he stated that Reno had already retreated from the timber by 1 P.M. Pvt. Jacob Hetler said they arrived on the field at 11 A.M. The Crow scout Goes Ahead said Reno took battle position in the valley between 8 and 9 in the morning, and Pvt. Gustave Korn said Reno attacked the village as early as 8 A.M.! There were almost as many different times given for the start of the battle as there were participants.[489] The Indians, with their frequent time estimations of around noon, were much more consistent than the white men were.

Author William Graham was concerned about the time discrepancies, especially noting that the early accounts of the fight seemed to set the hour of Reno's attack earlier in time than did the later accounts. He could not account for the variances and asked Gen. Edward Godfrey about them. Godfrey answered that it was likely that everyone was just too busy to take an accurate account of the hours.[490]

W. Kent King, an author who seemed to relish conspiracy theories, argued that the time variances were the result of a deliberate cover-up engineered by those such as Reno, Benteen, and "higher-ups," who sought to hide Benteen's dalliance in getting to the battlefield or Reno's tardiness in going to Custer's aid. Later times were entered into the record as a deliberate whitewash. If the battle started at 2 P.M. instead of noon, Benteen couldn't be accused of wasting two hours in getting to Reno. If they all met on the hilltop at 4 P.M. instead of 2 P.M., Reno had much less time to go to Custer's assistance. Were these officially sanctioned attempts to deceive, and did the "conspiracy" go as high as the presidency, as King would have us believe?[491] That may be pushing the intrigue a bit too far.

Some of the discrepancies may be the result of a simpler explanation. Lieutenant Wallace's official watch was set on Chicago time, which was one and a half hours earlier than the time under the Montana noonday sun. That will account for some of the time discrepancies. The time zones that we are so familiar with today were unknown in 1876. For many reasons, including a need to keep standardized timetables for the smooth operation of the railroads, a Prime Meridian Conference had been held in Washington, D.C., and the result was a world system of standard zones based on Greenwich Mean Time. The United States standardized in 1883, but in 1876, exact time was not as important as it is today. In 1876, even perceptions of time were experienced differently. The run of the seasons, the solar and lunar cycles, and the experience of living day to day was much different in 1876 than it was in 1776, and the variance was even more pronounced between 1876 and 1976. The world operated at a slower pace in the nineteenth century than it does today. Therefore, we must be wary when judging time perceptions of the men of 1876 while standing on "the farther shore" of a different century.[492]

Combat Stress

Yet there was more to the time variances than being in Montana with watches set on Chicago time. Many of the time problems could very well have been the result of fear and stress-related perception alterations. Recording the correct time for the start of the battle was a task that seemed simple, yet proved difficult.

While the measure of time, a noun, would seem to be a fairly objective proposition, the measure of adjectives such as "near" and "deep" have proven more troublesome. We have already seen that the "nearness" of Custer to the river meant different things to different people. "Deep" also caused similar problems. How deep is a "deep ravine"?

Numerous ravines cut up the hills along the Little Bighorn. There are many descriptive terms for them, including gullies, gulches, valleys, draws, cutbanks, arroyos, barrancas, ditches, washes, and so on. We have read that Pvt. Jacob Adams called the low hollow of the hospital area on Reno Hill a small basin. Young Hawk saw it as a ravine. Lieutenant Wallace called it a "swale of the ravine." It was a "depression" to Lt. Edward G. Mathey. Jacob Adams called the area below Custer Hill a large basin. Colonel Gibbon called it a gentle valley. DeRudio called the area a ravine, as did Moylan and McDougall. It was a gully to Roy and Hardy and Thompson. To Lieutenants McClernand and Hare it was a coulee. To several Cheyennes it was a big basin.

One would not be able to visualize the ravine's proportions from the soldiers' renditions, but one can ascertain a trend in the adjectives. The ravine does not appear to be as deep and imposing the further in time one is removed from the battle. The inaccessible pit seen by a gravedigging soldier in June 1876 was a ravine, a gully, a valley, or a slope to those visiting the field one, two, or five years later. The only eyewitnesses to comment on scramble marks or fingerprints in the dirt were 7th Cavalry survivors. No one else of the Montana or Dakota Columns saw any such thing. Colonel Gibbon, on the field June 29 but not subject to the ordeal experienced by the 7th Cavalry, saw the terrain as a gentle valley. To Mike Sheridan, who removed the officers' remains one year after the battle, there was no deep ravine at all—it was just a path toward the river marked by a line of dead. Montana pioneer Granville Stuart visited the area in 1880 and saw gradual, short-grass slopes and small sags that a horse could easily gallop over. Other visitors who described the area mentioned slopes, valleys, and gullies, with the adjective "deep" absent more often than not.[493] Time had softened the ravine's terror—at least for those who were not members of the 7th Cavalry.

For the battle survivors, exaggerated terrain was still a reality. This is not at all odd. The men of 1876 exercised their senses and perceptions under less than calm, objective circumstances. They had just been subjected to a traumatic three-day ordeal. They faced exhaustion, thirst, terror, and death. Some had not eaten for days. Parties were organized to take canteens to the river for water to assuage the suffering wounded men, acts of desperation that resulted in additional wounds and death for some, and Medals of Honor for the lucky survivors. And what of the wounded? Major Reno wanted to abandon them during the siege and make a run for it.[494] Thinking about the likely end result of that option could be horrifying.

As trying as the physical suffering was, the mental anguish may have been worse. As the nighttime bonfires glowed and flickered in the Indian village below, accompanied by beating drums, singing, dancing, and an occasional punctuated scream, the troopers lying in the blackness were subject to their own terpsichorean mental play. Lieutenant Godfrey reported that the men thought they saw and heard columns of troops approaching over the hills. They thought they heard horses and even trumpet calls. A response was sounded by one of their own trumpeters; shots were fired as signals. A civilian packer mounted a horse, galloped along the line, and shouted that General Crook was coming. It was all a "phantasma of their imaginations."[495]

Apparitions went bump in the night. Things crept by in the darkness. The eerie atmosphere on the hilltop was punctuated by a soldier's scream. One man went insane and had to be tied up like a hog. There was no pretending, said Private Windolph, that the men on Reno Hill were not disorganized and downright frightened. Men hid; some faked being wounded, and others buried their faces in the dirt and froze. The soldiers were like animals, thought Custer's striker, Pvt. John Burkman. They just followed the directions of their officers, but when the officers were too frightened to think straight it affected the men, and the "skeer got into our innards too."[496]

By mid-morning on June 27, the mob on the hill was at the end of its tether, and the appearance of the Terry-Gibbon column was a prayer come true. Lt. Edward Maguire reported that when they ascended the bluffs and met the survivors, the welcome they received would have moved the most callous. "Officers and men relieved their surcharged natures by hysterical shouts and tears." Colonel Gibbon commented on the ecstatic reaction the soldiers had at their rescue, the suffering they had gone through, the long, anxious hours they had waited for succor, the delusions they had experienced, and how their imaginations had affected their judgment. Pvt. John Sivertsen of Company M wrote that even the men of the rescuing forces were caught up in the moment. When General Terry and his command came up on the bluffs, the regiment formed a circle around him and cheered. "The gray-haired commander took off his hat and wept like a child."[497]

There had been a story circulated about trooper Mike Madden of K Company, who supposedly joked about his leg being amputated, telling the doctor that for another swig of whiskey he could cut off his other leg. Pvt. William H. White of Troop F of the 2nd Cavalry was there. He assisted Madden after the operation and was with him almost all the time. Madden was pale, weak, quiet, and very serious. White "neither heard nor heard of any such jollifying talk."[498] No one on the hill was in a joking mood.

The next morning, the men of the 7th Cavalry had to march north four miles to Custer's field. They were not quite through with their ordeal. What might have been their psychological makeup at that juncture? Certainly they did not relish a work detail to bury the putrescent corpses of what had been live comrades just a few days earlier. Though a few officers, enemies of Custer, cared not whether he lived or died, most of the soldiers were emotionally broken. First Lt. John Carland of Company B, 6th Infantry, recorded that when Terry looked upon Custer's body "the tears coursed down his face" and he said, "The Flower of the Army is gone at last." Major Reno wrote that when the survivors of the 7th got to Custer's field, it "was the first time I saw them give way. The brave fellows cried like children when they saw the mutilated bodies of their comrades of the day before." Pvt. David E. Dawsey of Company D wrote in a letter to his mother, "When the red devils got Custer they cut the heart out of this Regiment. It is not often a soldier wastes tears over an Officer, but I saw maney [sic] an old hand wipe his eyes with his blouse sleeve . . . the day we bureyed [sic] Custer."[499]

The troops were severely affected, and the demoralization did not quickly dissipate. After Terry's column met up with Crook's on August 10, Lieutenant Bourke recorded the poor showing made by Terry's men: they were fatigued, despondent, showed a lack of self-reliance, a lack of cohesion, and a lack of spirit to the point of demoralization. The massacre had fallen on them "as a wet blanket." The pall of gloom was injurious, spreading to members of the 5th Cavalry. Lt. Charles King, the regimental adjutant, reported that the Custer massacre so preyed upon the minds of some of the men that three were driven insane, two from his own veteran Company K.[500]

There was no glory at all in this phase of warfare, if there ever was such a thing in any type of war. For General Sherman, all war was "hell," and Indian fighting was the hardest kind of war. John Gibbon was certainly disillusioned. To him, the labors performed in an Indian war far exceeded those in a so-called civilized war. The troops engaged didn't even get credited with "glory." All glory meant on the frontier was being shot at by an Indian from behind a rock, and then getting your name spelled wrong in the newspapers.[501]

The enlisted men thought nothing of glory when confronted with Custer's dead. Certainly they cared nothing for the ephemeral, fleeting rush of a saber charge, or for following their officers into the sunset for God, Country, or Regiment. They wanted nothing to do with going for a brevet or a coffin. What the enlisted men thought of, said Private Windolph, "was how good a nice cold bottle of beer would taste right now." Pvt. Edward A. Pigford of Company M had a similar reaction. No one could imagine the terrible time the men went through, he said. "We were the most desperate men you ever heard of. . . . What wouldn't I have given for a drink of whiskey that day. . . . I'd have given all the money I ever expected to have for just one big swig of good licker [*sic*]."[502]

Instead of safety, rest, food, or drink, the survivors were rewarded with decaying and rotting corpses, maggots, blue-bottle flies, and vomit. It was enough to deeply affect even those who had not experienced the terror the 7th's survivors had. Lt. Gustavus C. Doane of Company E, 2nd Cavalry, who was instrumental in constructing litters to evacuate the wounded, saw enough of the burials to realize that a decent interment was impossible. There were only a half a dozen shovels in the entire command. All the troopers did was "scatter a token of dust and sagebrush on the bodies, then slip away in horror." Lt. William L. English of Company I of the 7th Infantry was, like Lieutenant Doane, with the Montana Column when it came upon Custer's field on June 27. The stench of the dead bodies and horses was fearful, English confided in his field diary. The scene had an even greater impact on Capt. Walter Clifford. The air was thick with the stench of festering bodies, and a brooding sorrow hung like a pall over every thought, he wrote. The smell was like a deadly poison, permeating his clothing and filling his lungs with pollution at every breath. They must hide their slain comrades from sight and leave. "A little delay on this death-stricken ground and we will remain forever." Insects crawled over everything, living and dead. Clifford couldn't eat. He couldn't sleep. "Let us bury our dead and flee from this rotting atmosphere," he pleaded.[503]

But the men couldn't flee, at least not quite yet. They got down on their knees and used knife blades, tin cups, and fingers to dig out poor graves for the horrid things that lay before them. Is it any wonder their perceptions and judgments were impaired?

Even in the best of times, soldiers did not make good dirt shovelers. Those subject to too much of it began to think of themselves as failures, and would seek respite in drink or desertion. In the course of a soldier's monotonous daily routine, he would avoid work whenever he could. He would traditionally kill time and avoid tasks. "No soldier ever overworks." Avoiding duty, "working the angles," and "goldbricking" was an admired and accepted norm.[504]

The burial of 200 bodies, a task that might have been accomplished with relative ease by several well-fed, well-rested, well-equipped companies, was a labor of Hercules to the seven surviving companies of the 7th Cavalry. And even to those well-fed, well-rested, well-equipped companies that returned to the field in subsequent years to complete the job, their task had evolved into the labor of Sisyphus, the poor fellow condemned forever to roll a heavy stone uphill only to have it fall back down every time he neared the top.

Besides the normal soldierly habit of avoiding an unpleasant work detail, other physical factors involved in the poor burials included exhaustion, lack of proper tools, and a need to expedite the evacuation of the wounded. Perhaps even more important reasons for the poor burials had mental and psychological origins, the very problems one might be less likely to admit.

The fear was still present. Kent King argued that a major cause for the shoddy burials was that the soldiers were still terrified that the Indians, obviously strong and undefeated, would return at any time to finish them off too. There was a hint of cowardice here, and shame. The neglect of the dead was disgraceful, but the shame would not fall on the enlisted men, it would rest on the shoulders of the officers.[505] The fear that caused them to abandon the dead would have to be rationalized into more logical, physical excuses.

Any soldier, any man, may have a difficult time admitting his fear. Yet, these men were suffering from its effects. Lieutenant Godfrey was well aware of the problem. Some men will always be overcome and lose all self-possession, he said. They will be wild-eyed, always wanting a place to hide, always having to be watched and driven. On the retreat from Weir Point, his own Company K turned tail with the order "Every man for himself!" and ran the last 300 yards back to Reno's perimeter.[506]

Though there was no name for it at the time, besides the general word "cowardice," some men were afflicted by one form or another of war neuroses, the nineteenth-century version of the "shell shock" of the Great War, the "combat fatigue" of World War II, or the "thousand-yard stare" of soldiers from all ages who have been through too much for too long. Stress and fear have been a constant companion in war, and soldiers' reactions to them have been remarkably consistent over the past 5,000 years. Though the psychiatric and emotional symptoms accompanying battle stress were noted, their dynamics were not understood.[507]

One study of a group of men with battle neuroses in World War II reads as if it could have directly pertained to the men besieged on Reno Hill. The constant threat of injury and death had its cumulative effect on their mental state, the analysts concluded. Men trapped in foxholes with an insistent, relentless threat hanging over them soon broke down. When the fighting was uncertain or the possibility of defeat imminent, their morale cracked and they were almost useless as an organized force able to carry out an assignment. Bad leadership was also a contributing factor in their breakdown. It was immensely deteriorating to their morale, especially as evidenced in the U.S. Army, where relations between men and their officers were based on personal, not traditional, loyalties.[508]

A hypothesis has been advanced that nearly all of Reno's men suffered from almost every major symptom of combat stress now known to military psychiatry, and Reno himself became a psychiatric casualty when he succumbed to acute battle shock syndrome. Reno's deterioration began almost immediately after being splattered in the face with the blood and brains of the scout Bloody Knife, who had just been struck in the head by a bullet. Reno may have been unfit for command for the remainder of the day. Some of his men were paralyzed by fear; others were seized with extreme, uncontrollable shaking. One went into convulsions. Another was thought to have suffered from acute neurasthenia and was lying face down on the ground, conscious but unresponsive to kicks and shoves by his comrades. Soldiers feigned illness to get off the front line and scurried off to the dubious safety of the "rear" hospital area. Some sat and cried. Captain Moylan reportedly "blubbered" like an urchin. About the only release from battle stress that Reno's men could not utilize was desertion, and only because there was no place to go.[509]

Those not succumbing to immediate onsets of battle shock syndrome will still show evidence of gradual combat shock after a time, and there is no statistical difference in breakdowns between raw and experienced troops. Combat reactions develop in stages and can be characterized by anxiety and a state of fluctuating fear that manifests itself in sweating, tremors, incessant urination, inability to eat, intense thirst, and vomiting. If the conditions causing the battle stress are not removed, the symptoms may change to a complete physical exhaustion that no amount of sleep or rest will eliminate. All the symptoms of the earlier stage may reappear with increased intensity. The soldier will lose all of his military skills, will avoid responsibility, and may not be able to accomplish even rudimentary tasks such as loading his weapon. His mental processes will deteriorate until he cannot react to the most elementary situations. He may enter a vegetative mental state that approaches catatonia.[510] The survivors of the Reno and Benteen battalions evidenced any number of these symptoms, running the gamut from mild to severe.

Another study gathered data to support the fact that men under battle stress may shun physical effort and lose their ability to process information and make decisions. Some of the symptoms in the early stages of mental breakdown in combat include general psychomotor retardation with difficulty of concentration and response, apprehensiveness, a reluctance to accept responsibility, a tendency to become confused, and impaired judgment. Perception disturbances include alterations of the five senses, ranging from hypersensitivities to insensitivities. Men will hallucinate and receive sensory perceptions without corresponding environmental input. They will experience delusions and misinterpret incoming sensory data. And, most pertinent to our discussion, they will "derealize," which involves complex distortions of the environment and spatial and temporal relations, so that the environment appears changed or altered.[511] In other words, both *time and terrain* will become distorted.

It is no secret that men can go insane from battle, or that there are men in every military unit that are either psychologically and emotionally unfit for combat, or will quickly become so after a period of prolonged stress. Almost all soldiers will eventually break in battle. Only the time it takes will vary. For poorly led individuals with low morale, the time needed for breakdown may be only a few hours.[512]

Besides the extreme cases of battle stress, there can be more subtle perception and judgment impairments that are not so outwardly manifest. In these cases, a man's horizons become foreshortened. There is nothing more important than what is in front of his own eyes, and everything in that range has the potential of affecting him. He may see and categorize even inanimate objects as friendly or threatening. A man's senses can become stronger than his decision-making processes based on conscious reflection.[513]

Fear-induced exaggeration will alter a man's senses and make him error-prone. It may make him go mad. Only a soldier's comrades, sharing the same experiences and witnessing his conduct, can possibly overcome that fear. But if men know their leaders are afraid, they will become even more fearful.[514]

If the men, their comrades, and all the officers are in the same situation, there is no "test group," no norm to emulate. Men are herdlike. They will react in a manner similar to the rest of the group and be subject to the same mass experience, including hallucinations and loss of their sense of time. In a crisis, people are imitative.[515]

If the entire group is psychologically ill-equipped to overcome the adverse conditions impacting on them, there is little hope for the individual trying to maintain a sense of sanity. In fact, most casualties in warfare are psychological to some extent. Only a few days in a psychologically intolerable situation will break down the majority of men. Because battle is a moral conflict, its study is necessarily social and psychological. After a time, personal survival regulates one's actions, and how a man can best overcome an obstacle in his path will become his prime concern. A soldier may come to view a situation in diametric opposition to his commander. Orders, scruples, or convention may be cast to the winds. Small-group psychology becomes the order of the day, and peer pressure rules a man's behavior.[516]

Space Warp

What does all this mean in the context of our gravedigging soldiers? We have cited samples from clinical studies, field observations, and personal experiences, and we can discern a common denominator. Men subjected to conditions of battle stress and fear are very likely to experience their environment in terms divorced from reality both in temporal and spatial terms. We have mentioned some of the temporal alterations, with battle time estimates for Reno's fight varying from early morning to mid-afternoon. The spatial distortions were no less a factor. Even the band of men that successfully goes through an engagement and takes its losses bravely, showing little or no signs of combat psychoses during the fight, may become wholly demoralized when the time comes to bury its own dead.[517] By that stage at the Little Bighorn, it is very possible that a significant number of exhausted survivors were experiencing the terrain on Custer's field as much more imposing and inaccessible than it really was.

In addition to the physical and mental stress affecting the men's perceptions, there was a true psychological need to believe that events occurred in a certain way. The first public accounts of the defeat, released through the newspapers within a few weeks of the fight, fostered images of "slaughter pens" and "ambuscaded ravines." The country was bombarded with stories of defeat in a ravine. New York's *Daily Graphic* and *Times* described the battle area replete with mountain ranges and deep canyons, and graphically illustrated the stories with more of the same. Even poet Walt Whitman lyrically visualized the fight in one of "Far Dakota's Canyons."[518]

What did the Oglala Crazy Horse think about Custer dying in one of those conjured canyons? According to his medicine man, Chipps, Crazy Horse indicated that the idea that Custer or his command marched in or died in any ravine was "without particle of foundation."[519] Yet, the public had obtained a false impression of events, and the impressions were not easily corrected. One year after the fight, when Lt. Homer Wheeler made his appearance on the battlefield with the 5th Cavalry, he was surprised by the true nature of the terrain as compared with his prior conception of it. He wrote to his uncle in a letter dated August 6, 1877, that "It was not near as rough as represented. In fact a General could not have had a Battle ground manufactured to order to suit him better."[520] To men such as Crazy Horse and Lieutenant Wheeler the terrain was not imposing at all, but the great majority of Americans could not see the field for themselves and continued to harbor their false notions. The soldiers of the 7th Cavalry would have no reason to disillusion them. An incorrect public impression may have been the necessary salve to help ease their troubled minds.

Had they not done a good job in burying the dead? Well, they did the best they could. Besides, digging in one of Dakota's canyons was not an easy task. It would not be in the men's best interest to admit the real situation. The dead on Reno Hill were buried much better, and during a siege when their own survival was extremely doubtful. They had even buried some horses to form barricades near the hospital depression. Why couldn't they have done the same for Custer's dead? Were they afraid? There was no understanding of psychological casualties in 1876. The explanation for such a dereliction of duty would have been cowardice. Were they cowards? The great majority were not, but the entire situation was enough to produce ulcer-inducing cognitive dissonance, a psychological conflict resulting from inconsistencies between one's beliefs and one's actions. It occurs when conflicting data are unresolved. As a remedy, a person might close his mind to any information that might disturb the "correctness" of his action. The person will attempt to reduce his "dissonance" by acquiring new cognitive elements consonant with his original cognition.[521] On the Little Bighorn, the exhausted survivors responded predictably. Facts, or rather memories of those facts, were altered. Details were invented. Many events on the field became entirely transformed.

Men's perceptions are more than a passive analysis. All that we see, hear, taste, and touch has been filtered and distorted as we process it. Disparate events are glued together to create an apparently complete vision, but in fact, perception and memory are full of illusion and error. Memory is a practiced re-creation of events rather than a faithful replay of what our senses recorded. A well-remembered scene is only a few vague images badly spliced together. A well-remembered event has dredged-up details filled in with enough general knowledge to make a reasonably whole simulation. We "paint in" details with educated guesses, and the "guesses" we supply are directly related to the questions we are asked.[522]

For example, a memory experiment was conducted in which subjects were shown a film of a mock car collision. When the experimenters began using the word "smash" to describe the event, the witnesses' estimates of the car's speed increased and they "remembered" that there must have been shattered glass in the accident. In the film a green car drove by the crash scene. Most subjects correctly said the car was green, but the questioners later began referring to a blue car driving past. Within the hour another set of questions was asked. The subjects that had correctly remembered a green car during the first half hour had, after only a few suggestions of a blue vehicle, begun to honestly "remember" the passing car as blue.[523] One may well wonder how many of Walter Camp's interviewees, from He Dog to Lieutenant McDougall, had their memories "painted" by Camp's persistent suggestions of "28 in a gully?"[524]

What this illustrates is that a man's memory is "creative." What is remembered is not the single element of experience, but a "schema" to which other impulses are attached. A new impulse will not necessarily set up a reaction in a fixed temporal order. It will, rather, enable one to go direct to the particular past response that is most relevant to the need of the moment. Very little of a man's memory is literally observed; a lot of it is distorted as far as the actual facts are concerned. When a subject is asked to remember a complex situation, one of the first things to emerge is largely a construction based on his predilections. What a man "remembers" is usually strongly slanted toward his needs and attitudes.[525]

More simply stated, the soldiers at the Little Bighorn could ease their consciences by "remembering" exaggerated spatial dimensions. They could come to believe that the very dimensions of a ravine they were forced to dig graves in made their task impossible before they even began. This rationalization can be explained as a method of lessening their cognitive dissonance, or, in a layman's terms, it can be explained as nothing more than a survival lie.[526]

To place the problems faced by the 7th Cavalry survivors into a late-twentieth-century context, we may also relate their symptoms to what has been described as post-traumatic stress disorder (PTSD). This mental disorder affects groups of people experiencing life-threatening traumas, such as those occurring in military combat. Many times the survivors will harbor guilt feelings about surviving when others did not, or about things they had to do in order to survive. There is an avoidance of situations that may arouse recollections of the trauma, and a diminished responsiveness to the external world, known as "psychic numbing" or "emotional anesthesia." At times there may be "psychogenic amnesia" of aspects of the trauma, selective perceptions, and a constriction and inflexibility of thought. An enduring adaptation response of a PTSD survivor is to perceive a continued threat in his or her environment and a need to utilize cognitive maneuvers and coping mechanisms to remove that perceived threat. Perhaps threat removal is an explanation of why the 7th Cavalry survivors wanted so badly to finish the gravedigging and flee the field, and of how they coped with their trauma by "numbing" out the unpleasantness and selectively remembering what would ease their consciences.[527]

The men doing the gravedigging on June 28 were not overly concerned with doing a commendable job in burying their comrades, and the reasons for their shoddy work were not purely physical ones such as the lack of spades and shovels. Their mental state exaggerated the obstacles in their path. The sensory image of bodies strewn along a gentle ravine became altered and magnified so that they appeared to lie in an inaccessible pit.

And even if this fiction were only half believed by the men, they may have rationalized their remaining doubts. A task of moderate difficulty became an impossibility. Why spend hours scratching in the hard-baked Montana soil with knife and fingers to cover those terrible objects that were dead anyway? Why not just kick some dirt and sage over them and say they were in a place impossible to get to? The terrain—seen through the eyes of men in a state of mind where perception distortions were common, where there was a real need to avoid another unpleasant task, and where rationalization and other psychological defense mechanisms were in operation—was transformed into larger-than-life proportions. Men almost exclusively remembered a deep ravine, but in fact, most of the bodies lying downslope from Custer Hill were found in the relatively shallow valley of Cemetery Ravine.

Of course, ascribing psychological reasons for men's actions is necessarily a speculative exercise. We do not know the innermost thoughts and motivations that dictated how they acted at the time or what they wrote later. We do not have enough of a portfolio built up on them and cannot analyze them as their more famous leader, George Armstrong Custer, has been psychoanalyzed.[528] Even if we could, Custer's supposed narcissistic personality disorder, his dichotomous actions involving senior authority figures, or a Freudian analysis of his men will not alone explain the outcome of his final battle.

For whatever reasons—physical or psychological, a simple case of misinterpretation, or a combination of all of these—we find that a significant number of 7th Cavalry survivors found bodies in Cemetery Ravine and passed on ambiguous testimony that all too often has been interpreted as pertaining to Deep Ravine. What the psychological factors discussed here may provide, however, is the cement necessary to mend the apparent breach between the historical record and the physical record. That linkage may allow us to move one small step closer to unlocking some of the secrets of the Battle of the Little Bighorn.

After the many burial and reburial details of 1876 to 1881, after the planting of the marble tombstones in 1890, and after the gravestone additions and adjustments over the years, a satisfactory end result was finally achieved. Lieutenant Colonel Sheridan once collected all the officers' remains. Captain Sanderson removed horse bones and soldier bones from the field and placed them in a cordwood mound on the hilltop. Lieutenant Roe removed and reinterred all the enlisted men's remains and placed them in a mass grave below the granite monument. No one from these expeditions ever found the remains of bodies in Deep Ravine. No one ever removed the remains of bodies from Deep Ravine. It is no mystery that searchers in the latter decades of the twentieth century cannot find evidence of remains in Deep Ravine. Few, if any, bodies were ever there.

John A. Cockerill, a *New York Herald* correspondent, walked the Custer battlefield in the early 1890s. It was a moving experience. As he stood on the field he wrote that the great brown hills were flooded with sunlight and the silence was as oppressive as the mystery that surrounded the troopers' deaths. "I tried to form some idea of the awful sensation which must have come to each of these brave fellows as he realized the horror of the situation. That death awaited every man. . . . The requiem of the winds over the graves there can never be sadder than on that golden evening when I turned my back upon this battlefield, at once the most pathetic and most mysterious of all that our sun shines upon."[529]

In 1928, Thomas B. Marquis stood at a cluster of markers with a Cheyenne warrior who had participated in the fight so many years before. The old Indian, because of superstition, reverence, or unspoken reasons of his own, balked at approaching any closer than 30 to 40 feet from the marble slabs. He would not go among the stones to talk. The markers were death sites. The spirits there were still strong.[530]

Today, long after Cockerill and Marquis and the old Cheyenne perceived the mystery, long after all the warriors and soldiers have perhaps passed on to a place where all their questions are answered, Custer's field has hardly changed. It is still a place where visitors do not walk alone, where the buffalo grass whispers in secret conversations with the wind, undulating with the hushed passage of apparitions. It is a place where one might instinctively turn his head to look for something—something that can be seen only after it has passed on. Standing in a far-off lonely coulee, spectral visitors still make fleeting appearances, but only for the believers.

No doubt the future will witness the unearthing of more bits and pieces of Indian and 7th Cavalry relics. More clues to the puzzle of what actually occurred that day will be found, but the fate of the bodies of 28 men once seen in a ravine should no longer perplex us. They are not missing; they never have been missing. For over 100 years they have been resting atop Custer Hill in the mass grave with their comrades who fell beside them long ago on that desperate afternoon in 1876. There is a sad side, however, to the resolution of any enigma. Perhaps now the tiny white tombstones rising spectrally from the grassy slopes in the sun have become just a touch less mysterious.

Custer Hill from Deep Ravine Trail. —Bill and Jan Moeller

Appendix: The Men of Company E

Officers

DE RUDIO, Charles Camilus, 1st Lieutenant. Assigned to Company E, but on duty with Company A during the Little Bighorn battle. Born August 26, 1832, Belluno, Italy. Educated at the Austrian Military Academy and served on staff of General Garibaldi in Italy. Participated in Civil War in 79th New York and 2nd U.S. Colored Infantry. Hid along river for two days during Reno siege. Retired 1896. Died in Los Angeles in 1910.

REILY, William Van Wyck, 2nd Lieutenant. Assigned to Company E, but on detached duty with Company F at the Little Bighorn. Born December 12, 1853, Washington, D.C. Attended Georgetown College and the Naval Academy, but resigned in 1872. Joined Company E in January 1876. His remains were exhumed in 1877 and reinterred in Washington, D.C.

SMITH, Algernon Emory, 1st Lieutenant. Commanding Company E, on detached duty from Company A. Born September 17, 1842, Newport, NY. Fought in the Civil War at Ft. Wagner, Drewry's Bluff, and Petersburg and was severely wounded at Ft. Fisher in January 1865, where he was brevetted major. Killed at the Battle of the Little Bighorn, his remains were exhumed in 1877 and reinterred at Ft. Leavenworth. Survived by his wife, Henrietta.

STURGIS, James Garland, 2nd Lieutenant. Second in command of Company E, on detached duty from Company M. Born January 24, 1854, Albuquerque, NM. Son of Col. Samuel D. Sturgis, the commanding officer of the 7th Cavalry. Graduated from West Point in 1875 and joined the regiment in October. Killed on June 25, but his body was never officially identified.

Enlisted Men

ABBOTS, Harry, Private. Born in New York City, 1853. Enlisted in 1875, former occupation listed as bricklayer. Hazel eyes, dark hair, dark complexion, 5' 9". Was on extra duty as a hospital attendant at Ft. Lincoln during the campaign. Discharged in December 1877 for disability.

ACKISON, David, Private. Born in Troy, NY, 1852. Enlisted in 1873, previously a railroader. Gray eyes, brown hair, fair complexion, 5' 5". Sick with consumption, Ackison was transported back to Ft. Buford on the *Far West*. Discharged in 1878.

BAKER, William H., Private. Born in Pope County, IL, 1849. Second enlistment in 1875, prior service in 3rd U.S. Artillery. Blue eyes, brown hair, fair complexion, 5' 9". Killed.

BARTH, Robert, Private. Born in Uforzheim, Germany, 1851. Enlisted in 1872, previous occupation was a jeweler. Gray eyes, brown hair, fair complexion, 5' 10". Killed.

BERWALD, Frank, Private. Born in Poland, 1851. Enlisted in 1873, previous occupation was a blacksmith. Gray eyes, brown hair, florid complexion, 5' 5". With the pack train on June 25. Discharged as a sergeant of good character in January 1878.

BOYLE, Owen, Private. Born in Waterford, Ireland, 1843. Enlisted in 1874 and listed previous occupation as a soldier. Gray eyes, dark hair, fair complexion, 5' 6". Served in U.S. Civil War. Killed.

BROGAN, James, Private. Born in Pittsburgh, PA, 1850. In his second enlistment when killed. Hazel eyes, brown hair, ruddy complexion, 5' 8".

BROMWELL, Latrobe, Private. Born in Frederick County, MD, 1847. Previously a clerk, he enlisted in 2nd U.S. Cavalry in 1870 and reenlisted in the 7th in 1875. Was at Powder River Camp during the Little Bighorn campaign. Gray eyes, light hair, light complexion, 5' 6". Reenlisted four more times. Was chief cook at the Training School for Cooks and Bakers at Ft. Riley until retirement in 1909.

BROWN, George C., Corporal. Born in Baltimore, MD, 1851. Enlisted in 1872, previous occupation listed as a candymaker. Brown eyes, brown hair, ruddy complexion, 5' 5". Killed.

BRUNS, August, Private. Born in Brunswick, Germany, 1838. Previous occupation was a musician. Participated in the 1874 Black Hills Expedition. Was on detached service at Ft. Lincoln during the Little Bighorn campaign. Hazel eyes, dark hair, sallow complexion, 5' 8". Discharged in 1880. Died in 1910 in Mandan, ND.

CHAPMAN, William H., Private. Born in Glastonbury, CT, 1852. Enlisted in March 1876, previous occupation listed as a farmer. Transferred from Company B in the field June 1. Possibly remained at Powder River Camp during the battle. Deserted in October 1876 and surrendered in 1886. Gray eyes, dark hair, ruddy complexion, 5' 9".

CONNOR, Edward, Private. Born in Clare, Ireland, 1846. Second enlistment in 1872. Hazel eyes, brown hair, ruddy complexion, 5' 8". Killed.

DARRIS, John, Private. Born in Goshen, NY, 1846. Served in the Civil War in the 1st New Jersey Cavalry. Abandoned wife and two children to enlist in the 7th Cavalry in 1875. Previous occupation variously listed as a farmer or a fireman. Blue eyes, brown hair, dark complexion, 5' 6". Possibly succumbed in Deep Coulee, where skeleton with arrowhead embedded in cervical vertebrae and boot with initials "J. D." were found in 1920s.

DAVIS, William, Private. Born in Vandalia, IL, 1851. Enlisted in 1874, previous occupation was a laborer. Deserted February 25, 1875, and apprehended February 28, 1875. Gray eyes, brown hair, fair complexion, 5' 6". Killed.

EAGAN, (Hagan) Thomas P., Corporal. Born in Ireland, 1847. Enlisted 1873, previous occupation a laborer. Gray eyes, sandy hair, light complexion, 5' 5". Killed.

FARRELL, Richard, Private. Born in Dublin, Ireland, 1851. Enlisted in 1875, previous occupation was a laborer. Gray eyes, brown hair, fair complexion, 5' 8". Body identified in deep gully by Frank Berwald.

GILBERT, Julius, Private. Born in Belfort, France, 1853. Enlisted in 1874, previous occupation was a farmer. Hazel eyes, brown hair, fair complexion, 5' 7". Was on detached service at Ft. Lincoln during the campaign. Discharged as a private of good character in 1879.

HEIM, John, Private. Born in St. Louis, MO, 1852. Enlisted in 1875, formerly a clerk. Brown eyes, light hair, fair complexion, 5' 1". Killed.

HENDERSON, John, Private. Born in Cork, Ireland, 1849. Second enlistment in 1875. Gray eyes, light hair, fair complexion, 5' 7". Killed.

HENDERSON, Sykes, Private. Born in Armstrong County, PA, 1844. Second enlistment in 1872. Brown eyes, brown hair, fair complexion, 5' 8". Killed.

HILEY, John S., Private. Born in Rugby, England, May 28, 1849. Enlisted in 1872 in New York under his brother-in-law's name. Listed previous occupation as a clerk. Real name was John Stuart Forbes. He was of noble birth and is listed in Foster's *Peerage and Baronetage, 1883.* Apparently left home because of gambling difficulties. Killed.

HOHMEYER, Frederick, 1st Sergeant. Born in Darmstadt, Germany, 1849. In third enlistment. Gray eyes, light hair, dark complexion, 5' 7½". Body identified in deep gully by Frank Berwald and by Captain

McDougall from name stitched on sock. His widow married Latrobe Bromwell.

HOWARD, Frank, Private. Born in Waukegan, IL, 1850. Enlisted in 1872, previous occupation was a farmer. Was on detached service at Ft. Lincoln during the campaign. Brown eyes, black hair, dark complexion, 5' 8". Discharged in 1877. Died November 27, 1911, at Cloverdale, CA.

HUBER, William, Private. Born in Wurtemburg, Germany, 1853. Enlisted in 1874, listed previous occupation as a gunsmith. Gray eyes, light brown hair, fair complexion, 5' 7". Body identified in deep gully by Frank Berwald.

HUTTER, Anton, Private. Born in Bavaria, Germany, 1851. Enlisted in 1872, formerly a laborer. Was in a Washington, D.C., insane asylum in June 1876. Hazel eyes, dark hair, fair complexion, 5' 10". Discharged in 1878.

JAMES, John, Private. Born in Rome, Italy, 1848. Enlisted in 1872, former occupation listed as a soldier. Gray eyes, brown hair, dark complexion, 5' 7". Was with the pack train during the Little Bighorn fight. Discharged in 1877 as a corporal of good character.

JAMES, William, B., Sergeant. Born in Pembrokeshire, Wales, 1849. Enlisted 1872, previous occupation was a coachman. Hazel eyes, light hair, light complexion, 5' 9". Killed.

KIMM, John G., Private. Born in New York City, 1848. Third enlistment in 1872. Served in the Civil War in the 20th New York Independent Battery. Gray eyes, black hair, florid complexion, 5' 10". Was with the pack train at the Little Bighorn. Discharged in 1877. Died in 1909 and is buried at Mt. Home National Cemetery, Tennessee.

KNECHT, Andy, Private. Born in Cincinnati, OH, April 12, 1852. Enlisted in 1873, previous occupation was a butcher. Hazel eyes, light brown hair, light complexion, 5' 6". Killed.

LANGE, Henry, Private. Born in Hanover, Germany, December 17, 1851. Enlisted in 1872, previous occupation was a laborer. Gray eyes, light hair, light complexion, 5' 8". Was with the pack train during the battle. Discharged in 1877. Died in 1928 in Chicago. Buried at Mt. Hope Cemetery in Cook County, IL.

LIDDIARD, Herod T., Private. Born in London, England, 1851. Enlisted in 1872, formerly a boatman. Was with the pack train and was killed during the siege of Reno's hilltop. Blue eyes, light hair, fair complexion, 5' 5".

MASON, Henry S., Corporal. Born in Brownville, IN, 1847. Second enlistment in 1875. Gray eyes, sandy hair, fair complexion, 5' 11". A sergeant in Company F on the 1874 Black Hills Expedition, Mason was reduced to private for gross neglect of duty. Killed.

McCANN, Patrick, Private. Born in Monahan, Ireland, 1853. Enlisted in 1874, formerly a laborer. Was in confinement at Ft. Lincoln, one year without pay, from May 2, 1876. Missed the battle. Gray eyes, brown hair, fair complexion, 5' 6".

McELROY, Thomas, Trumpeter. Born in Neagh, Ireland, 1845. Served in U.S. Civil War and was wounded. Enlisted in 7th Cavalry in 1875, previous occupation was a musician. Blue eyes, dark hair, ruddy complexion, 5' 5". His widow, Nora, married John Furey, later a member of Company E. Killed.

McKENNA, John, Private. Born in Limerick, Ireland, 1843. Enlisted in 1874, previous occupation was a hostler. Assigned to Company E, but transferred to Company I. Was not in the Little Bighorn battle and is not listed on the muster roll for June 30, 1876. Discharged in 1879. Hazel eyes, dark hair, medium complexion, 5' 8".

MEYER, Albert H., Corporal. Born in Germany, 1852. Enlisted in 1873, previous occupation listed as a bartender. Blue eyes, light hair, fair complexion, 5' 8". Body identified by Frank Berwald in deep gully.

MILLER, Henry, Blacksmith. Born in Baltimore, MD, 1844. Enlisted in 1871, occupation was a blacksmith. Blue eyes, brown hair, light complexion, 5' 9". Possibly at Powder River Camp during fight. Discharged in November 1876.

MOONIE, George A., Trumpeter. Born in Boston, MA, 1855. Enlisted 1875, previous occupation was a clerk. Hazel eyes, dark hair, fair complexion, 5' 6". Killed.

MURPHY, Lawrence, Sergeant. Born in Kerry, Ireland, 1849. Enlisted in 1871. Blue eyes, brown hair, fair complexion, 5' 5". Possibly at Powder River Camp during battle. Discharged in December 1876. Also served in 2nd U.S. Cavalry, 1882-86. Died of syphilis, U.S. Soldiers' Home, Washington, D.C., 1888.

O'CONNOR, Patrick, Private. Born in Langford, Ireland, July 1851. Enlisted in 1873, previous occupation was a shoemaker. Blue eyes, light hair, fair complexion, 5' 5". Killed.

O'TOOLE, Francis, Private. Born in County Mayo, Ireland, 1839. Enlisted in 1872, cited previous occupation as a soldier. Was an orderly with General Terry's headquarters during the Little Bighorn campaign.

Discharged as a sergeant of good character in 1877. Blue eyes, brown hair, fair complexion, 5' 9".

OGDEN, John S., Sergeant. Born in Newberry, MA, 1845. In second enlistment. Gray eyes, light hair, light complexion, 5' 8". Possibly killed near Medicine Tail ford.

PANDTLE, Christopher, Private. Born in Germany, June 15, 1849. Enlisted in 1872, previous occupation was a sawyer. Was on extra duty as a hospital attendant from May 1, 1876. Missed the battle. Discharged in 1877. Brown eyes, light hair, fair complexion, 5' 4". Became a U.S. citizen in 1894. Died of stomach cancer in Gardenville, WA, June 4, 1923. Cremated and ashes scattered.

REES, William H., Private. Born in Washington, PA, 1838. Enlisted in 1872, previous occupation was a laborer. Gray eyes, sandy hair, fair complexion, 6' 1". Body possibly identified near Deep Ravine.

REESE, William, Private. Born in Philadelphia, PA, 1846. Enlisted in 1873, former occupation listed as a brushmaker. Possibly was at Powder River Camp during the battle. Discharged in 1878 as a farrier of good character. Blue eyes, light brown hair, fair complexion, 5' 10".

RILEY, James F., Sergeant. Born in Baltimore, MD, 1845. Blue eyes, brown hair, fair complexion, 5' 11". Was with pack train on June 25. Wounded in back and left leg during Reno's hilltop fight. Transported back to Ft. Lincoln on the *Far West*. Discharged after expiration of second enlistment in August 1876.

ROOD, Edward, Private. Born in Tiago County, NY, 1848. Enlisted in 1873, previous occupation was a fireman. Hazel eyes, black hair, dark complexion, 5' 7". Killed.

SCHELE, Henry, Private. Born in Hanover, Germany, 1843. Second enlistment in 1872. Blue eyes, light hair, fair complexion, 5' 6". Killed.

SHIELDS, William, Saddler. Born in Vincennes, IN, 1841. In third enlistment. Gray eyes, brown hair, fair complexion, 5' 8". At Powder River Camp during battle. Discharged in September 1879. Died in 1888 and is buried at Ft. Sill, Oklahoma.

SMALLWOOD, William, Private. Born in Jonesville, IN, 1852. Enlisted in 1874, previously a farmer. Brown eyes, brown hair, dark complexion, 5' 8". Killed.

SMITH, Albert A., Private. Born in Queens County, NY, 1839. Enlisted in 1873, stated previous occupation was a soldier. Gray eyes, brown hair, fair complexion, 5' 5". Killed.

SMITH, James (1), Private. Born in Tipperary, Ireland, 1842. Third enlistment in 1874. Hazel eyes, brown hair, ruddy complexion, 5' 6". Killed.

SMITH, James (2), Private. Born in Lynn, MA, 1847. Enlisted in 1874, former occupation was a shoemaker. Hazel eyes, black hair, dark complexion, 5' 4". Killed.

SPENCER, Abel B., Farrier. Born in Rock County, WI, 1845. Enlisted in 1872, former occupation was a farmer. Hazel eyes, dark hair, dark complexion, 5' 7". At Powder River Camp during battle. Discharged in January 1877.

STAFFORD, Benjamin F., Private. Born in Boston, MA, 1846. Enlisted in 1873, previous occupation was a currier. Brown eyes, black hair, fair complexion, 5' 5". Killed.

STELLA, Alexander, Private. Born in Athens, Greece, 1853. Enlisted in 1874, previous occupation was a cook. Brown eyes, black hair, dark complexion, 5' 6". Killed.

TORREY, William A., Private. Born in Weymouth, MA, 1850. Enlisted in 1872, previous occupation was a bootmaker. Gray eyes, light hair, fair complexion, 5' 4". Killed.

VAN SANT, Cornelius, Private. Born in Cincinnati, OH, 1850. Enlisted in 1872, previous occupation was a clerk. Blue eyes, brown hair, fair complexion, 5' 7". Killed.

WALKER, George, Private. Born in Providence, RI, 1852. Enlisted in 1874, previously a hostler. Gray eyes, brown hair, florid complexion, 5' 6". Killed.

WELLS, John S., Sergeant. Born in Rose, OH, 1833. In second enlistment. Blue eyes, light hair, light complexion, 5' 9". Listed previous occupation as a soldier. Was on furlough during the Little Bighorn campaign. Reenlisted several more times and deserted in 1885.

WOODRUFF, Jerry, Private. Born in Montjoy, PA, 1848. Second enlistment in 1875, previous occupation was a soldier. Was on detached service at Ft. Lincoln during the campaign. Gray eyes, brown hair, florid complexion, 5' 6". Discharged in 1880 as a private of excellent character.

Compiled from Carroll, ed., *They Rode With Custer*; Hammer, *Men With Custer*; O'Neil, ed., *They Lie Buried*; and Overfield, *The Little Big Horn, 1876.*

Notes

Preface

1. John Lukacs, *Historical Consciousness or the Remembered Past* (New York: Schocken Books, 1985), 54-56.

2. James Patrick Dowd, *Custer Lives!* (Fairfield, WA: Ye Galleon Press, 1982).

3. William A. Graham, *The Custer Myth: A Source Book of Custeriana* (Harrisburg, PA: The Stackpole Company, 1953; reprint, Lincoln: University of Nebraska Press, 1986), v.

4. Frazier Hunt and Robert Hunt, *I Fought With Custer: The Story of Sergeant Windolph, Last Survivor of the Battle of the Little Big Horn* (New York: Scribner's, 1947; reprint, Lincoln: University of Nebraska Press, 1987), 2.

5. Robert M. Utley, *Frontier Regulars: The United States Army and the Indian, 1866-1891* (New York: MacMillan Publishing Company, 1973), 37; Richard Upton, *The Custer Adventure* (El Segundo, CA: Upton & Sons, 1990), 20; W. S. Nye, *Carbine and Lance: The Story of Old Fort Sill* (Norman: University of Oklahoma Press, 1969), 80; Jay Smith, "A Hundred Years Later," in *Custer and His Times.* (El Paso: Little Big Horn Associates, 1981), 125.

6. Robert M. Utley, ed., *Life in Custer's Cavalry: Diaries and Letters of Albert and Jennie Barnitz 1867-1868* (Lincoln: University of Nebraska Press, 1987), 20; George Armstrong Custer, *My Life on the Plains or, Personal Experiences with Indians* (Norman: University of Oklahoma Press, 1962); Graham, *Myth*, 219.

Chapter 1

7. James A. Sawicki, *Cavalry Regiments of the U.S. Army* (Dumfries, VA: Wyvern Publications, 1985), 58.

8. Melbourne C. Chandler, *Of Garryowen in Glory: The History of the 7th U.S. Cavalry* (Annandale, VA: Turnpike Press, 1960), 2-3; Charles K. Mills, *Rosters from the 7th U.S. Cavalry Campaigns, 1866-1896* (Bryan, TX: J. M. Carroll & Company, 1983).

9. Thomas W. Dunlay, *Wolves for the Blue Soldiers: Indian Scouts and Auxiliaries with the United States Army, 1860-90* (Lincoln: University of Nebraska Press, 1987), 25-26.

10. Utley, *Regulars*, 119-20.

11. Gary M. Thomas, *The Custer Scout of April, 1867* (Kansas City, MO: Westport Printing, 1987) 1-2; Brian W. Dippie, ed., *Nomad: George A. Custer in "Turf, Field and Farm"* (Austin: University of Texas Press, 1980), 123.

12. Utley, *Barnitz*, 44-53.

13. Custer, *My Life*, 64.

14. Utley, *Barnitz*, 270.

15. Custer, *My Life*, 66.

16. Lawrence A. Frost, *The Court-Martial of General George Armstrong Custer* (Norman: University of Oklahoma Press, 1968), 41; Custer, *My Life*, 73.

17. John M. Carroll, "Major Wickliffe Cooper, 7th U.S. Cavalry—Was it Murder or Suicide?" *Research Review: The Journal of the Little Big Horn Associates* 3 (December 1986): 13.

18. Marguerite Merington, ed., *The Custer Story: The Life and Intimate Letters of George A. Custer and His Wife Elizabeth* (Lincoln: University of Nebraska Press, 1987), 205.

19. Frost, *Court-Martial*, 59-64.

20. Ibid., 70-71.

21. Randy Johnson and Nancy P. Allen, *Find Custer! The Kidder Tragedy* (Lockport, IL: Printing Plus, 1988), 30, 65; John M. Carroll, ed., *Ten Years with General Custer Among the Indians (and other writings by John Ryan)* (Bryan, TX: J. M. Carroll & Company, 1980), 16; Custer, *My Life*, 108-12.

22. Chandler, *Garryowen*, 5.

23. Frost, *Court-Martial*, 91.

24. Chandler, *Garryowen*, 6.

25. Utley, *Barnitz*, 270.

26. Ibid., 276.

27. Custer, *My Life*, 160-61.

28. Utley, *Barnitz*, 190.

29. Robert C. Carriker, *Fort Supply Indian Territory* (Norman: University of Oklahoma Press, 1970) 10-12.

30. Blaine Burkey, *Custer, Come at Once!* (Hays, KS: Thomas More Prep, 1976), 44.

31. Merington, *Letters*, 216-17.

32. Lawrence A. Frost, "Two Sides of a General," in *Custer and His Times, Book Three* (El Paso, TX and Conway, AR: Little Big Horn Associates and University of Central Arkansas Press, 1987), 128-38; Paul L. Hedren, "The Custer Library," *Research Review: The Journal of the Little Big Horn Associates* 8, no. 4 (Winter 1974): 5-11.

33. Gregory J. W. Urwin, *The United States Cavalry: An Illustrated History* (Dorset, England: Blandford Press, 1983), 73.

34. Custer, *My Life*, 208.

35. Elizabeth A. Lawrence, *His Very Silence Speaks* (Detroit: Wayne State University Press, 1989), 45-47.

36. Utley, *Barnitz*, 204-5; Charles K. Mills, *Harvest of Barren Regrets: The Army Career of Frederick William Benteen, 1834-1898* (Glendale, CA: Arthur H. Clark Company, 1985), 156; Carroll, *Ten Years*, 44.

37. Stan Hoig, *The Battle of the Washita: The Sheridan-Custer Indian Campaign of 1867-69* (Lincoln: University of Nebraska Press, 1979), 78-79.

38. Ibid., 124-25; Mills, *Rosters*; DeB[enneville] Randolph Keim, *Sheridan's Troopers on the Borders: A Winter Campaign on the Plains* (Lincoln: University of Nebraska Press, 1985), 114-18.

39. Ibid., 144-48; Hoig, *Washita*, 141, 155, 204.

40. Carriker, *Fort Supply*, 26; Chandler, *Garryowen*, 25.

41. David L. Spotts, *Campaigning with Custer and the Nineteenth Kansas Volunteer Cavalry on the Washita Campaign, 1868-69* (Lincoln: University of Nebraska Press, 1988), 136-40; Mills, *Barren Regrets*, 185.

42. David Dixon, "Custer and the Sweetwater Hostages," in *Custer and His Times, Book Three* (El Paso, TX and Conway, AR: Little Big Horn Associates and University of Central Arkansas Press, 1987), 92-102.

43. Chandler, *Garryowen*, 30.

44. Ibid., 32-33.

45. Georg Wenzel Schneider-Wettengel, "Dutchie in the 7th," in *Custer and His Times* (El Paso: Little Big Horn Associates, 1981), 248.

46. Chandler, *Garryowen*, 36.

47. Ernest L. Reedstrom, *Bugles, Banners and Warbonnets* (New York: Bonanza Books, 1986), 248-49; Randy Steffen, *The Horse Soldier, 1876-1943*, vol. 2, *The Frontier, the Mexican War, the Civil War, the Indian Wars, 1851-1880*. (Norman: University of Oklahoma Press, 1978), 75-77.

48. Reedstrom, *Bugles*, 250-51, 276.

49. Lawrence A. Frost, *Custer's 7th Cavalry and the Campaign of 1873* (El Segundo, CA: Upton & Sons, 1986), 66-68.

50. Ibid., 83-84.

51. Donald Jackson, *Custer's Gold: The United States Cavalry Expedition of 1874* (Lincoln: University of Nebraska Press, 1972), v, 120-21.

52. Reedstrom, *Bugles*, 282-83.

53. Ronald H. Nichols, "The Springfield Carbine at the Little Big Horn," in 2nd Annual Symposium (Hardin, MT: Custer Battlefield Historical & Museum Assn., 1988), 54-61; Reedstrom, *Bugles*, 257.

54. Chandler, *Garryowen*, 43.

55. Kenneth M. Hammer, *The Glory March* (Monroe, MI: Monroe County Library System, 1980).

56. Don Rickey, Jr., *Forty Miles a Day on Beans and Hay* (Norman: University of Oklahoma Press, 1963), 17; Sandy Barnard, *Digging Into Custer's Last Stand* (Terre Haute, IN: AST Press, 1986), 55; Reedstrom, *Bugles*, 14.

57. Doug Keller, "Myths of the Little Big Horn," in 2nd Annual Symposium (Hardin, MT: Custer Battlefield Historical & Museum Assn., 1988), 48; John S. Gray, *Centennial Campaign: The Sioux War of 1876* (Fort Collins, CO: Old Army Press, 1976), 291; Lawrence A. Frost, *Custer Legends* (Bowling Green, OH: Bowling Green University Press, 1981), 190; Joe Sills, Jr., "The Recruits Controversy: Another Look." *Greasy Grass* 5 (May 1989): 4-8.

58. Hammer, *Glory*.

59. Ibid.

Chapter 2

60. John S. duMont, *Custer Battle Guns* (Canaan, NH: Phoenix Publishing, 1988), 90.

61. Carroll, *Ten Years*, 178; Lawrence A. Frost, *General Custer's Libbie* (Seattle: Superior Publishing Company, 1976), 246.

62. Carroll, *Ten Years*, 182.

63. William A. Graham, *The Reno Court of Inquiry: Abstract of the Official Record of Proceedings* (Harrisburg, PA: The Stackpole Company, 1954), 76, 146.

64. Edward S. Godfrey, "Custer's Last Battle," *Century Magazine* (January 1892; reprint, Golden, CO: Outbooks, 1986): 35.

65. Graham, *Abstract*, 103.

66. Kenneth M. Hammer, *Custer in '76: Walter Camp's Notes on the Custer Fight* (Norman: University of Oklahoma Press, 1976), 95, 248.

67. W. Kent King, *Tombstones for Bluecoats: New Insights Into the Custer Mystery*, vol. 4 (Marion Station, MD: n.p., 1981), 166.

68. Edward J. McClernand, *On Time for Disaster: The Rescue of Custer's Command* (Lincoln: University of Nebraska Press, 1989; reprint of *With the Indian and the Buffalo in Montana, 1870-1878* [Glendale, CA: Arthur H. Clark, 1969]), 92.

69. John Gibbon, *Gibbon on the Sioux Campaign of 1876* (Bellvue, NE: Old Army Press, 1970; [reprint of series in *The American Catholic Quarterly Review* (April-October 1877]), 40.

70. Richard G. Hardorff, *Markers, Artifacts and Indian Testimony: Preliminary Findings on the Custer Battle* (Short Hills, NJ: Don Horn Publications, 1985), 59; Hammer, *Camp's Notes*, 207.

71. John M. Carroll, ed., *A 7th Cavalry Scrapbook*, vol. 1 (Bryan, TX: J. M. Carroll & Company, 1978), 15.

72. John M. Carroll, ed., *The Benteen-Goldin Letters on Custer and His Last Battle* (Lincoln: University of Nebraska Press, 1991), 29-30.

73. Earl A. Brininstool, *Troopers with Custer: Historic Incidents of the Battle of the Little Big Horn* (Harrisburg, PA: The Stackpole Company, 1952; reprint, Lincoln: University of Nebraska Press, 1989), 61.

74. Hardorff, *Markers*, 8; John S. Gray, *Custer's Last Campaign: Mitch Bouyer and the Little Big Horn Reconstructed* (Lincoln: University of Nebraska Press, 1991), 393.

75. King, *Tombstones*, 3:135.

76. Charles Kuhlman, *Legend Into History* (Harrisburg, PA: The Stackpole Company, 1951), 187, 237.

77. John M. Carroll, ed., *A Very Real Salmagundi; Or, Look What I Found this Summer* (Bryan, TX: J. M. Carroll & Company, n.d.), 55.

78. King, *Tombstones*, 3:iii.

79. Lauren Brown, *Grasslands* (New York: Alfred A. Knopf, 1985), 56-59.

80. Ibid., 20.

81. Barnard, *Digging*, 11-15.

82. Jane McIntosh, *The Practical Archaeologist* (London: Paul Press, 1986), 8.

83. Douglas D. Scott et al., *Archaeological Perspectives on the Battle of the Little Big Horn* (Norman: University of Oklahoma Press, 1989), 8-10.

84. Barnard, *Digging*, 20.

85. Greg Bence, "The Enigma of Sergeant Butler," *Research Review: The Journal of the Little Big Horn Associates* 8, no. 1 (Spring 1974): 1-4; R. L. "Pinky" Nelson, "Sergeant Butler's 'Travelling' Marker," *Research Review: The Journal of the Little Big Horn Associates* 8, no. 1 (Spring 1974): 5-9; Hardorff, *Battle Casualties*, 110, 113-14. The exact location of Sergeant Butler's marker and the rationale for placing it there is one of many controversial subjects about the battle. Butler may have been killed on the retreat from the ford, may have been cut off from Company L when Indians attacked up Deep Coulee, may have been escaping from the battlefield, or may have been sent as a courier to get assistance from Reno. The latter explanation seems to carry the most weight today. Butler's "marker" has been one of the most peripatetic on the battlefield. Trumpeter John Martin of Company H and Lt. Edward S. Godfrey of Company K reported finding Butler's body near

Medicine Tail ford. Researcher Walter M. Camp, after studying many soldier accounts, concluded that Butler's body was found "on the second little hill north of the first ravine beyond Ford B—⁶⁄₁₀ of a mile beyond Ford B." In 1905, Butler's remains were transferred to the cemetery proper. In 1916, Godfrey placed a white stake on the spot where he remembered finding Butler's body. A marble marker was set at the "Godfrey Memory Spot" in 1917. In the early 1940s, battlefield Superintendent Edward S. Luce located an iron stake some distance away from the Godfrey marker, then later became convinced it was the correct site of Butler's original grave. A study done by Assistant Engineer Aubrey L. Haines of the Yellowstone Park staff seemed to confirm Luce's placement. The new spot was 3,000 feet from the river, as opposed to topographer R. B. Marshall's 1891 plot of 1,925 feet from the water. In 1949, Luce, Edward L. Nye, and six others moved the marker. It is now near the crest of the divide separating Medicine Tail Coulee from Deep Coulee. Whether it is in the right place is still debatable. Sgt. Stanislaus Roy of Company A remembered finding the body of Cpl. John Foley of Company C in the same area. In fact, it was Foley's body that lay on the rise, while Butler's was in the ravine beyond. Today, the Butler marker may more accurately depict the death site of Corporal Foley.

86. Jerome A. Greene, *Evidence and the Custer Enigma: A Reconstruction of Indian-Military History* (Golden, CO: Outbooks, 1986), 39; Henry Weibert and Don Weibert, *Sixty-Six Years in Custer's Shadow* (Billings, MT: Falcon Press Publishing Company, 1985), 147. Greene speculated that the boot with the initials "J. D." may have been from Pvt. John Duggan of Company L. I believe that since Company E has been more definitely placed in the area, Pvt. John Darris is a more likely candidate.

87. Weibert and Weibert, *Sixty-Six*, 148.

88. Hardorff, *Markers*, 31-36.

89. Weibert and Weibert, *Sixty-Six*, 149; Elwood L. Nye to Edward S. Luce, July 17, 1946; R. G. Cartwright to Edward S. Luce, July 26, 1946; Edward S. Luce to Regional Director, NPS, August 14, 1946. TL photocopies from National Archives, National Park Service Central Classified File, Civil Reference 1933-1949. Boxes 2129-2131, Record Group 79.

90. George Bird Grinnell, *The Fighting Cheyennes* (New York: Charles Scribner's Sons, 1915; reprint, Norman: University of Oklahoma Press, 1956), 350-51. David Humphreys Miller, *Custer's Fall: The Indian Side of the Story* (New York: Duell, Sloan & Pearce, 1957; reprint, Lincoln: University of Nebraska Press, 1985), 127-29.

91. Greene, *Enigma*, 22-24.

92. Ibid., 55-59.

93. Scott et al., *Perspectives*, 26-35.

94. Ibid., 44-45.

95. Douglas D. Scott and Melissa Connor, "Post-Mortem at the Little Big Horn," *Natural History* 6, no. 95 (June 1986): 50; Jim Robbins, "Unearthing Little Big Horn's Secrets," *National Parks* 60, nos. 11-12 (November-December 1986): 21; Robert Paul Jordan, "Ghosts of the Little Big Horn," *National Geographic* 170, no. 6 (December 1986): 796; Scott et al., *Perspectives*, 25.

96. Douglas D. Scott and Richard A. Fox, Jr., *Archaeological Insights into the Custer Battle: An Assessment of the 1984 Field Season* (Norman: University of Oklahoma Press, 1987), end-pocket map; Greene, *Enigma*, 55-60; Don Weibert, *Custer, Cases and Cartridges: The Weibert Collection Analyzed* (Billings, MT: Author, 1989), 38, 308.

97. Scott and Fox, *Insights*, 35, 119.

98. Robbins, "Unearthing," 21.

99. Scott and Fox, *Insights*, 35.

100. Scott et al., *Perspectives*, 44, 235.

101. David Alt and Donald W. Hyndman, *Roadside Geology of Montana* (Missoula, MT: Mountain Press Publishing Company, 1986), 363-66.

102. Scott et al., *Perspectives*, 230-35.

103. Ibid., 236-41.

104. "Custer Rediscovered," *Bismarck* (ND) *Tribune*, special edition dated "Summer of 84," photocopy.

105. Scott et al., *Perspectives*, 226, 230.

106. King, *Tombstones*, 3:iii.

107. Robert T. Bray, *Report of the Archaeological Investigations of the Reno Benteen Hill in 1958* (Brooklyn: Arrow & Trooper Publishing Company, n.d.), 7-8, 13, 15, 17.

108. Carroll, *Ten Years*, 158.

109. T. Lindsay Baker and Billy R. Harrison, *Adobe Walls: The History and Archaeology of the 1874 Trading Post* (College Station: Texas A&M University Press, 1986), 135-36, 144-47, 250, 290.

110. Fred H. Werner, *The Summit Springs Battle* (Greeley, CO: Werner Publications, 1991), 149-59.

111. Barnard, *Digging*, 54-55.

112. Ibid., 33-34.

113. Scott et al., *Perspectives*, 33.

114. Donald Johanson and James Shreeve, *Lucy's Child: The Discovery of a Human Ancestor* (New York: Avon Books, 1989), 20; McIntosh, *Archaeologist*, 92; Don Lessem, *Dinosaurs Rediscovered: New Findings Which Are Revolutionizing Dinosaur Science* (New York: Touchstone, 1992), 267-68.

Chapter 3

115. Miller, *Custer's Fall*, 246.

116. William A. Graham, *The Story of the Little Big Horn: Custer's Last Fight* (New York: The Century Company, 1926; reprint, Lincoln: University of Nebraska Press, 1988), 86; Graham, *Myth*, 3.

117. Brininstool, *Troopers*, 27; Fred Dustin, *The Custer Tragedy: Events Leading up to and Following the Little Big Horn Campaign of 1876* (Ann Arbor, MI: Edwards Brothers, Inc., 1939; reprint, El Segundo, CA: Upton & Sons, 1987), 118.

118. Frost, *Custer Legends*, 99.

119. Dunlay, *Wolves*, 64.

120. Thomas B. Marquis, *Keep the Last Bullet for Yourself* (Algonac, MI: Reference Publications, 1976), 158.

121. Kuhlman, *Legend Into History*, 110.

122. Thomas B. Marquis, *Custer on the Little Big Horn* (Algonac, MI: Reference Publications, 1967), 106.

123. Graham, *Myth*, 88-89.

124. Tom O'Neil, ed., *Garry Owen Tid Bits III* (Brooklyn, NY: Arrow & Trooper Publishing Company, 1991), 10-11.

125. Graham, *Myth,* 91-92.

126. Ibid., 93-96.

127. Usher L. Burdick, ed., *David F. Barry's Indian Notes on the Custer Battle* (Baltimore: The Proof Press, 1937), 9-15.

128. Graham, *Myth,* 77.

129. Richard G. Hardorff, *Lakota Recollections of the Custer Fight: New Sources of Indian-Military History* (Spokane: Arthur H. Clark Company, 1991), 95.

130. Joseph K. Dixon, *The Vanishing Race: The Last Great Indian Council* (Garden City, NY: Doubleday, Page & Company, 1913), 175-77.

131. Hardorff, *Markers,* 26, 59.

132. Greene, *Enigma,* 49.

133. Graham, *Myth,* 61-62.

134. Hammer, *Camp's Notes,* 209-10.

135. John G. Neihardt, *Black Elk Speaks: Being the Life Story of a Holy Man of the Oglala Sioux* (Lincoln: University of Nebraska Press, 1979), 125-27.

136. Graham, *Myth,* 81-85.

137. James McLaughlin, *My Friend the Indian* (Seattle: Superior Publishing Company, 1970), 43-46.

138. Hammer, *Camp's Notes,* 197-200.

139. Stanley Vestal, *Warpath: The True Story of the Fighting Sioux Told in a Biography of Chief White Bull* (Boston: Houghton Mifflin, 1934; reprint, Lincoln: University of Nebraska Press, 1984), 192-200.

140. Hardorff, *Lakota,* 107-26; Wayne Wells, "Little Big Horn Notes: Stanley Vestal's Indian Insights," *Greasy Grass* 5 (May 1989): 13-19.

141. Hardorff, *Lakota,* 113; Wells, "Vestal's Insights," 16.

142. Hardorff, *Lakota,* 112-15; Wells, "Vestal's Insights," 13-16.

143. Hardorff, *Lakota,* 126.

144. Hammer, *Camp's Notes,* 201-2.

145. Graham, *Myth,* 97-98.

146. Hardorff, *Lakota,* 49-52.

147. M. I. McCreight, *Firewater and Forked Tongues: A Sioux Chief Interprets U.S. History* (Pasadena: Trail's End Publishing Company, 1947), 112-14.

148. Hammer, *Camp's Notes,* 214-15.

149. Raymond J. DeMallie, ed., *The Sixth Grandfather: Black Elk's Teachings Given to John G. Neihardt* (Lincoln: University Of Nebraska Press, 1985), 185-87.

150. Hardorff, *Lakota,* 37-45.

151. Hammer, *Camp's Notes,* 205-7.

152. Hardorff, *Lakota,* 75-77.

153. Ibid., 143-49.

154. Ibid., 163-73.

155. Ibid., 153-59.

156. Neihardt, *Black Elk*, 119-24.

157. DeMallie, *Sixth Grandfather*, 191-92.

158. Graham, *Myth*, 109-10.

159. "Yellow Nose Tells of Custer's Last Stand," *Bighorn Yellowstone Journal* 1, no. 3 (Summer 1992): 14-17.

160. Hunt and Hunt, *Windolph*, 212-14.

161. Dixon, *Vanishing Race*, 181-83.

162. Hardorff, *Lakota*, 137-38.

163. "Two Moons Recalls the Battle of the Little Big Horn," *Bighorn Yellowstone Journal* 2, no. 1 (Winter 1993): 9-13.

164. Grinnell, *Fighting Cheyennes*, 346.

165. Ibid., 349-51.

166. Ibid., 351-54.

167. Hammer, *Camp's Notes*, 212-13.

168. Thomas B. Marquis, *Wooden Leg: A Warrior Who Fought Custer* (Lincoln: University of Nebraska Press, 1931), 224-42, 380.

169. Marquis, *Last Bullet*, 159.

170. Marquis, *Custer on Little Big Horn*, 80-92.

171. Peter J. Powell, *Sweet Medicine: The Continuing Role of the Sacred Arrows, the Sun Dance, and the Buffalo Hat in Northern Cheyenne History*, vol. 1 (Norman: University of Oklahoma Press, 1969), 112-17.

172. John Stands In Timber and Margot Liberty, *Cheyenne Memories* (Lincoln: University of Nebraska Press, 1967), 194-200.

173. Ibid., 202.

174. Ibid., 205, 209.

175. Ibid., 199.

176. Dixon, *Vanishing Race*, 181; Hardorff, *Lakota*, 125; Michael Moore and Michael Donahue, "Gibbon's Route to Custer Hill," *Greasy Grass* 7 (May 1991): 30.

177. Gray, *Custer's Last*, 373-77.

178. Graham, *Myth*, 10-11.

179. Ibid., 374.

180. Carroll, *Scrapbook*, 11:4-5.

181. Hammer, *Camp's Notes*, 156-59.

182. Ibid., 162-65.

183. Ibid., 166-68.

184. Ibid., 172.

185. Graham, *Myth*, 13-14.

186. Ibid., 18-19.

187. O. G. Libby, ed., *The Arikara Narrative of the Campaign Against the Hostile Dakotas—June, 1876* (Glorieta, NM: Rio Grande Press, 1976), 108-9.

188. Hardorff, *Markers,* 21-22; John S. Gray, "A Vindication of Curly," in 4th Annual Symposium (Hardin, MT: Custer Battlefield Historical & Museum Assn., 1990), 23.

189. Kuhlman, *Legend,* 165-66.

190. Thomas B. Marquis, narr., *Memoirs of a White Crow Indian,* by Thomas H. Leforge, (Lincoln: University of Nebraska Press, 1974), 250.

191. Robert M. Utley, *Custer and the Great Controversy: The Origin and Development of a Legend* (Pasadena, CA: Westernlore Press, 1962), 88.

192. David Hackett Fischer, *Historians' Fallacies: Toward a Logic of Historical Thought* (New York: Harper & Row, 1970), 9-10.

193. Lukacs, *Historical Consciousness,* 83.

194. Bruce A. Trinque, letter to author, November 2, 1991.

195. Marquis, *Last Bullet,* 166.

196. George M. Clark, *Scalp Dance: The Edgerly Papers on the Battle of the Little Big Horn* (Oswego, NY: Heritage Press, 1985), 24; Hardorff, *Markers,* 24.

197. Robert E. Doran, "Battalion Formation and the Custer Trail," in 3rd Annual Symposium (Hardin, MT: Custer Battlefield Historical & Museum Assn., 1989), 10; Greene, *Enigma,* 18; Hardorff, *Markers,* 24; Joe Sills, Jr., "Were There Two Last Stands?" in 2nd Annual Symposium (Hardin, MT: Custer Battlefield Historical & Museum Assn., 1988), 14.

198. Edwin C. Rozwenc, ed., *The Causes of the American Civil War* (Boston: D.C. Heath & Company, 1961).

Chapter 4

199. Mills, *Barren Regrets.*

200. The purpose of the court of inquiry was to establish the conduct of Maj. Marcus A. Reno at the Battle of the Little Bighorn. Less than a year after the fight, Frederick Whittaker published a biography of George Custer in which he charged Reno of cowardly conduct that led to the death of Custer and his men. Whittaker requested that a military committee of the House of Representatives conduct an investigation. Reno welcomed the opportunity to clear his name, but Congress adjourned without taking action. Reno wrote to President Rutherford B. Hayes requesting a court of inquiry. The request was granted, and the court convened at the Palmer House in Chicago from January 13 to February 11, 1879. The affair was not a court-martial, but an investigative inquiry. The court members included Col. John H. King, 9th Infantry; Col. Wesley Merritt, 5th Cavalry; and Lt. Col. W. B. Royall, 3rd Cavalry. First Lt. Jesse M. Lee, 9th Infantry, served as the court recorder, and Reno's counsel was Lyman D. Gilbert. After all was said and written, the court findings stated that while Reno could have done better, "there was nothing in his conduct which requires the animadversion from this Court." Ronald H. Nichols, ed., *Reno Court of Inquiry: Proceedings of a Court of Inquiry in the Case of Major Marcus A. Reno Concerning His Conduct at the Battle of the Little Big Horn River on June 25-26, 1876* (Crow Agency, MT: Custer Battlefield Historical & Museum Assn., 1992), v, vi, 629. Hereafter cited as Nichols, *Reno Court.*

201. Graham, *Abstract,* 146.

202. Gray, *Centennial,* 305. Custer's last order, written by his adjutant, read: "Benteen. Come on. Big Village. Be Quick, bring packs. W. W. Cooke. p.s. Bring pac[k]s." The order has been a subject of controversy ever since, not the least of which is the question of just how "quick" Benteen responded.

203. *The Reno Court of Inquiry: From the Official Records of the Office of the Judge Advocate General, U.S. Army. Additional Notes from the Files of the* Chicago Times. *A Copy from that of Edward S. Luce by Lawrence Frost, May 1950*, 503. Lawrence A. Frost's entirely hand-typed copy of the Court record is now located in the Custer Room of the Monroe County Library System in Monroe, Michigan. Hereafter cited as Frost, *Reno Court.*

204. Robert M. Utley, ed., *The Reno Court: The Chicago Times Account* (Fort Collins, CO: Old Army Press, 1983), 327. Hereafter cited as Utley, *Reno Court.*

205. Frost, *Reno Court*, 503.

206. Dan L. Thrapp, *Victorio and the Mimbres Apaches* (Norman: University of Oklahoma Press, 1974), 264.

207. Hammer, *Camp's Notes*, 135-36.

208. Gregory F. Michno, "Crazy Horse, Custer, and the Sweep to the North," *Montana The Magazine of Western History* 43, no. 3 (Summer 1993): 42-53.

209. Hammer, *Camp's Notes*, 95.

210. Nichols, *Reno Court*, 418.

211. Hammer, *Camp's Notes*, 102.

212. Hunt and Hunt, *Windolph*, 4.

213. Ibid., 109-10.

214. Hammer, *Camp's Notes*, 86-87.

215. Graham, *Abstract*, 109, 112.

216. Frost, *Reno Court*, 377.

217. Adolph Roenigk, *Pioneer History of Kansas* (Lincoln, KS: n.p., 1933), 290.

218. Walter Mason Camp, "Camp Manuscripts," Folder 9, Box 2, Lilly Library, Indiana University, Bloomington, IN. Hereafter cited as "Camp Mss."; Hammer, *Camp's Notes*, 116-17.

219. Utley, *Barnitz*, 269.

220. Frost, *Custer's Libbie*, 245.

221. Graham, *Abstract*, 76.

222. Frost, *Reno Court*, 272.

223. Scott et al., *Perspectives*, 226.

224. Gray, *Custer's Last*, 395.

225. Nichols, *Reno Court*, 535.

226. Hardorff, *Markers*, 57; Richard G. Hardorff, *The Custer Battle Casualties: Burials, Exhumations and Reinterments* (El Segundo, CA: Upton & Sons, 1989), 105.

227. Hammer, *Camp's Notes*, 72. Although we are indebted to Camp for his many interviews with battle participants, either an excessive exhuberance to prove a point or a failing memory caused him to make some questionable statements in his later years. In a 1920 letter to Godfrey, Camp wrote of one of his favorite topics, the placement of the gravemarkers. Perhaps forgetting that he had asked Godfrey about this very subject in 1909, and that Godfrey referred him to McDougall, Camp wrote: "There are 17 or 18 too many markers in the group at the monument, too many in the group around Keogh's marker, too many between the monument and the river, and none in the big gully where 28 ought to be. I discovered these dead in the gully with Capt. McDougall in 1909, and he was clear that there were only 9 dead between the end of the ridge and the gully. . . ." When could Camp have discovered dead in a gully with McDougall? Godfrey wrote to McDougall about the

subject. McDougall responded on May 18, 1909. Godfrey passed the information to Camp, and Camp wrote to McDougall. Although gravely ill, McDougall talked to Camp, perhaps in June 1909. On July 3 he was dead in his Vermont home. It is safe to say that McDougall did not leave his deathbed, rush out to Montana, discover dead with Camp, and rush back home to die. Perhaps we can just kindly believe that Camp confused some of his numbers and some of his witnesses. This Camp to Godfrey letter appears in John M. Carroll, ed., *A Very Real Salmagundi; or Look What I Found this Summer* (Bryan, TX: J. M. Carroll & Company, n.d.), 55-56.

228. Greene, *Enigma* [citing Jacques Barzun and Henry F. Graff, *The Modern Researcher* (New York: Harcourt, Brace & World, 1957)], 47.

229. Nichols, *Reno Court*, 454.

230. Utley, *Reno Court*, 344.

231. Graham, *Myth*, 220.

232. Rickey, *Forty Miles*, 311.

233. Carroll, *Ten Years*, 179, 181-82.

234. Brininstool, *Troopers*, 39.

235. Ibid., 61-63.

236. Hardorff, *Battle Casualties*, 100-101.

237. Ibid., 121; Moore and Donohue, "Gibbon's Route," 29.

238. Nichols, *Reno Court*, 33-34.

239. Utley, *Reno Court*, 63-4; James Willert, "The Reno Court of Inquiry of 1879: Focus on Wallace," *Research Review: The Journal of the Little Big Horn Associates* 2, no. 4 (December 1985): 3.

240. Utley, *Reno Court*, 82.

241. Ami Frank Mulford, *Fighting Indians in the 7th U.S. Cavalry: Custer's Favorite Regiment* (Corning, NY: Paul Lindsley Mulford, 1879), 149.

242. Walter M. Camp, "Walter Camp Collection," Mss. 57, Box 3, Harold Lee Library, Brigham Young University, Provo, Utah. Hereafter cited as "Camp Collection."

243. Nichols, *Reno Court*, 494-95.

244. Godfrey, "Custer's Last," 35.

245. Ibid, 23, 35.

246. Graham, *Myth*, 376; John M. Carroll, ed. *The Two Battles of the Little Big Horn* (New York: Liveright, 1974), 113.

247. Du Mont, *Battle Guns*, 88.

248. Hardorff, *Markers*, 56.

249. Hammer, *Camp's Notes*, 77.

250. Graham, *Myth*, 95; Carroll, *Two Battles*, 2, 35-37, 105.

251. Hammer, *Camp's Notes*, 68.

252. Willert, "Focus on Wallace," 3.

253. Nichols, *Reno Court*, 304; Utley, *Reno Court*, 264.

254. Nichols, *Reno Court*, 299; Utley, *Reno Court*, 262.

255. Nichols, *Reno Court*, 304; Utley, *Reno Court*, 264.

256. Graham, *Myth*, 276-78.

257. Cyrus T. Brady, *Indian Fights and Fighters* (McClure, Philips & Company, 1904; reprint, Lincoln: University of Nebraska Press, 1971), xiii; Carroll, *Benteen-Goldin Letters*, xi.

258. Carroll, *Benteen-Goldin Letters*, 19.

259. Ibid., 26-32.

260. Jacob Adams, *A Story of the Custer Massacre* (Carey, OH: Pamphlet reprint by Robert G. Hayman, 1965), 9, 25, 31, 34.

261. Bruce Liddic, ed., *I Buried Custer: The Diary of Thomas W. Coleman* (College Station, TX: Creative Publishing Company, 1979), 21.

262. "That Fatal Day: An Interview with Private John Dolan," in *That Fatal Day: Eight More With Custer* (Howell, MI: Powder River Press, 1992), 9.

263. Kenneth M. Hammer, *Men With Custer: Biographies of the 7th Cavalry, June 25, 1876* (Fort Collins, CO: Old Army Press, 1972), 121.

264. "Camp Collection," Mss. 57, Box 4.

265. Gregory J. W. Urwin, *Custer Victorious: The Civil War Battles of General George Armstrong Custer* (Rutherford, NJ: Fairleigh Dickinson University Press, 1983), 53.

266. Hammer, *Camp's Notes*, 138-40.

267. Ibid., 140.

268. Francis B. Taunton, *Custer's Field: "A Scene of Sickening Ghastly Horror."* (London: Johnson-Taunton Military Press, 1990), 37.

269. Gregory J. W. Urwin, "'Custar Had Not Waited for Us': One of Gibbon's Doughboys on the Custer Battle," in *Custer and His Times, Book Three*, 188; "Camp Collection," Mss. 57, Box 3; John M. Carroll, ed., *Who Was This Man Ricker and What Are His Tablets That Everyone Is Talking About?* (Bryan, TX: J. M. Carroll & Company, 1979), 72-73; Alfred B. Johnson, "Custer's Battlefield," *Bighorn Yellowstone Journal* 2, no. 4 (Autumn 1993): 20; John Lanahan, "From the Sioux Country," *Bighorn Yellowstone Journal* 2, no. 4 (Autumn 1993): 21.

270. Graham, *Myth*, 249-50.

271. Hammer, *Camp's Notes*, 95-97.

272. Ibid., 91.

273. Scott et al., *Perspectives*, 73-74.

274. Roger Darling, *A Sad and Terrible Blunder* (Vienna, VA: Potomac-Western Press, 1990), 109.

275. Ibid., 236.

276. Gibbon, *Sioux Campaign*, 29.

277. John S. Gray, "Captain Clifford's Story—Part 2," *Westerners Brand Book: Chicago Corral of Westerners* 26 (March 1969-February 1970): 81-82.

278. Thomas R. Buecker, "A Surgeon at the Little Big Horn: The Letters of Dr. Holmes O. Paulding," in *The Great Sioux War 1876-1877: The Best From Montana The Magazine of Western History,* ed. Paul L. Hedren (Helena: Montana Historical Society Press, 1991), 124-25, 128, 130.

279. Ibid., 139.

280. Hammer, *Camp's Notes*, 248.

281. King, *Tombstones*, 4:155.

282. Ibid., 4:166.

283. Graham, *Abstract*, ix, xiii.

284. W. Kent King, *Massacre: The Custer Cover-Up* (El Segundo, CA: Upton & Sons, 1989), 26-28; Brian W. Dippie, "Of Bullets, Blunders, and Custer Buffs," *Montana The Magazine of Western History* 41, no. 1 (Winter 1991): 80.

285. Nichols, *Reno Court*, 8.

286. Ibid., 15-16.

287. Utley, *Reno Court*, 42-43; Nichols, *Reno Court*, 15-17.

288. Charles Francis Roe, "Custer's Last Battle," in *Custer Engages the Hostiles* (Fort Collins, CO: Old Army Press, 1973), n.p; Carroll, *Two Battles*, 27-29.

289. Roe, "Custer's Last," 9-10; Carroll, *Two Battles*, 202-4.

290. George Schneider, ed., *The Freeman Journal: The Infantry in the Sioux Campaign of 1876* (San Rafael, CA: Presidio Press, 1977), 58-66.

291. Loyd J. Overfield II, *The Little Big Horn, 1876: The Official Communications, Documents and Reports* (Lincoln: University of Nebraska Press, 1990), 125.

292. Carroll, *Scrapbook*, 2:14-16.

293. Libby, *Arikara Narrative*, 58; Mari Sandoz, *The Battle of the Little Bighorn* (New York: J. B. Lippincott Company, 1966); Craig Repass, *Custer for President?* (Fort Collins, CO: Old Army Press, 1985); Robert Kammen, Joe Marshall, and Frederick Lefthand, *Soldiers Falling Into Camp: The Battles at the Rosebud and the Little Big Horn* (Encampment, WY: Affiliated Writers of America, 1992), 33, 142, 203.

294. Dee Brown, *The Year of the Century: 1876* (New York: Scribner's, 1966), 222-23.

295. McClernand, *On Time for Disaster*, 64-65.

296. Ibid., 91-93.

297. Gibbon, *Sioux Campaign*, unnumbered introduction by Capt. Michael J. Koury.

298. Hardorff, *Battle Casualties*, 94, 121-22; Oliver Knight, *Following the Indian Wars: The Story of the Newspaper Correspondents Among the Indian Campaigners* (Norman: University of Oklahoma Press, 1960), 211-12.

299. Stands In Timber, *Memories*, 196.

300. Moore and Donahue, "Gibbon's Route," 22-31.

301. Gibbon, *Sioux Campaign*, 39-40.

302. Richard Upton, *Fort Custer on the Bighorn, 1877-1898: Its History and Personalities as Told and Pictured by Its Contemporaries* (Glendale, CA: Arthur H. Clark Company, 1973), 289.

303. Graham, *Myth*, 374.

304. King, *Tombstones*, 2:83, 92.

305. Graham, *Myth*, 375.

306. John S. Gray, "Nightmares to Daydreams," *By Valor and Arms: Journal of American Military History* 1 (Summer 1975): 32.

307. Frost, *Reno Court*, 666-68.

308. John S. Gray, "Photos, Femurs, and Fallacies. Pts. 1 and 2," *Westerners Brand Book: Chicago Corral of Westerners* 20 (August 1963): 43.

309. John S. Gray, "Last Rites for Lonesome Charley Reynolds," *Montana The Magazine of Western History* 13, no. 3 (Summer 1963): 50-51.

310. Gray, "Photos," 43.

311. Philetus W. Norris, "Custer's Remains," *Bighorn Yellowstone Journal* 1, no. 2 (Spring 1992): 3-4.

312. Dan L. Thrapp, *Encyclopedia of Frontier Biography*, vol. 2, G-O (Lincoln: University of Nebraska Press, 1988), 1064.

313. Joseph Mills Hanson, *The Conquest of the Missouri: The Story of the Life and Exploits of Captain Grant Marsh* (New York: Murray-Hill Books, 1909), 379.

314. Gray, "Photos," 48.

315. King, *Tombstones*, 2:55, 57.

316. Frost, *Custer's Libbie*, 242.

317. Carroll, *Scrapbook*, 9:23-24.

318. King, *Tombstones*, 2:75, 98.

319. Hugh Lenox Scott, *Some Memories of a Soldier* (New York: The Century Company, 1928), 47.

320. Ibid., 48.

321. Hanson, *Conquest*, 378-80.

322. Barry Johnson, ed., "With Gibbon Against the Sioux in 1876: The Field Diary of Lt. William English," *English Westerners Brand Book* 9, no. 1 (October 1966): 5.

323. Marquis, *White Crow*, 239-40.

324. Ibid., 283-84, 311-12.

325. Paul A. Hutton, *Phil Sheridan and His Army* (Lincoln: University of Nebraska Press, 1985), 328-29.

326. Marquis, *White Crow*, 282.

327. Graham, *Myth*, 370.

328. Bill O'Neal, *Encyclopedia of Western Gunfighters*, (Norman: University of Oklahoma Press, 1979), 211-13; Paul I. Wellman, *A Dynasty of Western Outlaws* (New York: Pyramid Books, 1964), 180.

329. Homer Croy, *Trigger Marshall: The Story of Chris Madsen* (New York: Duell, Sloan & Pearce, 1958), 13-15.

330. Homer W. Wheeler, *Buffalo Days: The Personal Narrative of a Cattleman, Indian Fighter and Army Officer* (Indianapolis: Bobbs-Merrill, 1925; reprint Lincoln: University of Nebraska Press, 1990), 169, 184.

331. Fred H. Werner, *The Beecher Island Battle: September 17, 1868* (Greeley, CO: Werner Publications, 1989), 51-52, 120.

332. Graham, *Myth*, 371.

333. Gray, *Custer's Last*, 389.

334. Joseph C. Porter, *Paper Medicine Man: John Gregory Bourke and His American West* (Norman: University of Oklahoma Press, 1986), 1-2. 12; William H. Goetzmann, *Exploration and Empire: The Explorer and the Scientist in the Winning of the American West* (New York: W. W. Norton & Company, 1966).

335. Hardorff, *Battle Casualties*, 54-55.

336. Nancy T. Koupal, ed., "Diary of Fred M. Hans," *South Dakota Historical Collections* 40 (1980): 4-5, 44-45.

337. Ibid., 47-49.

338. King, *Tombstones*, 2:78. King insisted that Mike Sheridan lied time and again about finding and identifying the officers' graves. After a year of carnage by predators and Nature's elements, King asked, "how could *any* person hope to scrape out hidden stake tops?"

339. Robert G. Rosenberg, letter to author, December 14, 1991.

340. Andrew Ward, "The Little Bighorn," *American Heritage* 43, no. 2 (April 1992): 82.

341. Mulford, *Fighting Indians*, 147-49.

342. Hardorff, *Battle Casualties*, 59-61.

343. Ibid., 62.

344. Ibid., 63.

345. William Allen, *Adventures With the Indian and Game or 20 Years in the Rocky Mountains* (Chicago: A. W. Bowen & Company, 1903), 67-71.

346. Robert Vaughn, *Then and Now; or 36 Years in the Rockies* (Minneapolis: Tribune Printing Company, 1900), 316.

347. Don Rickey, Jr., *History of Custer Battlefield* (Billings, MT: Custer Battlefield Historical & Museum Association, 1967), 66, 70.

348. Colgate Hoyt, "An Account of a Trip Through the Yellowstone Valley in 1878," ed. Carroll Van West, *Montana The Magazine of Western History* 36, no. 2 (Spring 1986): 23, 25, 28-29. A point of comparison might be made between Miles's march and Custer's march to the battlefield, keeping in mind the latter's condemnation for supposedly driving his exhausted horses and men in a race to be the first to hit the Indian camp. Both expeditions trailed along the Yellowstone and up the Rosebud. Hoyt said his party consisted of about 150 people, including a reporter, three officers' wives, a surgeon, two young ladies from St. Paul, three children, private wagons, ambulances, and an eight-piece band. Yet they were well fed, well attended, and kept to what Hoyt intimated was a fairly leisurely marching pace of about 25 miles a day—about the same as Custer averaged.

349. Nelson A. Miles, *Personal Recollections and Observations of General Nelson A. Miles* (Chicago: The Werner Company, 1897), 286-89.

350. Graham, *Myth*, 370; Gray, "Photos," 49-50.

351. Gray, "Nightmares," 36-37.

352. Ibid., 37-38.

353. Elmo Scott Watson, "Photographing the Frontier," *English Westerners Brand Book* 8, no. 2 (January 1966): 7.

354. James Brust, "Fouch Photo May be First," *Greasy Grass* 7 (May 1991): 4-5. James Brust, "Into the Face of History," *American Heritage* 43, no. 7 (November 1992): 107.

355. Neil C. Mangum, ed., *Register of the Custer Battlefield National Monument Photograph Collection* (Custer Battlefield Historical & Museum Association, 1984), 30-35.

356. Wilson Bryan Key, *Subliminal Seduction: Ad Media's Manipulation of a Not So Innocent America* (New York: New American Library, Penguin, 1974), 58-59, 104-7.

357. William A. Frassanito, *Antietam: The Photographic Legacy of America's Bloodiest Day* (New York: Charles Scribner's Sons, 1978), 14, 288.

358. Charles Royster, *The Destructive War: William Tecumseh Sherman, Stonewall Jackson, and the Americans* (New York: Random House, 1993), 240-41.

359. Watson, "Photographing the Frontier," 8.

360. Charles F. Roe, "Report of August 6, 1881, to Asst. Adjt. General, Dept. of Dakota," (Little Bighorn Battlefield National Monument Files, photocopy); "Camp Mss.," Folder 11, Box 2.

361. Charles F. Roe, letter to Walter M. Camp, October 6, 1908, Little Bighorn Battlefield National Monument Files.

362. Hammer, *Camp's Notes*, 250.

363. Rickey, *Custer Battlefield*, 67-68.

364. Gray, *Custer's Last*, 412.

365. Ibid., 413-14.

366. Owen J. Sweet, "Report on the Custer Battlefield, May 15, 1890," Little Bighorn Battlefield National Monument Files.

367. Ibid.

368. Owen J. Sweet, letters to Walter M. Camp, November 24, 1912, and January 13, 1913, Little Bighorn Battlefield National Monument.

369. Sweet, "Report 1890."

370. Ibid.

371. Sweet to Camp, November 24, 1912, and January 13, 1913.

372. Hammer, *Camp's Notes*, 252-53.

373. Carroll, *Salmagundi*, 55.

374. "Camp Mss.," Folder 9, Box 2.

375. Ibid.

376. Paul A. Hutton, "'Correct in Every Detail': General Custer in Hollywood," *Montana The Magazine of Western History* 41, no. 1 (Winter 1991): 56; Paul A. Hutton, "Hollywood's General Custer: The Changing Image of a Military Hero in Film," *Greasy Grass* 2 (May 1986): 15-21.

Chapter 5

377. Douglas D. Scott, ed., *Papers on Little Big Horn Battlefield Archaeology: The Equipment Dump, Marker 7, and the Reno Crossing* (Lincoln: J & L Reprint Company, 1991), 116-20.

378. Ibid., 177-78.

379. Sandy Barnard, *Shovels and Speculation* (Terre Haute: AST Press, 1990), 23-28. The discovery of the remains led to the filming of a production called "Custer's Last Trooper," in which facial reconstructions and old photographs pointed to Ed Botzer as the "last trooper." The remains were formally interred at the Little Bighorn Battlefield Cemetery on June 23, 1991.

380. Scott, *Papers*, 169-70, 182.

381. Ibid., 190-92.

382. Richard A. Fox, Jr., conversation with author, June 27, 1992.

383. Scott et al., *Perspectives*, 28, 34.

384. Ibid., 74, 79.

385. Ibid., 74, 80.

386. Ibid., 73.

387. Ibid., 74.

388. Ibid., 72-73.

389. Ibid., 77.

390. Ibid., 59-61.

391. Chandler, *Garryowen*, 429-30; Overfield, *Communications*, 166-68; Gray, *Centennial*, 289.

392. "Camp Mss.," Folder 10, Box 2.

393. Scott and Connor, "Post-Mortem," 51.

394. Scott and Fox, *Insights,* end-pocket map shows about 120 army and Indian weapon-related items and other nonweapon artifacts; Greene, *Enigma*, 68, indicates several hundred bullets and cartridges.

395. Scott and Fox, *Insights*, 122; Scott et al., *Perspectives*, 130.

396. Jordan, "Ghosts," 796; Barnard, *Digging*, 33; Neil C. Mangum, "Destruction, Examination, and Reconstruction: A Review of the Archaeological Survey Conducted on Custer Battlefield, 1983-85," in *Custer and His Times, Book Three*, 158.

397. Scott and Fox, *Insights*, 47-48.

398. Gibbon, *Sioux Campaign*, 41; Daniel O. Magnussen, *Peter Thompson's Narrative of the Little Big Horn Campaign 1876: A Critical Analysis of an Eyewitness Account of Custer's Debacle* (Glendale, CA: Arthur H. Clark Company, 1974), 260. Magnussen remarked, "There was no mention of the river and Gibbon was describing the scene on Battle Ridge just prior to mentioning Bouyer."

399. Lowell Smith, ed., "Bones Identified as Bouyer's," *LBHA Newsletter* 20, no. 8 (November 1986): 6.

400. Scott et al., *Perspectives*, 84, 88.

401. Gray, *Custer's Last*, 394-95.

402. Rickey, *Custer Battlefield*, 69-70.

403. Kuhlman, *Legend*, xi.

404. Douglas D. Scott, letter to author, April 18, 1991.

405. Jordan, "Ghosts," 790; Robert M. Utley, *Custer Battlefield: A History and Guide to the Battle of the Little Big Horn*. Handbook 132. (Washington, D.C.: National Park Service, 1988), 64.

406. Gray, *Custer's Last*, ix.

407. Richard A. Fox, Jr., letter to author, July 17, 1993; in this letter Fox indicated that the Park Service did force the removal of contour intervals from the survey map for security reasons.

408. Gray, *Custer's Last*, 386.

409. Ibid., 387-95.

410. Bruce A. Trinque, letter to author, November 15, 1991.

411. Richard A. Fox, Jr., "The Keogh Episode: Archaeology and the Historical Record," in *Myles Keogh*, ed., John P. Langellier, Kurt H. Cox, and Brian C. Pohanka (El Segundo, CA: Upton & Sons, 1991), 145.

412. Scott et al., *Perspectives*, 88. Though digs are time-consuming and expensive, the archaeologists have argued for continued excavations.

413. Richard Allan Fox, Jr., *Archaeology, History, and Custer's Last Battle: The Little Big Horn Reexamined* (Norman: University of Oklahoma Press, 1993), 329.

414. Ibid., 208, 219; Fox to author, July 17, 1993. Fox states that some of the inconsistencies in this instance (such as gravemarkers 40 and 41 appearing as a single, and extras added to the lower line) are the result of the hazards of using CAD plots on small-scale maps when objects are close together. Indeed, one study has shown that because of advances in low-cost computer graphics, inadvertent yet serious cartographic errors can appear respectable and accurate. Maps based on electronic data files can be highly erroneous and should be used with caution. The warning "garbage in, garbage out" is instructive, but sometimes erroneous data cannot be discovered until they have been used for a while. See Mark Monmonier, *How to Lie with Maps* (Chicago: University of Chicago Press, 1991), 2, 57.

415. Douglas D. Scott, letter to author, May 16, 1991; Fox to author, July 17, 1993.

416. Kuhlman, *Legend*, 181-86.

417. Taunton, *Custer's Field*, 12.

418. Ibid., 15.

419. Scott and Fox, *Insights*, 47; Fox to author, July 17, 1993. Although a coauthor with Scott in 1987, Fox never agreed with the viability of a South Line as stated in *Insights*.

420. Taunton, *Custer's Field*, preface, 15.

421. "Camp Mss.," Folder 16, Box 6.

422. McClernand, *Disaster*, 92.

423. Weibert and Weibert, *Sixty-Six*, 58-64.

424. Ibid., 122.

425. In the Weiberts' defense, see Don Weibert, *Custer, Cases and Cartridges: The Weibert Collection Analyzed* (Billings, MT: Author, 1989). In this study, Weibert dropped the Bouyer-kills-Custer scenario and utilized more Indian accounts, concluding that the artifacts showed the Indians sought safety in distance and the resulting fight took place over long ranges—a good point against the panic-rout hypothesis.

426. King, *Tombstones*, 3:114-16.

427. Reedstrom, *Bugles*, 197-99.

428. Philip St. George Cooke, *Cavalry Tactics: or, Regulations for the Instruction, Formations, and Movements of The Cavalry of the Army and Volunteers of the United States*, vol. 1 (Philadelphia: J. B. Lippincott & Company, 1862), 159.

429. Utley, *Reno Court*, 41.

430. King, *Tombstones*, 3:117-122.

431. Greene, *Enigma*, 36-37.

432. Ibid., 42.

433. Kuhlman, *Legend*, 118, 183.

434. Jay Smith, "What Did Not Happen at the Battle of the Little Big Horn," *Research Review: The Journal of the Little Big Horn Associates* 6, no. 2 (June 1992): 13.

435. Graham, *Myth*, 115; Hardorff, *Markers*, 62.

436. Carroll, *Two Battles*, 108; Marquis, *Wooden Leg*, 268. The Cheyennes who died as a result of wounds received in this sector of the fight were Lame White Man, Noisy Walking, Open Belly, Limber Bones, and Black Bear.

437. Hardorff, *Markers*, 63.

438. See the numerous Indian accounts already examined, e.g., Two Moon, Flying By, Foolish Elk, White Bull, Iron Hawk, He Dog, and Standing Bear, plus Greg Michno, "Little Big

Horn Mystery Solved," *Research Review: The Journal of the Little Big Horn Associates* 6, no. 1 (January 1992): 12-13.

439. Hardorff, *Markers*, 44.

440. Ibid., 53, 54, 65; Hardorff, *Lakota*, 51. A portion of upper Deep Ravine branches nearly 400 yards from Custer Hill, but this section is completely void of gravemarkers and is several hundred yards short of the deep-walled section.

441. Hardorff, *Markers*, 54.

442. Hardorff, *Lakota*, 45.

443. Ibid., 77.

444. Ibid., 113, 115.

445. Hardorff, *Markers*, 59; See also, Richard G. Hardorff, *Hokahey! A Good Day to Die: The Indian Casualties of the Custer Fight* (Spokane: Arthur H. Clark Company, 1993), 47, 67, 73, 77. In this latter study, Hardorff continues to alternately accept or reject Wooden Leg's testimony.

446. Hardorff, *Markers*, 58; Hardorff, *Battle Casualties*, 95, 111, 115; Bruce A. Trinque, letter to author, March 21, 1993. Trinque indicates that Private Berwald "knocks into a cocked hat" Hardorff's statement that only two out of five bodies identified in Deep Ravine came from Company E. Berwald saw four bodies from E: Frederick Hohmeyer, William Huber, Richard Farrell, and Albert Meyer. Pvt. Francis O'Toole also identified the body of William Rees. With the possible addition of Captain McDougall's identification of Robert Hughes (Company K) and Private Lynch's naming of Timothy Donnelly (Company F) as being found in the ravine, we maintain a range of Company E dead from five out of five to five out of seven—71 percent to 100 percent. Contrary to Hardorff's assertion, Company E's presence in that area is fairly established.

447. Hardorff, *Markers*, 58.

448. Scott et al., *Perspectives*, 41.

449. Fox, *Archaeology, History*, 126, 185, 214, 227.

450. Fischer, *Historians' Fallacies*, 47. Fischer explains that this occurs when an attempt is made to sustain a factual proposition with negative evidence, such as when a historian declares that there is no evidence that X is the case, and then proceeds to affirm that not-X, therefore, must be the case. A lack of evidence for X does not prove the existence of not-X.

451. Fox, *Archaeology, History*, 181, 353.

452. Ibid., 186. It appears to me that the Cheyenne oral traditions, as per Powell and Stands In Timber, favors Company E being in the basin rather than Company F.

453. Ibid., 187-88. In fact, Freeman's map does not indicate any company made a stand on Cemetery Ridge. Fox contends that Freeman's map lacks scale, and a mark resembling a "1" far to the north "is indisputably on Cemetery Ridge." Freeman's scale may not be exact, but it is fairly accurate nonetheless. For example, the stand at "2" in Cemetery Ravine is a good representation of its actual location and distance between Custer Hill and the Deep Ravine ford. The stand at "4" on Calhoun Hill is in about the right place and distance between Custer Hill and Medicine Tail ford. Yet the mark that Fox claims is Freeman's "1" is farther north of Custer Hill than Medicine Tail ford is south of it—which means Fox's "1" is over 1½ miles north of Custer Hill. Since Cemetery Ridge begins only a few hundred yards west of Custer Hill, it is not at all reasonable to conclude this northern "1" represents a stand by a company on Cemetery Ridge. Part of the problem may stem from Fox's use of the drawing of Freeman's map in the 1977 Presidio Press version of Freeman's journal, in which the actual "1" is very indistinct. Fox left the actual "1" off his map and assumed a stray

mark resembling a "1" far to the north near the map's compass needle was the "1" Freeman referred to. In a direct reproduction of the map from Freeman's journal (fig. 11) the "1" shows up much clearer. It is not on Cemetery Ridge, but lies just south of the "7" in what appears to be Calhoun Coulee, a location where Fox (in *Archaeology, History,* 155-56) argues Company C may have been attacked.

454. Ibid., xv-xvi.

455. Scott and Fox, *Insights,* 47-48, 122-23; Scott et al., *Perspectives,* 123-24, 130.

456. Fox, *Archaeology, History,* 86, 124, 214.

457. Fox letter, 7-17-93.

458. Fox, *Archaeology, History,* 215.

459. Scott et al., *Perspectives,* 57, 87.

460. Fox, *Archaeology, History,* 215; Scott et al., *Perspectives,* 87.

461. Fox, *Archaeology, History,* 208, 213.

462. In past decades such historians as Marquis, Kuhlman, Graham, Utley, Powell, John Stands In Timber, Mangum, and Scott have traditionally placed the Lame White Man attack between Deep Ravine and Custer Hill. More recent interpretations, however, such as those by Hardorff and Fox, have argued for moving the attack site; since 1991 battlefield brochures have indicated the attack took place along Greasy Grass Ridge and in Calhoun Coulee.

463. Marquis, *Wooden Leg,* 231-32.

464. Ibid., 241-43.

465. Ibid., 380.

466. Marquis, *Last Bullet,* 157; National Park Service Central Classified File, Civil Reference, 1933-1949, National Monuments Custer Battlefield, Boxes 2129-2131, Record Group 79, National Archives, Washington, D.C. In the above files is a War Department Quartermaster form number 173, dated June 10, 1926, which states the Custer Battlefield Reservation is one mile square and is completely enclosed by a barbed wire fence attached to cedar posts extending five feet above ground level and spaced twelve feet apart with 2x8 boards for top rails. Also scattered in the boxes are numerous aerial photos taken between 1932 and 1935 showing the fence surrounding the field.

467. Marquis, *Wooden Leg,* 228-34; Fox, *Archaeology, History,* 136; Fox to author, July 17, 1993. Fox contends that Wooden Leg was not in the Lame White Man attack, but came on the field late, only in time to participate in the fighting in the Keogh sector. This does not appear to be borne out by Wooden Leg's narrative, which is consistently voiced in first person terms, i.e., "We forded the river . . . we fell in with the others . . . we urged on our horses . . . I swerved up a gulch to my left . . . I saw some Cheyennes going ahead of me . . . we were lying down in gullies . . . we kept creeping in closer . . . I got off and crept with them . . . I went back and got my horse. . . ." It is clear Wooden Leg was on the field to witness the Lame White Man attack.

468. Marquis, *Last Bullet,* 159; Fox, *Archaeology, History,* 149; Fox to author, July 17, 1993. Fox paraphrased Marquis's quote as ". . . the charge proceeded about 500 yards down the draw." Omitting the key part of the quote, "from the present monument," makes it easier to argue for changing the attack site. Fox indicated he submitted a second printing correction for this oversight but added that Marquis was only interpreting and was not presenting direct testimony.

469. "Camp Mss.," Folder 5, Box 7. On Camp's map, "C" is Greasy Grass Hill and "D" is Calhoun Hill. For those who have never had the opportunity to read Camp's writing

in its original form, some actual-size, sample tracings of his "notes" may be enlightening. The sample on the right from Lilly Library, Indiana University, concerns testimony from an individual designated on different pages as either the wife of Kill Assiniboine or Little Assiniboine.

470. Ward, "Little Bighorn," 84; Fox, *Archaeology, History,* 150-51, 167-68, 217, 300-303. There has been much ado about how Indians "saw" Battle Ridge running either east-west or north-south. It has been argued that Wooden Leg and Kate Bighead viewed the ridge in east-west terms and that Indians had a different conception of directions than did whites. In fact, it appears that a great number of Indians, including Runs The Enemy, Two Eagles, Red Hawk, Respects Nothing, Flying Hawk, Young Two Moon, Soldier Wolf, and Standing Bear, saw the ridge in north-south terms, the same as whites. There was no uniform, monolithic Indian perception of the terrain.

471. Scott et al., *Perspectives,* 106-111, 129.

472. Bruce A. Trinque, "The Cartridge-Case Evidence on Custer Field: An Analysis and Re-Interpretation," in 5th Annual Symposium (Hardin, MT: Custer Battlefield Historical & Museum Assn., 1991), 71-74.

473. Robert M. Utley, *Cavalier in Buckskin: George Armstrong Custer and the Western Military Frontier* (Norman: University of Oklahoma Press, 1988), 189-90.

474. William Hedley, "'ps Bring Pacs': The Order That Trapped the Custer Battalion," in 4th Annual Symposium (Hardin, MT: Custer Battlefield Historical & Museum Assn., 1990), 56-57, 66.

475. O'Neil, *Garry Owen III,* 10; Graham, *Myth,* 75, 89, 97, 103; Hardorff, *Lakota,* 95, 167, 169, 173, 184; Two Moon, "Recalls Battle," 10; Marquis, *Wooden Leg,* 230; Carroll, *Ricker,* 16-19.

476. Hutton, *Phil Sheridan,* 144-52.

477. Walter Millis, *Arms and Men: A Study in American Military History* (New York: New American Library, 1956); Bruce Catton, *Reflections on the Civil War* (Garden City, NY: Doubleday, 1981); Trevor N. Dupuy, *The Evolution of Weapons and Warfare* (Indianapolis: Bobbs-Merrill Company, 1980); Grady McWhiney and Perry D. Jamieson, *Attack and Die: Civil War Military Tactics and the Southern Heritage* (Tuscaloosa: University of Alabama Press, 1982); Paddy Griffith, *Rally Once Again: Battle Tactics of the American Civil War* (Wiltshire, England: Crowood Press, 1987). Herman Hattaway and Archer Jones, *How the North Won: A Military History of the Civil War* (Urbana: University of Illinois Press, 1983), 500; Royster, *Destructive War,* 355-56.

478. Griffith, *Rally*, 99-104.

479. Alvin M. Josephy, Jr., *The Civil War in the American West* (New York: Alfred A. Knopf, 1991), 149; Roger Darling, *General Custer's Final Hours: Correcting A Century of Misconceived History* (Vienna, VA: Potomac-Western Press, 1992), ix; D. A. Kinsley, *Custer Favor the Bold: A Soldier's Story* (New York: Promontory Press, 1992), 217; Frost, *Custer's 7th*, 66; Jay Smith, "What Did Not Happen," 13.

480. Ian Knight, *Brave Men's Blood: The Epic of the Zulu War, 1879* (London: Greenhill Books, 1990); Donald Morris, *The Washing of the Spears* (New York: Simon and Schuster, 1965); Terry C. Karselis, "Disaster in Duplicate: An Examination of the Similarities Between the Battle of Isandhlawana and the Little Big Horn," in 5th Annual Symposium (Hardin, MT: Custer Battlefield Historical & Museum Assn., 1991).

481. Michael Barthorp, *War on the Nile: Britain, Egypt and the Sudan 1882-1898* (Dorset, England: Blandford Press, 1984); Philip Ziegler, *Omdurman* (New York: Dorset Press, 1987); Byron Farwell, *Queen Victoria's Little Wars* (New York: Harper & Row, 1972).

482. Fischer, *Historians' Fallacies*, 224-25.

483. Tim Mulligan, "Custer and the Little Big Horn: A Needed Perspective," *Research Review: The Journal of the Little Big Horn Associates* 8, no. 1 (Spring 1974): 13; Hutton, *Phil Sheridan*, 328.

484. Trinque to author, November 15, 1991.

485. Kuhlman, *Legend*, 165; Fischer, *Historians' Fallacies*, 306.

Chapter 6

486. Scott et al., *Perspectives*, 84, 88, 130.

487. Joe Sills, Jr., "Weir Point, Another Perspective," *Research Review: The Journal of the Little Big Horn Associates* 3, no. 2 (June 1986): 25.

488. Nichols, *Reno Court*, 25, 74. One might wonder why so much stock has been placed in Wallace's time estimates. He was questioned by the court recorder at Reno's inquiry. Was his watch accurate, or was it maybe an hour slow or fast? Wallace answered, "I am not sure about that. It may have been fast or it may have been slow. I never have claimed that it was the local time of the place."

489. Overfield, *Communications*, 25; Graham, *Abstract*, 64; Hammer, *Camp's Notes*, 92; William Hedley, "'We've Caught them Napping': The Little Big Horn Time Warp," in 3rd Annual Symposium (Hardin, MT: Custer Battlefield Historical & Museum Assn., 1989), 58-59; Nichols, *Reno Court*, 96; Libby, *Arikara*, 101; Jacob Hetler, "Account of Service of Jacob Hetler Who Spent Five Years in Service with Company D, 7th U.S. Cavalry, and Who Served Under General Custer," *Winners of the West* 12, no. 12 (November 1935): 3; Dixon, *Vanishing Race*, 167; Gustave Korn, "The Custer Battle," *Winners of the West* 13, no. 2 (January 1936): 1.

490. Graham, *Myth*, 215.

491. King, *Massacre*.

492. Don Gifford, *The Farther Shore: A Natural History of Perception 1798-1984* (New York: Vintage Books, 1991), 98, 122-23.

493. Gibbon, *Sioux Campaign*, 40; Graham, *Myth*, 374; Granville Stuart, *Pioneering in Montana: The Making of a State, 1864-1887* (Lincoln: University of Nebraska Press, 1977), 120-21; Hardorff, *Battle Casualties*, 60; Allen, *Indians and Game*, 67; Gray, "Nightmares," 37-38; Sweet to Camp, November 24, 1912.

494. John M. Carroll, ed., *Custer's Chief of Scouts: The Reminiscences of Charles A. Varnum* (Lincoln: University of Nebraska Press, 1987), 95; Graham, *Myth*, 192; Carroll, *Two Battles*, 16-17.

495. Gibbon, *Sioux Campaign*, 32; Godfrey, "Custer's Last," 30.

496. Evan S. Connell, *Son of the Morning Star* (New York: Harper & Row, 1984), 58; Hunt and Hunt, *Windolph*, 96; Glendolin Damon Wagner, *Old Neutriment: Memories of the Custers* (Lincoln: University of Nebraska Press, 1989) 163.

497. Dowd, *Custer Lives*, 261; Gibbon, *Sioux Campaign*, 32; Chandler, *Garryowen*, 70; Jesse Brown and A. M. Willard, *Black Hills Trails: A History of the Struggles of the Pioneers in the Winning of the Black Hills* (Rapid City, SD: Rapid City Journal Company, 1924), 203.

498. Marquis, *Custer on Little Big Horn*, 40.

499. John Carland, "The Massacre of Custer," *Bighorn Yellowstone Journal* 1, no. 4 (Autumn 1992): 4; Marcus Reno, "From Major Reno," *That Fatal Day: Eight More With Custer* (Howell, MI: Powder River Press, 1992), 14; Robert J. Ege, *Settling the Dust: The Custer Battle—June 25, 1876* (Greeley, CO: Werner Publications, 1981).

500. James Willert, ed., *Bourke's Diary: From the Journals of 1st Lt. John Gregory Bourke June 27-Sept. 15, 1876* (La Mirada, CA: Author, 1986), 114-17; Charles King, *Campaigning With Crook* (Norman: University of Oklahoma Press, 1964), 88-89.

501. Knight, *Following the Indian Wars*, 5; Gibbon, *Sioux Campaign*, 61.

502. Hunt and Hunt, *Windolph*, xiii; Earle R. Forrest, *Witnesses at the Battle of the Little Big Horn* (Monroe, MI: Monroe County Library System, 1986), 24.

503. Orrin H. Bonney and Lorraine G. Bonney, *Battle Drums and Geysers*, part 1 (Houston, TX: n.p., 1970), 59; Johnson, "Diary of Lt. English," 6; Gray, "Clifford's Story," 82.

504. Reedstrom, *Bugles*, 6; Rickey, *Forty Miles*, 94, 133.

505. King, *Tombstones*, 2:83.

506. Edward S. Godfrey, "Cavalry Fire Discipline," *By Valor and Arms: The Journal of American Military History* 2, no. 4 (1976): 32, 36.

507. Richard Gabriel, *The Painful Field: The Psychiatric Dimension of Modern War* (Westport, CT: Greenwood Press, 1988), 9, 22.

508. Roy R. Grinker and John P. Spiegel, *War Neuroses* (1945; reprint, New York: Arno Press, 1979), 69; Roy R. Grinker and John P. Spiegel, *Men Under Stress* (New York: McGraw-Hill Company, 1945).

509. Richard A. Gabriel, *No More Heroes: Madness and Psychiatry in War* (New York: Hill & Wang, 1987), 63-66; Gabriel, *Painful Field*, 119-20.

510. Gabriel, *No Heroes*, 84-89; Gabriel, *Painful Field*, 129.

511. George L. Engel, *Psychological Development in Health and Disease* (Philadelphia: W. B. Saunders Company, 1962), 284, 327.

512. Rickey, *Forty Miles*, 301, 330; John Keegan and Richard Holmes, *Soldiers: A History of Men in Battle* (New York: Elisabeth Sifton Books, Viking Penguin, 1986), 156.

513. S. L. A. Marshall, *Men Against Fire: The Problem of Battle Command in Future War* (Gloucester, MS: Peter Smith, 1978), 113, 120.

514. Paul Fussell, *Wartime: Understanding and Behavior in the Second World War* (Oxford: Oxford University Press, 1989), 22. 273; Marshall, *Men Against Fire*, 48.

515. William Manchester, *Goodbye Darkness: A Memoir of the Pacific War* (New York: Dell, 1979), 83, 86-87.

516. John Keegan, *The Face of Battle* (Middlesex, England: Penguin Books, 1976), 44, 302-3, 341.

517. Marshall, *Men Against Fire*, 179.

518. Bruce A. Rosenberg, *Custer and the Epic of Defeat* (University Park: Pennsylvania State University Press, 1974), 128, 260; Brian W. Dippie, "Brush, Palette and the Custer Battle: A Second Look," *Montana The Magazine of Western History* 24, no. 1 (Winter 1974): 64-66.

519. Carroll, *Ricker*, 48-49.

520. H. W. Wheeler, "Custer Battlefield in '77," *Westerners Brand Book: Chicago Corral of Westerners* 4, no. 11 (January 1948): 67.

521. Rosenberg, *Epic of Defeat*, 218-19. The stress of war produced the same psychological conflicts in no less a personage than Robert E. Lee. See Hattaway and Jones, *How the North Won*, 373.

522. John McCrone, *The Ape That Spoke: Language and the Evolution of the Human Mind* (New York: William Morrow and Company, 1991), 68-69, 72-74, 114-16.

523. Ibid., 118.

524. Hammer, *Camp Notes*, 72, 207.

525. Rosenberg, *Epic of Defeat*, 260-61.

526. Michael Fellman, *Inside War: The Guerilla Conflict in Missouri During the American Civil War* (New York: Oxford University Press, 1989), 48-49.

527. American Psychiatric Association, *Diagnostic and Statistical Manual of Mental Disorders DSM III-R* (Washington, D.C.: American Psychiatric Press, 1987), 236-37, 248-50; Eva Kahana et al., "Coping with Extreme Trauma," in *Human Adaptation to Extreme Stress from the Holocaust to Vietnam*, ed. John P. Wilson, Zev Harel, and Boaz Kahana (New York: Plenum Press, 1988), 62-67, 70; Margaret A. Stavick, letter to author, January 4, 1994. Stavick, who has been very successful in winning disability awards for Vietnam veterans, suggested the likelihood that 7th Cavalry troopers were suffering from PTSD. She has a work in progress on George Custer's stress disorders and believes battle survivors were not paying attention to the terrain at all and did not know what, where, or who they were burying, let alone being able to remember the "deepness" of a ravine. She believes "psychic numbing" played a great part in the burials; the men simply blocked out of their minds what they didn't want to remember. Stavick thinks it is "asking too much of the survivors of this battle to remember in which ravine/gully the dead were buried." It is interesting to note that another recent work on a nineteenth-century soldier, Gen. Ranald S. Mackenzie, makes use of the PTSD angle. Author Charles M. Robinson III contends that Mackenzie, of the 4th Cavalry, became a psychiatric casualty when he cracked after the funeral of his men following the November 25, 1876, fight with Dull Knife's Cheyennes. His condition deteriorated to the point that he was "retired" from the service and committed to an asylum in 1884. Rather than syphilis being the cause of Mackenzie's condition, Robinson argues that he was more likely suffering from PTSD. See Charles M. Robinson III, *Bad Hand: A Biography of General Ranald S. Mackenzie* (Austin, TX: State House Press, 1993), 223, 323-26, 333-38.

528. Charles K. Hofling, *Custer and the Little Big Horn: A Psychobiographical Inquiry* (Detroit: Wayne State University Press, 1981).

529. Herbert Coffeen, *The Custer Battle Book* (New York: Carlton Press, 1964), 55.

530. Marquis, *Last Bullet*, 164.

Bibliography

Adams, Jacob. *A Story of the Custer Massacre.* Pamphlet reprint by Robert G. Hayman. Carey, OH: 1965.

Allen, William. *Adventures With the Indians and Game or 20 Years in the Rocky Mountains.* Chicago: A. W. Bowen & Company, 1903.

American Psychiatric Association. *Diagnostic and Statistical Manual of Mental Disorders DSM III-R.* Washington, D.C.: American Psychiatric Press, 1987.

Alt, David, and Donald W. Hyndman. *Roadside Geology of Montana.* Missoula, MT: Mountain Press Publishing Company, 1986.

Baker, T. Lindsay, and Billy R. Harrison. *Adobe Walls: The History and Archaeology of the 1874 Trading Post.* College Station: Texas A&M University Press, 1986.

Barnard, Sandy. *Digging Into Custer's Last Stand.* Terre Haute, IN: AST Press, 1986.

———. *Shovels and Speculation.* Terre Haute, IN: AST Press, 1990.

Barthorp, Michael. *War on the Nile: Britain, Egypt and the Sudan 1882-1898.* Dorset, England: Blandford Press, 1984.

Bence, Greg. "The Enigma of Sergeant Butler." *Research Review: The Journal of the Little Big Horn Associates* 8, no. 1 (Spring 1974): 1-4.

Bonney, Orrin H., and Lorraine G. Bonney. *Battle Drums and Geysers.* Part 1. Houston, TX: N.p., 1970.

Bradley, James H.. *The March of the Montana Column: A Prelude to the Custer Disaster*, edited by Edgar I. Stewart. Norman: Uinversity of Oklahoma Press, 1961.

Brady, Cyrus T. *Indian Fights and Fighters.* McClure, Philips & Company, 1904. Reprint, Lincoln: University of Nebraska Press, 1971.

Bray, Robert T. *Report of the Archaeological Investigations of the Reno Benteen Hill in 1958.* Brooklyn, NY: Arrow & Trooper Publishing Company, n.d.

Breisach, Ernst. *Historiography: Ancient, Medieval, and Modern.* Chicago: University of Chicago Press, 1983.

Brininstool, E. A. *Troopers With Custer: Historic Incidents of the Battle of the Little Big Horn.* Harrisburg, PA: The Stackpole Company, 1952. Reprint, Lincoln: University of Nebraska Press, 1989.

Brown, Dee. *The Year of the Century: 1876.* New York: Scribner's, 1966.

Brown, Jesse, and A. M. Willard. *The Black Hills Trails: A History of the Struggles of the Pioneers in the Winning of the Black Hills.* Rapid City, SD: Rapid City Journal Company, 1924.

Brown, Lauren. *Grasslands.* New York: Alfred A. Knopf, 1985.

Brust, James. "Fouch Photo May Be First." *Greasy Grass* 7 (May 1991): 2-9.

———. "Into the Face of History." *American Heritage* 43, no. 7 (November 1992): 104-13.

Buecker, Thomas R. "A Surgeon at the Little Big Horn: The Letters of Dr. Holmes O. Paulding." In *The Great Sioux War 1876-1877: The Best From Montana The Magazine of Western History,* edited by Paul L. Hedren, 123-151. Helena: Montana Historical Society Press, 1991.

Burdick, Usher L., ed. *David F. Barry's Indian Notes on the Custer Battle.* Baltimore: The Proof Press, 1937.

Burkey, Blaine. *Custer, Come at Once!* Hays, KS: Thomas More Prep., 1976.

Camp, Walter M. "Camp Manuscripts." Lilly Library, Indiana University, Bloomington, IN.

———. "Walter Camp Collection." Harold Lee Library, Brigham Young University, Provo, UT.

Carland, John. "The Massacre of Custer." *Bighorn Yellowstone Journal* 1, no. 4 (Autumn 1992): 2-5.

Carriker, Robert C. *Fort Supply Indian Territory.* Norman: University of Oklahoma Press, 1970.

Carroll, John M. "Major Wickliffe Cooper, 7th U.S. Cavalry—Was it Murder or Suicide?" *Research Review: The Journal of the Little Big Horn Associates* 3 (December 1986): 6-17.

———, ed. *The Benteen-Goldin Letters on Custer and His Last Battle.* Lincoln: University of Nebraska Press, 1991.

———, ed. *A Bit of 7th Cavalry History with All Its Warts.* Bryan, TX: J. M. Carroll & Company, 1987.

———, ed. *Custer's Chief of Scouts: The Reminiscences of Charles A. Varnum.* Lincoln: University of Nebraska Press, 1987.

———, ed. *The Lt. Maguire Maps.* Bryan, TX: J. M. Carroll & Company, n.d.

———, ed. *A Seventh Cavalry Scrapbook.* Vols. 1-13. Bryan, TX: J. M. Carroll & Company, 1978-79.

———, ed. *Ten Years with General Custer Among the Indians (and other writings by John Ryan).* Bryan, TX: J. M. Carroll & Company, 1980.

———, ed. *They Rode With Custer.* Mattituck, NY: J. M. Carroll & Company, 1987.

———, ed. *The Two Battles of the Little Big Horn.* New York: Liveright, 1974.

———, ed. *A Very Real Salmagundi; Or, Look What I Found this Summer.* Bryan, TX: J. M. Carroll & Company, n.d.

———, ed. *Who Was This Man Ricker and What Are His Tablets That Everyone Is Talking About?* Bryan, TX: J. M. Carroll & Company, 1979.

Catton, Bruce. *Reflections on the Civil War.* Garden City, NY: Doubleday, 1981.

Chandler, Melbourne C. *Of Garryowen in Glory: The History of the 7th U.S. Cavalry.* Anandale, VA: Turnpike Press, 1960.

Clark, George M. *Scalp Dance: The Edgerly Papers on the Battle of the Little Big Horn.* Oswego, NY: Heritage Press, 1985.

Coffeen, Herbert. *The Custer Battle Book.* New York: Carlton Press, 1964.

Connell, Evan S. *Son of the Morning Star.* New York: Harper & Row, 1984.

Cooke, Philip St. George. *Cavalry Tactics: Or, Regulations for the Instruction, Formations, and Movements of The Cavalry of the Army and Volunteers of the United States.* Vol. I. Philadelphia: J. B. Lippincott & Company, 1862.

Croy, Homer. *Trigger Marshall: The Story of Chris Madsen.* New York: Duell, Sloan & Pearce, 1958.

Custer, George Armstrong. *My Life on the Plains or, Personal Experiences with Indians.* Norman: University of Oklahoma Press, 1962.

Darling, Roger. *Benteen's Scout to-the-Left.* El Segundo, CA: Upton & Sons, 1987.

———. *General Custer's Final Hours: Correcting a Century of Misconceived History.* Vienna, VA: Potomac-Western Press, 1992.

———. *A Sad and Terrible Blunder.* Vienna, VA: Potomac-Western Press, 1990.

DeMallie, Raymond J., ed. *The Sixth Grandfather: Black Elk's Teachings Given to John G. Neihardt.* Lincoln: University of Nebraska Press, 1985.

Dippie, Brian W. "Brush, Palette and the Custer Battle: A Second Look." *Montana The Magazine of Western History* 24, no. 1 (Winter 1974): 64-66.

———. "Of Bullets, Blunders, and Custer Buffs." *Montana The Magazine of Western History* 41, no. 1 (Winter 1991): 76-80.

———, ed. *Nomad: George A. Custer in Turf, Field and Farm.* Austin: University of Texas Press, 1980.

Dixon, David. "Custer and the Sweetwater Hostages." In *Custer and His Times, Book Three,* 82-108. El Paso, TX and Conway, AR: Little Big Horn Associates and University of Central Arkansas Press, 1987.

Dixon, Joseph K. *The Vanishing Race: The Last Great Indian Council.* Garden City, NY: Doubleday, Page & Company, 1913.

Dolan, John. "That Fatal Day: An Interview with Private John Dolan." In *That Fatal Day: Eight More with Custer,* 7-9. Howell, MI: Powder River Press, 1992.

Doran, Robert E. "Battalion Formation and the Custer Trail." 3rd Annual Symposium. Custer Battlefield Historical & Museum Association, 1989.

Dowd, James Patrick. *Custer Lives!* Fairfield, WA: Ye Galleon Press, 1982.

DuMont, John S. *Custer Battle Guns.* Canaan, NH: Phoenix Publishing, 1988.

Dunlay, Thomas W. *Wolves for the Blue Soldiers: Indian Scouts and Auxiliaries with the United States Army, 1860-90.* Lincoln: University of Nebraska Press, 1987.

Dupuy, Trevor N. *The Evolution of Weapons and Warfare.* Indianapolis: Bobbs-Merrill Company, 1980.

———. *Understanding War: History and Theory of Combat.* New York: Paragon House Publishers, 1987.

Dustin, Fred. *The Custer Tragedy: Events Leading up to and Following the Little Big Horn Campaign of 1876.* Ann Arbor, MI: Edwards Brothers, 1939; reprint, El Segundo, CA: Upton & Sons, 1987.

Ege, Robert J. *Settling the Dust: The Custer Battle—June 25, 1876.* Greeley, CO: Werner Publications, 1981.

Engel, George L. *Psychological Development in Health and Disease.* Philadelphia: W. B. Saunders Company, 1962.

Farwell, Byron. *Queen Victoria's Little Wars.* New York: Harper & Row, 1972.

Fellman, Michael. *Inside War: The Guerilla Conflict in Missouri During the American Civil War.* New York: Oxford University Press, 1989.

Fischer, David Hackett. *Historians' Fallacies: Toward a Logic of Historical Thought.* New York: Harper & Row, 1970.

Forrest, Earle R. *Witnesses at the Battle of the Little Big Horn.* Monroe, MI: Monroe County Library System, 1986.

Fougera, Katherine Gibson. *With Custer's Cavalry.* Lincoln: University of Nebraska Press, 1986.

Fox, Richard A., Jr. *Archaeology, History, and Custer's Last Battle: The Little Big Horn Reexamined.* Norman: University of Oklahoma Press, 1993.

———. "The Keogh Episode: Archaeology and the Historical Record." In *Myles Keogh,* edited by John P. Langellier, Kurt H. Cox, and Brian C. Pohanka, 142-53. El Segundo, CA: Upton & Sons, 1991.

Frassanito, William A. *Antietam: The Photographic Legacy of America's Bloodiest Day.* New York: Charles Scribner's Sons, 1978.

Frost, Lawrence A. *The Court Martial of General George Armstrong Custer.* Norman: University of Oklahoma Press, 1968.

———. *Custer Legends.* Bowling Green, OH: Bowling Green University Popular Press, 1981.

———. *Custer's 7th Cavalry and the Campaign of 1873.* El Segundo, CA: Upton & Sons, 1986.

———. *General Custer's Libbie.* Seattle: Superior Publishing Company, 1976.

———. *The Reno Court of Inquiry: From the Official Records of the Office of the Judge Advocate General, U.S. Army. Additional Notes from the Files of the* Chicago Times. *A Copy from that of Edward S. Luce by Lawrence Frost, May 1950.*

———. "Two Sides of a General." In *Custer and His Times, Book Three,* 121-47. El Paso, TX and Conway, AR: Little Big Horn Associates and University of Central Arkansas Press, 1987.

Fussell, Paul. *Wartime: Understanding and Behavior in the Second World War.* Oxford: Oxford University Press, 1989.

Gabriel, Richard A. *No More Heroes: Madness and Psychiatry in War.* New York: Hill & Wang, 1987.

———. *The Painful Field: The Psychiatric Dimension of Modern War.* Westport, CT: Greenwood Press, 1988.

Gibbon, John. *Gibbon on the Sioux Campaign of 1876,* edited by Michael J. Koury. Bellevue, NE: Old Army Press, 1970.

Gifford, Don. *The Farther Shore: A Natural History of Perception 1798-1984* New York: Vintage Books, 1991.

Godfrey, Edward S. "Custer's Last Battle 1876." *Century Magazine* (January 1892). Reprint, Golden, CO: Outbooks, 1986.

———. "Cavalry Fire Discipline." *By Valor and Arms: The Journal of American Military History* 2, no. 4 (1976): 30-36.

Goetzmann, William H. *Exploration and Empire: The Explorer and the Scientist in the Winning of the American West.* New York: W. W. Norton & Company, 1966.

Graham, William A. *The Custer Myth: A Source Book of Custeriana.* Lincoln: University of Nebraska Press, 1953.

———. *The Reno Court of Inquiry: Abstract of the Official Record of Proceedings.* Harrisburg, PA: The Stackpole Company, 1954.

———. *The Story of the Little Big Horn: Custer's Last Fight.* New York: Century Company, 1926. Reprint, Lincoln: University of Nebraska Press, 1988.

Gray, John S. "Captain Clifford's Story—Part II." *Westerners Brand Book: Chicago Corral of Westerners* 26 (March 1969-February 1970): 81-83.

———. *Centennial Campaign: The Sioux War of 1876.* Ft. Collins, CO: Old Army Press, 1976.

———. *Custer's Last Campaign: Mitch Boyer and the Little Big Horn Reconstructed*. Lincoln: University of Nebraska Press, 1991.

———. "Last Rites for Lonesome Charley Reynolds." *Montana The Magazine of Western History* 13, no. 3 (Summer 1963): 40-51.

———. "Nightmares to Daydreams." *By Valor and Arms: The Journal of American Military History* 1 (Summer 1975): 31-39.

———. "Photos, Femurs, and Fallacies. Pts. 1 and 2." *Westerners Brand Book: Chicago Corral of Westerners* 20 (August 1963): 41-51.

———. "A Vindication of Curly." 4th Annual Symposium. Custer Battlefield Historical & Museum Association, 1990.

Greene, Jerome A. *Evidence and the Custer Enigma: A Reconstruction of Indian-Military History*. Golden, CO: Outbooks, 1986.

———. *Slim Buttes, 1876: An Episode of the Great Sioux War*. Norman: University of Oklahoma Press, 1982.

Griffith, Paddy. *Rally Once Again: Battle Tactics of the American Civil War*. Wiltshire, England: Crowood Press, 1987.

Grinker, Roy R., and John P. Spiegel. *Men Under Stress*. New York: McGraw-Hill Company, 1945.

———. *War Neuroses*. 1945. Reprint, New York: Arno Press, 1979.

Grinnell, George Bird. *The Fighting Cheyennes*. New York: Scribner's, 1915. Reprint, Norman: University of Oklahoma Press, 1956.

Hammer, Kenneth M. *Custer in '76: Walter Camp's Notes on the Custer Fight*. Norman: University of Oklahoma Press, 1976.

———. *The Glory March*. Monroe, MI: Monroe County Library System, 1980.

———. *Men With Custer: Biographies of the 7th Cavalry, June 25, 1876*. Ft. Collins, CO: Old Army Press, 1972.

Hanson, Joseph Mills. *The Conquest of the Missouri: The Story of the Life and Exploits of Captain Grant Marsh*. New York: Murray-Hill Books, 1909.

Hardorff, Richard G. *The Custer Battle Casualties: Burials, Exhumations and Reinterments*. El Segundo, CA: Upton & Sons, 1989.

———. *Hokahey! A Good Day to Die! The Indian Casualties of the Custer Fight*. Spokane: Arthur H. Clark Company, 1993.

———. *Lakota Recollections of the Custer Fight: New Sources of Indian-Military History*. Spokane: Arthur H. Clark Company, 1991.

———. *Markers, Artifacts and Indian Testimony: Preliminary Findings on the Custer Battle*. Short Hills, NJ: Don Horn Publications, 1985.

Hattaway, Herman, and Archer Jones. *How the North Won: A Military History of the Civil War*. Urbana: University of Illinois Press, 1983.

Hedley, William. "'ps Bring Pacs': The Order That Trapped the Custer Battalion." 4th Annual Symposium. Custer Battlefield Historical & Museum Association, 1990.

———. "'We've Caught them Napping': The Little Big Horn Time Warp." 3rd Annual Symposium. Custer Battlefield Historical & Museum Association, 1989.

Hedren, Paul L. "The Custer Library." *Research Review: The Journal of the Little Big Horn Associates* 8, no. 4 (Winter 1974): 5-11.

——. *First Scalp for Custer: The Skirmish at Warbonnet Creek, Nebraska, July 17, 1876.* Lincoln: University of Nebraska Press, 1987.

Hetler, Jacob. "Account of Service of Jacob Hetler Who Spent Five Years in Service with Co. D, 7th U.S. Cavalry, and Who Served under General Custer." *Winners of the West* 12, no. 12 (November 1935): 3.

Hofling, Charles K. *Custer and the Little Big Horn: A Psychobiographical Inquiry.* Detroit: Wayne State University Press, 1981.

Hoig, Stan. *The Battle of the Washita: The Sheridan-Custer Indian Campaign of 1867-69.* Lincoln: University of Nebraska Press, 1979.

Hoyt, Colgate. "An Account of a Trip Through the Yellowstone Valley in 1878," edited by Carroll Van West. *Montana The Magazine of Western History* 36, no. 2 (Spring 1986): 22-35.

Hunt, Frazier, and Robert Hunt. *I Fought With Custer: The Story of Sergeant Windolph, Last Survivor of the Battle of the Little Big Horn.* New York: Scribner's, 1954. Reprint, Lincoln: University of Nebraska Press, 1987.

Hutton, Paul A. "'Correct in Every Detail': General Custer in Hollywood." *Montana The Magazine of Western History* 41, no. 1 (Winter 1991): 29-56.

——. "From Little Big Horn to Little Big Man: The Changing Image of a Western Hero in Popular Culture." *Western Historical Quarterly* 7, no. 1 (January 1976): 19-45.

——. "Hollywood's General Custer: The Changing Image of a Military Hero in Film." *Greasy Grass* 2 (May 1986): 15-21.

——. *Phil Sheridan and His Army.* Lincoln: University of Nebraska Press, 1985.

Jackson, Donald. *Custer's Gold: The United States Cavalry Expedition of 1874.* Lincoln: University of Nebraska Press, 1972.

Johanson, Donald, and James Shreeve. *Lucy's Child: The Discovery of a Human Ancestor.* New York: Avon, 1989.

Johnson, Alfred B. "Custer's Battlefield." *Bighorn Yellowstone Journal* 2, no. 4, (Autumn 1993): 17-20.

Johnson, Barry, ed. "With Gibbon Against the Sioux in 1876—The Field Diary of Lt. William English." *English Westerners Brand Book* 9, no. 1 (October 1966): 1-9.

Johnson, Randy, and Nancy P. Allen. *Find Custer! The Kidder Tragedy.* Lockport, IL: Printing Plus, 1990.

Jordan, Robert Paul. "Ghosts of the Little Big Horn." *National Geographic* 170, no. 6 (December 1986): 787-813.

Josephy, Alvin M., Jr. *The Civil War in the American West.* New York: Alfred A. Knopf, 1991.

Kahana, Eva, et al. "Coping with Extreme Trauma." In *Human Adaptation to Extreme Stress from the Holocaust to Vietnam,* edited by John P. Wilson, Zev Harel, and Boaz Kahana. New York: Plenum Press, 1988.

Kammen, Robert, Joe Marshall, and Frederick Lefthand. *Soldiers Falling Into Camp: The Battles at the Rosebud and the Little Big Horn.* Encampment, WY: Affiliated Writers of America, 1992.

Karselis, Terry C. "Disaster in Duplicate: An Examination of the Similarities Between the Battle of Isandhlawana and the Little Big Horn." 5th Annual Symposium. Custer Battlefield Historical and Museum Association, 1991.

Keegan, John. *The Face of Battle.* Middlesex, England: Penguin Books, 1976.

Keegan, John, and Richard Holmes. *Soldiers: A History of Men in Battle.* New York: Elisabeth Sifton Books, Viking Penguin, 1986.

Keim, DeB[enneville] Randolph. *Sheridan's Troopers on the Border: A Winter Campaign on the Plains.* Philadelphia: 1870. Reprint, Lincoln: University of Nebraska Press, 1985.

Keller, Doug. "Myths of the Little Big Horn." 2nd Annual Symposium. Custer Battlefield Historical & Museum Association, 1988.

Key, Wilson Bryan. *Subliminal Seduction: Ad Media's Manipulation of a Not So Innocent America.* New York: New American Library, Penguin, 1974.

King, Charles. *Campaigning with Crook.* Norman: University of Oklahoma Press, 1964.

King, W. Kent. *Massacre: The Custer Cover-Up.* El Segundo, CA: Upton & Sons, 1989.

———. *Tombstones for Bluecoats: New Insights Into the Custer Mystery.* Vols. 1-4. Marion Station, MD: N.p., 1980-81.

Kinsley, D. A. *Custer Favor the Bold: A Soldier's Story.* New York: Promontory Press, 1992.

Knight, Ian. *Brave Men's Blood: The Epic of the Zulu War, 1879.* London: Greenhill Books, 1990.

Knight, Oliver. *Following the Indian Wars: The Story of the Newspaper Correspondents Among the Indian Campaigners.* Norman: University of Oklahoma Press, 1960.

Korn, Gustave. "The Custer Battle." *Winners of the West* 13, no. 2 (January 1936): 1.

Koupal, Nancy T., ed. "Diary of Fred M. Hans." *South Dakota Historical Collections* 40 (1980): 4-5, 42-50.

Kuhlman, Charles. *Legend Into History.* Harrisburg, PA: The Stackpole Company, 1951.

Lanahan, John. "From the Sioux Country." *Bighorn Yellowstone Journal* 2, no. 4, (Autumn 1993): 21-22.

Lawrence, Elizabeth A. *His Very Silence Speaks.* Detroit: Wayne State University Press, 1989.

Lessem, Don. *Dinosaurs Rediscovered: New Findings Which Are Revolutionizing Dinosaur Science.* New York: Touchstone, 1992.

Libby, O. G., ed. *The Arikara Narrative of the Campaign Against the Hostile Dakotas—June, 1876.* Glorieta, NM: Rio Grande Press, 1976.

Liddic, Bruce, ed. *I Buried Custer: The Diary of Pvt. Thomas W. Coleman.* College Station, TX: Creative Publishing Company, 1979.

Lukacs, John. *Historical Consciousness or the Remembered Past.* New York: Schocken Books, 1985.

Magnussen, Daniel O. *Peter Thompson's Narrative of the Little Big Horn Campaign 1876: A Critical Analysis of an Eyewitness Account of Custer's Debacle.* Glendale, CA: Arthur H. Clark Company, 1974.

Maguire, Edward. *Reconnaissances and Explorations—Report of the Secretary of War.* Annual report of Lt. Edward Maguire, Corps of Engineers, for the fiscal year ending June 30, 1876. 44th Cong., 2nd sess., vol. 2, pt. 3, bk. 1745, app. OO.

Manchester, William. *Goodbye Darkness: A Memoir of the Pacific War.* New York: Dell, 1979.

Mangum, Neil C. "Destruction, Examination, and Reconstruction: A Review of the Archaeological Survey Conducted on Custer Battlefield, 1983-85." In *Custer and His Times, Book Three,* edited by Gregory J. W. Urwin and Roberta E. Fagan, 149-74. El Paso, TX and Conway, AR: Little Big Horn Associates and University of Central Arkansas Press, 1987.

———, ed. *Register of the Custer Battlefield National Monument Photograph Collection.* Custer Battlefield Historical & Museum Association, 1984.

Marquis, Thomas B. *Custer on the Little Big Horn.* Algonac, MI: Reference Publications, 1967.

———. *Keep the Last Bullet for Yourself.* Algonac, MI: Reference Publications, 1976.

———. *Wooden Leg: A Warrior Who Fought Custer.* Lincoln: University of Nebraska Press, 1931.

———, narr. *Memoirs of a White Crow Indian,* by Thomas H. Leforge (1928). Lincoln: University of Nebraska Press, 1974.

Marshall, S. L. A. *Men Against Fire: The Problem of Battle Command in Future War.* Gloucester, MA: Peter Smith, 1978.

McClernand, Edward J. *On Time for Disaster: The Rescue of Custer's Command.* Lincoln: University of Nebraska Press, 1989.

McCreight, M. I. *Firewater and Forked Tongues: A Sioux Chief Interprets U.S. History.* Pasadena, CA: Trail's End Publishing Company, 1947.

McCrone, John. *The Ape That Spoke: Language and the Evolution of the Human Mind.* New York: William Morrow & Company, 1991.

McIntosh, Jane. *The Practical Archaeologist.* London: Paul Press, 1986.

McLaughlin, James. *My Friend the Indian.* Seattle: Superior Publishing Company, 1970.

McWhiney, Grady, and Perry D. Jamieson. *Attack and Die: Civil War Military Tactics and the Southern Heritage.* Tuscaloosa: University of Alabama Press, 1982.

Merington, Marguerite, ed. *The Custer Story: The Life and Intimate Letters of George A. Custer and His Wife Elizabeth.* Lincoln: University of Nebraska Press, 1987.

Michno, Greg. "Crazy Horse, Custer, and the Sweep to the North." *Montana The Magazine of Western History* 43, no. 3 (Summer 1993): 42-53.

———. "Little Big Horn Mystery Solved." *Research Review: The Journal of the Little Big Horn Associates* 6, no. 1 (January 1992): 7-19, 31.

Miles, Nelson A. *Personal Recollections and Observations of General Nelson A. Miles.* Chicago: The Werner Company, 1897.

Miller, David Humphreys. *Custer's Fall: The Indian Side of the Story.* New York: Duell, Sloan & Pearce, 1957. Reprint, Lincoln: University of Nebraska Press, 1985.

Millis, Walter. *Arms and Men: A Study in American Military History.* New York: New American Library, 1956.

Mills, Charles K. *Harvest of Barren Regrets: The Army Career of Frederick William Benteen, 1834-1898.* Glendale, CA: Arthur H. Clark Company, 1985.

———. *Rosters From the 7th U.S. Cavalry Campaigns, 1866-1896.* Bryan, TX: J. M. Carroll & Company, 1983.

Monmonier, Mark. *How to Lie with Maps.* Chicago: University of Chicago Press, 1991.

Moore, Michael, and Michael Donahue. "Gibbon's Route to Custer Hill." *Greasy Grass* 7 (May 1991): 22-31.

Morris, Donald. *The Washing of the Spears.* New York: Simon and Schuster, 1965.

Mulford, Ami Frank. *Fighting Indians in the 7th U.S. Cavalry: Custer's Favorite Regiment.* Corning, NY: Paul Lindsley Mulford, 1879.

Mulligan, Tim. "Custer and the Little Big Horn: A Needed Perspective." *Research Review: The Journal of the Little Big Horn Associates* 8, no. 1 (Spring 1974): 10-14.

National Park Service Central Classified File. Civil Reference 1933-1949. Record Group 79, National Archives. Washington, D.C.

Neihardt, John G. *Black Elk Speaks: Being the Life Story of a Holy Man of the Oglala Sioux.* Lincoln: University of Nebraska Press, 1979.

Nelson, R. L. "Pinky." "Sergeant Butler's 'Travelling' Marker." *Research Review: The Journal of the Little Big Horn Associates* 8, no. 1 (Spring 1974): 5-9.

Nichols, Ronald H. "The Springfield Carbine at the Little Big Horn." 2nd Annual Symposium. Custer Battlefield Historical & Museum Association, 1988.

————, ed. *Reno Court of Inquiry: Proceedings of a Court of Inquiry in the Case of Major Marcus A. Reno.* Crow Agency, MT: Custer Battlefield Historical & Museum Association, 1992.

Norris, Philetus W. "Custer's Remains." *Bighorn Yellowstone Journal* 1, no. 2 (Spring 1992): 2-6.

Nye, W. S. *Carbine and Lance: The Story of Old Fort Sill.* Norman: University of Oklahoma Press, 1969.

O'Neal, Bill. *Encyclopedia of Western Gunfighters.* Norman: University of Oklahoma Press, 1979.

O'Neil, Tom, ed. *They Lie Buried.* Brooklyn, NY: Arrow & Trooper Publishing Company, 1991.

————. *Garry Owen Tid Bits III.* Brooklyn, NY: Arrow & Trooper Publishing Company, 1991.

Overfield, Loyd J., II. *The Little Big Horn, 1876: The Official Communications, Documents and Reports.* Lincoln: University of Nebraska Press, 1990.

Pohanka, Brian C. "Profile: Lieutenant William Van Wyck Reily, 7th U.S. Cavalry." *Greasy Grass* 2 (May 1986): 9-11.

Porter, Joseph C. *Paper Medicine Man: John Gregory Bourke and His American West.* Norman: University of Oklahoma Press, 1986.

Powell, Peter J. *Sweet Medicine: The Continuing Role of the Sacred Arrows, the Sun Dance, and the Buffalo Hat in Northern Cheyenne History.* Vol. 1. Norman: University of Oklahoma Press, 1969.

Reedstrom, Ernest L. *Bugles, Banners, and Warbonnets.* New York: Bonanza Books, 1986.

Reno, Marcus. "From Major Reno." *That Fatal Day: Eight More With Custer.* Howell, MI: Powder River Press, 1992.

Repass, Craig. *Custer for President?* Ft. Collins, CO: Old Army Press, 1985.

Rickey, Don, Jr. *Forty Miles a Day on Beans and Hay.* Norman: University of Oklahoma Press, 1963.

————. *History of Custer Battlefield.* Billings, MT: Custer Battlefield Historical & Museum Association, 1967.

Robbins, Jim. "Unearthing Little Big Horn's Secrets." *National Parks* 60, no. 11-12 (November-December 1986): 17-23.

Robinson, Charles M., III. *Bad Hand: A Biography of General Ranald S. Mackenzie.* Austin, TX: State House Press, 1993.

Roe, Charles Francis. "Custer's Last Battle." In *Custer Engages the Hostiles.* Ft. Collins, CO: Old Army Press, 1973.

Roenigk, Adolph. *Pioneer History of Kansas.* Lincoln, KS: N.p., 1933.

Rosenberg, Bruce A. *Custer and the Epic of Defeat.* University Park: Pennsylvania State University Press, 1974.

Royster, Charles. *The Destructive War: William Tecumseh Sherman, Stonewall Jackson, and the Americans.* New York: Random House, 1993.

Rozwenc, Edwin C., ed. *The Causes of the American Civil War.* Boston: D. C. Heath & Company, 1961.

Sandoz, Mari. *The Battle of the Little Bighorn.* New York: J. B. Lippincott Company, 1966.

————. *Crazy Horse: The Strange Man of the Oglalas.* Lincoln: University of Nebraska Press, 1961.

Sawicki, James A. *Cavalry Regiments of the U.S. Army.* Dumfries, VA: Wyvern Publications, 1985.

Schneider, George, ed. *The Freeman Journal: The Infantry in the Sioux Campaign of 1876.* San Rafael, CA: Presidio Press, 1977.

Schneider-Wettengel, Georg Wenzel. "Dutchie in the 7th." In *Custer and His Times*, 247-52. El Paso: Little Big Horn Associates, 1981.

Scott, Douglas D., and Melissa Connor. "Post-Mortem at the Little Big Horn." *Natural History* 95, no. 6 (June 1986): 48-54.

Scott, Douglas D., and Richard A. Fox, Jr. *Archaeological Insights into the Custer Battle: An Assessment of the 1984 Field Season.* Norman: University of Oklahoma Press, 1987.

Scott, Douglas D., Richard A. Fox, Jr., Melissa A. Connor, and Dick Harmon. *Archaeological Perspectives on the Battle of the Little Big Horn.* Norman: University of Oklahoma Press, 1989.

Scott, Douglas D., ed. *Papers on Little Big Horn Battlefield Archaeology: The Equipment Dump, Marker 7, and the Reno Crossing.* Lincoln: J & L Reprint Company, 1991.

Scott, Hugh Lenox. *Some Memories of a Soldier.* New York: The Century Company, 1928.

Sills, Joe, Jr. "The Recruits Controversy: Another Look." *Greasy Grass* 5 (May 1989): 2-8.

————. "Weir Point, Another Perspective." *Research Review: The Journal of the Little Big Horn Associates* 3, no. 2 (June 1986): 25-28.

————. "Were There Two Last Stands?" 2nd Annual Symposium. Custer Battlefield Historical & Museum Association, 1988.

Smith, Jay. "A Hundred Years Later." In *Custer and His Times*, 101-45. El Paso: Little Big Horn Associates, 1981.

————. "What Did Not Happen at the Little Big Horn." *Research Review: The Journal of the Little Big Horn Associates* 6, no. 2 (June 1992): 6-13.

Smith, Lowell, ed. "Bones Identified as Bouyer's." *LBHA Newsletter* 20, no. 8 (November 1986): 6.

Spotts, David L. *Campaigning With Custer and the Nineteenth Kansas Volunteer Cavalry on the Washita Campaign, 1868-69.* Lincoln: University of Nebraska Press, 1980.

Stands In Timber, John, and Margot Liberty. *Cheyenne Memories.* Lincoln: University of Nebraska Press, 1967.

Steffen, Randy. *The Horse Soldier, 1776-1943.* Vol. 2, *The Frontier, the Mexican War, the Civil War, the Indian Wars, 1851-1880.* Norman: University of Oklahoma Press, 1978.

Stewart, Edgar I. *Custer's Luck.* Norman: University of Oklahoma Press, 1955.

Stewart, Edgar I., and Jane R. Stewart, eds. *Field Diary of Lt. Edward Settle Godfrey.* Portland: Champoeg Press, 1957.

Stuart, Granville. *Pioneering in Montana: The Making of a State, 1864-1887.* Lincoln: University of Nebraska Press, 1977.

Taunton, Francis B. *Custer's Field: "A Scene of Sickening Ghastly Horror."* London: Johnson-Taunton Military Press, 1990.

Thomas, Gary M. *The Custer Scout of April 1867.* Kansas City, MO: Westport Printing, 1987.

Thrapp, Dan L. *Encyclopedia of Frontier Biography.* Vol. 2, G-O. Lincoln: University of Nebraska Press, 1988.

———. *Victorio and the Mimbres Apaches.* Norman: University of Oklahoma Press, 1974.

Trinque, Bruce A. "The Cartridge-Case Evidence on Custer Field: An Analysis and Re-Interpretation." 5th Annual Symposium. Custer Battlefield Historical & Museum Association, 1991.

"Two Moons Recalls the Battle of the Little Big Horn." *Bighorn Yellowstone Journal* 2, no. 1 (Winter 1993): 9-13.

Upton, Richard. *The Custer Adventure.* El Segundo, CA: Upton & Sons, 1990.

———. *Fort Custer on the Bighorn, 1877-1898: Its History and Personalities as Told and Pictured by Its Contemporaries.* Glendale, CA: Arthur H. Clark Company, 1973.

Urwin, Gregory J. W. "'Custar Had Not Waited for Us': One of Gibbon's Doughboys on the Custer Battle." In *Custer and His Times, Book Three,* edited by Gregory J. W. Urwin and Roberta E. Fagan, 175-91. El Paso, TX and Conway, AR: Little Big Horn Associates and University of Central Arkansas Press, 1987.

———. *Custer Victorious: The Civil War Battles of General George Armstrong Custer.* Rutherford, NJ: Fairleigh Dickinson University Press, 1983.

———. *The United States Cavalry: An Illustrated History.* Dorset, England: Blandford Press, 1983.

Utley, Robert M. *Cavalier in Buckskin: George Armstrong Custer and the Western Military Frontier.* Norman: University of Oklahoma Press, 1988.

———. *Custer and the Great Controversy: The Origin and Development of a Legend.* Pasadena, CA: Westernlore Press, 1960.

———. *Custer Battlefield: A History and Guide to the Battle of the Little Big Horn.* Handbook 132. Washington, D.C.: National Park Service, 1988.

———. *Frontier Regulars: The United States Army and the Indian, 1866-1891.* New York: Macmillan Publishing Company, 1973.

———. "Gossip and Scandal." *Research Review: The Journal of the Little Big Horn Associates* 3, no. 1 (June 1989): 18-19.

———, ed. *Life in Custer's Cavalry: Diaries and Letters of Albert and Jennie Barnitz, 1867-1868.* Lincoln: University of Nebraska Press, 1987.

———, ed. *The Reno Court: The Chicago Times Account.* Ft. Collins, CO: Old Army Press, 1983.

Vaughn, Robert. *Then and Now; or 36 Years in the Rockies.* Minneapolis: Tribune Printing Company, 1900.

Vestal, Stanley. *Warpath: The True Story of the Fighting Sioux Told in a Biography of Chief White Bull.* Boston: Houghton-Mifflin, 1934. Reprint, Lincoln: University of Nebraska Press, 1984.

Wagner, Glendolin Damon. *Old Neutriment: Memories of the Custers.* Lincoln: University of Nebraska Press, 1987.

Watson, Elmo Scott. "Photographing the Frontier." *English Westerners Brand Book* 8, no. 2 (January 1966): 1-8.

Weibert, Don. *Custer, Cases and Cartridges: The Weibert Collection Analyzed.* Billings, MT: Author, 1989.

Weibert, Henry, and Don Weibert. *Sixty-Six Years in Custer's Shadow*. Billings, MT: Falcon Press Publishing Company, 1985.

Wellman, Paul I. *A Dynasty of Western Outlaws*. New York: Pyramid Books, 1964.

Wells, Wayne. "Little Big Horn Notes: Stanley Vestal's Indian Insights." *Greasy Grass* 5 (May 1989): 9-19.

Werner, Fred H. *The Beecher Island Battle, September 17, 1868*. Greeley, CO: Werner Publications, 1989.

———. *The Summit Springs Battle*. Greeley, CO: Werner Publications, 1991.

Wheeler, Homer W. *Buffalo Days*. Indianapolis: Bobbs-Merrill, 1925. Reprint, Lincoln: University of Nebraska Press, 1990.

———. "Custer Battlefield in '77." *Westerners Brand Book: Chicago Corral of Westerners* 4, no. 11 (January 1948): 67-68.

Willert, James. *Bourke's Diary from Journals of 1st Lt. John Gregory Bourke, June 27-September 15, 1876*. La Mirada, CA: Author, 1986.

———. "The Reno Court of Inquiry of 1879: Focus on Wallace." *Research Review: The Journal of the Little Big Horn Associates* 2, no. 4 (December 1985): 3-23.

"Yellow Nose Tells of Custer's Last Stand." *Bighorn Yellowstone Journal* 1, no. 3 (Summer 1992): 14-17.

Ziegler, Philip. *Omdurman*. New York: Dorset Press, 1987.

Letters Received by Author in Westland, MI:

Richard A. Fox, Jr., July 17, 1993.

Robert G. Rosenberg, December 14, 1991.

Douglas D. Scott, April 18, 1991, and May 16, 1991.

Margaret A. Stavick, January 4, 1994.

Bruce A. Trinque, November 2, 1991; November 15, 1991; and March 21, 1993.

Index

Gregory Michno was born in Detroit, Michigan, in 1948. After receiving a B.S. in social science from Michigan State University in 1970, he traveled west and earned a master's in history in 1973 from the University of Northern Colorado. He remains keenly interested in western history and often takes his wife, Susan, and his two children, Amanda and Nathaniel, on research trips to the West from their Westland, Michigan, home.

Greg was drawn to the mysterious fate of Custer's Gray Horse Company after learning that archaeological digs in the 1980s at the Little Bighorn battlefield failed to turn up any trace of the men supposedly killed in Deep Ravine. In spite of living a thousand miles away and working full-time for the Michigan Department of Social Services, he found enough "spare time" to apply his research and reasoning skills toward solving this lingering mystery. He volunteered as a Deep Ravine Trail guide in 1991 and wrote a piece for the January 1992 issue of *Research Review: The Journal of the Little Big Horn Associates* entitled "Little Big Horn Mystery Solved," which won the 1993 Larry Frost Award for best article. Now, after much additional work, he offers a detailed account of his findings. His next contribution to understanding the Custer battle, a work in progress tentatively entitled "Lakota Noon," promises to shed light on Indian movements during the fight.